P9-DVJ-525

Withdrawn from Collection

An Environmental History of Canada

Laurel Sefton MacDowell

An Environmental History of Canada

UBCPress · Vancouver · Toronto

© UBC Press 2012

All rights reserved. No part of this publication may be reproduced, stored in a retrieval system, or transmitted, in any form or by any means, without prior written permission of the publisher, or, in Canada, in the case of photocopying or other reprographic copying, a licence from Access Copyright, www.accesscopyright.ca.

20 19 18 17 16 15 14 13 12   5 4 3 2 1

Printed in Canada on FSC-certified ancient-forest-free paper (100-percent post-consumer recycled) that is processed chlorine- and acid-free.

Library and Archives Canada Cataloguing in Publication

MacDowell, Laurel Sefton
    An environmental history of Canada / Laurel Sefton MacDowell.

Includes bibliographical references and index.
Also issued in electronic format.
ISBN 978-0-7748-2102-5

    1. Human ecology – Canada – History. 2. Natural resources – Canada – History. 3. Canada – Environmental conditions – History. 4. Environmental policy – Canada. I. Title.

GF511.M33 2012   304.20971   C2012-903170-4

Canadä

UBC Press gratefully acknowledges the financial support for our publishing program of the Government of Canada (through the Canada Book Fund), the Canada Council for the Arts, and the British Columbia Arts Council.

UBC Press
The University of British Columbia
2029 West Mall
Vancouver, BC V6T 1Z2
www.ubcpress.ca

For Carl Berger

Contents

Acknowledgments / ix

Introduction / 1

Part 1: Aboriginal Peoples and Settlers

1   Encountering a New Land / 11

2   Settling the Land and Transforming the "Wilderness" / 40

Part 2: Industrialism, Reform, and Infrastructure

3   Early Cities and Urban Reform / 75

4   The Conservation Movement / 96

5   Mining Resources / 120

6   Cars, Consumerism, and Suburbs / 140

Part 3: Harnessing Nature, Harming Nature

7   Changing Energy Regimes / 163

8   Water / 188

9   The Contested World of Food and Agriculture / 215

Part 4: The Environmental Era

10   The Environmental Movement and Public Policy / 243

11   Parks and Wildlife / 268

12   Coastal Fisheries / 286

13   The North and Climate Change / 305

Conclusion / 326

Index / 331

Acknowledgments

THIS BOOK BEGAN in the early 1990s, when I started to rethink Canadian history from an environmental perspective. I developed an undergraduate course in Canadian environmental history and a graduate course in North American environmental history, and I organized a conference on the new field of environmental history. I then began to write this book.

Many people have influenced and assisted me. A special thanks to Elizabeth Jewett for help with the photos. Ben Bradley, Colin Coates, Harriet Friedmann, Richard Hoffman, George Warecki, Alexander Murray, and the Toronto Environmental History group read and commented on earlier versions of several chapters. Thanks to Richard White for his advice about the photos and maps. Thanks to my daughter,

Jen MacDowell, who searched for and copied many articles, saving me a lot of time.

I particularly want to thank Randy Schmidt, senior editor at UBC Press, for his patience and support through a lengthy review and revision process. More recently, I worked with copy editor Lesley Erickson, production editor Holly Keller, and cartographer Eric Leinberger to bring the book to press. It has been a large task, but I appreciate their excellent work.

I am dedicating this book to Carl Berger – my friend, teacher, colleague, and husband. Carl studied the natural world long before there was a field of environmental history. Together, we have bird-watched, gardened, and walked in forests, fields, and deserts. These experiences have influenced me and inform this history.

An Environmental History of Canada

Introduction

North Americans have not yet learned the difference between yield and loot.

— CARL SAUER, GEOGRAPHER, "THEME OF PLANT AND ANIMAL
DESTRUCTION IN ECONOMIC HISTORY," 1938

WHAT IS ENVIRONMENTAL history? More specifically, what is Canadian environmental history? History, in general, is the study of the human past on the planet. But there are many branches of historical inquiry. Political historians analyze policies and the actions of leaders; economic historians examine economic phenomena and institutions and how they have affected history; and social historians use categories such as class, gender, race, and ethnicity to understand the lives of different groups of people. For environmental historians, nature is an agent in human development and social change. These historians focus on the interdependent relationship between people and the natural world, human beings and their environment, and human society and the planet.

Environmental history is a relatively new field that emerged in the 1970s and took on steam in the 1980s; by 2000 historians such as John McNeill were calling attention to the enormous pressure that humans were placing on the planet. Historian Richard Grove (2007, 76) observes that scholars were "increasingly concerned to look back at the history of global environmental degradation and the impact of capitalism and imperialism on world ecologies." In North America, influenced in large part by the modern environmental movement, historians began to examine the past to determine how and why the current state of environmental despoliation had occurred. To answer these questions, they had to rethink US and Canadian history.

Environmental history began as an offshoot of intellectual history and is associated with the publication of Samuel Hays' *Conservation and the Gospel of Efficiency* (1959) and Roderick Nash's *Wilderness and the American Mind* (1967). Historians of the American West such as Walter Prescott Webb and James Malin recognized the physical environment's effects on society. Donald Worster's *Nature's Economy* (1994), an intellectual history of thinkers' ideas about nature and ecology, led to his work on the effect of human action on the environment in *Dust Bowl* (2004), a book about the American West in the 1930s. In *Rivers of Empire* (1992), Worster traced the manipulation of rivers to irrigate western lands, produce wealth, and lay the basis of modern western American society. Historians interested in the roots of modern environmentalism, such as Robert Gottlieb and Adam Rome, examined early "pollution fighters" in the 1960s, the evolving environmental movement, and issues of environmental justice that related the variables of class, gender, and ethnicity to environmental history. Historian Carolyn Merchant, biographer Linda Lear, and others wrote women into environmental history. Shepard Krech III and Richard White examined indigenous people's attitudes to nature in contrast to those of Europeans.

By the 1980s, environmental history was a vibrant interdisciplinary field. Historians in Canada and the United States experimented by borrowing theories and methods from anthropology, archaeology, historical geography, Aboriginal studies, and various scientific fields. Some drew on science methods to "read" ecological footprints on the land – such as scorch marks in rocks, tree rings, or bones from excavation sites – to reinterpret the past. Others examined how perceptions of the wilderness or the environment had helped to shape, or construct, nature and the landscape. Still others studied the influence of war and government policy on the environment.

The fruit of these lines of inquiry proved original and provocative. For example, William Cronon's classic study, *Changes in the Land* (1983), about colonial New England, recounted how settlers' use of the land had differed from that of indigenous peoples, whom settlers marginalized as they transformed the environment. *Ecological Imperialism* (1986), Alfred Crosby's work

on the Columbian exchange – the massive exchange of ideas, diseases, agricultural goods, and slave labour between the eastern and western hemispheres after 1492 – looked at the theme of indigenous-newcomer contact not from the perspective of imperialism or colonialism but through a lens focused on the environmental consequences of these exchanges. Stephen J. Pyne, in *Fire in America: A Cultural History of Wildland and Rural Fire* (1982), analyzed the relationship between culture and nature through the use of fire, whereas Thomas Dunlap, in *Nature and the English Diaspora* (1999), examined English settlers' ideas about nature and later conceptions of conservation and ecology. Other environmental historians explored the relationship between the economy and the environment and the economy's effect on environmental policy and politics. Finally, Martin Melosi and others insisted that environmental history should include the urban environment, and they broadened both environmental history and urban history by examining consumer culture and urban waste and the changing infrastructure of cities and their spatial effect on local communities.

Canadian environmental history was perhaps sparked by Ramsay Cook's comment in 1990 that early Canadian historians such as W.L. Morton and Arthur Lower had been sensitive to the environment but had not studied it explicitly as a theme (Cook 1990). Harold Innis, a political economist and pioneer in communications studies, for example, had developed the staples thesis to explain the history of Canadian resource development and exploitation, but he did not explore the effect of this development on the environment. Donald Creighton's Laurentian hypothesis (that Canadian economic and national development derived from the gradual exploitation of key staples such as fur, timber, and wheat) and J.M.S. Careless's metropolitan-hinterland thesis (that large urban communities dominate surrounding territory through economic means) likewise overlooked the effects of historical change on the Canadian landscape. Carl Berger's intellectual history *Science, God and Nature in Victorian Canada*; Suzanne Zeller's *Land of Promise, Promised Land: The Culture of Victorian Science in Canada,* which links landscape to science and technology; and William Waiser's biography of botanist John Macoun, *The Field Naturalist,* are examples of studies that explore the theme of nature but are not environmental histories. Likewise, Canadian historical geographers, influenced by R. Cole Harris, Conrad Heidenreich, and others, concentrated on tracing Canada's geographical evolution over time, as exemplified by the three-volume *Historical Atlas of Canada*. Environmental historian Graeme Wynn suggests that the discipline's prominence perhaps delayed the inception of environmental history in Canada by drawing prospective scholars away from history.

In the 1990s, however, US envirometal history began to influence Canadian historians. Several conferences held in Canada showcased existing work by US and Canadian environmental historians and explored new directions for research. At McGill University in Montreal, the Arpents Environmental History Group started a network for environmental historians in 2003. The following year, the American Society for Environmental History held its first meeting in Canada, in Victoria, British Columbia. These early developments led to financial support from universities and the first appointments in environmental history. The Social Sciences and Humanities Research Council, for instance, began to fund the Network in Canadian History and the Environment (NICHE). This explosion of interest in Canadian environmental history was reflected in scholarly journals. *BC Studies* published an entire issue on the environment in 2004, and in 2007 the American journal *Environmental History* devoted an issue to Canada.

Environmental historians from around the world met in Denmark in 2009 for the First Global Environmental History Conference. Throughout the decade, ecology – the branch of biology that deals with how organisms relate to one another and to their environments – emerged as a lens through which environmental historians could rethink the past. They began to use it as a metaphor and as a model to distinguish their approach from historical geography.

Canadian environmental historians quickly differentiated themselves from their US counterparts. Whereas American environmental history has been shaped by the work of Cronon, Webb, and Malin on the western frontier and by historical studies on conservation, Canadian environmental history has been influenced by Innis's staple thesis, Creighton's Laurentian hypothesis, and Careless's metropolitan-hinterland thesis. Armed with a different national history and historiographical tradition, Canadian environmental historians reassessed these early theories of and approaches to the past, offered new explanatory frameworks, and focused on Canada's history as a northern nation.

The growing complexity of environmental issues at the end of the twentieth century, including environmental health and climate change, has opened historians' eyes to new subjects and issues, and North American historians took note when European historians urged them to apply more social theory to environmental history. These concerns are reflected in a range of new studies and approaches: from revisionist narratives of Canadian resources development that take into account environmental policy, to studies of the importance of provincial and national parks, to the ideas and backgrounds of leaders in environmental campaigns. The increasing prominence of global environmental issues suggests that Canadian environmental history will only become more important as the twenty-first century progresses.

In a rapidly globalizing world, environmental historians are also examining developments within a comparative or transnational perspective. This research suggests that environmental history may work best on a regional or global scale rather than on a national one. In their introduction to *Ecology and Empire: Environmental History of Settler Societies,* Tom Griffiths and Libby Robin argue (1997, 12) that national histories are limited in that they "need continually to fragment or enlarge the national perspective and to scrutinize and reflect upon the intersections of nature and nation." This book acknowledges this limitation but also recognizes that all Canadians, from students to concerned citizens, need an environmental history of the northern half of North

America. It is true that Canadians are "the other North Americans." But even though Canada's economic and cultural history has become more intertwined with that of the United States, particularly in the second half of the twentieth century, Canada has a different climate, distinctive geographical features such as the Canadian Shield, its own history, a parliamentary system of government and politics, and unique elements such as Crown lands that have affected the exploitation of resources. More importantly, Canada is an immense country that has natural resources such as forests, fish, and water and diverse ecosystems that are increasingly essential to the world.

This book explores how Canada's landscape changed over thousands of years. When glaciers retreated, ending the Ice Age, they left behind a geography that influenced Canada and its history profoundly. This text re-examines well-known subjects in Canadian history – Aboriginal peoples and their first contacts with Europeans, the fur trade, settling the land, the creation of a transportation infrastructure, and the growth of cities – in ways that emphasize the interaction between people and their environment. Today, *sustainable development* is a buzzword for policy makers, but it did not play a large part in Canadian history. Although Aboriginal people lived lives linked intimately to the environment – to plants, animals, and landscapes – they were relegated to reserves after the arrival of European settlers, who sought to conquer the land, not only for survival but also for profit. In the nineteenth century, voters supported politicians and businesses intent on making the nation prosperous and powerful through the development of agriculture, industry, and resources. *Sustained economic growth*, not sustainable development, has been the driving force in Canadian history. The growth of consumerism in the late twentieth century has only further desensitized Canadians to the natural world, even though we continue to depend upon it for our survival.

Sustained economic growth has been a driving force in history, yet in the past, as in the present, some people questioned whether Canada's bountiful environment was as inexhaustible as the development ethos suggested. In the late nineteenth century, Canadian intellectuals, scientists, naturalists, and civil servants were in the vanguard of the conservation movement. Their belief that exploitation must be balanced by conservation led Canada to adopt early legislation to regulate hunters and resource extractors and to preserve forests, watersheds, and wildlife. Policy makers, however, were motivated as much by commercial gain as they were by a concern for the environment. National parks not only protected nature, they also became sites for multiple activities, including logging, tourism, and recreation, by the late twentieth century.

The 1960s and early 1970s witnessed renewed protests against environmental degradation. In 1962, for instance, Rachel Carson, an American writer, published *Silent Spring* to raise an alarm about the effects of DDT and other chemical pollutants. She found a massive audience of readers in both the United States and Canada. A decade later, a small group of activists set sail from Vancouver, British Columbia, aboard the *Phyllis Cormack* to draw attention to US underground nuclear testing off the coast of Alaska. These activists, the founders of Greenpeace, helped to foster "a new environmental way of thinking," one that favours human stewardship rather than domination of nature (McNeill 2000, 337). Annual celebrations such as Earth Day and growing awareness of climate change have transformed environmentalism into a mainstream movement. The perplexing issue of how to repair damage to what we now recognize is a fragile planet and forestall a turbulent and threatening future is a growing concern.

Debates about the Kyoto Accord and climate change suggest, however, that the Canadian government's response to modern environmental issues and the enforcement of regulations continue to be lax. Part of the problem is our very disconnection from nature and our over-reliance on and confidence in technology as a solution to problems. As this book shows, hubris is a recurring theme in Canadian history. The collapse of the Newfoundland cod fishery in 1992 is only the most recent example. Quick fixes designed to sustain economic growth rather than preserve nature are no solution. But prosperity, enjoyed far from the crushing poverty of developing countries, makes it difficult for Canadians to appreciate the urgent need to create a sustainable society. The message of conservation articulated early in the twentieth century remains unfulfilled.

Learning new ways to live that leave a lighter human imprint on the environment, developing new energy sources, and reusing resources rather than wasting them are challenges that Canadians and people around the world must meet in the twenty-first century. Because the commercial drive remains strong, living sustainably will require re-education. This environmental history of Canada brings to light the grave consequences of the development ethos as it played out throughout Canadian history, not to condemn, but so we can begin to develop strategies to create a liveable, sustainable environment in the future.

Works Cited

Cook, Ramsay. 1990. "'Cabbages Not Kings': Towards an Ecological Interpretation of Early Canadian History." *Journal of Canadian Studies* 25, 4: 5-16.

Griffiths, Tom, and Libby Robin, eds. 1997. *Ecology and Empire: Environmental History of Settler Societies.* Edinburgh: Keele University Press.

Grove, Richard. 2007. "The Great El Nino of 1789-93 and Its Global Consequences." *Medieval History Journal* 10, 1 and 2: 75-98.

McNeill, John R. 2000. *Something New under the Sun: An Environmental History of the Twentieth-Century World.* New York: W.W. Norton.

Sauer, Carl O. 1938. "Theme of Plant and Animal Destruction in Economic History." In *Land and Life,* edited by John Leighly, 145-54. Berkeley: University of California Press.

For Further Reading

Dunlap, Thomas. 1999. *Nature and the English Diaspora: Environment and History in the United States, Canada, Australia, and New Zealand.* New York: Cambridge University Press.

Hays, Samuel. 1959. *Conservation and the Gospel of Efficiency: The Progressive Conservation Movement, 1890-1920.* Cambridge: Harvard University Press.

Malin, James. 1956. *The Grasslands of North America: Prolegomena to Its History.* Lawrence, KS: J.C. Malin.

Nash, Roderick. 1967. *Wilderness and the American Mind.* New Haven, CT: Yale University Press.

Webb, Walter Prescott. 1931. *The Great Plains.* Waltham, MA: Ginn and Company.

Canadian Environmental History

Campbell, Claire Elizabeth. 2005. *Shaped by the West Wind: Nature and History in Georgian Bay.* Vancouver: UBC Press.

Colpitts, George. 2002. *Game in the Garden: A Human History of Wildlife in Western Canada.* Vancouver: UBC Press.

Evenden, Matthew D. 2004. *Fish versus Power: An Environmental History of the Fraser River.* New York: Cambridge University Press.

Forkey, Neil S. 2003. *Shaping the Upper Canadian Frontier: Environment, Society and Culture in the Trent Valley.* Calgary: University of Calgary Press.

Hodgins, Bruce W., Jamie Benidickson, and Peter Gillis. 1982. "Ontario and Quebec Experiments in Forest Reserves, 1883-1930." *Journal of Forest History* 26, 1: 20-33.

Killan, Gerald. 1993. *Protected Places: A History of Ontario's Provincial Parks System.* Toronto: Dundurn Press.

Loo, Tina. 2006. *States of Nature: Conserving Canada's Wilderness in the Twentieth Century.* Vancouver: UBC Press.

MacEachern, Alan. 2001. *Natural Selections: National Parks in Atlantic Canada, 1935-1970.* Montreal and Kingston: McGill-Queen's University Press, 2001.

Morse, Kathryn. 2003. *The Nature of Gold: An Environmental History of the Klondike Gold Rush.* Seattle: University of Washington Press.

Nelles, H.V. 1974. *The Politics of Development: Forests, Mines and Hydro-Electric Power in Ontario, 1849-1941.* Toronto: Macmillan of Canada.

Piper, Liza, and John Sandlos. 2007. "A Broken Frontier: Ecological Imperialism in the Canadian North." *Environmental History* 12, 4: 759-95.

Sandwell, R.W. 2009. "History as Experiment: Microhistory and Environmental History." In *Method and Meaning in Canadian Environmental History,* edited by Alan MacEachern and William J. Turkel, 124-38. Toronto: Nelson Education.

Stelter, Gilbert A., and Allan F.J. Artibise, eds. 1984. *The Canadian City: Essays in Urban and Social History.* Ottawa: Carleton University Press.

Stuart, Richard. 1994. "'History Is Concerned with More Than Ecology, But It Is Concerned with Ecology Too': Environmental History in Parks Canada." Paper presented at the Canadian Historical Association annual meeting, Winnipeg, Manitoba, June.

Warecki, George. 2000. *Protecting Ontario's Wilderness: A History of Changing Ideas and Preservation Politics, 1927-1973*. New York: Peter Lang.

Wynn, Graeme. 2004. "'Shall We Linger Along Ambitionless?' Environmental Perspectives on British Columbia." *BC Studies* 142-43: 5-67.

–. 2007. *Canada and Arctic North America: An Environmental History*. Santa Barbara: ABC-CLIO.

International and Transnational Perspectives

Evans, Sterling. 2006. *Borderlands of the American and Canadian Wests: Essays on the Regional History of the 49th Parallel*. Calgary: University of Calgary Press.

Griffiths, Tom, and Libby Robin, eds. 1997. *Ecology and Empire: Environmental History of Settler Societies*. Edinburgh: Keele University Press.

Grove, Richard. 2007. "The Great El Nino of 1789-93 and Its Global Consequences." *Medieval History Journal* 10, 1 and 2: 75-98.

McNeill, John R. 2000. *Something New under the Sun: An Environmental History of the Twentieth-Century World*. New York: W.W. Norton.

Sorlin, Sverker, and Paul Warde. 2007. "The Problem of Environmental History: A Rereading of the Field." *Environmental History* 12, 1: 107-30.

Weart, Spencer R. 2008. *The Discovery of Global Warming*. Cambridge, MA: Harvard University Press.

White, Richard. 1999. "The Nationalization of Nature." *Journal of American History* 86, 3: 976-86.

US Environmental History

Cronon, William. 1983. *Changes in the Land: Indians, Colonists and the Ecology of New England*. New York: Hill and Wang.

Crosby, Alfred. 1986. *Ecological Imperialism: The Biological Expansion of Europe, 900-1900*. New York: Cambridge University Press.

–. 2003. *The Columbian Exchange: Biological and Cultural Consequences of 1492*. Santa Barbara: Praeger.

Gottlieb, Robert. 2005. *Forcing the Spring: The Transformation of the American Environmental Movement*. New York: Island Press.

Hurley, A., ed. 1997. *Common Fields: An Environmental History of St. Louis*. St. Louis: Missouri Historical Society.

Krech, Shepard, III. 1999. *The Ecological Indian: Myth and History*. New York: W.W. Norton.

Lear, Linda. 1997. *Rachel Carson: Witness for Nature*. New York: Henry Holt and Company.

Melosi, Martin. 2001. *Effluent America: Cities, Industry, Energy, and the Environment*. Pittsburgh: University of Pittsburgh Press.

Merchant, Carolyn. 1990. *The Death of Nature: Women, Ecology and the Scientific Revolution*. San Francisco: Harper.

Opie, John. 1998. *Nature's Nation: An Environmental History of the United States*. New York: Harcourt Brace College Publishers.

Pyne, Stephen J. 1982. *Fire in America: A Cultural History of Wildland and Rural Fire*. Princeton, NJ: Princeton University Press.

Rome, Adam. 2003. "'Give Earth a Chance': The Environmental Movement and the Sixties." *Journal of American History* 90, 2: 525-54.

White, Richard. 1985. "American Environmental History: The Development of a New Historical Field." *Pacific Historical Review* 54, 3: 297-335.

Worster, Donald. 1992. *Rivers of Empire: Water, Aridity and the Growth of the American West*. New York: Oxford University Press.

–. 1994. *Nature's Economy: A History of Ecological Ideas*. Cambridge: Cambridge University Press.

–. 2004. *Dust Bowl: The Southern Plains in the 1930s*. New York: Oxford University Press.

PART 1

Aboriginal Peoples and Settlers

1
Encountering a New Land

Fossil records suggest that in the past 500 million years, there have been five waves of extinction when large numbers of species died out ... most recently, when the dinosaurs disappeared, 65 million years ago. Preeminent scientists believe that humans are currently causing the sixth great extinction in the history of life on Earth.

— DAVID R. BOYD, ENVIRONMENTAL LAWYER, *UNNATURAL LAW*, 2003

THE LAND WE now know as Canada evolved over millions of years, and humans have inhabited it for only a fraction of that time. During ice ages, vast sheets of ice and snow covered much of the northern hemisphere. A unique combination of natural forces came together to create land bridges that drew humans to the continent. Climate change influenced the movement and social development of peoples throughout North and South America. Aboriginal peoples, in turn, developed patterns of subsistence living that were finely adapted to local environments and natural resources such as buffalo, elk, deer, and fish. A thousand years ago, European explorers began to encounter the so-called New World for the first time. Over the next eight hundred years, news of the region's riches spread slowly throughout Europe. Speculators, in the form of fishermen, explorers, and fur traders, soon followed. This chapter explores how these long-term developments transformed the

environment and the way in which people – both Aboriginal and European – perceived it.

The Land before People

In the not-so-distant past, North America was a different place than it is today. But then, as now, a combination of geography, ecology, geology, climate change, and accident shaped the continent's turbulent history. During the Mesozoic era (245-65 million years ago), the environment evolved in the absence of humans, and dinosaurs roamed a land that we would not recognize today. The Rocky Mountains did not yet exist, a huge seaway divided the continent in half, and the climate was warm and lush. Small shrubs grew where today we find towering pines, and magnolia, Asian gingko, and palm trees dotted Alberta's Badlands.

The Mesozoic era came to an end around 65 million years ago when an asteroid hit what is today known as the Yucatan Peninsula.

GLOBAL WARMING IN HISTORICAL PERSPECTIVE

In the distant past, as in the present, the smallest shift in ocean currents, the earth's tilt, the movement of the earth's crust, or gases in the atmosphere could cause massive climate change. Climatologists have identified what they call the Medieval Warm Period (or Little Climatic Optimum), which stretched from 900 to 1300 CE, and the Little Ice Age (1300-1870), which was characterized by wetter, cooler temperatures. Over the past two centuries, a number of scientists – Joseph Fourier (in 1824), Svante Arrhenius (in 1894), and Guy Arrhenius (in 1894), and Guy Stewart Callendar (in 1938) – have warned that increased carbon dioxide emissions would cause temperatures to rise. Today, although we are due for another cooling period, greenhouse gases are instead heating up the planet. The Keeling Curve, a graph that shows ongoing change in the concentration of carbon dioxide in the atmosphere as measured at Mauna Loa Observatory, shows that the global carbon dioxide level was 315 parts per million (ppm) in 1958, 365 ppm in 1997, and 392 ppm in 2011.

Hot rock shot into the atmosphere and started huge fires. The resulting smokescreen destroyed about 80 percent of all species in North America. Most of what remained was rock and clay, but tiny fern spores – "the species that won back the continent" – survived inside rocks (Flannery 2001) as did herbs and palms located in remote, sheltered areas that acted as refuges for them. The Arctic Circle, located far from the blast, was one protective region. There was no ice at the pole, and flora – conifers, small flowering plants, and deciduous trees – began to move slowly southward in a gradual greening process.

Those animal species that survived extinction included reptiles such as lizards and snakes that burrowed in the land and amphibians such as frogs and toads that could survive for a time on dead matter in aquatic ecosystems. The water itself protected these creatures from the asteroid's intense heat. But it was mammals that shaped the post-asteroid order. Following the extinction of their most dangerous predators, the dinosaurs, the mammals that survived grew larger and more varied, and each new species filled a vacuum in the new ecosystem.

Over millions of years, climate change and continental drift – the gradual movement, formation, or re-formation of the continents relative to one another described by the theory of plate tectonics – influenced the distribution of flora and fauna, resources such as fossil fuels and minerals, and the movement of animals. Sixty million years ago, the movement of the earth's crust also joined the two North American continental halves together. Continental drift caused North America to join with Greenland and Asia at various times. New animal species such as huge flightless birds and amphibians arrived from both the east and the west. The mammals included primitive creatures that resembled hippos, elephants, lions, and horses. Fourteen million years after the dinosaurs disappeared, the continent was once again repopulated, this time with giant mammals that evolved quickly as they hunted in tropical forests. When temperatures cooled, biodiversity decreased and species immigration slowed, despite the presence of land bridges. Cooling caused rainforests to give way to deciduous trees, and drier weather promoted the development of grasslands in open spaces. Most large mammal species disappeared or migrated to South America, which joined North America about 30 million years ago.

During the Pleistocene epoch (2.9 million to 12,000 years ago), waves of glaciation shaped the North American environment. Scholars continue to debate the causes of the Ice Age, but causative variables included changes in ocean currents and the tilt of the planet, the movement of the earth's crust,

and volcanic activity. The last intense freeze occurred between approximately 35,000 and 12,000 years ago, a period known as the Wisconsin Glacial Episode. What is now Canada was covered in massive ice sheets (the Alaskan, the Laurentide in the northern interior, and the Cordilleran along the Pacific Coast) that were several kilometres deep. The pressure of advancing and retreating ice pushed enormous rocks hundreds of kilometres, gouged out holes for lakes, built up rock for mountains, and deposited huge quantities of sediment. It transformed the geology, landscape, vegetation, and water systems of North America.

During the Pleistocene epoch, a land bridge about 1,400 kilometres wide formed across the Bering Strait. Known as Beringia, the landmass stretched from present-day Yukon through Alaska to northeast Asia (see Figure 1.1). Beringia was a productive ecosystem that supported a diverse mosaic of plants, shrubs, and grasslands and large populations of grazing animals and their predators. The area experienced about twenty freezes and thaws during the Pleistocene era that periodically supported the movement of animals over the land bridge. Woolly mammoths (see Figure 1.2), giant ground sloths, muskoxen, camels, broad-fronted moose, and giant beaver crossed into North America pursued by saber-toothed cats, giant short-faced bears, and wolves.

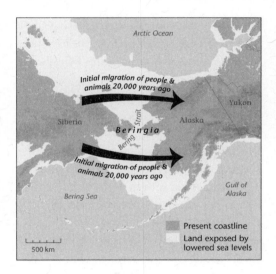

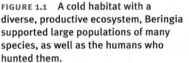

FIGURE 1.1 A cold habitat with a diverse, productive ecosystem, Beringia supported large populations of many species, as well as the humans who hunted them.

FIGURE 1.2 **Woolly mammoths crossing Beringia into North America. Archaeologists discovered the bones of these ancient creatures, along with other animals, in Yukon.**
Courtesy of the SFU Museum of Archaeology and Ethnology

The Arrival of Humans

Humans were late to reach the Americas, the last continents they inhabited. Ice sheets blocked movement into North America from Beringia until around 13000 BCE (before the Common Era), when parts of the Northwest Pacific Coast began to deglaciate. Global warming encouraged the growth of vegetation in what is now Canada. Meltwater channels formed, and lichens, mosses, and small shrubs began to sprout on moraines, masses of rocks and sediment carried down by glaciers. Over time, corridors running from north to south formed, large glacial lakes took shape, and boreal forest began to evolve. The process, however, was slow. North America was not fully deglaciated until around 5000 BCE.

Most scientists believe modern humans *(Homo sapiens)*, in pursuit of game, began entering North America via the Bering land bridge. Although no human bones have been found in Canada to support this hypothesis, it has been borne out by the 1993 discovery of a projectile point in Alaska. Carbon dating of archaeological evidence – fluted points, microblades, burins, and flakes – at the Bluefish Caves in northeastern Yukon also suggests that small hunting groups sporadically occupied the area between 25,000 and 12,000 years ago. One theory is that the Clovis people, named for their fluted stone spear points, crossed Beringia and then spread southward. As warming temperatures melted the ice sheets, the sea eventually rose to cover the Bering land bridge around 11000 BCE. It is possible that people continued to come to North America by navigating the narrow channel in boats or rafts and that the Bering land bridge was not the only entry point for early people.

When the Clovis hunters reached the Great Plains, they encountered vast numbers of enormous mammals, which they hunted for food and material resources. Their arrival coincided with the extinction of ancient animals, including the mammoth and mastodon. Although some scholars attribute these animals' extinction to global warming, which disrupted plant and animal ecosystems and dried up watering places, others, such as geochronologist Paul Martin, liken the development to a blitzkrieg. According to

this theory, our first ancestors devised long Clovis points to slaughter large game efficiently. Following the mass killing and extinction of many mammal species, however, the Clovis people disappeared within three hundred years. The recent discovery of nanodiamonds in the boundary sediment layer suggests, however, that a medium-sized comet might have hit Earth about 13,000 years ago, killing species and temporarily reversing the effects of global warming.

The Development of Cultural Areas

The Clovis people were of a single stock, but dental and genetic evidence reveals that they became more differentiated as they spread throughout North America and developed into three successor peoples – the Amerinds, the Na-Dené, and the Aleut-Inuit peoples – who used smaller spear points to hunt. Early peoples in North America had to adapt to a dramatically changing environment. Plants disappeared or changed, and new migrant animals filled niches left by extinctions. Bison, elk, moose, and grizzly bear became fauna distinct to North America and the predecessors of contemporary wildlife. A warmer climate fostered the emergence of distinct regions: grasses in the interior; lichen woodland as far northwest as the Mackenzie River Valley; a vast boreal forest dominated by balsam, jack pine, birch, and white pine; and a forest of elm, hemlock, maple, and beech in the cool temperate area of the Great Lakes–St. Lawrence region. By 3000 BCE, when climate change slowed, humans enjoyed a more stable environment. Vegetation existed farther north than today, but as temperatures cooled after 2000 BCE,

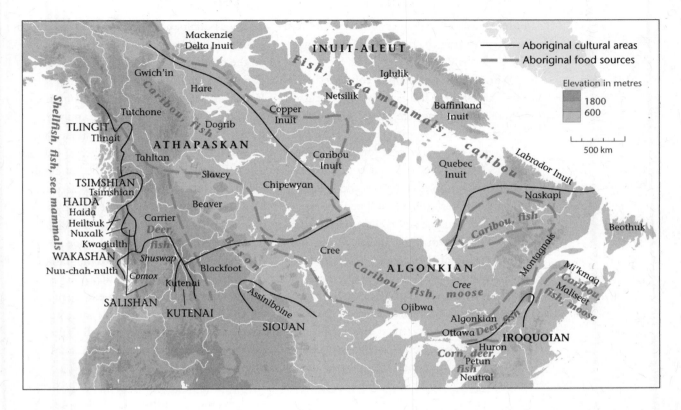

FIGURE 1.3 Indigenous peoples in northern North America spoke different languages and occupied approximately these areas at the time of European contact.

the treeline retreated southward by as much as three hundred kilometres in places. By 500 BCE, environmental conditions were similar to those experienced by Europeans when they first arrived in North America in 1000 CE.

The changing environment influenced the movement of generations of people across northern North America. Their adaptations to new regions – the Arctic, tundra, woodlands, and coastal regions – created different societies and cultures that shared certain characteristics (see Figure 1.3). The climate remained cool, and the environment could not sustain many people. Although warmer areas such as the Pacific Interior and the St. Lawrence Valley supported farming, the majority of people were hunter-gatherers

who relied on relatively simple technology and dispersed, seasonal, and unpredictable food supplies. Despite a harsh environment, they were self-sufficient, relied on their intimate knowledge of the land and resources, and developed patterns of subsistence living finely adapted to local environments. They also developed trade networks within and among tribes.

The peoples of the Pacific Coast and Interior were primarily fishers who relied on spears, hooks, nets, and weirs. Some followed the salmon along the Fraser, Thompson, and upper Columbia Rivers and lived in temporary huts covered in rush mats. More sedentary peoples spent most of the year in pit houses, made of logs and covered in sod, along riverbanks. They feasted, participated in religious and healing ceremonies, and told stories featuring characters such as Coyote, the trickster.

Northwest Coast peoples consumed enormous amounts of fish but sustained healthy fisheries by holding ceremonies to delay fishing until the salmon spawned. Such rituals were a mark of respect for the "salmon people," whom they believed were much like themselves but lived in houses and villages under the water. Animals and people were essentially the same and could transfer from one type of life form to another. When the salmon voluntarily left their villages and offered themselves to humans, all groups celebrated their coming. After the feast, they carefully returned the fish bones to the water so the salmon would return once again. Northwest Coast peoples likewise talked to and thanked the animals they hunted and the cedar trees they stripped of bark for clothing and baskets.

Although the peoples of the Pacific Northwest were constantly on the move during their seasonal hunting and fishing activities, they developed more settled and hierarchical communities as their food supplies became more abundant. Because they enjoyed a moderate climate by Canadian standards, their art and construction techniques flourished, and their populations expanded. They used trees from old-growth forests to make large cedar houses, and their regionally distinctive wooden carvings of ravens, thunderbirds, and other powerful creatures reflected their artistic and spiritual sensibilities.

Over the Rocky Mountains to the east, the Plains Indians likewise developed "increasingly effective subsistence strategies over the millennia" (Ray 1996, 13). Huge herds of buffalo, or bison, which ranged across parkland or grasslands, depending on the position of vegetative communities, dominated these hunters' lives. Plains Indians moved on a seasonal basis in pursuit of animals, and their dependency on the buffalo meant they had to manipulate the environment to enhance its ability to support herds. Early peoples followed the buffalo on foot and used dogs and travois to carry supplies and carcasses. The men used projectile points on spears, darts (atlatls), and then bows and arrows to hunt. As they became more familiar with the buffalos' migration patterns, they began to lure them into enclosures in winter or to stampede them off cliffs in summer. They used the same kill sites, such as Head-Smashed-In-Buffalo-Jump in southern Alberta, for thousands of years.

The centrality of the buffalo to the lives of Plains Indians influenced their cosmology, customs, and spirituality. Plains Indians viewed the buffalo as the provider, as a link between the creator and humans. The Sun Dance, a ritual in preparation for the hunt, revolved around the central image of the buffalo. Plains Indians also constructed large medicine wheels on hilltops throughout the northern Prairies for easier communication with the spirits. Composed of circles with lines of stones radiating out like spokes, medicine wheels were used to attract rain and buffalo and, possibly, to mark burial sites. During hunts, Plains Indians made offerings to the buffalo spirits because they believed the boundaries between people and animals were blurred. Following the hunt, they often used every part of the animal: the meat for food, the bones for tools, the hides and fur for clothing, the skins for making mobile lodgings (teepees), buffalo chips for cooking fuel, bladders for receptacles, and sinews for bow strings and cordage.

In the Eastern Woodlands and Subarctic, Aboriginal peoples can be grouped into two language families: Algonkian or Iroquoian. The Algonkians hunted, fished, and gathered berries and nuts for sustenance. In this harsh climate, they roamed incessantly in search of animals for food and clothing. When Europeans first made contact with the Algonkians on the Atlantic coast at the end of the fifteenth century, these nomadic forest peoples had occupied the same places for generations. From Yukon to Labrador, various groups hunted within territorial boundaries that remained fluid. They assumed that all phenomena, including the dead and animals, had spirit power. The hunt was a spiritual quest in which the hunter's soul spirit would lead him to game that had agreed to be slain. The hunters' sense of kinship with game animals suffused Algonkian culture. Their respect for nature and taboos controlled and moderated human behaviour. Hunters were occasionally wasteful, but their culture often inhibited them from overexploiting wildlife. Their mobile lifestyle also led them to adopt the canoe; light, portable housing; and a few easy-to-carry utensils. This way of life limited their possessions and stores of food, and it probably helped keep their population levels low. Their patterns of living were well suited to their environment.

The Iroquoian "forest" peoples were likewise diverse but "inhabited a single ecological zone of deciduous forest with coniferous admixture." Their material culture and societies resulted from a noteworthy "correlation

THE HORSE AND THE TRANSFORMATION OF PLAINS SOCIETIES

The Blackfoot Confederacy, or Niits'tapi, composed of tribes that inhabit present-day Montana and southern Alberta, first encountered the horse around 1730. Spanish explorers brought the horse to the New World by ship in the sixteenth century, and the animals eventually spread north. The Blackfoot traded some to their neighbours, the Cree and Assiniboine, by 1750. The horse transformed the buffalo hunt and, with it, Plains Indians. As the kill became more efficient, tribes became wealthier and enjoyed a higher standard of living. Wealth and power, combined with increased mobility, led to more intertribal warfare and the development of warrior societies.

between ecological, linguistic, and cultural boundaries" (Trigger 1969, 6, 14). The Wenro, Erie, Neutral, and Petun peoples lived north of the Great Lakes, where they grew and traded tobacco. The powerful Huron Confederacy (called Wendat, meaning "islanders" or "peninsula dwellers") lived near Penetanguishene on Lake Huron. The confederacy consisted of four nations – People of the Bear, People of the Rocks, the Cord People, and the Deer People – names all drawn from the natural world.

The Huron were distinctive in that they lived on the northern limits of fertile land that could be cultivated, and they practised intensive agriculture. They used the slash-and-burn method to clear areas of forests and weeds. They then intercropped, or planted together, the "three sisters" – beans, corn, and squash – on large, well-spaced mounds. Archaeological evidence of ridged, furrowed, and raised fields suggests that they used various techniques to reduce frost hazards. They also kept gardens for emergency seed supplies in case crops failed. After ten to twelve years of cultivation, they abandoned

DORSET ARTWORK: REFLECTIONS OF A HARSH ENVIRONMENT

The Dorset people's artwork, like Inuit art in general, reflects a culture shaped by a harsh, cruel environment, one in which animals were the main source of survival. Their artwork consisted of small sculptures of humans, animals, and birds carved in bone, antler, ivory, soapstone, and wood. These figures had a magical or religious significance, and the Dorset possibly used them as amulets to ward off evil spirits or in shamanic rituals. Carvers often depicted the largest predator in their world, the polar bear. Their sculptures of bears with slit throats filled with red ochre and ivory slivers perhaps played a key role in hunting rituals.

exhausted fields to lie fallow. The Huron learned to make various tuberous plants edible, they tapped maple trees for sap to convert to sugar, they wove mats and baskets from reeds, and they turned clay into cooking pots. Because their more sedentary lifestyle and food crops sustained more people, the Huron were more numerous than the northern Algonkian hunter-gatherer societies with whom they traded. They numbered about thirty thousand people at the time of contact with Europeans.

In the Arctic, Aboriginal peoples moved through a harsh environment on a seasonal basis to hunt seal, caribou, muskox, and small birds and animals. The Dorset, a Paleo-Eskimo culture that lived along the coast of Labrador and Newfoundland, developed sturdy hide kayaks for water travel, sleds for snow travel, and made harpoons and small tools out of stone, bone, wood, and ivory. Their rectangular soapstone lamps burned oil from whale blubber for heat and light. The Dorset people's precarious existence depended on hunting seal and walrus in the spring and summer and fishing for Arctic

char in the summer. Even with small numbers, people sometimes starved during the scarce winter months. In the summer, they lived in tents made of seal or muskox skins. In the winter, they built sod and stone huts in the ground. When they hunted seals, they probably built igloos on sea ice. After living for about five centuries in the Arctic, some Dorset communities disappeared as a result of environmental distress, brought on by a cooling period between 550 BCE and 400 CE. When temperatures rose again after 400 CE, they enjoyed a more predictable environment and a surge of creativity in the arts.

Around 1000 CE, the Thule, ancestors of the modern Inuit, moved rapidly across the Arctic from the west and displaced or absorbed the Dorset. Warmer temperatures and changing ice conditions provided the Thule with an opportunity to move eastward through sea ice passages in pursuit of sea mammals, including whales, seals, and walrus. The Thule also had more advanced technology and better weaponry than the Dorset, including projectile-point tools and spears. Thule hunters travelled on water in skin boats and used dog sleds and bows and arrows to hunt caribou on land. Their decorative art was functional and less spiritual than Dorset creations.

The Beothuk, who inhabited Newfoundland at the time of contact, likewise eked out a living in their inhospitable environment. With ingenuity and inventiveness, they used available resources to build half-moon-shaped birch bark canoes, complex conical dwellings called *mamateeks,* and fences to hunt caribou. They covered the *mamateeks* with birch bark and, in winter, insulated them with dried moss and banked them with soil. The Beothuk population was small but viable. The island's limited resources, however, could not accommodate other peoples, such as the Mi'kmaq. The situation led to competition and hostility between the two peoples.

Aboriginal Perceptions of and Approaches to the Land

Aboriginal peoples adapted to new environments out of necessity. They also modified their environments to suit their needs. They marked the land with rocks, paths, and settlements. They used fire for multiple purposes: for heat and light; to clear fields and campsites; as a weapon; for communication; to enhance the production of certain foods and medicinal plants; to attract, hunt, and drive wildlife; and to improve grazing for horses after they acquired them. By setting fire to prairie grasslands, for example, Aboriginal people created and maintained fire-succession ecosystems. They kept back forests and enhanced soils. In forested areas, they created edge habitats that attracted deer and combatted insect infestations. These practices, which sometimes escaped their control, nevertheless reflected their ecological knowledge of the land and their ability to manipulate it.

Aboriginal people's integration with the environment and knowledge of the natural world led them to view their surroundings from both material and spiritual perspectives. Besides living off the land, Aboriginal peoples developed cultural customs, religious ideas, and myths and taboos to live safely and to better understand their place in the world. They inhabited a vast, dark, and silent

THE THULE: MOVERS OF BOULDERS

The Thule used rocks for many purposes: to hold down tents and boats, to identify winter villages, to build cairns for their dead, to protect meat supplies, and to build dams or weirs to intercept runs of Arctic char. They also built *inuksuit* (plural of *inukshuk*), rocks piled to resemble humans, to mark a featureless snow-covered landscape or to channel caribou toward waiting hunters. By moving boulders, the Thule altered the landscape and left numerous traces of their presence for modern archaeologists.

land occupied by other species. Spirits, they believed, inhabited these species and had varying degrees of power. Aboriginal people sought to live harmoniously with the spirits by making offerings to them, along with beseeching prayers and gifts. They prayed to ward off diseases caused by evil spirits and to ensure their own safety when crossing dangerous river passages.

Aboriginal peoples' distinctive customs and art expressed their fear of the environment and respect for its animate and inanimate inhabitants. Feasts, ceremonies, traditions, and stories, including creation narratives, were part of indigenous peoples' spiritual lives and religious ideas. They reflected their relationship with nature and helped to integrate their societies. Their animistic religions – religions in which all things, animate or inanimate, have souls or spirits – did not distinguish between human, plant, and animal. They respected and placated them all. Although Aboriginal people hunted animals, they shared their environment with them and developed rituals to show their respect. Within their worldview, human beings did not hold a special place in the cosmos – they were but one element among many in an integrated environment. This worldview meant accommodation with other species and with nature. Pre-contact farming and hunter-gatherer societies understood their environment. They had to if they hoped to maintain their culture, a food supply, and a manageable population level. They were people who "adapted to their environment and worked out a code of behaviour for living compatibly with their world" (Miller 1989, 13).

Early Explorers: The Norse

Unlike self-sufficient Aboriginal peoples, who lived in sync with their surroundings, the first Europeans to reach the North American continent were traders who came to exploit the new land. Land hunger, trade, and the desire for wealth and fame – if necessary, through piracy and war – motivated the Norse to move overseas. A land shortage in Scandinavia placed limits on crops and animal husbandry. Their agriculture-based economy needed new pastures and grass for grazing animals, and global warming in the centuries between 800 and 1200 CE facilitated their explorations.

The Norse landed in what is today the Arctic and Newfoundland and Labrador in 1000 CE. They stayed a relatively short time, but they traded on return voyages. And although they had only a slight environmental impact on the land, their brief stay in the so-called New World resulted in the earliest meeting of Aboriginal peoples (called Skraelings by the Norse) and Europeans. Unlike European explorations of centuries later, which resulted in permanent settlements, the incursion of the Norse ended when Aboriginal people drove them out. While in the New World, the Norse depended on their own technology – including their magnificent ships, weapons, and iron tools – to maintain themselves, acquire resources, and complete trading expeditions. But they were not self-sufficient, and they could not survive without Aboriginal allies to teach them the geography, assist them in acquiring trade goods, and instruct them in skills to live in such a harsh environment. Aboriginal peoples retained control of their environment.

Leif Eiriksson, son of Eirik the Red, is credited with the first landings in North America. He landed on and named three areas: Helluland, the "land of flat stones," on the east coast of Baffin Island; Markland, the "land of forests and timber," in central Labrador; and Vinland, "a warm and bountiful land," most likely the northern tip of Newfoundland, the site of the Norse village L'Anse aux Meadows. Indigenous peoples had used the site around the village for hunting and fishing for thousands of years. When Leif's brother Thorvald encountered indigenous people, probably Dorset or Thule, during the second expedition to Vinland in 1004, he provoked hostilities and died from an arrow wound. His crew retreated, wintered at Leifsbudir, a settlement founded by Leif, and sailed home in the spring.

Other Norse traders and explorers likewise encountered Aboriginal peoples, such as the early Algonkians (Point Revenge and Beothuk peoples), as they sailed through icy waters along the windy eastern shores of Baffin Island, Newfoundland, and Labrador. Thorfinn Karlsefni, of Iceland, reached

Helluland and Markland between 1003 and 1015 and explored other areas, which he named. He and his crew acquired trade items, such as polar bear pelts, walrus tusks, narwhal horns, and eider ducks. Later, on a trip to Europe, Karlsefni sold his ship's figurehead, carved of maple from Vinland, to a man from Bremen. It was possibly the first crafted import from North America to Europe. Karlsefni, too, tried to colonize Vinland, but he also encountered Aboriginal people, probably Beothuk. He bartered either milk or red cloth for furs. An outbreak of hostilities, however, caused the Norse to abandon their outpost after only a few years. They returned to their more established colonies in Greenland, settled by the Danes in 986, and made no further colonization efforts in North America. Brief trips (perhaps to Labrador or Baffin Island) for timber and furs ceased after cooler temperatures and ice killed expedition members from Iceland in 1347.

Throughout the period of Norse explorations, Aboriginal peoples and the Norse encountered each other only sporadically. The Thule's encounters with the Norse in both Greenland and in what would become Canada suggest a relationship defined by occasional trade and conflict. Trade was mutually beneficial: the Thule wanted iron, and the Norse wanted animal hides and ivory. By the thirteenth century, the Thule had meteoric iron and had acquired smelted iron, which they valued for tools and tips on weapons. These most northern hunter-gatherers traded occasionally with the Norse but were not interested in lengthy connections. They drove the Norse out of the continent. Perhaps the contact was too brief.

Perhaps the climate, on the eve of the Little Ice Age, which would overtake Europe and North America from around 1300 to 1870, was too cool. It seems the Norse were not carriers of European pathogens. For whatever reason, Aboriginal people were not exposed to European diseases. Consequently, they did not suffer the destabilization and depopulation that followed the Columbian exchange.

European Expansionism

The early Norse period of exploration was largely forgotten in Europe. Although the Norse maintained settlements in Greenland until about the mid-fifteenth century, they abandoned their sailing route to North America when increasing ice in the Atlantic made sailing too dangerous. With the exception of annual voyages across the Atlantic by European fishermen, European exploration did not begin in earnest until the late fifteenth century, when Christopher Columbus's voyage across the Atlantic Ocean in 1492 and John Cabot's rediscovery of North America in 1497 led to general awareness of the American continents.

These so-called discoveries coincided in western Europe with the emergence of imperialism, the policy of extending a nation's authority by territorial acquisition or economic and political hegemony over other nations. The process of imperial expansion led European states with advanced technologies to invade remote lands occupied by migratory farmers and hunter-gatherers, whom they displaced. These incursions were premised on notions of superiority, conquest, and environmental exploitation for commercial gain. Unlike Aboriginal peoples,

Europeans believed, as both Greek philosophy and Christianity taught them, that their minds and spirit made them superior to nature, which was for human benefit, if only it could be mastered. Although Aboriginal people admired aspects of European technology that could make their lives easier, Europeans held the myopic view that indigenous people were inferior beings that lacked both society and culture. Upon hearing of the New World, Europeans instinctively looked for exploitable goods. They started with fish and then moved to furs. The history of Canada, consequently, is partly a story of resources exploitation.

The Early Fisheries

At about the same time that the Norse abandoned their settlements in Greenland, Spanish, Portuguese, Italian, French, and English sailors entered the North Atlantic in search of fish. Although knowledge of western lands, in general, had faded in Europe and had been consigned to saga texts, it had lived on in the stories and knowledge of ordinary fishermen. With the Norse settlements, fishermen pursued whales, fished for cod, and traded European goods for falcons, polar bears, and ivory along the coast. Years after the Norse retreated, European fishers continued to arrive annually to harvest cod, seals, and whales. The Catholic Church had stimulated a burgeoning market for Atlantic cod *(Gadus morhua)* by declaring fish a suitable food for meatless religious holy days. When the building of larger ships enabled travel for longer distances, the cod fishery expanded. Despite high casualty rates in the frigid northern seas, more European fishers sent out ships, which returned with enormous hauls. John Cabot's successful voyage to Newfoundland in 1497 further publicized the immense marine resources of the northwest Atlantic.

The profitable Grand Banks fishery, located southeast of Newfoundland on the North American continental shelf, supplied cod to Europe and drove further exploration. The fishery was an open-access resource, and nations mingled fairly amicably, except in times of war. By the late sixteenth century, hundreds of fishing and whaling fleets with thousands of men set sail for the Grand

BASQUE FISHERMAN AND OVERFISHING IN THE GRAND BANKS

Basques were among the earliest fishermen to arrive in Newfoundland. They hunted whales and found the Grand Banks bountiful with cod. They enjoyed friendly relations with some coastal peoples, such as the Montagnais, but poor relations with the Inuit. The Basques sometimes traded European goods for seal skins, and they developed a pidgin dialect to communicate with indigenous peoples. When explorer John Cabot wrote about the abundance of cod in the region, he noted that Aboriginal peoples called it *baccalaos*. This was not an Aboriginal word but rather a derivation of *bakalaua*, a Euskara or Basque word. In other words, Basque fishermen had established a presence in the New World long before Cabot's visit. In the sixteenth century, Basque whalers affected the environment by contributing to the precipitous decline in bowhead whales, the extinction of right whales and southern walrus, and the depletion of seabird colonies. They harvested enormous amounts of cod. Given that both whales and cod feed on crustacean zooplankton, it is possible that smaller whale populations actually increased cod stocks around the end of the sixteenth century.

Banks each year. In 1578, for example, English merchant Anthony Parkhurst estimated that there were nearly 400 ships in Newfoundland – 150 were French, 100 Spanish (Basque), 50 Portuguese, 30 to 50 English, and 20 to 30 Basque. They processed an estimated 75,000 tonnes of fish annually. The trade required unprecedented skills and large amounts of capital and labour. Europeans adapted their fishing practices to meet the harsh conditions of the new environment. Each country acquired favourite fishing spots and used various fishing tools and methods in their fisheries. Fishermen developed fish oil and wet cod for northern European markets and dried cod for markets in southern Europe and the West Indies. Merchants managed fishers, and governments, in turn, managed merchants. The fur trade began as part of the fishery but later developed into a separate industry.

Codfish stocks remained abundant in the Newfoundland fishery despite prolonged colder temperatures during the Little Ice Age and fluctuations in catches. It is difficult to estimate the size of catches, but they were greater than any catch made by the small Inuit population, and advances in gear technology increased catch levels over time. The catch level remained sustainable throughout the seventeenth and eighteenth centuries, probably because of relatively low-tech fishing methods. Much like their modern counterparts, early fishermen reacted to reduced catches by either moving to new fishing areas or changing their methods. Biologists have recently suggested that continued, intense, unregulated fishing depleted stocks and might have encouraged cod

migration. Because the capture of large fish influences the rate of reproduction among cod, even the early fisheries' "moderate" catches would have altered the age, gender composition, and overall size of Atlantic cod.

Although the fishermen were only sojourners in the New World, they explored and made their mark on the coastal regions of Newfoundland. Fishing crews landed on Terra Nova to rest, to gather fresh water and wood, and to dry fish on the shores. Migratory fishers in the dry fisheries needed cabins, wharves, flakes to dry fish, washing cages, and sometimes oil vats. They stripped trees from old-growth boreal forests, took more wood than they needed, left much to rot, and sometimes started forest fires, which destroyed flora and fauna. The environmental damage was limited, however, because they did not move too far inland. But by 1620 the forests were noticeably less dense.

European fishers had a more permanent effect on those Aboriginal people who had to compete with them for summer fishing sites. Some made special trading or raiding trips to obtain goods from fishermen. Fishermen traded iron, cloth, and arms for furs, which returned to Europe with the large cod catches. By the late sixteenth century, European traders were meeting the Mi'kmaq regularly at summer rendezvous sites to barter, and the Mi'kmaq were changing their hunting patterns to engage in this trade. The Beothuk, in contrast, lost their summer fishing sites to the Europeans and came to depend more and more on the interior for resources. Meagre resources, infectious diseases, and violent encounters with Europeans drove them to extinction.

European Explorers Chart a New Environment

The impact of European expansion was limited to a small geographical area during the era of the early fisheries, a situation that changed once European rulers turned their sights on the New World. Competitive expansionary politics in Europe, scientific curiosity, technological developments in navigation (compasses, quadrants, and astrolabes), and larger ships spurred explorers westward. Cartographers recorded new discoveries on maps as the European world became more connected by trade and commerce. From the beginning, Europeans viewed the New World as a bountiful land. In particular, they sought a shorter sea passage to Asia – the famed Northwest Passage – and new resources to exploit. Their acquisitiveness extended to scientific inquiries that facilitated imperial aims.

The Age of Exploration began in northern North America in 1497, when Britain sponsored Genovese merchant John Cabot's (Giovanni Caboto) search for the Northwest Passage to Asia. The exact place of Cabot's landing is unknown, but the possibilities range from the Strait of Belle Isle to Cape Breton. This first recorded European landing since the Norse led to a better cartographic understanding of what Europeans soon realized was a large continent.

Perhaps because early explorers such as Cabot and Jacques Cartier did not venture far beyond coastlines, their early impressions were of an unending, abundant "wilderness," an earthly paradise or pristine environment inhabited by only a few people. This notion of abundance persisted and set the stage for

wasteful behaviour by fur traders, loggers, and settlers. While sailing near the Grand Banks in 1497, for example, Cabot noted that the fish were so abundant they slowed the boat. In 1501, Gaspar Corte-Real, the Portuguese explorer, recorded that he saw plentiful game – caribou, foxes, sables, otters, wolves, and tigers (probably black leopards) – in Newfoundland. In 1534, when Cartier, exploring for France, approached what he called the Isle of Birds (Funk Island) off the coast of Newfoundland, he described a land where bears swam out to feed on birds and where gannets, murres, and puffins nested. The great auk, the original "penguin," now extinct, he observed, was as large as a goose, "being black and white with a beak like a crow's." Its small wings rendered it incapable of flying (Cook 1993, xvii). The crew killed over a thousand murres and great auks. Sir Humphrey Gilbert, an English explorer who landed in Newfoundland in 1583, wrote that nature made up for the terrible cold weather "with incredible quantity and no less variety of all kinds of fish in the sea and fresh waters, as trouts, salmons and other fish to us unknown; also cod which alone draweth many nations thither." He observed that the many creatures "may induce us to glorify the magnificent God, who hath superabundantly replenished the earth with creatures serving *for the use of man,* though man hath not used the fifth part of same" (Payne 1900, 30).

Despite their initial fear of the unknown and wild animals, explorers evaluated the new environment for exploitable commodities. When Italian explorer Giovanni da Verrazano explored the East Coast from Newfoundland to the Carolinas for the French Crown in 1524, he searched the forests for suitable wood and examined rocks for minerals. Both Cabot and Corte-Real commented that the region's tall trees would be ideal for ships' masts. Old-growth forests, now almost beyond our comprehension, were a new, valuable source of wood because timber in Europe was becoming a scarce commodity. When Cartier abandoned his settlement on the St. Lawrence and returned to France in 1542, he took with him pyrites and quartz that he thought were gold and diamonds. As Martin Frobisher sailed through the eastern Arctic in 1576 in search of the Northwest Passage, he collected 203 tonnes of mineral samples, which later proved worthless. Although members of several expeditions met Aboriginal people who wanted to trade furs, the trade did not begin in earnest until fashion trends in Europe increased demand for fur.

Although the New World in general was viewed as bountiful, explorers described northern regions in less flattering terms. Although Verrazano, reminded of Vergil's *Arcady*, referred to southern regions as Arcadia, Cartier described Labrador's barren coast as the "land God gave to Cain." A member of Frobisher's expedition remarked, "In place of odiferous and fragrant smells of sweet gums and pleasant notes of musical birds, which other countries in more temperate zones do yield, we tasted the most boisterous Boreal blasts mixed with snow and hail in the months of June and July, nothing inferior to our intemperate winter" (Honour 1975, 16). The comment is one of the earliest recorded complaints about Canada's weather. Because imports from the north — cod, pelts, and wood — were not as enticing as gold from Spanish conquests or spices from the East Indies, the French and British Crowns did not encourage permanent settlements until changing markets made Canada a valuable source of raw materials.

First Contacts

Europeans' entry into the New World overturned thousands of years of Aboriginal predominance in only a few hundred years. First contact, the first meeting of two cultures, was a long process in Canada that took centuries as explorers and fur traders charted the new environment. These first encounters, described by Europeans as "discoveries," began in 1498, when Cabot bartered a pair of Venetian earrings and a sword with Labrador Algonkians and gave netting needles to Inuit. The first recorded encounter on the Pacific Coast occurred nearly three hundred years later, in 1774, when the Spanish navigator Juan Perez exchanged clothes, beads, and knives for sea otter skins from the Haida. Four years later, James Cook spotted the West Coast from aboard the *Resolution* and discovered that Russian fur-trading companies had hunted sea otter and walrus in the region for years. He sailed past the Strait of Juan de Fuca to Nootka Sound, where men in huge canoes greeted him and traded fine sea otter skins for a few nails. His crew then headed north to the limits of the North American coast in the Arctic in search of an opening into the continent. First contacts ended in 1910 when the Copper Inuit met explorer Vilhjalmur Stefansson near Victoria Island in the Arctic.

Explorers' accounts of first contacts reflect their cultural bias, which influenced how they viewed the landscape and the people who inhabited it. Explorers proclaimed their

FIGURE 1.4 "Cartier Plants a Cross at Gaspe 1534": Symbols of possession, such as Cartier's fifty-foot wooden cross, justified European expansion but made Aboriginal people hostile or suspicious of European encroachments on their environment.

Charles W. Jefferys, illustrator, *The Picture Gallery of Canadian History* (Toronto: Ryerson, 1950), 1:73

THE MYTH OF DISCOVERY, HISTORY, AND ENVIRONMENTAL HISTORY

The idea that Europeans had discovered or found an empty new continent justified their desire to conquer it. Until recently, historians upheld this myth of discovery by estimating, incorrectly, that the Aboriginal population at first contact had been low. New, scientific methods have raised estimates substantially. It is now estimated that 60 to 100 million lived in North and South America combined and that 4 to 11 million people lived in North America alone. The indigenous population of northern North America was relatively sparse, about 500,000 people, and lacked cities, as Europeans understood them, but Canada was, nevertheless, a land inhabited by diverse peoples who had complex material cultures and spiritual beliefs, people who manipulated their environment with fire and by hunting, cultivating, harvesting, and gathering food. This misconception about population numbers made contact a momentous process because it justified Europeans' aggressive intrusion into the new environment. Environmental historians continue to view contact as important, but they examine it from the perspective of how imperialism and colonialism affected the peoples and landscape of the New World.

"discoveries" with symbols of possession – such as Cabot's English flags and Cartier's fifty-foot wooden cross with a French coat of arms – and claimed territory on behalf of their sovereigns without regard for Aboriginal peoples (see Figure 1.4). Cartier saw no reason to ask permission to explore or establish settlements. He, like most Europeans, believed that Aboriginal people had wasted the land by not rendering it productive. In another kind of possession, he and other explorers gave European names to flora, fauna, and places, without a care that they already had Aboriginal names.

Contact, however, was a momentous two-way process of discovery and acculturation. Both cultures had only a rudimentary understanding of the world's geography, were vulnerable to food scarcity, and were fearful of their uncertain environments. Europeans had more advanced technology, but unlike indigenous peoples, they had poor personal hygiene and a poor understanding of medicine. Many Europeans had grown up in crowded, filthy cities and showed signs of ill health and poor physical development. By comparison, Aboriginal people were physically strong and healthy.

Whereas written European accounts of first contacts predominated in traditional historical narratives, oral accounts passed from generation to generation among Aboriginal people. In 1633, a young Montagnais who lived along the St. Lawrence related his grandmother's story of seeing French ships for the first time. The Montagnais thought the "floating islands" were inhabited by supernatural spirits and mistook the sails for clouds and the cannon discharges for thunder. During other first contacts, Aboriginal people likewise treated Europeans who appeared at the "edge of the water, woods, plains, or desert" as powerful spirits or shamans (Axtell 1992, 26, 35-37). And they interpreted European technology as having extraordinary spiritual power. They examined cloth, metal goods, compasses, and books with fascination. At first, they responded most positively to trinkets such as glass beads, which they buried with their dead because they associated them with natural materials that brought physical, spiritual, and social well-being.

Aboriginal peoples welcomed the newcomers by giving their boats the best anchorages. They carried Cartier ashore so he would not get wet, seated guests on skins or mats, and entertained them with speeches, dancing, singing, and games. Aboriginal people recognized that these encounters with Europeans might have serious consequences and tried to assimilate the "aliens" into their society to ensure peace. In the east, they smoked the calumet pipe with their visitors because tobacco was sacred and lifted their prayers to heaven. Across the land, they offered marriages and the adoption of children, perhaps because they sensed that the newcomers' power could be a double-edged sword. Europeans at first depended on Aboriginal people for information about the environment. They engaged them as guides, translators, and provisioners and were careful not to offend for fear of being abandoned in the woods or attacked. Aboriginal people had the upper hand in the relationship, as indicated by European efforts to learn their languages. But as Europeans learned more, they became more dominant, and unlike the Norse, they kept coming.

FIGURE 1.5 Hudson's
Bay Company canoe
manned by voyageurs
passing a waterfall
Frances Anne Hopkins, artist, 1869,
Library and Archives Canada,
Frances Anne Hopkins fonds,
C-002771

The Columbian Exchange

Environmental transformation and cultural
change began as soon as the peoples from the
two hemispheres met. As historian William
Cronon notes, two human communities
confronted each other for the first time, and
two sets of ecological relationships came to
inhabit one world. The massive exchange of
ideas, diseases, and agricultural goods and
the intermingling of North American and
European biota – animal and plant life – that
followed first contacts quickly shattered the
relationship between Aboriginal peoples and
their environment.

The Columbian exchange was an uneven
exchange. Europeans affected the New World
more than Aboriginal peoples influenced the
Old. Cartier made notes on edible fruits and
nuts and took slips of trees and seeds to
France for the king's garden at Fontainebleu.
Most expeditions had naturalists. In 1792,
for example, Archibald Menzies, a surgeon-
botanist, arrived on the West Coast with
British explorer George Vancouver. He was
the first European to describe, catalogue, and
collect West Coast trees, plants, and seeds,
which he took to England for his mentor,

Joseph Banks, the director of the Royal
Gardens at Kew, who had been on Cook's
first voyage. In the 1820s, James Douglas,
an explorer and naturalist, sent plants, including the Sitka spruce, to Britain. Europeans gained corn, potatoes, and tobacco
from the New World and absorbed indigenous peoples' knowledge about plants into
European botany and medicine.

The exchange of knowledge and new
plants and crops went both ways. Samuel de
Champlain, who founded New France and
Quebec City in 1608, encouraged the growth
of French crops such as wheat and barley in
his colony along the St. Lawrence. They did
well in the fertile, previously untilled soil.
When settlers and missionaries migrated,
they carried seeds and brought domesticated
animals, such as cattle and pigs, previously
unknown to Aboriginal people. Ships not
only carried explorers and settlers, they also
carried weeds, insects, and diseases that ran
rampant and transformed the ecological
systems of the New World and the health
of Aboriginal people.

European diseases caused drastic declines in indigenous populations – in some
communities, only 10 percent of people

survived – and assisted European occupation and conquest. Pre-contact Aboriginal societies had by no means been disease-free, but because Aboriginal people lived in small mobile groups and in a cool climate free of domesticated animals, they were relatively safe. Archaeological findings indicate that some undernourished peoples suffered from endemic pathologies – diseases restricted to certain areas or populations – but the effects of such diseases were insignificant compared to Old World pathogens, against which indigenous peoples lacked antibodies. When Jesuit priests brought measles to the Huron in 1636 and smallpox in 1640, the epidemics cut the Huron population in half within a few years. Drastic population declines unhinged and destabilized Aboriginal societies. They caused starvation, conflict, and the merger of different groups when survivors adopted refugees and orphans. Territories were cleared of people, cleared land reverted to woods, and wildlife increased. Newcomers moved in, only to start the process all over again.

Historians tend to view the Columbian exchange negatively, as a form of biological imperialism. In the 1930s, geographer Carl Sauer lamented the extensive biological changes brought on by contact between what he called the ecological islands of Asia, Africa, Europe, and the Americas. More recently, historian William H. McNeill has argued that the unification of the planet inaugurated by Columbus either damaged or destroyed local forms of life, human and nonhuman, and made possible political conquest and settlement (McNeill 1976). Alfred Crosby, who coined the term *Columbian exchange*, writes of the "cataclysmic loss

DISEASES IN THE NEW WORLD

The spread of diseases – including smallpox, cholera, measles, influenza, and tuberculosis – from Europeans to Aboriginal peoples was an ongoing process that accompanied, if not preceded, European expansion throughout the continent. Between 1760 and 1820, for example, fur traders introduced diseases to the Plains Indians. The smallpox epidemic of 1781 killed at least a third of almost every band. Between 1819 and 1839, measles reduced the Cree from 3,000 to 1,600 people, and smallpox spread among the Assiniboine. A smallpox epidemic in 1862-63 reduced the population of the Queen Charlotte Islands by almost 90 percent.

of Native life from imported diseases" and "the extinction of more species of life forms in the last 400 years than the usual processes of evolution might kill off in a million" years. The result? "A more impoverished genetic pool" (Crosby 1994, 180). Such pessimism is understandable, given the plight of indigenous peoples and the downward trajectory of the planet's environmental health to the present. But the interaction between ecology and empire is a complex historical process that defies simplistic interpretations. The results of the Columbian exchange were not simply destructive. The New World's ecosystems proved to be resilient and dynamic. Pre-contact Aboriginal societies were viable and sustainable, but so too were postcontact European settler societies. In some cases, Europeans' drive for wealth and expansion led to the productive management of resources, improved living standards, and increased population numbers.

The Competition for Furs

When Europeans encountered the New World, they not only brought new diseases and flora and fauna, they also "thrust commercialized human predation across the North Atlantic Ocean. Commercial hunting proved to be the most lucrative way to exploit the northernmost regions of the Americas" (Richards 2005, 463). The trade in furs – sea otter, beaver, buffalo – depended on long-term, shifting alliances between French and English traders and Aboriginal peoples that transformed the environment by depleting wildlife, hastening the spread of disease, disrupting ecosystems, and marginalizing indigenous peoples. The fur trade began casually on the Atlantic Coast around 1580, when European fishers and whalers traded goods for furs. It quickly developed into an enormous separate industry fuelled by European fashions, particularly an insatiable demand for hats made from felted beaver fur. Hunters depleted beaver populations in Europe and Russia and turned to North America as an opportune new source for the fur. By 1750, beaver pelts amounted to about 40 percent of all skins sent abroad from North America.

Competition for furs and the exhaustion of beaver fields heightened imperial rivalries between France and England and sparked further exploration of the continent. The territorial reach of the trade quickly exceeded the limits of settlement. Encouraged by traders, Aboriginal hunters pursued beaver in the Maritimes, up the St. Lawrence, along eastern interior rivers such as the Saguenay, St. Maurice, and Ottawa, through the Great Lakes, and beyond the forested areas of the Canadian Shield onto the Great Plains. The fur trade eventually extended over the Rocky Mountains to the Pacific Coast and north into the Athabasca region (see Figure 1.6).

When furs brought to France by fishermen began to turn a reliable profit, the Crown set its sights on establishing an overseas empire and a large-scale fur trade, which would operate from a base in the Gulf of St. Lawrence. Champlain, following Cartier's route, surveyed the area between 1603 and 1635 and chose the location for permanent settlements. Meanwhile, the British were busy founding the populous and prosperous Thirteen Colonies on the Atlantic seaboard to the south and searching for the Northwest Passage in the North. In 1610, explorer Henry Hudson discovered a passage into the interior – Hudson Bay – to rival the St. Lawrence River. Growing imperial rivalry led the British to establish the Hudson's Bay Company (HBC) in 1670 and fur-trading posts on both Hudson and James Bays. Over the next century, the French competed effectively with the British by expanding the trade westward along the continent's northern rivers to the Great Lakes and beyond. Wars between France and England and their Aboriginal allies resulted in the Iroquois' destruction of Huronia in 1648; the British expulsion of the French Acadians from present-day Nova Scotia, New Brunswick, and Prince Edward Island; and the Conquest of New France in 1763.

After the Conquest, French traders founded the North West Company (NWC) in Montreal and resumed the spatial expansion of the trade. Between 1774 and 1821, when the HBC gained a monopoly over the trade, French traders built 351 posts, the HBC 250. When the United States gained independence from Britain in 1776, the British lost trade in the American West and, in response, expanded the fur trade north into

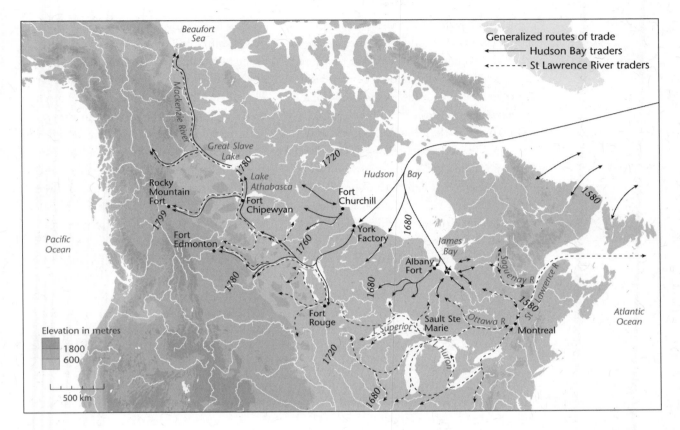

FIGURE 1.6 Major fur trade routes. Competition between the British and French led fur traders to develop different routes through the interior. Settlements both preceded and emerged to service the trade.

the Subarctic and west to the Pacific Coast. Peter Pond, American fur trader and a founder of the North West Company, reached the Athabasca country by land in 1778. The following decade, Aboriginal guides led Scottish fur trader Alexander Mackenzie through the interior, north to Great Slave Lake, and up what would be named the Mackenzie River to the Beaufort Sea. On behalf of the North West Company, Mackenzie evaluated the river systems for use as fur trade routes to the Pacific. In 1793, Aboriginal guides led him to the Pacific Ocean, completing the European penetration of northern North America. Simon Fraser built the first fur trade post west of the Rockies in 1805.

The expansion of the trade had an environmental impact that extended far beyond the exhaustion of beaver populations. The expanding trade required infrastructure such as forts and trading posts, ports for York boats on Hudson Bay, and roads that reshaped the landscape. By the late 1700s, the St. Lawrence fur trade's long supply lines included roads built around portages on the Ottawa River, a canal at Sault Ste. Marie, ships on Lake Superior, and supply bases farther west. Fur trade expansion intensified conflict among Aboriginal hunters and between the French and British, which meant more fortified posts and garrisons. Various Aboriginal groups competed for middleman status. European traders depended on middlemen to retrieve furs from interior tribes in exchange for European goods. Middlemen then delivered the pelts to the posts in exchange for more European goods. The trading companies took sides to secure fur trade routes and to maintain cooperation from Aboriginal people, who guided traders, hunted, trapped, and prepared furs. Conflict among Aboriginal groups resulted in more aggressive hunting and more efficient depletion of resources. Wars between Aboriginal groups became more deadly after traders introduced firearms.

Spatial expansion, imperial rivalry, and war marked the fur trade as it opened up the interior and revealed its main waterways and major geographical regions. The notion of abundance promulgated by explorers persisted. The partners of trading companies maintained a rapacious view of the natural world and a sense of entitlement in relation to their Aboriginal partners, whom they pressured to overharvest wildlife. Many voyageurs, the ordinary men who transported furs, did not want to control the landscape, but they served those who did. The voyageurs were mobile people who believed in nonaccumulation. In this sense, they were similar to Aboriginal hunter-gatherers, but they worked on contract for European commercial companies intent on profit through plunder.

The Fur Trade's Impact on Aboriginal People

Because the fur trade turned fur-bearing animals into commodities, Aboriginal people's approach to the natural world changed radically as they participated in it. As they moved toward commercial hunting, power shifted in favour of Europeans, just as the physical location of Aboriginal groups themselves shifted. Tribes and nations adapted to their role in the trade by changing their spatial distribution. Declining game resources in forested areas and lethal diseases forced Aboriginal people away from Hudson Bay. The Assiniboine and Cree, who once occupied the Eastern Woodlands, pushed west onto the Great Plains. They became buffalo hunters who acquired horses from the Blackfoot and guns from traders.

The fur trade was "perhaps the single most important conduit for contact" and changed Aboriginal peoples' behaviour, hunting practices, and relationship to the environment (Richards 2005, 474). European markets and imperial rivalries drove the trade, but Aboriginal peoples' desire for European goods was persistent, cumulative, and in the case of guns and alcohol, devastating. In the early years, when furs could be obtained without difficulty, trade goods made Aboriginal peoples' lives easier. They could exploit the French-English rivalry to receive gifts and better-quality goods suitable to the northern climate and conditions. As Aboriginal people became dependent on European goods, however, some forgot the old ways. The Montagnais were among the first nations to stop making pottery or cooking in bark containers. It was easier to acquire European goods "in exchange for skins which cost them almost nothing" (Denys 1908 [1672], 442). The Upland Assiniboine and Cree came to value guns so highly and became "so accustomed to using them that they had forgotten how to use bows and arrows as early as 1716" (Ray 1974, 72).

The purpose of hunting changed, and new patterns of living replaced self-sufficient subsistence lifestyles. For example, before 1760, Aboriginal people in the West lived in three distinct habitats – the woodlands, parkland borders, and the grasslands. They followed animals into the parkland in the winter and onto the grasslands in the summer. Their ability to exploit all three zones gave them "a great deal of ecological flexibility," which allowed them to adjust to changing conditions (Ray 1996, 46). This flexibility was important because the availability of resources fluctuated with periodic outbreaks of disease and short-term changes in climate or rainfall. Hunters lost this ability when they ceased their seasonal food quests at traditional sites and adopted the rhythms of the fur trade, which were shaped by market demand for specific furs.

The fur trade companies did not, as a rule, encourage Aboriginal people to practise conservation of wildlife. They simply moved when animals had been depleted in a region. The Hudson's Bay Company even had hunters decimate all wildlife in areas where there might be competition for furs. In the Northwest, when wildlife populations declined, the company did attempt to introduce conservation measures for economic reasons. The policy failed, however, partly because prestige and pensions depended on the numbers of furs officials brought in. Traders therefore judged their short-term interests to be more important than conservation. These measures also came too late for Aboriginal trappers. Some expressed concern about killing methods and the scope of the hunt, but they were dependent on the company for food and wages and often in debt to the companies.

Increased commercial hunting and more efficient weapons such as repeating rifles acquired from Europeans changed the culture of hunting among Aboriginal people and probably affected the traditional spiritual relationship between Aboriginal people and wildlife. Whether Aboriginal people were conservationists or wasteful before contact is a matter of debate. Historian Shepard Krech III believes Aboriginal North Americans had ecological knowledge of the environment, which helped them manipulate it. They expressed their kinship with other species through "narratives, songs, poems, parables, performances, rituals, and material objects" (Krech 1999, 211). But such knowledge was cultural rather than ecological in a modern sense. Aboriginal peoples' behaviour varied depending on the circumstances and could be either conservationist or wasteful. Before contact, for instance, Plains Indians were known to use only parts of the buffalo, rather than the whole animal, if it was undernourished or if its flesh was dry. And buffalo jumps, the pre-contact practice of running buffalo over cliffs, killed hundreds of animals at a time. The fur trade, by making Aboriginal people dependent on the trade, fundamentally altered their circumstances.

Wildlife Depletion

The fur trade depleted North American wildlife. Modern biologists, using historical records, estimate that traders and middlemen slaughtered millions of animals. The trade put the greatest pressure on the North American beaver, which became "prey to one of the longest sustained hunts for a single species in world history" (Richards 2005, 467).

Beaver live in deciduous forests, and Canada's forests were extensive. Estimates of the pre-contact beaver population in North America range from 10 to 100 million. Although beaver are prolific – reproducing two to five kits each year and taking two and a half years to reach maturity – they are vulnerable to hunters because they tend to stay in one place and do not hibernate. Hunters killed approximately 286,000 per year, and diseases (such as an epidemic in 1800 among western beaver) killed off the remainder nearly to extinction.

As the fur trade moved from east to west, it left behind ecosystems altered beyond recognition. Beavers, nature's hydraulic engineers, create dams, ponds, meadows, and useful ecosystems for other wildlife. Beaver dams shape environments by ensuring water supplies and stabilizing stream flows. When beaver populations declined, their dams broke, changing surrounding landscapes and destroying the habitat of other wildlife species. Beaver numbers did not begin to rise until after the 1840s, when Europeans switched from felt to silk hats and when market demand shifted to other furs, such as marten, fox, and muskrat.

Provisioning the fur trade also led to the depletion of other fur-bearing animals. The HBC hired Homeguard Cree to provision its posts. These contract hunters provided traders with moose, caribou, deer, rabbits, and geese. Traders themselves hunted and fished for wildlife to supply their posts and sustain them on journeys. The HBC's policy of self-sufficiency helped reduce its overhead costs, but it depleted species that fell outside of commercial trade. For instance, it is estimated that traders and provisioners at one post could kill up to two hundred partridges a day. In 1709-10, eighty company men at one post, over one winter, consumed ninety thousand partridges, twenty-five thousand hares, thousands of geese, and fish and deer. These numbers seem high, but traders were engaged in heavy work. A single man could consume between six and twelve pounds of meat per day, and posts often fed guests and Aboriginal visitors.

The extermination and disappearance of the buffalo in the United States and Canada remains a grim narrative in the history of wildlife. A number of factors contributed to overhunting. Plains Indians cultures centred on the buffalo hunt, and the introduction of the horse and firearms only made the hunt more efficient. A market for buffalo robes began to develop in the 1830s when other fur-bearing animals had been depleted.

THE SWAN TRADE

The Hudson's Bay Company did not restrict its business to fur-bearing animals. It marketed swan skins to the European garment industry and sold swan and goose feathers for the production of quill pens. Overhunting contributed to the decline of trumpeter and tundra swans in North America. Between three thousand and five thousand swans were shot annually, to the point where "the swan flight into James Bay had almost disappeared by 1783-85" and swans became scarce in the interior (Houston, Houston, and Reeves 2003, 189-98).

Buffalo hides were used for robes and as a source of leather for industrial belts. To acquire trade goods such as guns, Plains Indians hunted more buffalo. The Hudson's Bay Company, which realized robes were being traded south of the border, raised their prices and actively encouraged the buffalo robe trade to keep American traders south of the forty-ninth parallel. Once Plains Indians became enmeshed in trade, it is estimated that they began to harvest buffalo at about twice the rate they would have for subsistence.

The Metis, people of mixed European-Aboriginal descent and the offspring of the trade, were searching for a way to support themselves as the fur trade dwindled. Buffalo hunts became an important aspect of Metis social organization, identity, and lifestyle. The Metis also began to take on a middle-man position, buying robes and meat for pemmican from Plains Indians and selling them to the HBC or American companies. In 1840 alone, they drove 1,210 Red River carts, each loaded with a nine-hundred-pound load, to Minneapolis.

Overhunting by American hunters and sportsmen and by Aboriginal and Metis hunters, combined with the US army's policy of exterminating buffalo to starve Plains Indians into submission, pushed buffalo to the brink of extinction by the late 1870s. Prior to contact, it is estimated that 60 million buffalo roamed North America in two vast herds, one northern, one southern. By 1890, there were fewer than one hundred.

With the buffalo gone, many realized that the land could no longer support the Plains Indians' traditional way of life. In 1871, Plains Cree chiefs asked the HBC's chief factor, W. J. Christie, about the Canadian government's intentions. The chiefs wanted to know what the transfer of the HBC lands to the new nation of Canada in 1870 meant for them. The numbered treaties, which were negotiated between 1871 and 1876, extinguished Aboriginal claims to the grasslands, parklands, and woodlands of the Canadian Prairies. Marginalized on reserves with poor diets, many Plains Indians died. About one-sixth of the Blackfoot in Canada perished between 1879 and 1881. Others suffered the effects of disease, displacement, and dispossession. These developments were the direct result of the spatial expansion of the fur trade and the depletion of animals.

THE PERIOD OF European exploration, Aboriginal-European contact, and the Columbian exchange initiated a process of enormous environmental and cultural change that was as significant as the movement of plants, wildlife, and people before the Ice Age and after its conclusion, when people started residing in North America. The environment was transformed as people's perceptions of it changed. The fur trade slaughtered millions of animals and destroyed ecosystems to line the pockets of merchants and provide Europeans with warm, durable, and fashionable clothing. Although western European consumers benefitted, Aboriginal peoples were left with little to sustain them when the trade contracted and when political and economic developments ushered in a new wave of settlers.

Works Cited

Axtell, James. 1992. *Beyond 1492: Encounters in Colonial North America.* New York: Oxford University Press.

Boyd, David R. 2003. *Unnatural Law: Rethinking Canadian Environmental Law and Policy.* Vancouver: UBC Press.

Cook, Ramsay. 1993. *The Voyages of Jacques Cartier.* Toronto: University of Toronto Press.

Crosby, Alfred W. 1994. *Germs, Seeds, and Animals: Studies in Ecological History.* Armonk, NY: ME Sharpe.

Denys, Nicholas. 1908 [1672]. *The Description and Natural History of the Coasts of North America (Arcadia).* Translated and edited by William F. Ganong. Toronto: Champlain Society.

Flannery, Tim. 2001. *The Eternal Frontier: An Ecological History of North America and Its Peoples.* London: William Heinemann.

Honour, Hugh. 1975. *The New Golden Land: European Images of America from the Discoveries to the Present Time.* New York: Pantheon Books.

Houston, C. Stuart, Mary Houston, and Henry M. Reeves. 2003. "Appendix E: The Nineteenth-Century Trade in Swan Skins and Quills." In Stuart Houston, Tim Ball, and Mary Houston, *Eighteenth-Century Naturalists of Hudson Bay,* 188-99. Montreal and Kingston: McGill-Queen's University Press.

Krech, Shepard, III. 1999. *The Ecological Indian: Myth and History.* New York: W.W. Norton McMillan.

McNeill, William Hardy. 1976. *Plagues and People.* Garden City, NY: Anchor.

Miller, J.R. 1989. *Skyscrapers Hide the Heavens: A History of Indian-White Relations in Canada.* Rev. ed. Toronto: University of Toronto Press.

Payne, Edward John, ed. 1900. *Voyages of the Elizabethan Seamen to America: Select Narratives from the "Principal Navigations" of Hakluyt.* London: Clarendon Press.

Ray, Arthur. 1974. *Indians in the Fur Trade: Their Role as Trappers, Hunters, and Middlemen in the Lands Southwest of Hudson's Bay, 1660-1870.* Toronto: University of Toronto Press.

–. 1996. *I Have Lived Here since the World Began: An Illustrated History of Canada's Native Peoples.* Toronto: Key Porter Books.

Richards, John F. 2005. *The Unending Frontier: An Environmental History of the Early Modern World.* Berkeley: University of California Press.

Trigger, Bruce. 1969. *The Huron Farmers of the North.* Toronto: Holt, Rinehart and Winston.

For Further Reading

The Land before People

Christianson, Gale E. 1999. *Greenhouse: The 200-Year Story of Global Warming.* New York: Walker and Company.

Flannery, Tim. 2001. *The Eternal Frontier: An Ecological History of North America and Its Peoples.* London: William Heinemann.

Hoffecker, John F., and Scott A. Elias. 2003. "Environment and Archeology in Beringia." *Evolutionary Anthropology* 12, 1: 34-49.

Steinberg, Ted. 2002. *Down to Earth: Nature's Role in American History.* New York: Oxford University Press.

Weart, Spencer R. 2008. *The Discovery of Global Warming.* Cambridge, MA: Harvard University Press.

The Arrival of Humans

Cinq-Mars, Jacques. N.d. "The Bluefish Caves." *Canadian Encyclopedia.* http://www.thecanadianencyclopedia.ca/.

Dixon, E. James. 2001. "Human Colonization of the Americas: Timing, Technology and Process." *Quaternary Science Reviews* 20, 1-3: 277-99.

Fladmark, K.R. 1979. "Routes: Alternate Migration Corridors for Early Man in North America." *American Antiquity* 44, 1: 55-69.

Haynes, C. Vance. 1980. "The Clovis Culture." *Canadian Journal of Anthropology* 1, 1: 115-21.

Kennett, D.J., et al. 2009. "Nanodiamonds in the Younger Dryas Boundary Sediment Layer." *Science* 323, 5910: 94.

McNeill, William Hardy. 1976. *Plagues and People.* Garden City, NY: Anchor.

Wynn, Graeme. 2007. *Canada and Arctic North America: An Environmental History.* Santa Barbara: ABC-CLIO.

The Development of Cultural Areas

Binnema, Theodore. 2004. *Common and Contested Ground: A Human and Environmental History of the Northwestern Plains.* Toronto: University of Toronto Press.

Dick, Lyle. 2009. "People and Animals in the Arctic: Mediating between Indigenous and Western Knowledge." In *Method and Meaning in Canadian Environmental History,* edited by Alan MacEachern and William J. Turkel, 76-101. Toronto: Nelson.

Evenden, Matthew. 2004. *Fish versus Power: An Environmental History of the Fraser River.* New York: Cambridge University Press.

Fagan, Brian. 2008. *The Great Warming: Climate Change and the Rise and Fall of Civilizations.* New York: Bloomsbury Press.

Fossett, Renee. 1997. *In Order to Live Untroubled: Inuit in the Central Arctic, 1550-1940.* Winnipeg: University of Manitoba Press.

Greenberg, Joseph H., C.G. Turner II, and S. Zegura. 1986. "The Settlement of the Americas: A Comparison of the Linguistic, Dental and Genetic Evidence." *Current Anthropology* 37, 5: 477-97.

Haines, Francis. 1938. "The Northwest Spread of Horses among the Plains Indians." *American Anthropologist* 40, 3: 429-37.

Harris, R. Cole, and Geoffrey Matthews, eds. 1987. *Historical Atlas of Canada.* Vol. 1, *From the Beginning to 1800.* Toronto: University of Toronto Press.

Heidenreich, Conrad. 1990. "The Natural Environment of Huronia and Huron Seasonal Activities." In *People, Places, Patterns, Processes: Geographical Perspectives on the Canadian Past,* edited by Graeme Wynn, 42-55. Toronto: Copp Clark Pitman.

Marshall, Ingeborg. 1996. *A History of Ethnology of the Beothuk.* Montreal and Kingston: McGill-Queen's University Press.

McMillan, Alan D. 1995. *Native Peoples and Cultures of Canada.* Vancouver: Douglas and McIntyre.

Morgan, R. Grace. 1980. "Bison Movement Patterns on the Canadian Plains: An Ecological Analysis." *Plains Anthropologist* 25, 88: 143-60.

Ray, Arthur. 1996. *I Have Lived Here since the World Began: An Illustrated History of Canada's Native Peoples.* Toronto: Key Porter Books.

Richards, John F. 2005. *The Unending Frontier: An Environmental History of the Early Modern World.* Berkeley: University of California Press.

Spry, Irene M. 1995. "Aboriginal Resource Use in the Nineteenth Century in the Great Plains of Modern Canada." In *Consuming Canada: Readings in Environmental History,* edited by Chad Gaffield and Pam Gaffield, 81-92. Mississauga, ON: Copp Clark.

Taylor, Joseph E., III. 1999. *Making Salmon: An Environmental History of the North West Fisheries Crisis.* Seattle: University of Washington Press.

Trigger, Bruce. 1969. *The Huron Farmers of the North.* Toronto: Holt, Rinehart and Winston.

Aboriginal Perceptions of and Approaches to the Land

Barrett, Stephen W., and Stephen F. Arno. 1982. "Indian Fires as an Ecological Influence in the Northern Rockies." *Journal of Forestry* 80, 10: 647-51.

Brody, Hugh. 2000. *The Other Side of Eden: Hunters, Farmers and the Shaping of the World.* Vancouver: Douglas and McIntyre.

Crowe, Keith J. 1991. *A History of the Original Peoples of Northern Canada.* Montreal and Kingston: McGill-Queen's University Press.

Dickasen, Olive. 1997. *Canada's First Nations: A History of the Founding Peoples from Earliest Times.* Toronto: Oxford University Press.

Kuhnlen, Harriet V., and Nancy J. Turner. 1991. *Traditional Plant Foods of Canadian Indigenous Peoples.* Philadelphia: Gordon and Breach.

Miller, J.R. 1989. *Skyscrapers Hide the Heavens: A History of Indian-White Relations in Canada.* Rev. ed. Toronto: University of Toronto Press.

Early Explorers: The Norse

Fagan, Brian. 2000. *The Little Ice Age: How Climate Made History, 1300-1850.* New York: Basic Books.

Jones, Gwyn. 1984. *A History of the Vikings.* Oxford: Oxford University Press.

McGhee, Robert. 1984. "Contact between Native North Americans and the Medieval Norse: A Review of the Evidence." *American Antiquity* 49, 1: 4-26.

Quinn, David B. 1975. *North America from Earliest Discovery to First Settlements: The Norse Voyages to 1612.* New York: Harper and Row.

Seaver, Kirsten A. 1996. *The Frozen Echo: Greenland and the Exploration of North America, ca. AD 1000-1500.* Palo Alto, CA: Stanford University Press.

The Early Fisheries

Bakker, Peter. 1989. "'The Language of the Coastal Tribes Is Half Basque': A Basque-American Indian Pidgin in Use between Europeans and Native Americans in North America ca. 1540–ca. 1640." *Anthropological Linguistics* 31, 3-4: 117-47.

Hutchings, Jeffrey A., and Ransom A. Myers. 1995. "The Biological Collapse of Atlantic Cod off Newfoundland and Labrador: An Exploration of Historical Changes in Exploitation, Harvesting Technology, and Management." In *The*

North Atlantic Fisheries: Successes, Failures, and Challenges, edited by Ragnar Arnason and Lawrence Felt, 37-93. Charlottetown: Institute of Island Studies.

Innis, H.A. 1931. "The Rise and Fall of the Spanish Fishery in Newfoundland." *Transactions of the Royal Society,* 3rd ser., 25, sec. 2: 51-70.

Pope, Peter E. 2009. "Historical Archaeology and the Maritime Cultural Landscape of the Atlantic Fishery." In *Method and Meaning,* edited by Alan MacEachern and William J. Turkel, 36-54. Toronto: Nelson.

Rastogi, Toolika, Moira W. Brown, Brenna A. McLeod, Timothy R. Frasier, Robert Grenier, Stephen L. Cumbaa, Jeya Nadarajah, and Bradley N. White. 2004. "Genetic Analysis of 16th-Century Whale Bones Prompts a Revision of the Impact of Basque Whaling on Right and Bowhead Whales in the Western North Atlantic." *Canadian Journal of Zoology* 82, 10: 1647-54.

Turgeon, Laurier. 1998. "French Fishers, Fur Traders and Amerindians during the 16th Century: History and Archaeology." *William and Mary Quarterly,* 3rd ser., 55, 4: 585-610.

European Explorers Chart a New Environment

Axtell, James. 1992. *Beyond 1492: Encounters in Colonial North America.* New York: Oxford University Press.

Biggar, Henry Percival. 1923. *The Voyages of the Cabots and the Corte-Reals to North America and Greenland, 1497-1503.* London: n.p.

Crosby, Alfred W. 1994. *Germs, Seeds, and Animals: Studies in Ecological History.* Armonk, NY: ME Sharpe.

Denevan, William. 1992. "The Pristine Myth: The Landscape of the Americas in 1492." *Annals of the Association of American Geographers* 82, 3: 369-85.

Honour, Hugh. 1975. *The New Golden Land: European Images of America from the Discoveries to the Present Time.* New York: Pantheon Books.

Payne, Edward John, ed. 1900. *Voyages of the Elizabethan Seamen to America: Select Narratives from the "Principal Navigations" of Hakluyt.* London: Clarendon Press.

Pope, Peter E. 1997. *The Many Landfalls of John Cabot.* Toronto: University of Toronto Press.

Sauer, Carl. 1971. *Sixteenth-Century North America: The Land and the People as Seen by the Europeans.* Berkeley: University of California Press.

First Contacts

Axtell, James. 1992. *Beyond 1492: Encounters in Colonial North America.* New York: Oxford University Press.

Coates, Colin M. 1993. "Like 'The Thames towards Putney': The Appropriation of Landscape in Lower Canada." *Canadian Historical Review* 54, 3: 317-43.

Cook, Ramsay, ed. 1993. *The Voyages of Jacques Cartier.* Toronto: University of Toronto Press.

Fisher, Robin. 1977. *Contact and Conflict: Indian-European Relations in British Columbia.* Vancouver: UBC Press.

Hough, Richard. 1995. *Captain James Cook: A Biography.* London: Coronet.

Pastore, Ralph. 1994. "The Sixteenth Century: Aboriginal Peoples and European Contact." In *The Atlantic Region to Confederation: A History,* edited by Philip A. Buckner and John G. Reid, 22-39. Toronto: University of Toronto Press.

Reid, John G. 1994. "1686-1720: Imperial Intrusions." In *The Atlantic Region to Confederation: A History,* edited by Philip A. Buckner and John G. Reid, 78-103. Toronto: University of Toronto Press.

The Columbian Exchange

Cronon, William. 1983. *Changes in the Land: Indians, Colonists and the Ecology of New England.* New York: Hill and Wang.

Crosby, Alfred W. 1994. *Germs, Seeds, and Animals: Studies in Ecological History.* Armonk, NY: ME Sharpe.

–. 2000. "Ecological Imperialism: The Overseas Migration of Western Europeans as a Biological Phenomenon." In *American Encounters: Natives and Newcomers from European Contact to Indian Removal, 1500-1850,* edited by Peter C. Mancall and James H. Merrell, 55-67. New York: Routledge.

Griffiths, Tom, and Libby Robin, eds. 1997. *Ecology and Empire: Environmental History of Settler Societies.* Edinburgh: Keele University Press.

Grove, Richard. 1995. *Green Imperialism: Colonial Expansion, Tropical Island Edens and the Origins of Environmentalism, 1600-1860.* Cambridge: Cambridge University Press.

Houston, Stuart, Tim Ball, and Mary Houston. 2003. *Eighteenth-Century Naturalists of Hudson Bay.* Montreal and Kingston: McGill-Queen's University Press.

McNeill, William Hardy. 1976. *Plagues and People.* Garden City, NY: Anchor.

Sauer, Carl O. 1938. "Theme of Plant and Animal Destruction in Economic History." In *Land and Life,* edited by John Leighly, 145-54. Berkeley: University of California Press.

Saunders, Richard. 1935. "The First Introduction of European Plants and Animals into Canada." *Canadian Historical Review* 16, 4: 388-406.

The Competition for Furs

Creighton, Donald. 1937. *The Empire of the St. Lawrence: A Study in Commerce and Politics.* Toronto: Ryerson Press.

Innis, Harold. 1970. *The Fur Trade in Canada.* Toronto: University of Toronto Press.

Podruchny, Carolyn. 2006. *Making the Voyageur World: Travelers and Traders in the North American Fur Trade.* Toronto: University of Toronto Press.

Richards, John F. 2005. *The Unending Frontier: An Environmental History of the Early Modern World.* Berkeley: University of California Press.

Trigger, Bruce. 1960. "The Destruction of Huronia: A Study in Economic and Cultural Change, 1609-1650." *Transactions of the Royal Canadian Institute* 33, 1: 14-45.

Trudel, Marcel. 1973. *The Beginnings of New France.* Toronto: McClelland and Stewart.

The Fur Trade's Impact on Aboriginal People

Krech, Shepard, III. 1999. *The Ecological Indian: Myth and History.* New York: W.W. Norton McMillan.

Martin, Calvin. 1974. "The European Impact on the Culture of a Northeastern Algonquian Tribe: An Ecological Interpretation." *William and Mary Quarterly* 3, 31: 3-26.

Ray, Arthur. 1974. *Indians in the Fur Trade: Their Role as Trappers, Hunters, and Middlemen in the Lands Southwest of Hudson's Bay, 1660-1870.* Toronto: University of Toronto Press.

Richards, John F. 2005. *The Unending Frontier: An Environmental History of the Early Modern World.* Berkeley: University of California Press.

White, Richard. 1991. *The Middle Ground: Indians, Empires, and Republics in the Great Lakes Region, 1650-1815.* Cambridge, MA: Cambridge University Press.

Wildlife Depletion

Colpitts, George. 2002. *Game in the Garden: A History of Wildlife in Western Canada to 1940.* Vancouver: UBC Press.

Dobak, William A. 1996. "Killing the Canadian Buffalo, 1821-1881." *Western Historical Quarterly* 27, 1: 33-52.

Hammond, Lorne. 1993. "Marketing Wildlife: The Hudson's Bay Company and the Pacific Northwest, 1821-1849." *Forest and Conservation History* 37, 1: 14-25.

Houston, C. Stuart, Mary Houston, and Henry M. Reeves. 2003. "Appendix E: The Nineteenth-Century Trade in Swan Skins and Quills." In Stuart Houston, Tim Ball, and Mary Houston, *Eighteenth Century Naturalists of Hudson Bay,* 188-99. Montreal and Kingston: McGill-Queen's University Press.

Morgan, R. Grace. 1980. "Bison Movement Patterns on the Canadian Plains: An Ecological Analysis." *Plains Anthropologist* 25: 143-60.

Richards, John F. 2005. *The Unending Frontier: An Environmental History of the Early Modern World.* Berkeley: University of California Press.

2

Settling the Land and Transforming the "Wilderness"

The 19th century was a special time for Canada ... The profound revolution in the century was the transformation of forest and grassland into farmland, accompanied by the growth of commercial centres in widely separated clusters of settlement.

— R. LOUIS GENTILCORE AND GEOFFREY J. MATTHEWS, EDS.,
HISTORICAL ATLAS OF CANADA, 1993

EXPLORATION, FISHERIES, AND the fur trade gave European imperial powers and ambitious commercial interests a tenacious foothold in the New World, a foothold that was deepened by the arrival of European settlers. The process began in New France at the beginning of the seventeenth century, and settlers gradually and sporadically spread across the northern half of North America over the next three centuries. Permanent settlements were a way for "expansive early modern states to impose new types of territoriality on frontier regions" (Richards 2005, 4). By peopling the land with Europeans, who came to conquer and transform forests and grasslands into farmland, these countries – first France, then England – fundamentally altered the population, land use, and ecology of northern North America. Aboriginal peoples were marginalized and relegated to reserves; European perceptions of the environment came to dominate; the land was surveyed for family plots, roads, railways,

and waterways; and forests were cleared to make way for crops and livestock, commercial centres, and for commercial gain in the lumber industry. By 1900, a new country, Canada, had taken shape.

Permanent Settlements

The process of claiming the land for permanent settlements was sporadic because France and Britain first focused on fish and fur resources and were slow to realize the new continent's agricultural potential. In addition, the northern half of North America was vast and populated by few people – Aboriginal or non-Aboriginal – compared to what would become the United States. The dry fisheries and the Basque whaling stations in Newfoundland remained temporary encampments for migrant fishermen until the seventeenth century. In 1610, however, the English set up the Newfoundland Company. The company gave land grants to permanent and semi-permanent residents in the belief that a permanent settlement would add security to the fishery. Settlers were migratory fishers who overwintered and then took up residence. The trade in harp seals also led to the appearance of British settlements along the northeast coast. By the 1670s, fishermen lived in thirty tiny English settlements, and residents were responsible for one-third of England's catch. St. John's, which was home to thirty families, was the largest settlement. By 1790, Newfoundland had a winter population of twenty thousand and an even larger summer population.

In Acadia, the name given to the northeastern portion of France's lands in North America, the French established the first permanent settlement in 1605 in what is now Nova Scotia's Annapolis Basin. Known as Port-Royal and the capital of Acadia until its fall in 1710, the settlement grew to include 1,400 farmers and fishers. The settlers did not encroach seriously on Aboriginal lands or economies, but contact and trade between the two peoples did exist. As agriculture grew more important, the territories and economies of both peoples became increasingly distinct, which perhaps contributed to their ongoing, relatively harmonious relationship. The French also established a garrison at Plaisance, Newfoundland, in 1658, in the hopes of competing with the English. By 1698, the French settlement had twenty-nine families and had established itself as the most stable fishing settlement north of New England.

Early settlers in the Atlantic region "focused on the commercial exploitation of the fisheries and the cultivation, at a subsistence level, of small areas of land" (Sanger 1977, 136). In Nova Scotia, settlers eked out an existence by draining marshlands, removing trees, and permanently altering the environment around the Bay of Fundy. Severe weather conditions and poor soil caused many to fail, but these early attempts proved that Europeans could survive in a land that their governments thought uninhabitable. Settlers supplemented fishing and cultivation with other subsistence activities such as berry picking; hunting wild game and fowl; procuring timber for buildings, repairs, and firewood; and grazing livestock. Because these resources were marginal, spatially segregated, and seasonal, settlers developed strategies to harvest them in an annual round. Although European settlers differed culturally from Aboriginal peoples, they too adopted a mobile lifestyle to survive in North America's harsh environment.

In the region that would eventually become the provinces of Quebec and Ontario, an area that belonged to France until the British Conquest of New France in 1763, establishing permanent settlements was likewise sporadic and shaped by imperial rivalries. Although France focused on the fur trade, it tried to strengthen its agricultural base in the St. Lawrence Valley in response to developments in British North America. England actively encouraged agricultural settlement in its colonies to the south, particularly the Thirteen Colonies. The region had a population of over 100,000 permanent settlers by 1650. The environment in northern North America, however, differed from that of both the Thirteen Colonies and western Europe so that the process of settlement and domination was slower because both the European and Aboriginal populations were small and because there was so much

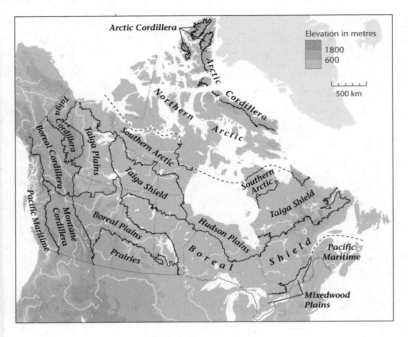

FIGURE 2.1 Ecological regions of Canada

Source: Natural Resources Canada, "The Atlas of Canada," http://atlas. nrcan.gc.ca/.

space. Life along the St. Lawrence meant long winters and a short, hot growing season of only about 150 days. Soils ranged from rich loam to clay to light sand, and drought was seldom a problem. The Canadian Shield, however, limited the amount of agricultural land available (see Figure 2.1). The region contained limestone plains, belts with steep slopes and thin soils, and poorly drained areas. French immigrants did not favour the region. Those French settlers who did come settled at Quebec (1608), Trois-Rivières (1634), and Montreal (1642). Only 2,500 Europeans lived in these tiny outposts along the St. Lawrence in the 1660s, and at the end of the French regime, that number had risen only to 70,000.

As European settlements in New France expanded, Aboriginal groups came into more frequent contact with settlers and lost more people to war and disease. Aboriginal

people visited Montreal during the annual fur fair, which, in turn, stimulated trade in other items. Aboriginal groups and the French "gradually congregated around a concept, a fort, a shore" (Harris and Matthews 1986, 113). Although Aboriginal people outnumbered the French in the town until 1668, the French did not allow them to have legal title to the land. Some Aboriginal people grew corn and lived in bark-and-branch mobile shelters near the missions. They supplied European settlers with game and fish, medicinal plants, and transportation, and they served as warriors when their rivals, the Iroquois, attacked. As the number of French farms increased, Aboriginal people (among them Huron refugees) retreated, and many relocated. Epidemics and disease reduced their number to between three and four thousand people, and they suffered extreme culture shock in the face of the Christian missionary's paternalism.

Following the Conquest of New France in 1763, immigration remained at a trickle until the American Revolution forced large numbers of British Loyalists to relocate to British North America: 34,000 settled in Nova Scotia, 2,000 in Prince Edward Island, and 10,000 in Quebec, which was called Lower Canada. Others settled in the new colonies of New Brunswick and Upper Canada (1791-1841; called Canada West from 1841-67 and Ontario thereafter). England recognized Aboriginal peoples' title to the land, which it purchased through treaties as needed. In the treaty-making process, Aboriginal people retained hunting and fishing rights, but the influx of farmers pushed them to the margins. The Six Nations, Britain's allies during the American Revolution, were ceded good land close to the Grand River, and the Mississauga settled on four reserves in the Trent Valley. In general, however, Aboriginal people retreated, and European newcomers benefitted by receiving land often cleared and readied for settlement. Aboriginal people were seen regularly on Ontario's lakes and in the settlement of York (the future Toronto) until the 1830s. They then became an infrequent sight in white settlements.

Surveys and Land Grants

European settlement in central Canada and the Atlantic region changed the landscapes and ecosystems of these areas in profound ways. Settlers had a proprietary attitude toward the land and evaluated it in terms of what could be exploited and what could be replaced with European organisms. Unlike Aboriginal hunter-gatherers, Europeans were sedentary and brought with them entrenched notions about private landownership. Early agricultural settlement proceeded through several stages – land surveys, land grants, and clearing – before actual farming began. Land surveys determined the size, shape, and location of farms and fields and the layout of roads. The pattern of land use varied from region to region, and history and culture as much as the terrain itself determined the design.

Surveys preceded land grants, but squatters existed in each region. In New France, farmers worked the land in long, narrow lots that gave each family access to the St. Lawrence River (see Figure 2.2). A ribbon of settlement gradually emerged, one that followed the contours of the land and waterways rather than a fixed legal definition of

land use. Settlers wanted to be close to the river to fish and to travel to village markets. To be independent but not isolated, they built farmhouses close together along the river. When France established the seigneurial system, a semi-feudal system of land distribution, in the seventeenth century, it had little influence on this pattern of settlement, but it did clarify social relationships and provide stability. The easy availability of land meant peasant farmers, or habitants, had access to the seigneur's forests in exchange for work, and they practised a more extensive type of agriculture compared to farmers in France. On the eve of the Conquest, there were about 250 seigneuries with different practices and social relationships. In general, however, the system supported small family farms. Land was cheap, but the cost of labour was high. Family members, including children, therefore did the majority of the work. Because the market for agricultural products was limited, these families practised subsistence farming with only small surpluses. New France was a society in which European institutions were adapted to suit the New World environment. As a consequence, Canadiens tended to be freer and more prosperous than their European counterparts.

The English had their own ideas about the landscape and landownership and put their cultural stamp on land after the Conquest. Nova Scotia in 1775 had twenty thousand inhabitants, including Acadians, New Englanders, and some German and British immigrants. These settlers farmed, fished, made crafts, or served in the military at Halifax, a town founded in 1749 as a counterweight to the French fortress at Louisbourg. Following the American Revolution, in 1783,

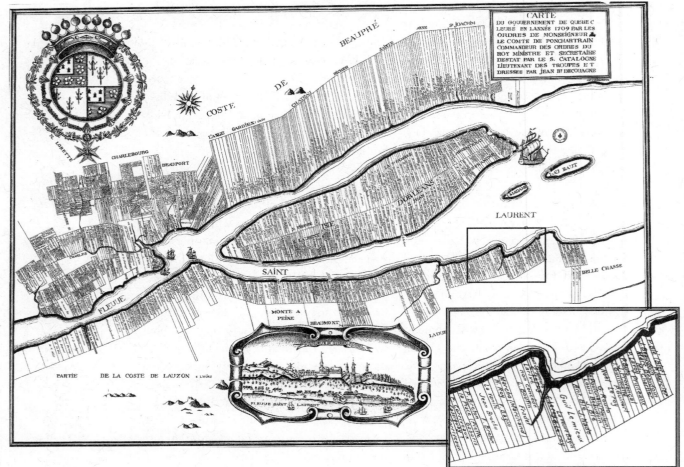

FIGURE 2.2 Land distribution in New France. This map from 1709 shows the distinctive elongated farms of New France and Quebec (see inset). These narrow river front lots bore little resemblance to land distribution patterns in the French rural landscape but left an indelible imprint on the landscape in North America.
Bibliothèque et Archives nationales du Québec

Britain and the United States settled the international boundary between Nova Scotia and Massachusetts, and over twenty thousand Loyalists settled on British lands. When the British established the colony of New Brunswick, they surveyed the land quickly and set aside forest reserves called the King's Forest. In both colonies, the Loyalists received free rations and land grants of various sizes, depending on their influence or military rank. The Loyalist migration created towns such as Parrtown (present-day Saint John) overnight. The families occupied vacant lands of varied quality, suffered cold temperatures, and

encountered "a much more disconcerting forest growth than they were used to" (MacKinnon 1986, 148).

About ten thousand Loyalists settled in Upper Canada. They were mostly small farmers from the eastern seaboard who settled along the St. Lawrence, the Bay of Quinte, and the Niagara frontier on free land grants of 100 to 200 acres. Larger grants went to military officers and government officials. The British supplied rations, some livestock, primitive implements, and seeds so the settlers could make a new start "in the wilderness."

FIGURE 2.3 Land distribution in Upper Canada, 1791. The distinctive chequered pattern of surveys in Upper Canada divided each township into 200-acre lots for farms (the light rectangles) but set aside about a third of the land for Crown reserves, which the government allocated for schools and other purposes, and for clergy reserves (the dark rectangles) to support the Anglican Church.

Gilbert Patterson, *Land Settlement of Upper Canada, 1783-1840*, Ontario Department of Public Records and Archives, 16th Report, 1920, Archives of Ontario

Following the War of 1812 between Britain and the United States, successive waves of mostly British and Irish immigrants arrived in the region. Treaties with Aboriginal peoples extended the colonial government's land holdings, which it opened up to these settlers. Officials surveyed the land, and as settlement moved inland, the British built colonization roads.

The method of land surveying used in Upper Canada laid out lots in a distinctive chequered pattern that dispersed settlers more than their counterparts in Lower Canada (see Figure 2.3). Family plots lay alongside Crown and clergy reserves in a system designed to support the Anglican Church. The English government hoped to build a stratified, orderly English society in contrast to the "democratic" republic to the south. In all regions of British North America, land was associated with freedom, social status, and economic security. This association motivated settlers to improve their lives by converting the countryside from a forested wilderness to an agricultural economy of small farmers. After the War of 1812, reforms reduced free land grants to 100 acres, the government taxed wild lands to force land speculators to develop or sell their properties, and it required those who took up land to build a house and fence, to maintain a road, and to clear five acres within a few years.

Clearing the Land

Most settlers believed they needed to subdue the wilderness. The dominant feature of the pre-settlement landscape was old-growth boreal forests. These forests consisted of cedar, hemlock, white and red pine, and northern hardwoods, including maple, oak, and beech, and they extended from the Atlantic region to the western edge of Lake Superior. Settlers developed an intimate relationship with these forests because settlement began as a process of deforestation. Settlers had no notion of ecology. They did not view trees as species that interacted with one another and with other plants, animals, and people. Inherited cultural ideas influenced their approach toward nature. Christianity provided support for their belief that humans had ascendancy over all other elements in the natural world. Settlers believed they had a right to exploit the environment, and their knowledge about the natural world, new technologies, and scientific methods provided the means to control it. Both religion and science strengthened

their justifications for human domination. If humans exploited nature and sold and traded its resources, they could end scarcity and make a profit (an idea central to capitalism in emerging industrializing societies). Such beliefs underpinned European dominance in this era, rationalized settlers' exploitative encounters with new lands, and brought them valuable resources. Settlers viewed ancient forests as resources whose destruction brought progress. They therefore felt no remorse because they were converting so-called wilderness into civilized communities and using the lands productively.

Overwhelmed by tall stands of virgin forest, settlers viewed trees as something to be conquered. Felling and removing them was hard, back-breaking labour, but settlers felt it needed to be done because trees took up space, sheltered unwanted wildlife and pests, attracted lightning, and occasionally fell, causing untold damage. To pioneers, forests were frightening places with wild animals such as bears and wolves and wild men whom they viewed as savages. From European folklore and literature, they had learned to view forests as eerie, awful places, places where the sound of the wind and the shadows cast by trees played tricks with the imagination. The idea of getting lost in the woods terrified them. Anna Jameson, a British traveller, wrote in *Winter Studies and Summer Rambles in Canada,* "A Canadian settler hates a tree, regards it as his natural enemy, as something to be destroyed, eradicated, annihilated by all and any means. The idea of useful or ornamental is seldom associated here with even the most magnificent of timber trees" (Jameson 1969 [1838], 51).

A BACKWOODSMAN'S VIEW OF NATURE

Gordon Sellar, a Scot who settled in Upper Canada, wrote, "It is the axe that has made Canada ... These beautiful fields are the speechless bequest of the men and women who redeemed them from savagery, at the cost of painful privation, of exhausting never ceasing toil, of premature decay of strength" (Sellar 1969, 101-2). In the backwoods of central Canada, Sellar portrayed farmers and woodsmen as pioneers of progress transforming the virgin wilderness into a fruitful garden. To Sellar, subduing the wilderness was an exalted calling.

In New France, indentured labourers or moonlighting military personnel often did the back-breaking work of clearing the forests. In the Atlantic region and Upper Canada, the work was done by independent yeoman, who also worked their own land, by labourers hired by farmers with capital, and by small-time farmers who cleared forests for cash. Labourers toiled in the hope of earning enough cash to take up a homestead, and many farmers also worked part-time in lumber camps in the winter. Seasonal labour "complemented and stabilized work on the farm" (Sandwell 1994, 26).

Clearing the land involved clear-cutting, girdling (removing a strip of bark around the circumference of a tree to kill it), and burning. Abraham Gesner – a lawyer, geologist, and inventor – described the system of clearing. Workers first cut the underbrush, often when the ground was frozen, and then removed small trees suitable for making fences. In the spring, they felled larger trees and cut them into logs. In the autumn, they used oxen to draw brushwood, limbs, and unused logs into large piles for burning. In Upper Canada, the farmers collected the ashes and stored them in waterproof log sheds until winter, when they were sold to potash factories. In New Brunswick, where there were no asheries, so the ashes were left to mix with the soil. From the 1820s in Upper Canada, "the typical involvement of a settler was to take logs to a nearby mill, have them cut into boards, and as payment leave a portion – usually a half – for the operator of the mill. For the most part, however, the settlers were more concerned with the destruction of the forest than its exploitation" (Glazebrook 1968, 41).

Clearing was the first step in a "natural" process of land improvement that continued for years (see Figure 2.4). Cutting left stumps that took about seven years to rot. Settlers then axed the stumps or used oxen to pull them out and pile them for burning. Samuel Strickland in Lakefield described a logging bee of twenty men who used five yokes of oxen to pile logs "until the heap is seven or eight feet high and 10 to 12 feet broad. All chips sticks and rubbish are placed on top ... In one day I cleared five acres and set fire at night ... On a dark night a hundred or two of these heaps, all on fire at once have a very fine effect and shed a broad glare of light. In the month of July in new settlements the whole country at night appears lit up by these fires" (Barker 2003, 67). Farmers also had to remove secondary growth. The average farmer cleared about one and a half acres per year. Over time, rough pioneer farms emerged in forests where Aboriginal people had hunted only years before. Larger homes, barns, and outbuildings replaced log houses. Forest gave way to stumps and then open fields. Roads, bridges, and railways eventually linked communities. Local entrepreneurs built sawmills, gristmills, and schoolhouses.

As settlers transformed the wilderness into a European agricultural landscape, they wasted untold natural resources. Claude-Thomas Dupuy, the intendant of New France (1726-28), noted that "les bruleurs de forets behave as if the trees were of no use ... They are scattering fires and starting fires everywhere to clear a concession of which no more than one-tenth will ever be cultivated" (Mackay 1985, 15). The destruction of the forests bewildered Aboriginal people. Kahkewaquonaby (Sacred Waving Feathers), later known as

Peter Jones, a Methodist missionary, wrote that indigenous people believed trees, rocks, water, plants, and wildlife were endowed with immortal spirits and possessed supernatural power "to punish anyone who wasted them." They "avoided cutting down living trees" because it pained them (Smith 1987, 11). Indigenous peoples' use and management of forest resources had been extensive, and included the use of fire, but it had been less than the reproduction and growth rates of the species involved. Non-Aboriginal travellers also made note of the ugliness of the dispersed log houses, rough fences made of split timbers, sloppy tillage, and a disfigured landscape strewn with wasted wood. But pioneers regarded forests as obstacles to development and felt a sense of triumph with the results of their hard work. One historian wrote, "I have no doubt whatever that a twenty-acre field was an infinitely greater joy to the backwoods settler at the time than the forest he had swept away" (Roe 1982, 42).

The Shanty in the Bush

Fifteen Years after Settlement

Thirty Years after Settlement

THE EVOLUTION OF A CANADIAN FARM

These illustrations were probably prepared as emigration propaganda

FIGURE 2.4 Evolution of the Canadian farm. These illustrations depict how the rural environment changed quickly as settlers pushed back forest, created farms, and built small communities.

E. Guillet, *Early Life in Upper Canada* (Toronto: University of Toronto Press, 1963), 37. Reprinted with the permission of the publisher

FROM SHELTERS TO PERMANENT RESIDENCES

The appearance of buildings and artifacts, often composed of materials from the natural world, signalled the permanence and culture of European settlers and their adaptations to a new environment. In New France, the landscape was dotted with temporary farmhouses that consisted of no more than a few posts, a thatch or bark roof, and a dirt floor. Habitants later built houses out of heavy planks placed horizontally or out of straw and mortar. In the early eighteenth century, fieldstone houses became popular. These farmhouses fused designs from France and varied in size, depending on the farmer's resources. After

Farming in Central and Eastern Canada

From the arrival of the first explorers and settlers, farmers sowed the land they cleared with imported seeds and plants in the hope of re-creating a European-style landscape in the wilderness. Whether they were French Canadians in the St. Lawrence Valley or Loyalists in the Maritime colonies or Upper Canada, farming was a long-term struggle to develop new techniques to grow old crops in the New World.

Samuel de Champlain experimented with crops at St. Croix in 1604, and he had ground in the St. Lawrence Valley prepared for gardens of grains and seeds in 1608. Louis Hébert, who supervised the gardens at Port-Royal, settled in New France as its first farmer. Aided by the rich soil near Quebec, he sowed wheat and vegetables in 1617 and gave information and species to Jacques-Philippe Cornut, author of *Canadensium Plantarum Historia* (1635). Champlain later wrote, "I travelled and saw well-cultivated land already sown and laden with good grain, gardens full of every sort of plant; cabbages, turnips, lettuce, purslane, sorrel, parsley as well as other vegetables as good and as forward as any in France" (Saunders 1935, 394). Although Hébert produced good crops with support from Champlain, the French government remained more interested in the fur trade. Jean Talon, intendant of New France (1665-72), however, tried to diversify the colony's economy by encouraging settlement. In 1670, he claimed that "almost all the European plants and animals that have since proved fundamental in Canadian life were now securely established" (Coates 2000, 4). Over the next century, as the population of New France increased gradually, farm families left their mark on the land as they carved out a new terrain to make it "productive."

Farmers in New France, however, quickly exhausted the fertile soil with overextensive agriculture and defective methods of tilling. Unlike intensive farming, extensive

1760, farmers adapted their house styles to the Canadian climate. French Canadian residences had long overhangs, plenty of windows, and cellars for storage.

In Upper Canada, settlers lived in tents, bark wigwams, or more commonly, rough shanty cabins. They built these cabins out of round logs with bark roofing. The cabins had no windows and only a covered opening for a door. Packed earth served as a floor, and a hole in the roof took the place of a chimney. Over time, farmers replaced these temporary shelters with small one-storey log houses, sometimes with a loft. Although they were an improvement, these houses lacked adequate foundations and often had uneven logs. Hand-squared logs had gaps that the farmers filled with wooden wedges and clay. They built chimneys from a mixture of stone, logs, and clay, and they finished roofs with handmade shingles. Settlers cut doorways and windows after the house was completed, and they filled them with doors and expensive glass as they could afford them. These draughty houses, lit by fires and homemade candles, were difficult to heat. But construction costs were low, and neighbours helped out during housing bees. "Handsome residences" – frame, brick, or stone houses – eventually replaced the shanties, depending on the availability of materials, labour, and financial resources. In the late nineteenth century, Canadians in older communities built fine buildings in the Georgian and Late Victorian styles.

THE POTATO

The British introduced the potato to Canada and French Canadian farmers after the Conquest. By 1831, the tuber accounted for 46 percent of crops. As wheat yields declined in Lower Canada, potatoes offered an easy alternative crop. Potatoes helped habitants feed their families, but they also had blights and depleted the soil.

agriculture is a system of crop cultivation that uses small amounts of labour and capital relative to the land being farmed. The crop yield in extensive agriculture depends primarily on the natural fertility of the soil, the terrain, the climate, and the availability of water. Because extensive agriculture produces a lower yield per unit of land than intensive agriculture, it requires large quantities of land to be profitable. Farmers in New France used a simple two-year rotation system for crops. Their poorly ploughed fields sprouted weeds, they did not plant grass or clover for cover, and they rarely used manure as fertilizer. Wheat midge and rust caused problems, and the coarse grains produced were suitable for the farmers' own use but not for export. The cold climate and short growing season hindered production, but after a recession in 1780-84, some wheat and flour went to the British market. By 1800, most of the 180,000 French speakers in the St. Lawrence Valley were subsistence farmers who relied on a few livestock and wheat, barley, oats, corn, and potatoes.

The failure to produce exports persisted under British rule, even though England imported wheat from Canada. The lack of exports perhaps reflected the limits of subsistence agriculture. Between 1803 and 1842, wheat production declined despite increased demand and higher prices. French Canadian farmers could not compete with the cheaper wheat being produced in Upper Canada. As the population increased, putting pressure on the land, farms were subdivided and fertile land became more and more scarce. French Canadian farmers diversified by growing more oats and hay to supply to vigorous local markets, which expanded and contributed to greater economic vitality. But agricultural practices in the St. Lawrence Valley changed slowly, and traditionalism was the bane of agricultural reformers in both Canada East and the French-speaking communities of Nova Scotia. In 1859, the first agricultural school opened in Quebec. It introduced innovations in dairy production, improved agricultural methods, and implemented an extensive drainage plan on its model farm to expand land under cultivation.

In the colonies settled by Loyalists, farmers at first planted seeds around stumps. These early crops grew well in virgin soil, but the farmers rarely rotated their crops or applied fertilizer, and they used crude implements. Pioneer farming in northern North America was not for the faint of heart. In the Maritimes, Loyalist farmers Jack Wiswall and Alexander Howe made immense efforts to grow crops quickly on relatively good land but produced barely enough food to feed their families. Others were destitute. They did not have the skills needed to grow crops in the demanding region: "Nature played an important role in the crushing of Loyalist hopes" (MacKinnon 1986, 182). In 1789, the Society for Promoting Agriculture in Nova Scotia published articles and created local societies to improve farming methods and encourage Loyalists not to abandon agriculture, not always with success. The Loyalists' enterprise eventually created local markets, and within a decade "the land was beginning to repay their efforts ... Those who accepted Nova Scotia on its terms managed to survive and to prosper" (Wynn 1990, 16). In New Brunswick, most farmers' wheat crops produced good yields. They planted potatoes every two or three years, and clover and timothy produced good hay. Critics, however, commented on the relatively backward, unremunerative state of agriculture in the region.

By 1800, over 75,000 people lived in Britain's four Atlantic colonies: Newfoundland, New Brunswick, Nova Scotia, and Prince Edward Island (which the British attained from France in 1763). The population was scattered and dependent on water transportation. Most people fished and farmed. The best farms were in the Fundy marshes, the Saint John Valley, and in Lunenburg, where farmers produced small surpluses and exported fish and furs. Most farming remained at the subsistence level, but a few farmers took small surpluses to local markets, which linked the towns to the countryside. The pioneering stage of farming ended in the mid-nineteenth century, when a larger population engaged in improved farming methods such as using manure as fertilizer, crop rotation (the successive planting of different crops on the same land to improve soil fertility and help control insects and diseases), and summerfallow (the practice of allowing land to remain unsown during the growing season). Nevertheless, the region's cool climate – made worse by occasional global climate disruptions, periodic blights, and crop failures – made farming difficult.

In Upper Canada, backwoods farming was so tough that only one family in five succeeded. By the 1830s, would-be farmers with capital bought partially cleared land closer to towns to avoid having to cut trees and clear land. Unlike French Canadian farmers, English farmers planted as much land as possible with wheat, their major crop. But the wheat fields were interspersed with European weeds such as wild mustard and oxeye daisy. Such weeds were so tenacious that the legislature passed the Canada Thistle Act in 1865, the first noxious weed act in British North America. As in other regions, farmers exhausted the soil with poor plowing techniques, crude tillage implements, and a failure to use crop rotation. They experimented with indigenous corn, squashes, and turnip and with most of the cereals of northern Europe (wheat, rye, oats, and buckwheat).

Subsistence agriculture was a mix of living off nature's bounty, raising imported livestock for meat and dairy products, and importing seeds and shrubs to produce crops. Farm wives planted vegetable gardens close to home, harvested wild berries and nuts, and cared for the livestock. They manufactured both cheese and butter until 1860, when butter and cheese making were industrialized and taken over by men. In 1863, the *Canadian Agriculturalist* proclaimed that "the rough era" of chopping and clearing the forest was over. The soil, however, was already exhausted. As established crops declined in

GARDENS IN THE WILDERNESS

The appearance of gardens on farmsteads indicated stability. Horticulturalists served as agents of plant mobility, and when settlers imported species, they shuffled the distribution of North American plants. In New France, Récollet and Jesuit missionaries observed, collected, and maintained holding gardens for indigenous plants, some of which they sent to the Jardin du Roi in France. Some seventeenth-century monastery gardens flourished and included orchards. Botanist-priests in Quebec included L'Abbé Léon Provancher in the nineteenth century and Frère Marie-Victorin in the twentieth century.

Early gardens in English-speaking British North America not only provided sustenance, they also fulfilled aesthetic needs. Settlers also planted gardens on newly cleared land near virgin forests to protect their homes from insects and wildlife. The Loyalists mainly grew vegetables, but by 1793 farmers also cultivated apple, peach, and cherry trees supplied by nurseries in Niagara. In addition to planting European herbs for cooking and medicine and flowers for decorative purposes, settlers also experimented with indigenous plants. They transplanted shrubs, ornamental trees such as rock elm and creepers, and yellow, white, and blue violets. These plants did not always flourish away from the forest's shade and soil. Honeysuckle, white spirea, and wild roses did, however, appear in gardens.

To European settlers, gardens were an indication of more advanced settlement and civilization. In *The Backwoods of Canada* (1835), Catharine Parr Traill, an English-Canadian author who wrote about life as a settler near Peterborough, wrote optimistically about the "phenomena of the uncultured forest, its botanical treasures, and its living occupants" as well as the changes that had taken place in the environment since her arrival in 1832 (Forkey 2003, 109). Her garden included domesticated indigenous plants, and she wreathed a hop vine mixed with scarlet creeper and morning glory around the pillars of her cabin. Like other English settlers, she saw nature as God's work, and her interest in natural history sustained her.

yields, farmers adapted British techniques to meet local conditions.

Farmers in Upper Canada developed local agricultural markets, and they exported some of their wheat and flour to Lower Canada and abroad. Local breweries and distilleries bought grain to produce beer and whisky, and from the 1830s onward, hundreds of mills of various kinds linked the farming and commercial worlds, helping to create communities and reflecting the region's developing prosperity. In the Kingston and York areas, farmers produced beef, some for the United States, and pork, peas, and potatoes.

In the second half of the nineteenth century, mechanization contributed to greater production and helped farmers in what is now called Ontario make the transition from subsistence to commercial agriculture. Farmers replaced sickles with reapers in the 1840s, and the hand-held flail gave way to mechanized threshers that separated the grain from the straw and chaff. This transition from handwork to mechanized harvesting peaked in the 1880s, a key decade for the sale of agricultural implements. Farm machinery was affordable (a self-binder in 1881 cost three hundred dollars but half that only one decade later), and farmers mechanized to produce more high-grade, consumer-oriented products to make a decent living. The technological improvements included mowers, seed drills, manure spreaders, potato diggers, cultivators, hay loaders, and disc harrows. Drawn by horses and then by steam- and gasoline-driven combustion engines, farm machinery worked the soil thoroughly and saved time and labour.

The number of acres being farmed peaked in the 1890s, and rural depopulation increasingly made farm labourers scarce. When the Prairies became Canada's major wheat-producing region, farmers in central Canada quickly turned to mixed farming and grew fodder crops to feed livestock. Mechanization increased productivity but visibly changed the landscape as small farms gave way to fewer larger ones. Farmers retired, and young people often chose life in the city. In some cases, unconnected farm lots merged under a single family who worked out of the old home; in others, farms passed into the hands of large corporations. Dairy farming helped to replenish soils exhausted from years of intense wheat production. It was better for the environment and considered more modern and scientific.

Three centuries of pioneer farming had a profound effect on the environment and landscape of central and eastern Canada. Like explorers and fur traders before them, settlers contrasted their industry and quest to be independent landowners with Aboriginal people's indolence. They viewed themselves as the embodiment of progress and civilization, which was symbolized by turning "wasted" land into manicured gardens and open fields. Their confidence, however, led to waste and carelessness. Farmers cut more trees than was necessary, started forest fires, practised extensive agriculture, and moved on to new areas rather than reusing land already cleared. As they reconfigured the land, they created a patchwork of settlements that displaced indigenous plants and depleted wildlife through deforestation, hunting, and fishing. The land was so abundant that early settlers could not imagine a shortage, but it came in the mid- to late nineteenth century, propelling some easterners to move west to begin the pioneer adventure all over again.

Settling the Prairies

Even before settlers began to arrive en masse on the Canadian Prairies, the region had become one of the most ecologically transformed places on Earth. It was also one of the least known to Canadians and Europeans. Before 1850, knowledge of the environment was speculative. Was it a desert or a Garden of Eden? Old World maps presented the interior as "nothing more than a narrow belt which would be somehow closely situated to the Asian continent" (Murray 1989, 14). Although Alexander Mackenzie's overland journey in 1793 had increased awareness of the size of the interior, an image of the West as an inaccessible wasteland inhabited by "savage" Aboriginal peoples, fur traders, and wild animals persisted. The Hudson's Bay Company encouraged this view even as it produced maps and sketches and gathered information for its own agricultural gardens and for Lord Selkirk's proposed settlement

FOREST FIRES

Forest fires in all regions increased as European colonists cleared land by burning trees and stumps. Loggers also took the trunks of old trees but left their tops and branches as debris, which easily caught fire. In 1825, a great fire near the Miramichi River in New Brunswick killed 160 people, 800 cattle, and wildlife. In 1851, an accidental fire destroyed most of the big pine country on the Bonnechere River, a tributary of the Ottawa. Following a fire, herbaceous plants and then second-growth trees grew back. Complete forest restoration, including the return of the original trees, took a long time, however. This final stage was rarely reached in settled areas.

at Red River. Company employees recorded the region's natural history and observed its weather. Their information and meteorological data spanned over three centuries. They knew that northwest North America was much colder in the winters and hotter in the summers than the same latitudes in Europe. Although they did not share the information at the time, their records today offer valuable information about the Little Ice Age (1300-1870), including the Brief Warmer Period (1830-70). Europeans in general continued to adhere to a rigid theory of latitudinal climate zones, in which the European climate was considered normal and the northern North American climate aberrant.

Attitudes toward the Prairies began to change as people took up permanent settlement in the region. In 1812, Lord Selkirk founded a small Scottish settlement at the confluence of the Red and Assiniboine Rivers to produce food for the Hudson's Bay Company's trading posts. From the beginning, the colonists faced an unpredictable climate, hostility from the North West Company, which feared the Hudson's Bay Company was trying to disrupt its access to Metis pemmican, and the anger of French- and English-speaking Metis, who disputed the settlers' right to "their" land, which they had settled in the French Canadian style of long river lots. In the first ten years, grasshoppers, floods, drought, and frost guaranteed that the colonists would harvest only two crops. Nevertheless, they adapted to the severe environment by experimenting with wheat seeds to develop a hardy mix that could mature early. Their subsistence-level agriculture produced poor crops and low-quality flour, butter, cheese, beef, and pork. Their limited, inefficient, and intensive methods could not form the basis of a large-scale agricultural economy. The settlement did prove, however, that growing crops and raising livestock were possible along the Red River. Whether farming could work in the more arid grasslands remained an unknown.

Beginning in the 1850s, a confluence of events caused public perceptions of the Prairies to shift from uninhabitable wilderness to potential settlement frontier. In 1848, Paul Kane, an artist who travelled throughout the region from 1846 to 1848, created a sensation when he exhibited 240 sketches of Aboriginal people and artifacts in Toronto. Kane's idealized oil paintings, along with the publication of his journal, *Wanderings of an Artist* (1859), depicted the region shortly before the indigenous way of life, the physical environment, and the economic and political bases of the region changed permanently. Kane's book appeared not long after Lorin Blodget, a physicist and writer, had published *Climatology in the United States* (1857), in which he likened the climate of the Northwest to that of western and northern Europe and concluded that the land could be farmed as far north as the sixty-fifth parallel. His work was timely, optimistic, and influential. Canadian expansionists such as George Brown, editor of the Toronto *Globe,* were seeking evidence that the region was suitable for settlement and agricultural development.

In 1857-58, two major government-funded scientific expeditions, a Canadian one led by Henry Youle Hind and a British one led by John Palliser, dispelled the idea that the region was a desert and gave credence to the expansionists' idea that the West could link

British North America and British Columbia into a new Canadian nation. Such unity would prevent the United States from fulfilling its "manifest destiny" to conquer the entire continent. The Palliser expedition described the parklands as a fertile belt good for agriculture and the grasslands as less than ideal. It identified Palliser's Triangle, an arid region unsuitable for cultivation south of the South Saskatchewan River. The two reports prepared by the Hind expedition described the region's geography and concluded that the Red and Saskatchewan River Valleys were fertile and arable. Hind was impressed with the region's clean air and vast sweep of treeless grasslands that forced him to carry wood and use buffalo dung for fires. He predicted the collapse of the area's buffalo-hunting economy and Aboriginal unrest. Like Palliser, Hind described the dry, fertile grasslands and viewed the parklands as a fertile belt, but he exaggerated the annual level of rainfall and the warm summer climate. He neglected to mention the shortness of the frost-free period, an important factor for cultivation, and did not notice or warn of summer frosts. He too identified a sterile southern plain characterized by dry, sandy soil and limited farming potential. The Hind and Palliser expeditions stimulated public interest in the West, increased pressure for a Canadian railway route to the Pacific, and in combination with the 1858 gold rush in British Columbia, persuaded politicians, businessmen, and speculators that the Prairies could be opened to settlement.

When the Hudson's Bay Company sold most of Rupert's Land and the North-West Territories to Canada (which had come together as a new nation composed of the

PRAIRIE GRASSLANDS AND THE DEMISE OF THE BUFFALO

Annexation of the West coincided with the disappearance of the buffalo. For thousands of years, millions of buffalo had swept across North America in large herds that destroyed everything in their path. When they grazed, they kept perennial tall grasses short. They rubbed and sometimes destroyed trees, slashed roots, and beat down shrubs; they caused erosion; and they marked the ground with deep ruts. They turned lakes, streams, and sloughs into mud holes, and they left enormous quantities of dung in their wake. Because they roamed widely, however, the land could recover. With their extermination, an era ended, and the environment changed. Grasses grew taller, providing luxuriant open ranges for cattle, particularly in what is now southern Alberta, the centre of Canada's ranching industry.

former British colonies in 1867), the federal government immediately sent out parties to mark the West's boundaries and to survey the new land. Their work helped promote the region as a potential settlement frontier. George Mercer Dawson, a geologist, was a member of both the International Boundary Survey and the Geological Survey of Canada. His *Report on the Geology and Resources of the Region in the Vicinity of the Forty-Ninth Parallel,* published in 1875, offered a cogent analysis of the area's potential. Botanist John Macoun and others convinced the public that the region was suitable for Western-style agriculture. Macoun, who was also part of the Geological Survey of Canada, exaggerated its potential. His reports stressed that it was covered with high and luxuriant prairie grasses, which he failed to link to the demise of the buffalo, and he attributed the land's treelessness to fires rather than dryness.

The Dominion Land Survey set the stage for an orderly system of settlement. The survey differed from its counterparts in

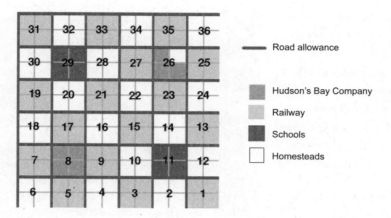

31	32	33	34	35	36
30	29	28	27	26	25
19	20	21	22	23	24
18	17	16	15	14	13
7	8	9	10	11	12
6	5	4	3	2	1

— Road allowance

▨ Hudson's Bay Company

▢ Railway

■ Schools

▢ Homesteads

FIGURE 2.5 The Dominion Land Survey began to be implemented in 1871. It applied a flat grid system to the settled areas of the four western provinces and used a one-square-mile land unit called a section (640 acres; 259 hectares). Townships had thirty-six sections of which a portion was used for homesteads (settlements) and the rest were lands granted to railways or the Hudson's Bay Company or set aside for schools. Settlers initially received a quarter-section (160 acres; 65 hectares) and eventually could extend their holdings. Every section was numbered and marked out with survey stakes with pegs to mark the quarter sections.

Ontario and Quebec. Surveyors staked out townships, ranges, and sections for future grants to settlers and railroad and colonization companies. Each township formed a six-by-six-mile square subdivided into thirty-six sections. Each section of land was a square mile (640 acres), and quarter sections were 160 acres each (see Figure 2.5). Policy makers envisaged that each family would take up a quarter section of land. Through the Dominion Lands Act (1872), which was based on the American Homestead Act, the Canadian government offered free land in the hopes of attracting settlers. Canada also gave vast lands to the Canadian Pacific Railway and the Hudson's Bay Company. Over time, "softly flowing landscapes of untrammeled rangeland vistas [would be replaced] with a new landscape marked by square quarter-section farmsteads, grid roads that owed little to geography, equally spaced townships along straight railway rights-of-way, unswerving fence links, rectangular vegetable gardens and linear shelterbelts" (Potyondi 1995, 113).

Before the arrival of settlers en masse, the federal government needed to deal with one final barrier to settlement – Aboriginal peoples. Its failure to consult with local people regarding the annexation of the West had sparked the Red River Resistance of 1869-70, which resulted in the creation of the small province of Manitoba and some land for the Metis community, much of which speculators acquired. The declining fur trade and end of the buffalo trade resulted in mass starvation and poverty for First Nations and Metis communities. Between 1871 and

1877, the Canadian government negotiated Treaties 1 to 7, which relocated First Nations to reserves and defined their relationship with the Canadian state. In exchange for the promise of security, First Nations agreed to give up huge tracts of land and resources. Some Aboriginal leaders, who had their own ideas about property ownership and land use, thought their people would continue to have access to the region's game. Dual usage of the land was impossible, however, when private property became the basis of western settlement and agricultural development. The treaties led to Aboriginal people's suspicions of the federal Indian Act, which had been passed in 1876, and the breakdown of negotiated arrangements contributed to the outbreak of the Northwest Rebellion in 1885.

The government's suppression of the rebellion and the completion of the Canadian Pacific Railway in 1886 signalled that the West was "open for business." By 1914, over 3 million immigrants – first from Ontario and then from Britain, eastern Europe, and the United States – had taken up the challenge. To gain ownership or a land patent, settlers were required to build a habitable dwelling and cultivate some land annually as evidence of "improvement." Early arrival and the acquisition of good, cheap, accessible land were "among the most important determinants of success" (Dick 1985, 26). The settlers' response to the new environment was not, however, always dictated by logic.

The Prairies were "an environment stranger than most could ever have imagined" (Rees 1988, 24). Canadian promotional brochures had promised rich soil and a tem-

THE PRAIRIES AS UNFINISHED NATURE

Newcomers often defined the Prairies' negatively – as unfinished nature. Many viewed the absence of trees as a deficiency rather than as a characteristic of the landscape. Europeans loved trees. They believed they held moisture, altered the climate, and attracted rain. Inspired by Arbor Day, which was started in 1872 in the United States, Canadian settlers planted trees in the North-West Territories (present-day Alberta and Saskatchewan) in 1884 and in Manitoba in 1886. Their beliefs about trees, however, had no scientific foundation. Trees shade the surface of the land and obstruct winds, but they do not affect air temperatures or precipitation levels. They inject some moisture into the air, but only a fraction of the total humidity. Settlers' persistent ideas about trees reflected their intense desire for rainfall. Their optimistic belief that a more moderate climate and rainfall would follow the plough died hard.

perate climate, but settlers found "a land that was flat, dry, sparsely treed and by old world standards, empty of people." The grasslands were desolate: "cold bare bleak in the extreme – no gardens, no fences, no roads ... loneliness, utter loneliness" (Rees 1988, 36). Many settlers compared the prairie landscape to an ocean, and they feared getting lost. When it came time to choose a homestead, the first settlers clung to water and wooded areas. They assumed the parklands had better soil, and they often chose land because it had a familiar landmark or was located near friends or family, rather than for the quality of the soil. Although the land survey dispersed settlers, they often located farmsteads at the interior corners of quarter sections to be closer to neighbours.

In the forty-year period before the First World War, most farmland was taken up, and farmers tamed it quickly. As in other regions, the settler's first task was to build a shelter.

With no wood, the grasslands presented a problem, but settlement occurred more quickly than in central and eastern Canada because farmers did not have to clear the land. In the northern parklands, settlers lived in tents or in tarpaper or wooden shacks; on the grasslands, they lived in huts made of sod. Sod huts were warmer in winter and cooler in summer than a wooden shack, and the sod was a free and natural part of the prairie. After 1896, if the homestead was located close to the railway, farmers could order a building kit from Eaton's. Over time, farmers erected barns and frame houses, and they used wooden ploughs to break the sod, the first step in the farming operation.

From the beginning, government officials, farmers, and scientists worked together – to advertise the region's potential, to develop dry-land farming techniques, and to increase production. The government, through its forest nursery at Indian Head, and the Canadian Pacific Railway, through 1,500 station gardens, encouraged farm beautification to demonstrate the land's fertility and to promote the "New West." Prairie agriculture was monoculture, the practice of producing one single crop over a large area, and wheat was king. Settlers, aided by government experimental stations, which were established in 1886, used Red Fife as a base to develop hardy, fast-growing wheat. In 1909, the Dominion cerealist, Charles Saunders, developed Marquis wheat, a short-season, rust-resistant variety that became the backbone of the early grain industry. By 1915, it accounted for 60 percent of all prairie wheat. The Indian Head station experimented and produced drought-resistant grain varieties for southern Saskatchewan, short-season varieties for the Peace River district, and rust-resistant varieties for Manitoba. Between 1901 and 1921, wheat production increased twenty times. In recognition that quarter sections were too small for this type of farming, the government amended the Dominion Lands Act, first to allow settlers to apply for a second homestead and in 1908 to permit farmers to pre-empt adjoining quarter sections. To take advantage of escalating wheat prices and increase yields, the government encouraged technological innovation, mechanization, and the development of hybrids.

Farmers saw themselves as principal actors in the clash between wilderness and civilization. Government pamphlets encouraged them in a "war on weeds" to destroy native plants to prepare a place for cultivated plants to grow (Evans 2002, 83). They ploughed, sowed seeds, dammed creeks, and killed off all potential nuisances, including weeds, gophers, coyotes, and insects. Weeds, pests, and plant diseases ruined crops, but monoculture, over time, encouraged the spread of ever-hardier varieties of weeds. Good husbandry techniques developed in England were of little use to farmers coping with the Canadian environment. They developed new techniques and enthusiastically embraced chemicals such as pesticides and herbicides when they became available.

Within a decade, serious soil erosion was a problem. In response, governments promoted farmer education, some mixed farming, crop diversification, and planting trees for windbreaks. Farmers responded, but enthusiasm for these new approaches waned with rising grain prices in the 1920s. Farmers reverted to cereal monoculture. Farm implements and mechanized farming pulverized the soil and changed its structure by eliminating small rocks and reducing its organic matter. Crop rotation slowed this process, but farmers eventually began to replace lost nutrients with chemical fertilizers rather than by more natural means. Cultivation caused water to evaporate, and many streams, sloughs, and ponds dried up. Periodic droughts meant poor crops. In the heat, thin soils formed crusts on the surface that could not absorb moisture. Farmers then had to contend with soil runoff. Winds contributed to soil erosion and caused drifting, which reached epic proportions in the 1930s. During that decade, prairie farmers experienced huge reverses from economic depression, drought, grasshopper plagues, and windstorms.

In the end, the cost of mechanization and the difficulties of turning the Prairies into viable farms contributed to rural depopulation and the destruction of an ecosystem. A homesteader who used horsepower could support a family, but a quarter section was too small to cover the costs of machinery. Between 1870 and 1927, the turnover rate of farms was 41 percent as a high proportion of farmers failed. Those who succeeded did so by increasing their land holdings and by buying better machinery, including chilled steel ploughs, seed drills, tractors, trucks, threshers, and combines. As the number of farmers declined steadily, the size of farms and crop yields grew. Mechanization and monoculture changed prairie lands into "an artificial, managed environment" (Potyondi 1994, 225). Farmers were not stewards of the land but rather engineers who manipulated the environment.

Within only a few decades, the Prairie's diverse vegetation cover disappeared: "The rich old level prairie, with a myriad of sweet and delicate flowers, was gone ... turned into farmers' fields of grain ... replaced with Canada thistle, Russian thistle, tumbleweeds" (Seton 1978, 299). Birds such as the Missouri skylark, the white-tailed longspur, and the prairie plover were "wholly routed by the plough." The striped gopher disappeared, but the yellow gopher, who built passageways deep underground, increased in number. As prairie fires, both natural and deliberately set, became less common, woodland areas expanded southward. Within one generation, an industrialized system of agriculture geared to the global market had transformed "the complex buffalo landscape," which had lasted twelve thousand years, to "a simplified ecosystem devoted to monoculture production" (Potyondi 1994, 214).

British Columbia

The settlement of British Columbia occurred later than in the other regions of Canada because of its distinctive history, geography, and ecology. Vancouver Island, the base of the Pacific fur trade, became a Crown colony of British North America in 1849. The Mainland, however, did not became a colony until 1858, when a large influx of American gold seekers forced the British to maintain their influence north of the forty-ninth parallel. The two colonies became one in 1866, and the British government directed patterns of land occupation until 1871, when British Columbia joined Canada.

British Columbia developed a distinctive agricultural industry that was secondary to logging, fishing, and mining. Geography was a factor in a region where "cityscape presses

RACISM IN BC AGRICULTURE

As in other parts of Canada, agriculture was both implicitly and explicitly racist. Farmers and governments displaced indigenous peoples before they transformed the "savage wilderness" into a European-style Eden. In British Columbia, however, farmers also tried to prevent Asian immigrants from owning land and farming. Asians nevertheless worked as labourers on farms, and by the 1920s Japanese-owned berry farms produced much of the province's small fruit.

against wilderness without the intermediate agrarian landscape so familiar in Europe and eastern North America" (Demeritt 1995-96, 29). However, the region also enjoyed a moderate climate that encouraged farming in certain areas, particularly in river valleys and on southeastern Vancouver Island and other islands. On Saltspring Island, settled in the late 1850s, large commercial farms exported farm produce, and small farmers augmented their agricultural labour with horticulture and seasonal work in the lumber and fishing industries. Between 1891 and 1921, 175,000 former British army officers and upper- and middle-class settlers, people who celebrated country living, settled at Victoria and in the Cowichan and Okanagan Valleys, giving the areas an English flavour. Britons constituted one-third of the province's population on the eve of the First World War. Imbued with Arcadian values derived from the English romantics such as John Ruskin, who "decried the Enlightenment domination of nature and the spiritual and moral decay it caused," these so-called gentlemen farmers cultivated flowering plants and fruit trees on small lots (Bennett 1998, 80). Growing fruit and grazing cattle in fenced gardens and pastures

transformed British Columbia. In the Okanagan, Aboriginal people were restricted to a reserve a fraction the size of their previous lands, and British orchardists converted the area's dry soil through irrigation to re-create their version of Eden. By 1905, fruit trees covered 11,735 hectares of the valley.

Agrarianism – the celebration of agriculture as both productive work and a source of wealth and independence for yeoman farmers – also encouraged settlers from central Canada and the United States to farm in the river valleys of the central Interior. By the 1890s, dairy farmers in Richmond, Surrey, Delta, and Langley in the lower Fraser Valley were working low land protected by dikes. The dry southern Interior was less suitable for farming, but some people cleared small plots of large trees, blasted stumps, and worked subsistence farms part-time as they held seasonal jobs in logging companies, sawmills, or canneries. As on the Prairies, settlers viewed farming as the act of carving civilization out of a savage wilderness. They persisted in the face of daunting challenges, and many were brought down by the high costs of drainage, land clearing, and irrigation. Some developed cooperatives; others sold out to larger farms. Although never a major industry in British Columbia, fruit and vegetable production on small farms fed a growing population. The value of local produce exceeded imports in 1911.

The Lumber Industry

By 1900, most of British Columbia's forests remained untouched, but old-growth forests in central and eastern Canada had disappeared. Settlers played a large role, but loggers and commercial logging companies were responsible for the majority of the devastation. As early as 1779, William Davidson of New Brunswick received the first contract from the British to cut down trees for ship masts. The deforestation that preceded or accompanied European agricultural settlement and the lumber industry's commercial interest in wood as a commodity created a reciprocal relationship between settlers and sawmill owners. In the mid-nineteenth century, lumber companies also began to move into areas with no settlers. To a greater extent than with fish or fur, and much like agriculture, the timber industry visibly transformed Canada's landscape as deforestation advanced along with settlers from the Atlantic region to central Canada and later to the northern Prairies and British Columbia.

England was the hub of the world timber trade, and wood quickly became one of the foundations of British North America's prosperity. When the French Revolution and the Napoleonic Wars (1793 to 1815) closed England's access to lumber in the Baltic, Canada became an important alternative supplier. The best trees were massive white pines or hemlock in New Brunswick and Upper Canada, red and white pine in the Ottawa Valley, pine and spruce in Lower Canada, and oak beyond the Welland Canal. Loggers harvested these trees in what historian Arthur Lower called the commercial assault on the forests. After the lumber industry culled trees in the Maritimes, it moved on to central Canada and later to the West. In central Canada, timber floated down rivers to the St. Lawrence, where it awaited shipment to England. The wood was used in the British shipbuilding industry for masts,

as planks and boards in general construction, and for firewood and potash. In 1811, 23,053 masts, 24,469 boatloads of oak, and 52,888 loads of pine were shipped from Quebec. Canada was Great Britain's wood yard, and Britain encouraged private investors and companies to build lumberyards and sawmills in support of the trade. Between 1820 and 1846, Canadian suppliers concentrated on ton timber (crudely squared pine trunks), deals (thick boards used for construction and ship decking), and planks (see Figure 2.6). Until 1857, they successfully pressured the British government to impose stiff duties on Baltic timber imports. When the tariff ended, however, Baltic imports surpassed imports from Canada. Demand for square timber also peaked in 1850 and then declined as wooden sailing vessels gave way to iron steamships and as lumbering degraded the forests.

The lumber industry survived. In the 1840s, the sawn lumber trade in central Canada and New Brunswick expanded to service the demands of settlers at home but particularly in the United States. The concentration of sawmills along rivers and their tributaries from Saint John in New Brunswick to the north shore of Lake Erie increased the industry's accessibility to white pine. Between 1860 and 1910, the Ottawa Valley led the way in lumber production and enriched lumber barons such as E.B. Eddy, an American entrepreneur, and J.R. Booth of Quebec in the process. Governments granted large companies long or renewable licences to cut huge tracts of Crown land. Communities such as Chaudière Falls in the Ottawa-Hull area served as the centre of the industry as it expanded to the "back settlements" of the

FIGURE 2.6 Lumber merchant J.R. Booth's rafts of pine timber sit in a cove in 1891 ready for loading onto a transatlantic ship. Loggers assembled square timber into small rafts that they floated down narrow waterways. As a river widened, they joined the rafts together to create immense floating platforms. Logging companies cleared brush along the routes of the river drives, dredged shallow rivers, and reordered the waterways to suit their unrestrained logging, destroying natural ecosystems in the process. At their destination, the loggers broke up the rafts for loading onto the ships.

John Thomson, photographer, Library and Archives Canada fonds, C-006073

FIGURE 2.7 Lumberjacks felling trees in a virgin Ontario forest in the nineteenth century. The northern boreal forests contained immense stands of hemlock, white and red pine, and cedar, along with northern hardwoods such as maple, oak, and beech, which dominated northern North America's pre-settlement landscape. With basic, though improving technology, lumberjacks did the dangerous work of cutting down these giant trees.

Library and Archives Canada, William Morell Harmer Collection, C-026244

Kawartha Lakes, to the "bush land" north of the Great Lakes, and to Georgian Bay.

The lumber industry was forced to expand constantly because the sustained attack on the forest lowered the quantity and quality of white pine (see Figure 2.7). When forests on the north shore of Lake Ontario became sparse in the 1850s, American and Canadian loggers moved to harvest forests around Georgian Bay and up the Bruce Peninsula. There, from the 1870s onward, sawmills operated year-round. Loggers hauled trees cut inland in winter along roads to the water. In the spring, they drove the logs to the bay. After the mills in Michigan ran out of nearby forests, US companies began rafting logs across Georgian Bay and Lake Huron. Canadians were indignant that Canadian logs were not being milled in Canadian communities. In 1897, the Ontario government passed legislation stipulating that all pine logs cut on its Crown lands had to be processed in the province. In 1900, it amended the legislation to include spruce pulpwood. The legislation simply encouraged US companies to jump the tariff wall. In Georgian Bay, for instance, "mills appeared like mushrooms in the middle of the forests, ate up the trees, and then disappeared" (Barry 1971, 93). The boom dwindled in 1905 but did not disappear until the 1940s. In the meantime, with so many mills in operation, wood manufacturing and the pulp-and-paper industry took off in southern Ontario and Quebec. Carpenters made shutters and furniture for a national market, and the pulp-and-paper industry harvested the remains of old-growth and second-growth forests. Both industries gave new impetus to deforestation.

Because lumbermen regarded timber as a one-crop commodity, they cut and moved on. Companies either expanded west into the northern forests of the Prairies or jumped the Prairies entirely to exploit British Columbia's huge timber stands. In a pattern similar to that of the fur trade, the lumber industry penetrated Canada's interior and opened up the country in a westward direction, "not as a line but as a series of expanding circles," an approach conditioned by the country's rugged geography (Lower 1936, 150). The lumber industry in British Columbia began as an

AN INTEGRATED TIMBER OPERATION IN BOBCAYGEON

Although the square timber trade peaked in the mid-nineteenth century, it did overlap with the sawn lumber trade. Mossom Boyd, for instance, built an integrated timber business that operated from 1849 to 1904 out of Bobcaygeon, Ontario. He shipped square timbers to the British market until the 1880s, driving them down the Trent waterway to Quebec. But from the 1850s he also shipped sawn lumber, which needed protection from water, by boat, wagon, and train for sale at the wholesale market in Albany, New York. Between 1869 and 1884, under contract with the Canada Land and Emigration Company in England, Boyd took out an annual average of forty thousand high-quality pine logs from the Haliburton region. His business needs stimulated transportation networks that helped end isolation in backwoods settlements but hastened deforestation.

offshoot of the Hudson's Bay Company. The company built a sawmill on Vancouver Island in 1848 and developed plans for an export trade to San Francisco. The gold rush also stimulated the industry because miners used wood for buildings, mineshafts, sluice boxes, and flumes. Private investors opened the first sawmill on the Mainland at Yale in 1858. In the 1860s, when corduroy roads and charred stumps remained a common sight on settlers' lands, lumbering was well under way at Burrard Inlet, in present-day Vancouver. In 1865, Edward Stamp leased 3,238 hectares (8,000 acres) of land at a penny an acre for twenty-one years, beginning a decades-long "assault on the gigantic trees of the virgin forest" (Mackay 1985, 25).

Lumber companies exported British Columbia's old-growth trees as lumber, laths, and shingles to international markets in Australia, New Zealand, San Francisco, and South America, whereas lighter cargo went to Mexico, China, England, and Hawaii. Beginning in the 1890s, the expanding export market included huge shipments of pine, cedar, hemlock, spruce, larch, and Douglas fir. Industry leaders and government officials viewed timber exports from British Columbia as "green gold" and paid little attention to regenerating what they considered an inexhaustible supply. The provincial government gave the industry generous terms for purchasing and leasing timberlands, 95 percent of which were Crown lands. "An Ordinance to Amend and Consolidate the Laws Affecting Crown Lands in British Columbia," passed in 1870, "regulated" logging through timber leases with enormous acreages. New legislation in 1888 granted thirty-year timber licences with an annual rent of ten cents per acre (0.4 hectares) and a royalty payment of fifty cents per 1,000 feet (305 metres). The system, which was highly lucrative, attracted US lumbermen to stands made accessible by the building of the Canadian Pacific Railway, the Crow's Nest Pass Railway, and newer lines in the interior. In 1895, 1903, and 1905, the government increased rates marginally and made cutting licences mandatory. When it stipulated that wood cut on Crown land had to be processed on Crown land, the number of mills, the amount of timber cut, and government revenues all increased.

Successive governments, supported by businessmen and large-property owners, continued to support the lumber industry. The government subsidized the construction of wagon roads and railways, paid the costs of reclamation schemes, and dispensed land, timber, and mineral rights. A provincial Royal Commission on Timber and Forestry in 1910 reported on the butchery and wastage of wood. The Forest Act of 1912 curbed the worst abuses, but the damage was done: 80 percent of Crown timberland had already been leased. In 1917, when British Columbia surpassed all other Canadian provinces in lumber production, its logging industry had already repeated the pattern of environmental damage practised in the East.

The Environmental Impact of Deforestation

Forest clearing was the "greatest single factor in the evolution of the North American landscape" (Williams 2006, 292). Clearing the land opened areas for farmland, reduced distances between settlements, and brought untold profits, but in the process a new land-scape emerged. Abraham Gesner wrote, "By such operations, the forests are leveled and their [the settlers'] solitudes are cheered by the light of day; the swamps and bogs are redeemed to the plough, the scythe and the sickle, and hill and valley resound with human labour and happiness, until the land is filled with villages, towns, and cities" (Gesner 1847, 252). Cutting forests, however, led to a scarcity of plants and wildlife that was noticeable by the mid-nineteenth century. This scarcity concerned settler and naturalist Catharine Parr Traill well before the conservation movement emerged, but hers was a minority view. In 1852, she wrote, "I am a great admirer of the indigenous flowers of the forest, and it is with a feeling strongly allied to regret, that I see them fading away from the face of the earth ... Man has altered the face of the soil – the mighty giants of the forests are gone, and the lowly shrub, the lovely flower, the ferns and mosses, that flourished beneath the shade, have departed with them" (Raglon 2005, 8).

From the daily activities of early settlers to the organized deforestation of the lumber barons, Canada's environment was altered without concern for future generations. Settlers viewed wood as an unlimited resource and used and abused it accordingly. They burned wood on the spot, used it for houses and fences, and made and sold some for potash. But they mostly used it for heat, energy, and cooking. Plumes of acrid smoke marked settlements as pioneers burned green wood for cooking and heating and as they cleared brush and trees. Settlers consumed huge amounts of wood: between twenty and thirty cords a year, a cord being a pile

of wood that when stacked tightly occupies a volume of 128 cubic feet (3.62 cubic metres). Pioneers used inefficient fireplaces for years before they turned to more efficient wood-burning stoves. Chopping, splitting, hauling, and stacking wood took time and energy, but it was also a profitable, and necessary, side-line for farmers.

Pioneers thought the forests were boundless, that waterways could absorb all damage, and that fish were abundant. They were insensitive to the lumber industry's adverse effects on the natural environment. Aside from stripping the land, the lumber industry transformed and polluted waterways, which were used as laneways, as storage areas, as power sources, and as waste-disposal units. During the square timber trade, workers blasted rocks from narrow brooks and sometimes used dynamite to break up logjams. Logging companies cleared brush along the routes of drives, dredged parts of the rivers that were shallow or filled with debris, and cleared beaver dams out of streams. Loggers built their own dams to flush cuttings through troublesome passages, and they used reservoir dams to regulate the flow of water. These man-made dams flooded huge areas of land and destroyed fish and plant cover. Lumber barons essentially reordered the waterways to suit unrestrained logging, and they destroyed natural ecosystems in the process. Log drives removed bankside soils, streamside vegetation, and streambed spawning gravel. With the removal of vegetation, soils eroded, riverbanks warmed, and new types of vegetation took over.

Sawdust also caused problems. When companies milled wood, bark and sawdust spewed into rivers and lakes, where they coated and destroyed fish feeding grounds and spawning areas. Sawdust also turned vast wetlands into deserts, which fish avoided. As early as 1850, the New Brunswick government had Moses Perley – lawyer, naturalist, and author – examine the state of the colony's fisheries. Perley reported that milldams and mill waste were having an adverse effect on salmon runs and spawning grounds flowing into the Bay of Fundy. Because stream fish require clean water within a narrow temperature range to reproduce, fish populations rapidly decreased or disappeared in logged-over areas throughout central and eastern Canada.

As pollution from sawmills worsened, some town officials pressed mill owners to clear waterways and save fish stocks, but they had difficulty preventing the ruinous effects of sawdust. In 1886, a divisional court blamed mill owners for allowing "sawdust, blocks, chips, bark and other refuse to fall into the River Ottawa, and thereby pollute the water and impede navigation. This refuse accumulates in great flowing masses, substantial enough occasionally for a man to walk upon" (McLaren 1984, 225). Officials urged the use of sawdust burners, which a few lumber

barons had introduced. In Alma Parish, New Brunswick, however, the lumber industry continued to have priority over the fishing industry. Mills on the Salmon and Point Wolfe Rivers engaged in environmentally destructive behaviour but were unwilling to do cleanups. A combination of vacillating public policy, public complacency, and organized lobbying by lumber barons contributed to government inaction. In Alma Parish, unsustainable methods eventually led to the disappearance of the forest, along with the lumber companies; the demise of salmon, trout, herring, and shad; and the gradual death of a community, as workers moved away. Many mill sites throughout Canada became towns where fish species had disappeared and did not return. Wildlife managers later introduced invasive alien species such as carp, smelt, and Pacific salmon. The lumber industry thus left permanent damage in its wake.

In central Canada, lumbermen managed to forestall government regulation, despite public concerns about fisheries and navigation. Over time, however, government passed effective, enforceable legislation. In the Ottawa Valley, for example, conflicts between

DESTRUCTION IN THE TRENT VALLEY

Lumbermen did not need permission to build dams, and without knowledge of ecosystems, their activities had disastrous consequences. In 1872, for instance, after loggers had denuded much of the land adjacent to rivers in the Trent system of forest cover, soil erosion became a problem. Heavy snow cover led to large, quick spring runoffs and flooding. Because the soil could no longer absorb water, water poured down the Trent system, taking out booms, piers, and slides. The Lumbermen's Committee had to rebuild the entire system on a smaller scale. When the Commission of Conservation surveyed the Trent Valley in 1912, mismanagement of timber resources and soil erosion remained a problem that adversely affected agriculturalists when they settled on the cleared land. "The slopes, once for the most part covered with valuable pine and hardwood forest, had been cut over. A large area, the pinery in particular, had been repeatedly subjected to fires and rendered liable to eventual total destruction" (Guillet 1957, xxvii).

lumber companies, which were opposed to any regulation, and conservationists, who viewed mill refuse as a nuisance to health, navigation, and recreation, lasted for years. Finally, in 1902, the largest sawdust polluter, the J.R. Booth Company, was forced to install equipment to stop materials from entering the Ottawa River. The case centred on the enforcement of antidumping regulations, which sportsmen supported to protect fish and spawning grounds. As the river deteriorated and methane explosions became commonplace, the lumber industry had rejected the use of chipping and grinding machines and asserted its right to pollute. In response, strategically placed politicians and civil servants opposed to sawdust pollution passed stronger regulations. Lumber companies, in turn, eventually began to use the waste as energy, and they diversified their businesses to include pulp-and-paper and wood byproducts. Booth was the last holdout, but his defiance was overcome once the government prepared to prosecute. This long struggle to control the lumber industry's waste-disposal practices demonstrated a change in Canadian attitudes toward the depletion of renewable resources and a consensus among decision makers that lumber refuse was destroying other businesses, damaging the environment, and degrading water quality.

No area in Canada in this period had a forestry inventory or conducted forestry on a sustained-yield basis. Corruption played a role in several provinces as public servants or politicians accepted bribes from lumber companies in return for favours. The concept of forests as renewable resources came late, but, in 1894, Hugh Watt, MLA for the

Cariboo region in British Columbia, suggested a commission to study forestry in the province. He claimed forests were not inexhaustible and not the property of one generation but rather a sacred trust to be used and preserved for future generations. Noting the connection between healthy forests and the survival of fish and game, Watt advocated conservation, the replanting of cut areas, and scientific forest management. Unlike earlier critics, Watt refrained from using incendiary language against "monopolists" in the lumber industry and instead focused on conservation. The provincial government, which "remained committed to industrialization," ignored his ideas, and industry leaders used the concept of conservation, when useful, to further their specific goals. "Business interests, rather than government, drove change" (Mackay 1985, 239).

To EARLY SETTLERS and businessmen, forests represented both the enemy and wealth. Trees were cut aggressively in largely unregulated activity because lumbering and agriculture were the mainstays of the Canadian economy. The transformation of the environment through deforestation, surveys, and land grants set the stage for orderly, rapid settlement and the larger process of nation building as former British colonies and territories came together into a single nation in the mid-nineteenth century. Indigenous peoples were confined to new "Native spaces" on reserves or in isolated, unpopulated areas, and natural landscapes gave way to inorganic grids defined by roads, fences, and farm boundaries. Agriculturists attempted to turn the wilderness into a European-style Garden of Eden, and regardless of whether they practised mixed farming in the Maritimes, Quebec, Ontario, or British Columbia or monoculture wheat production on the Prairies, they upset ecosystems. In concert with the logging industry, agriculturalists created new environments that would have been unrecognizable to the regions' original inhabitants.

Works Cited

Barker, Grace. 2003. *Timber Empire: The Exploits of the Entre-preneurial Boyds.* Huntsville: Fox Meadow Creations.

Barry, James. 1971. *Georgian Bay: The Sixth Great Lake.* Toronto: Clarke Irwin and Company.

Bennett, Jason Patrick. 1998. "Apple of the Empire: Landscape and Imperial Identity in Turn-of-the-Century British Columbia." *Journal of the Canadian Historical Association* 9, 1: 63-92.

Coates, Colin. 2000. *The Metamorphoses of Landscape and Community in Early Quebec.* Montreal and Kingston: McGill-Queen's University Press.

Demeritt, David. 1995-96. "Visions of Agriculture in British Columbia." *BC Studies* 108: 29-59.

Dick, Lyle. 1985. "Factors Affecting Prairie Settlement: A Case Study of Abernethy, Saskatchewan, in the 1880s." *Canadian Historical Association Historical Papers* 20, 1: 11-28.

Evans, Clinton L. 2002. *The War on Weeds in the Prairie West: An Environmental History.* Calgary: University of Calgary Press.

Forkey, Neil. 2003. *Shaping the Upper Canadian Frontier: Environment, Society and Culture in the Trent Valley.* Calgary: University of Calgary Press.

Gentilcore, R. Louis, and Geoffrey J. Matthews. 1993. *Historical Atlas of Canada.* Vol. 2, *The Land Transformed, 1800-1891.* Toronto: University of Toronto Press.

Gesner, Abraham. 1847. *New Brunswick: With Notes for Emigrants, Comprehending the Early History, an Account of the Indians.* London: Simmonds and Ward.

Glazebrook, G.P. de T. 1968. *Life in Ontario: A Social History.* Toronto: University of Toronto Press.

Guillet, E.C. 1957. *The Valley of the Trent.* Toronto: Champlain Society.

Harris, R. Cole, and Geoffrey J. Matthews. 1986. *Historical Atlas of Canada.* Vol. 1, *From the Beginning to 1800.* Toronto: University of Toronto Press.

Jameson, Anna Brownell. 1969 [1838]. *Winter Studies and Summer Rambles in Canada.* Toronto: McClelland and Stewart.

Lower, Arthur. 1936. *Settlement and the Forest Frontier in Eastern Canada.* Toronto: Macmillan.

Mackay, Donald. 1985. *Heritage Lost: The Crisis in Canada's Forests.* Toronto: Macmillan of Canada.

MacKinnon, Neil. 1986. *This Unfriendly Soil: The Loyalist Experience in Nova Scotia, 1783-1791.* Montreal and Kingston: McGill-Queen's University Press.

McLaren, John P.S. 1984. "'The Tribulations of Antoine Ratté': A Case Study of the Environmental Regulation of the Canadian Lumbering Industry in the Nineteenth Century." *University of New Brunswick Law Journal* 33: 203-59.

Murray, Jeffrey S. 1989. "The Map-Makers: Filling in the Blanks in Western America." *The Beaver* 69, 1: 14-27.

Potyondi, Barry. 1994. "Loss and Substitution: The Ecology of Production in Southwestern Saskatchewan, 1860-1930." *Journal of the Canadian Historical Association* 5: 213-35.

—. 1995. *In Palliser's Triangle: Living in the Grasslands, 1850-1930.* Saskatoon: Purich Publishing.

Raglon, Rebecca. 2005. "Little Goody Two-Shoes: Reassessing the Work of Catharine Parr Traill." In *This Elusive Land: Women and the Canadian Environment,* edited by Melody Hessing, Rebecca Raglon, and Catriona Sandilands, 4-18. Vancouver: UBC Press.

Rees, Ronald. 1988. *New and Naked Land: Making the Prairies Home.* Saskatoon: Western Producer Prairie Books.

Richards, John F. 2005. *The Unending Frontier: An Environmental History of the Early Modern World.* Berkeley: University of California Press.

Roe, Frank Gilbert. 1982. *"Getting the Know-How": Homesteading and Railroading in Early Alberta.* Edmonton: NeWest Press.

Sandwell, R.W. 1994. "Rural Reconstruction: Toward a New Synthesis in Canadian History." *Histoire sociale/Social History* 27, 53: 1-32.

Sanger, Chesley. 1977. "The Evolution of Sealing and the Spread of Permanent Settlement in Northeastern Newfoundland." In *The Peopling of Newfoundland: Essays in Historical Geography,* edited by John Mannion, 136-51. St. John's: Institute of Social and Economic Research.

Saunders, R.M. 1935. "The First Introduction of European Plants and Animals into Canada." *Canadian Historical Review* 16, 4: 388-406.

Sellar, Robert, ed. 1969. *A Scotsman in Upper Canada: The Narrative of Gordon Sellar.* Toronto: Clarke, Irwin, and Company.

Seton, Ernest Thompson. 1978. *Trail of an Artist-Naturalist.* New York: Arno Press.

Smith, Donald. 1987. *Sacred Feathers: The Reverend Peter Jones (Kahkewaquonaby) and the Mississauga Indians.* Toronto: University of Toronto Press.

Williams, Michael. 2006. *Deforesting the Earth: From Prehistory to Global Crisis (An Abridgment).* Chicago: University of Chicago Press.

Wynn, Graeme. 1990. "Exciting the Spirit of Accumulation among the 'Plodholes'": Agricultural Reform in Pre-Confederation Nova Scotia." *Acadiensis* 20, 1: 5-51.

For Further Reading

Permanent Settlements

Cronon, William. 1983. *Changes in the Land: Indians, Colonists, and the Ecology of New England.* New York: Hill and Wang.

Dunlap, Thomas R. 1999. *Nature and the English Diaspora: Environment and History in the United States, Canada, Australia, and New Zealand,* New York: Cambridge University Press.

Harris, R. Cole, and John Warkentin. 1974. *Canada before Confederation.* Toronto: Oxford University Press.

Hatvany, Matthew G. 2003. *Marshlands: Four Centuries of Environmental Change on the Shores of the St. Lawrence.* Sainte-Foy: Les Presses de l'Université Laval.

Sanger, Chesley. 1977. "The Evolution of Sealing and the Spread of Permanent Settlement in Northeastern Newfoundland." In *The Peopling of Newfoundland: Essays in Historical Geography,* edited by John Mannion, 136-51. St. John's: Institute of Social and Economic Research.

Traill, Catharine Parr. 1966. *The Backwoods of Canada.* Toronto: McClelland and Stewart.

Trudel, Marcel. 1973. *The Beginnings of New France, 1524-1663.* Toronto: McClelland and Stewart.

Surveys and Land Grants

Coates, Colin. 1993. "Like 'The Thames towards Putney': The Appropriation of Landscape in Lower Canada." *Canadian Historical Review* 74, 3: 317-43.

Craig, Gerald. 1963. *Upper Canada: The Formative Years, 1784-1841.* Toronto: McClelland and Stewart.

Forkey, Neil. 2003. *Shaping the Upper Canadian Frontier: Environment, Society and Culture in the Trent Valley.* Calgary: University of Calgary Press.

Harris, R. Cole. 1984. *The Seigneurial System in Early Canada: A Geographical Study.* Montreal and Kingston: McGill-Queen's University Press.

MacKinnon, Neil. 1986. *This Unfriendly Soil: The Loyalist Experience in Nova Scotia, 1783-1791.* Montreal and Kingston: McGill-Queen's University Press.

Clearing the Land

Bitterman, Rusty. 1993. "Farm Households and Wage Labour in the Northeastern Maritimes in the Early 19th Century." *Labour/Le Travail* 31 (Spring): 13-45.

Gesner, Abraham. 1847. *New Brunswick: With Notes for Emigrants, Comprehending the Early History, an Account of the Indians.* London: Simmonds and Ward.

Jameson, Anna Brownell. 1969 [1838]. *Winter Studies and Summer Rambles in Canada.* Toronto: McClelland and Stewart.

Little, J.I. 1999. "Contested Land: Squatters and Agents in the Eastern Townships of Lower Canada." *Canadian Historical Review* 80, 3: 381-412.

MacKinnon, Neil. 1986. *This Unfriendly Soil: The Loyalist Experience in Nova Scotia, 1783-1791.* Montreal and Kingston: McGill-Queen's University Press.

Russell, Peter A. 1983. "Forest into Farmland: Upper Canadian Clearing Rates, 1822-1839." *Agricultural History* 57, 3: 326-39.

Sellar, Robert, ed. 1969. *A Scotsman in Upper Canada: The Narrative of Gordon Sellar.* Toronto: Clarke, Irwin, and Company.

Farming in Central and Eastern Canada

Coates, Colin. 2000. *The Metamorphoses of Landscape and Community in Early Quebec.* Montreal and Kingston: McGill-Queen's University Press.

Dechêne, Louise. 1992. *Habitants and Merchants in 17th-Century Montreal.* Montreal and Kingston: McGill-Queen's University Press.

Derry, Margaret. 1998. "Gender Conflicts in Dairying: Ontario's Butter Industry, 1880-1920." *Ontario History* 90, 1: 31-47.

Forkey, Neil. 2003. *Shaping the Upper Canadian Frontier: Environment, Society and Culture in the Trent Valley.* Calgary: University of Calgary Press.

Harris, Cole. 2008. *The Reluctant Land: Society, Space, and Environment in Canada before Confederation*. Vancouver: UBC Press.

Lawr, D.A. 1972. "The Development of Ontario Farming, 1870-1914: Patterns of Growth and Change." *Ontario History* 64, 4: 239-51.

Ouellet, Fernand. 1980. *Lower Canada, 1791-1840: Social Change and Nationalism*. Toronto: McClelland and Stewart.

Saunders, R.M. 1935. "The First Introduction of European Plants and Animals into Canada." *Canadian Historical Review* 16, 4: 388-406.

Wilson, Bruce. 1981. *As She Began: An Illustrated Introduction to Loyalist Ontario*. Toronto: Dundurn Press.

Wynn, Graeme. 1990. "Exciting the Spirit of Accumulation among the 'Plodholes'": Agricultural Reform in Pre-Confederation Nova Scotia." *Acadiensis* 20, 1: 5-51.

Settling the Prairies

Careless, J.M.S. 1967. "The Toronto *Globe* and Agrarian Radicalism, 1850-1867." In *Upper Canadian Politics in the 1850s*, edited by Ramsay Cook, Craig Brown, and Carl Berger, 38-63. Toronto: University of Toronto Press.

Carter, Sarah. 1990. *Lost Harvests: Prairie Indian Reserve Farmers and Government Policy*. Montreal and Kingston: McGill-Queen's University Press.

Dick, Lyle. 1985. "Factors Affecting Prairie Settlement: A Case Study of Abernethy, Saskatchewan, in the 1880s." *Canadian Historical Association Historical Papers* 20, 1: 11-28.

Dunbar, G.S. 1993. "Isotherms and Politics: Perceptions of the Northwest in the 1850s." In *Prairie Perspectives 2*, edited by Anthony W. Rasporich and Henry C. Klassen, 80-101. Toronto: Holt, Rinehart and Winston.

Evans, Clinton L. 2002. *The War on Weeds in the Prairie West: An Environmental History*. Calgary: University of Calgary Press.

Friesen, Jean. 1986. "Magnificent Gifts: The Treaties of Canada with the Indians of the Northwest, 1869-76." *Transactions of the Royal Society of Canada* 5, 1: 41-51.

Ganzevoort, Herman. 1973. *A Dutch Homesteader on the Prairies: Willem de Gelder*. Toronto: University of Toronto Press.

Morton, W.L. 1949. "Agriculture in the Red River Colony." *Canadian Historical Review* 30, 4: 305-21.

—. 1964. *The Critical Years: The Union of British North America, 1857-1873*. Toronto: McClelland and Stewart.

Murray, Jeffrey S. 1989. "The Map-Makers: Filling in the Blanks in Western America." *The Beaver* 69, 1: 14-27.

Owram, Doug. 1980. *Promise of Eden*. Toronto: University of Toronto Press.

Potyondi, Barry. 1994. "Loss and Substitution: The Ecology of Production in Southwestern Saskatchewan, 1860-1930." *Journal of the Canadian Historical Association* 5: 213-35.

—. 1995. *In Palliser's Triangle: Living in the Grasslands, 1850-1930*. Saskatoon: Purich Publishing.

Rees, Ronald. 1988. *New and Naked Land: Making the Prairies Home*. Saskatoon: Western Producer Prairie Books.

Roe, Frank Gilberet. 1982. *"Getting the Know-How": Homesteading and Railroading in Early Alberta*. Edmonton: NeWest Press.

Waiser, W.A. 1989. *The Field Naturalist: John Macoun, the Geological Survey and Natural Science*. Toronto: University of Toronto Press.

British Columbia

Barman, Jean. 1991. *The West beyond the West: A History of British Columbia*. Toronto: University of Toronto Press.

Bennett, Jason Patrick. 1998. "Apple of the Empire: Landscape and Imperial Identity in Turn-of-the-Century British Columbia." *Journal of the Canadian Historical Association* 9, 1: 63-92.

Demeritt, David. 1995-96. "Visions of Agriculture in British Columbia." *BC Studies* 108: 29-59.

Hak, Gordon. 2000. *Turning Trees into Dollars: The British Columbia Coastal Lumber Industry, 1858-1913*. Toronto: University of Toronto Press.

Harris, Cole. 2002. *Making Native Space: Colonialism, Resistance, and Reserves in British Columbia*. Vancouver: UBC Press.

Marchak, M. Patricia. 1983. *Green Gold: The Forest Industry in British Columbia*. Vancouver: UBC Press.

The Lumber Industry

Armson, K.A. 2001. *Ontario Forests: A Historical Perspective*. Toronto: Fitzhenry and Whiteside.

Campbell, Claire Elizabeth. 2005. *Shaped by the West Wind: Nature and History in Georgian Bay*. Vancouver: UBC Press.

Lower, Arthur. 1936. *Settlement and the Forest Frontier in Eastern Canada*. Toronto: Macmillan.

Marchak, M. Patricia. 1983. *Green Gold: The Forest Industry in British Columbia*. Vancouver: UBC Press.

Pyne, Stephen J. 2007. *Awful Splendour: A Fire History of Canada*. Vancouver: UBC Press.

Wynn, Graeme. 1981. *Timber Colony: A Historical Geography of Early Nineteenth-Century New Brunswick*. Toronto: University of Toronto Press.

The Environmental Impact of Deforestation

Allardyce, Gilbert. 1972. "'The Vexed Question of Sawdust': River Pollution in Nineteenth-Century New Brunswick." *Dalhousie Review* 52, 2: 177-90.

Gillis, Peter. 2006. "Rivers of Sawdust: The Battle over Industrial Pollution in Canada, 1865-1903." In *Canadian Environmental History*, edited by David Freeland Duke, 265-84. Toronto: Canadian Scholars' Press.

Guillet, E.C. 1957. *The Valley of the Trent*. Toronto: Champlain Society.

Mackay, Donald. 1985. *Heritage Lost: The Crisis in Canada's Forests*. Toronto: Macmillan of Canada.

McLaren, John P.S. 1984. "'The Tribulations of Antoine Ratté': A Case Study of the Environmental Regulation of the Canadian Lumbering Industry in the Nineteenth Century." *University of New Brunswick Law Journal* 33: 203-59.

Williams, Michael. 2006. *Deforesting the Earth: From Prehistory to Global Crisis (An Abridgment)*. Chicago: University of Chicago Press.

PART 2

Industrialism, Reform, and Infrastructure

3
Early Cities and Urban Reform

One river or ravine or clump of trees by the water looks pretty much like another; it is when they build on it that men really put a distinctive hand on the landscape.

— ALAN GOWANS, URBAN HISTORIAN, "THE EVOLUTION OF ARCHITECTURAL STYLES IN TORONTO," 1984

CANADA REMAINED A predominantly rural, agricultural nation until 1920, when urban dwellers for the first time outnumbered their rural counterparts. Yet towns and cities grew in concert, first with agriculture and then with industrialism – the development of industries that manufactured large quantities of inexpensive goods and concentrated employment in urban factories. Much like the process of clearing and farming land before it, the Industrial Revolution, which began in England in the mid-eighteenth century and spread throughout the Western world over the next two centuries, introduced yet another period of "ecological restructuring, a new and significant chapter in the earth's environmental history" (Williams 2006, 136). Industrialism put Canada on the road to modern economic and national development, but it also reconfigured the landscape

AN ECOLOGICAL APPROACH TO URBANIZATION

In 1986, historian Theodore Steinberg noted that environmental historians had yet to explore the Industrial Revolution's impact on the environment and encouraged them to adopt an ecological perspective on the phenomenon. Economic historians had sketched the growth of industry. Historians of technology had examined innovations, inventions, patents, and their diffusion. Labour and social historians had focused on the human consequences of industrial development for ordinary men and women, including transformations in family life as people left rural communities for the city. Environmental historians, however, began to ask new questions. What was it like to live in a nineteenth-century city? How much air pollution was there in the home or at work? How frequently did disease wrack crowded urban neighbourhoods? What did early cities smell like? How did people get clean water or dispose of garbage?

In addition to studying urban pollution, environmental historians examine the spatial development of cities and the growth of urban infrastructure, services, and parks. They seek to understand how the complex, often subterranean, internal development of cities has affected people and the environment.

and polluted the environment as new energy sources (steam, coal, and hydroelectricity) fuelled the economy and manufacturing production, centred in Ontario and Quebec. In the eighty-year period between 1850 and 1930, Montreal made the transition from a small town of approximately fifty thousand people to a large industrial complex of nearly one million inhabitants. As railways and other transportation routes stretched across the nation, drawing early towns into a sprawling industrial complex, the pattern was repeated in other Canadian cities and led to similar problems: overcrowding, pollution, and unsanitary conditions but also to reform. Over time, people's attitudes toward the environment changed, as became evident in the early reform movement and in urban design.

The Growth of Cities

Canada's villages, towns, and cities evolved as and continue to be built environments that reflect different eras, peoples, cultures, and accommodations to the natural world. Aboriginal peoples came together in villages to fish, hunt, or farm; for defence purposes; or in response to pressure from Europeans. Likewise, European settlements began as tiny colonial outposts in the French and British Empires. Influenced by developments in the metropolis – Paris or London, depending on the era or empire – early Canadian centres emerged in places that allowed settlers to exploit the environment and its natural resources to maximum effect. Some towns were located near former Aboriginal trails and trading centres. After the American Revolution, for instance, the British founded York at the base of the Toronto Carrying-Place Trail, which Aboriginal people had used before and during the French regime (see Figure 3.1). These early towns housed military men, fur traders, and administrators. Over time, they developed into commercial communities linked to the two largest cities, Montreal and Toronto, and influenced the sizable regional hinterlands that surrounded and were served by them. The basic network of cities in central and eastern Canada had taken shape by the 1850s.

All early urban centres were walking cities. They were relatively compact areas based on mixed patterns of land use. There was little separation between the place of work and the home. In design and appearance, however, early towns reflected different political and cultural influences. The towns of New France, though North American outposts, resembled French provincial towns. Louisbourg, France's eighteenth-century naval fortress, had elaborate fortifications. Halifax, founded by the British in 1749 in an era of imperial rivalry, resembled "the towns of Ulster [Ireland], designed to subjugate and assimilate a hostile, non-urban local population," meaning

THE METROPOLITAN-HINTERLAND THESIS

Because Canada developed first as a colonial society, as an offshoot of the French and British Empires, and transformed itself from a colony to a transcontinental industrializing nation in the nineteenth century, metropolitanism – the impact of cities on development and society – became an important concept in Canadian history. Historian J.M.S. Careless noted that infrastructure such as police or railways emanated from the metropoles. For example, the North West Mounted Police and the Canadian Pacific Railway preceded settlement on the Canadian Prairies, Canada's hinterland. From the beginning of the nation-building process, Careless argued, cities had an indelible effect on the shape and direction of Canadian society and its transformation of the environment.

the Acadian French and Aboriginal people (Stelter and Artibise 1984, 13).

After the American Revolution, Loyalists founded "instant towns" in New Brunswick and Upper Canada to service a dispersed population of settlers. Kingston began as a fort, became a Loyalist refugee centre, and served briefly as the capital of the United Province of Canada (1841-67). York (Toronto), which had a strategic location on a harbour, became the capital city of a society that John Graves Simcoe, lieutenant-governor of Upper Canada, envisaged as a rigid social hierarchy based on the land. The colonial government situated officials on thirty-two large park lots (100 acres, or 40.5 hectares each) that faced the harbour. The profits from developing these lands created local elites. Early land assignments also influenced Montreal, where long, narrow seigneurial grants affected street patterns. Newer planned communities such as Goderich and Guelph, designed by the Canada Company, attempted to overcome the limitations of the monotonous grid. The Canadian superintendent of the company, John Galt, laid out the town like a European city centre with town squares, broad main streets, and smaller side streets. From the air, the town resembled a giant lady's fan, with the streets forming triangles. Thus, by 1850, cities in central and eastern Canada were of different ages, had diverse functions and appearances, and reflected various cultural influences.

Before 1870, settlements on the Prairies consisted of the Red River settlement and scattered forts, missions, and fur-trading posts – remote nodes with tiny populations that tended to concentrate near water sources. Red River, a dispersed and self-reliant

FIGURE 3.1 The Toronto Carrying-Place Trail. This portage route linked Lake Ontario with Lake Simcoe. The name came from the Mohawk term *toron-ten*, meaning "the place where the trees grow over the water."

Source: Percy J. Robinson, *Toronto during the French Regime, 1615-1793* (Toronto: University of Toronto Press, 1965), viii-ix. Reprinted with the permission of the publisher

FIGURE 3.2 Upper Main Street, Winnipeg, 1876. This wide thoroughfare in Winnipeg was characteristic of main streets in western cities. Prairie cities, like land grants for farms, conformed to the square grid superimposed on the western landscape by the Dominion Lands Act.
Archives of Manitoba, N21074

community, also had a tiny commercial nucleus in what is today downtown Winnipeg. The Council of Assiniboia, the administrative body of Rupert's Land from 1821 to 1870, sat in the newer community of Upper Fort Garry, at the intersection of the Red and Assiniboine Rivers. Once the Prairies became a part of Canada and settlers began to arrive, the region's urban centres boomed. Railway routes determined which towns would survive and which would perish. As crews built the Canadian Pacific Railway across the southern Prairies, towns such as Brandon appeared overnight. When the line passed through Calgary in 1883, the North West Mounted Police post transformed quickly into an urban centre that would compete with Edmonton for domination of the region. The Dominion Land Survey contributed to the planned look of prairie towns,

which had wide thoroughfares, numbered rather than named streets, and a universal grid pattern, whatever the terrain (see Figure 3.2). By 1901, three cities, twenty-seven towns, and fifty-seven villages held about 20 percent of the Prairie's population.

In British Columbia, location and function influenced the emergence of cities. Victoria, on the southern tip of Vancouver Island, was established in 1841 by the British as a fur-trading post and administrative centre. It became the capital of British Columbia after the province joined Canada. On the Mainland, a community called Gastown emerged around a sawmill located on a beautiful harbour. When the railway reached the Pacific Coast in 1886, the town was renamed Vancouver, which prospered as a commercial centre and evolved into the largest city in British Columbia.

In Canada as a whole, 45 percent of the population lived in towns and cities by 1911 (see Figure 3.3). Although Canadian cities borrowed from European and American models, urbanization coincided with industrialization, and urban buildings often reflected their unplanned and rushed nature in their utilitarian appearance and design. Sanitation and deodorization had already become a concern in Europe by the eighteenth century, when governments put drainage and sanitation systems in place to prevent diseases; paved roads in the classical fashion; and gave buildings ventilation features such as domes, cupolas, porticoes, and large windows and doors. European cities widened their streets and built vast squares with fountains, features that lasted for centuries. In Canada, by contrast, companies located factories and industries along waterways, a main energy source, with no consideration of aesthetics, public health, or the environment. Growth was desirable, and cities, particularly on the Prairies, were guilty of boosterism. They promoted their town or city to improve public perceptions and attract citizens and investors. Municipal councils gave industries financial bonuses to locate in their communities, and they took a hands-off approach to regulation, which proved to be disastrous for the environment.

Throughout Canada, agricultural hinterlands surrounded cities. The city and the countryside shared a reciprocal relationship centred on food consumption and production. Farmers sold agricultural produce at large city markets and, in return, bought urban goods. This interactive process meant that cities and city dwellers continued to be

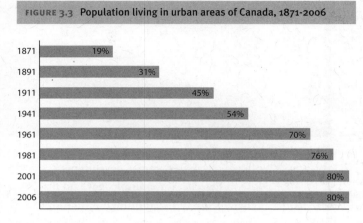

FIGURE 3.3 Population living in urban areas of Canada, 1871-2006

Year	Percent
1871	19%
1891	31%
1911	45%
1941	54%
1961	70%
1981	76%
2001	80%
2006	80%

Note: Before 1981, "urban population" refers to populations within centres of 1,000 people or more. For 1981 to 2006, it refers to persons living within centres with a population of 1,000 or more and within areas with at least 400 persons per square kilometre.

Source: Adapted from Human Resources and Skills Development Canada, "Indicators of Well-Being in Canada," http://www4.hrsdc.gc.ca/. Reproduced with the permission of the Minister of Public Works and Government Services Canada, 2012.

connected to nature and the bounty of the land, but it also meant that urban trends pervaded the rural environment. For example, when cities gave up gas streetlamps in favour of electrical light stands, rural electrification would follow a generation later.

Railways and Industrial Development

Industrialism and urbanization in Canada coincided with, and were made possible by, railway expansion. Railways not only provided transportation infrastructure, they were also the largest manufacturing companies. As railways linked communities, contributing to expanding markets for manufactured goods, industrialists moved their businesses to larger and larger centres in their search for better transportation facilities, abundant and cheap labour, and larger local markets. Cities

FIGURE 3.4 Toronto, in 1850, before the coming of the railway. Called York, the city was strategically located on a harbour, which suited John Graves Simcoe for military purposes but later also attracted railway and commercial interests.

Library and Archives Canada, W.H. Coverdale Collection of Canadiana, C-046109

offered a way to organize development. Joseph Flavelle, for example, gave up his general store in Peterborough, Ontario, to start a specialized meat-packing business. He relocated to Toronto in 1887 and emerged as a leader in the city's burgeoning business community. This pattern of business consolidation was repeated often, changing the spatial distribution of people and industry.

Railways linked urban centres to their hinterlands to exploit resources and ship them to markets. Railways had an immediate and permanent effect on both the city and the countryside. The arrival of the railway in Georgian Bay, for instance, was a turning point in the history of the Great Lakes. The railway supported the expansion of the area's shipping, timber, fishing, and tourism industries. Railway development also stimulated urban growth by facilitating the movement of rural workers and immigrants to the cities and the consolidation of the urban industrial workforce. In Toronto, for example, manufacturers from the 1880s onward built factories next to railway tracks, which "fanned out from the centre of the city near the waterfront," with a tangential line constructed across the northern edge of the built-up area (Gad 1988, 151). Railways also contributed to early suburban growth. For instance, an industrial suburb emerged at West Toronto Junction and became a s suburb of Toronto by 1914. Sometimes these early suburbs reinforced class and social inequalities by concentrating environmental harms in certain areas. When the Great Western Railway connected Hamilton to other border cities in the 1850s, its shops spread along the waterfront. Its presence attracted other industries, and the denser industrial environment meant extensive pollution in nearby working-class neighbourhoods, which were far removed from wealthier areas.

The railways' effect on the environment in general varied. Railways not only contributed to air pollution and noise, their tracks also disturbed the landscape as they pushed through all types of terrain. If the railway crossed a wetland, the crew filled it in; if a line went through a gulley, the crew built a bridge; if the crew encountered a hill, they tunnelled through it (see Figure 3.5). Trains also threw off sparks that started forest fires, a grave concern for early foresters and conservationists.

Infrastructure and Spatial Expansion

Industrialization, rapid population growth (from both natural increase and immigration), and the development of rail transportation systems transformed small preindustrial communities into crowded commercial centres that needed infrastructure – basic physical and organizational structures and facilities, such as roads, buildings, sewers, and power supplies. Light was important. For instance, in 1845, merchants in Saint John, New Brunswick, formed a joint stock company and won a contract from the municipal council to build a gasworks and provide city streets with lights. By the fall of the following year, all of the major thoroughfares had gas-lit lamps. Four years later, the company was providing gas to 140 street lamps and 750 private homes and businesses through 33.8 kilometres of pipes. The number of customers doubled over the next decade. Steam engines provided the major power source until the 1880s, when the introduction of electrical power lit up city streets, stimulated new businesses, and led to renovations in older factories. As electricity use increased, both cities and factories in core urban areas expanded, and lights in general contributed to greater mobility.

Street railways, which first appeared in US cities in the 1850s, likewise promoted the expansion of urban centres and, as an innovation in mass transit, came to symbolize urban progress. In 1861, Toronto's city council granted Alexander Easton a licence and a thirty-year franchise to operate a street railway system. Beginning with 9.7 kilometres of track on three lines that carried two thousand passengers each working day, the system expanded to 110 kilometres of track that carried from fifty thousand to sixty thousand passengers a day in 1891. Between 1891 and 1894, the system was converted to electricity, a process that left an indelible mark on the urban cityscape in the form of a profusion of wires and cables strung between posts. Street railways stimulated the growth of early suburbs and made spatial expansion a defining characteristic of early urban centres. Toronto was typical in the sense that "the desire to gain access to the centre of the city on the part of a few well-to-do suburbanites preceded the desire to escape the city by its residents" (Coheen 1970, 73). Just as immigrants gravitated to factories in city centres, political and economic elites committed to growth politics "shaped the legal and material foundations" of suburban growth through control over the ideology of local urban expansion" (Lewis 2004, 79). Rosedale and Yorkville, among the first Toronto suburbs, were middle-class enclaves. Eventually, some workers also chose to move away from the city centre and ride the streetcar to work.

FIGURE 3.5 Victoria railway locomotive on a trestle bridge in 1870 on a route between Fenelon Falls and Haliburton. In defiance of the natural landscape, and by necessity, rail lines were completely flat. In this case, railway crews built the bridge over a low area.
Library and Archives Canada, Canadian National Railway Company fonds, PA-117833

In Montreal from the 1860s onward, a combination of urban growth, the availability of suburban land, railways, and the decentralization of production facilities led to industrial suburbanization and satellite towns, which reshaped the city's geography. As the urban frontier moved out from Old Montreal, "the suburban manufacturing districts created in the earlier growth phase had been enveloped by the expanding city and new ones formed on the periphery" (Lewis 2004, 85). Suburbs in Montreal, as in other cities, were homogeneous, segregated by class and sometimes by ethnicity. By the 1880s in the West End, the industrial suburbs of St. Henri and Ste. Cunegonde and the satellite town of Lachine had emerged. Over the next ten years, East End districts formed another distinct nucleaus.

This pattern of cities annexing most or all of the earliest suburbs was repeated in all regions. In 1929, for example, Vancouver annexed extensive suburbs, including Point Grey and South Vancouver. Some communities that began as suburbs but were not incorporated, such as Mississauga, later became cities. Just as working-class housing surrounded industries in the city centre, so too did residential areas encircle outlying industrial districts.

Urban Living and Pollution

Nineteenth-century cities were distinctive environments that people at first viewed as unnatural, unhealthy, dangerous, and immoral. Many were ambivalent about urban centres, and rural folk in particular feared losing young people to them. Over time, however, as cities became more established, the urban lifestyle – characterized by conveniences, excitement, culture, and cosmopolitanism – captured the imagination of many.

The majority of people found it difficult to adapt to early cities because they were crowded, noisy, and filthy. In the countryside, people used compost heaps, which dispersed smells, to dispose of household waste and to fertilize gardens. They put wood ashes in gardens, and outhouses broke down human wastes. In the early cities, by contrast,

> Decaying garbage, kitchen slop, and the excrement of thousands of horses, cows and pigs filled the streets. Farmers' markets drowned in blood, animal carcasses and fish heads, rotting vegetables, and offal. Slaughterhouse wastes mingled with street refuse and accumulated in the lower regions of towns to become noxious cesspools. Buildings lacked indoor plumbing. In most cities it was common to store human excrement and other wastes in pails, which were then dumped in the streets or emptied into the nearest body of water. (Baldwin 1988, 221)

Smells from organic processes permeated houses and streets, and acid emissions from factories polluted the air.

Because cities developed faster than services such as sewers and water-treatment facilities, which cities usually implemented in wealthy areas first, the quality of life in poorer working-class areas was terrible. Poorly paid workers without job security resided in slums, which concerned urban reformers for health and humanitarian reasons. From a public health perspective, heavily populated areas characterized by substandard housing and squalid overcrowded conditions contributed to disease, which affected everyone, including the wealthy. Crowded unsanitary conditions led to outbreaks of tuberculosis and other diseases, resulted in unnecessary deaths, especially of small children, and added to noise pollution.

The urban environment, with its relatively dense population, over time evolved to meet the needs of people and industry, whereas, in less populated rural areas, people intermingled with other species, domesticated animals, and wildlife. At first, however, early cities retained certain rural characteristics. In the 1860s, pigs wandered in the main streets of Toronto (see Figure 3.6), which was nicknamed "Hog Town." In Montreal, "cows grazed in backyards and on street verges. Pigs scrounged in courtyards and alleys, and poultry could be heard and seen throughout the city" (Bradbury 1984, 13). Cattle, swine, and goats roamed city streets until the 1880s because working-class people in Toronto and Montreal were forced to raise animals and cut costs to maintain an adequate food supply (see Figure 3.7). These household practices reflected the persistence of rural ways in a new urban environment. They symbolized a transitional period when people were changing from agriculturalists to urban-industrial workers.

As populations and traffic increased, municipalities took action to promote cleaner streetscapes. They began by prohibiting the breeding or grazing of farm animals in city limits. Montreal's tougher bylaws, although sometimes not well enforced, controlled the slaughter of animals and required dog owners

to have a licence for their pets. The number of animals kept for food dropped dramatically between 1861 and 1891. A Toronto bylaw passed in 1890 sought to prevent animals, with the exception of horses, from running at large by imposing rules about fencing, providing pounds for runaways, and limiting the number of animals in each household. Cows, however, continued to be a visible element in urban environments until railways with refrigerator cars made the long-distance transfer of milk feasible. Municipalities then

FIGURE 3.6 Pigs rooting in the middle of Wellington Street in Toronto in the early 1860s. This early urban environment looked quite rural even though the city was growing quickly.
The Beaver (August-September 1987): 60, Library and Archives Canada, C-11384

FIGURE 3.7 The iron fence at Osgoode Hall Law School in York included narrow gates to keep out cows as they wandered by from nearby farms or town properties.
Canadian Architectural Archives, Accession #262A/99.01, Project PAN 61370, Image 136

restricted farm animals to stockyards before slaughter. Citizens knew of their presence from the distinctive acrid smell that permeated areas such as the Toronto Junction, a centre for the meat-packing industry.

In addition to waste and pollution from livestock and slaughterhouses, early city dwellers also experienced the environmental effects of industrial growth. In the 1830s, Britain, as the "workshop of the world," became the first country to experience industrial pollution. Industrialization and its effects quickly spread to North America, where the United States surpassed Britain in the volume of industrial output by 1890. Canada had a slower rate of industrialization, urban growth, and population increase than the United States, but its experience of industrial pollution was the same. Industries created atmospheric pollution – smoke and winter fogs – as well as acids, dusts, and odours. Chemical industries produced carbon and sulphur dioxide (from burning coal) and released hydrochloric acid into the air. Whereas hydrochloric acid polluted water, killed trees, and contributed to poor crops, calcium sulphide emissions filled cities with the smell of rotten eggs.

People who worked in factories laboured for long hours in increasingly disciplined workforces. Factory owners expected them to

THE HORSE IN THE MODERN CITY

Horses, an abundant fixture in early Canadian cities, remained a main source of transportation until the invention of the automobile. Rather than having to deal with pollution from exhaust and smog, earl city dwellers had to deal with copious amounts of horse manure. A single horse discharged gallons of urine and nearly twenty pounds of manure a day, which was a waste-disposal problem.

INDUSTRIAL TIME

The transition from preindustrial to industrial society not only changed the environment, it also divorced people from its natural rhythms. Streetlights and electricity meant that people no longer worked from sunrise to sunset, dividing their day between light hours and darkness, as had been the case in preindustrial communities. Instead, employers defined the workday in terms of minutes, hours, and work shifts, and many factories operated twenty-four hours a day. Industrial workers began to wear watches to keep track of time and to accustom themselves to the new rhythms of the industrial factory, which were based on the novel concept of saving time. Outside of the factories, the transcontinental railways forced small towns and cities to set their clocks. When the companies developed their schedules, all communities had to be on the same local time. Sir Sandford Fleming, a Canadian, invented standard time, "the unexpressed operating system of all interdependent technologies," twenty-four time zones, and the Greenwich meridian so the world would be on the same timeframe (Blaise 2001, 18). The 1884 Prime Meridian Conference confirmed the system.

be punctual, take brief meal breaks, and work at repetitive tasks on assembly lines, which were sometimes speeded up at the behest of time-study experts. Such regimentation, known as Taylorism, replaced the older rhythms of rural communities and was far removed from the powerful, slower, and more natural rhythms of Aboriginal hunter-gatherer societies.

Early factory inspectors' reports reveal the effects of industrialism in Canada. According to the Ontario Factories Act of 1886, inspectors were to report on industrial accidents and the number of hours worked by women and children. The inspectors, however, also described workplace environments. In 1888, for instance, one inspector noted overcrowding in factories and the presence of dangerous machinery and nails. He also wrote about the lack of ventilation and the dangers of open vats of chemicals. The inspector made note of whether the air was pure or foul and whether workers were affected "by the dust, vapors, fumes or gases resulting from the various processes carried on." The chief impurities in the air on his beat included carbonic acid and carbonic oxide, produced by coal stoves, candles, lamps, and gas. He concluded that "the great problem of supplying air in sufficient quantities without creating draft" and "removing that which is foul, under the varying conditions of a changeable climate such as Canada, has not received the attention it deserves from employers" (Ontario, Factory Inspector's Report, 1888, 6). In 1894, another inspector worked with the Board of Health to urge factories to introduce measures to avoid a cholera outbreak. Factories in the soap, wool, and cotton industries took some action, but confectionary factories, where syrup dripped over floors and starch dust coated everything, did nothing. The inspector concluded that, in older establishments, "the accumulation on the floors of grease, syrup, soap and other matters" was so great that it would be impossible to keep them clean (Ontario, Factory Inspector's Report, 1894, 9).

Early court cases about work-related accidents also open a window on industrial workplaces and their impact on the environment. From the 1860s to the mid-1880s, workers in Ontario launched a number of lawsuits for compensation for work-related accidents. Most cases centred on the railway industry because the Grand Trunk and the Great Western Railways employed the largest number of people. These workers used steam-powered heavy machinery without guards. Thousands were hurt or died, impoverishing their families. Because English common law worked against workers' rights on the job, the pattern before 1886, the year the government passed protective legislation, was that workers sometimes won their case before a jury but always lost on appeal. In 1884, in Cumminsville, Halton County, workers filed a case against the Hamilton Powder Company, which made 250 kegs a day of high-grade blasting powder for the Canadian Pacific Railway. When the manager raised the quota to 360 kegs per day, the antiquated powder grinders overheated, threw a spark, and ignited loose powder on the mill floor. The resulting fire exploded kegs of ground powder, which shook buildings many kilometres away in Hamilton. The blast killed five men and injured and permanently disabled others. It, and other industrial incidents, also destroyed the environment: "All of the factory's main buildings were smoldering rubble," and "the mature elm and maple trees that had ringed the site were toppled over like broken matchsticks" (Kostal 1988, 9).

The Public Health Movement

Early cities gave off foul odours from slaughterhouses, breweries, and bakeries and from the chemical treatment of organic matter to make glue, tallow, and fertilizer. Municipalities accumulated organic waste and routinely dumped it into the nearest body of water, which they assumed could absorb it. Until the mid-nineteenth century, people viewed waste as an inconvenience and an eyesore but not as a major sanitation problem. Developments in England and the United States and epidemics of cholera, typhoid, smallpox, and other diseases, however, helped give rise to the public health movement, which pressed for safer, more sanitary cities. The British Poor Law Commission Report of 1842 had established a connection between communicable diseases and filthy environmental conditions. Three decades later, in 1869, Britain established a Sanitary Commission and passed public health laws to reduce diseases in cities. North American cities copied these initiatives.

Before the 1880s, however, contagionists and anticontagonists disagreed about how diseases spread. Contagionists believed disease spread among persons in direct contact and favoured quarantines and isolation of the sick. Anticontagonists, whose views held more weight until the scientific breakthroughs of Louis Pasteur, thought disease was simply "in the air." They linked sickness to pestilential miasmas – gases caused by putrefying matter such as excrement and corpses or by sewers and cesspools. The miasmic theory drove sanitation reform in Europe and North America when people tried to eliminate conditions that generated miasmas. Reformers "purified" or disinfected cities by removing garbage, eliminating standing water, and cleaning streets and basements to prevent the fumes of rotting matter from contaminating the air. Theirs was a fearful, foreboding view of the environment, one full of unseen dangers from foul air and water. Pasteur's experiments in the 1860s and 1870s, however, led to the germ theory of disease – the idea that bacteria cause illness. The theory helped public health officials understand the causes of disease and push for improved sanitation practices and water supplies in the nineteenth century. In the twentieth century, death rates from disease fell further once laboratories discovered vaccines and cities implemented immunization programs.

In Canada, doctors, reformers, and some municipal politicians came to understand, particularly after epidemics, that citizens' health and safety depended on state-owned and state-regulated sanitation facilities, including indoor toilets, sewer systems, clean drinking water, and waste-disposal programs. Reformer Herbert Ames, in his study of working-class conditions in Montreal, *The City Below the Hill* (1897), loathed outdoor toilets, protesting that "that relic of rural conditions, that unsanitary abomination, the out-of-door-pit-in-the-ground privy, is still to be found in the densely populated heart of our city." Montreal in 1896 had 5,800 privies, 3,000 fewer than in 1891. Ames found the situation inexcusable since "there is not a street or lane in our nether city which has not a water service. Only a few small alleys are without a drainage system." He wanted the Birmingham pail system adopted in Montreal, "whereby all night-soil is collected and removed once in every 24 hours," to eliminate the most objectionable aspects of privies (Ames 1972, 47).

As in the British and American movements, Canadian urban reformers focused on civic government, clean water, slums, and public health. They sought improvements by drawing on the expertise of town planners, boards of health, and civil engineers. Reformers, however, had to compete with developers and business owners, who sought maximum profits, and boosters, who had a radically different vision of urban development. Civic officials ignored new planning ideas such as radial roads because of the expense. They remained fiscally conservative when they considered human waste disposal, water supply issues, and sanitation services: they cut corners on design by combining rather than separating storm water and sanitary pipes; they relied too much on the absorptive capacity of running water to dilute and purify waste; and they were reactionary rather than pre-emptive, doing nothing until a health crisis or public pressure forced them to act.

Water and Waste-Disposal Systems

Developing waste-disposal and sewage and water systems posed numerous challenges for municipalities and brought into play clashing ideas about nature, the nature of the state and urban governance, and notions of environmental justice. Small rural communities used private wells for water, outdoor

EARLY AWARENESS OF AIR POLLUTION

Early reformers and public health officials focused on the water supply and the quality of sewers for waste-disposal systems, but industrial air pollutants did gain some attention before the First World War and led to poorly enforced legislation. Public health officers blamed industrial diseases on unsanitary workplaces, poor ventilation, and poisoning from phosphorus, lead, arsenic, mercury, brass, silica, and the fumes of wood alcohol. Factory inspectors noted the poor quality of workplace air and the effects of chemicals. And members of smoke abatement leagues in industrial cities worried about the health effects of smog, caused by burning coal in homes and industries. The war, however, drew attention away from the issue. Once the conflict ended, engineers treated emissions as something to be managed rather than reduced. In general, air pollution did not become a major public concern until the 1960s, when it became a quality-of-life issue.

GARBAGE DISPOSAL

Crowded, growing cities needed efficient garbage disposal systems. At first, cities hired contractors – called dustmen – to cart away debris and waste. In Montreal, the civic government in 1760 ordered residents to pile their refuse in front of their houses. Collectors eventually picked it up and dumped it in the St. Lawrence River. As late as 1910, Kingston's medical health officer deplored the city's lack of organized garbage collection and disposal. He complained that household and commercial solid refuse littered the urban landscape and that the smell of decomposing waste permeated the air in the summer. Sanitary reformers pressured the city for garbage service, but citizens used limestone quarries and Kingston's large harbour for household waste. The city depended on private contractors until 1915, when it hired its own small crew to implement a weekly collection service, set up a municipal dump on a marshy lot, and constructed an incinerator. The City of Hamilton, by contrast, used garbage as landfill to reclaim heavily polluted areas along the waterfront and, in the north end, to create a park.

privies or outhouses, compost heaps and fires for household garbage, and private waste-disposal heaps for human and farm waste. In larger towns and cities, however, where people disposed of human waste in streets or harbours, water contamination quickly emerged as a problem and spawned health problems and social and political conflicts.

The development of municipal services in Saint John, New Brunswick, followed a path similar to that of other Canadian cities, but Saint John was one of the few cities to construct early permanent sewers. Neighbourhood groups, concerned about water quality, pressed the municipal council for sewers in 1817. Councillors responded slowly because of financial concerns, and the council delayed action until epidemics and public debates over private or public ownership of sewers forced it to act. At the time, the city had a primitive water system. Wealthy residents had private wells, whereas each ward had a municipal well. In the 1830s, following a cholera epidemic, citizens stated they would pay for a continuous supply of fresh country water. Their demand for reform coincided with the city's need to provide more water for street cleaning and for fire-fighting purposes. The city built a rudimentary wood sewer system, and a private company, supported by the council, secured a water supply and laid iron pipes to transport it to the community. Within a decade, the fire hydrant had replaced the private well, but piped water remained a luxury for the majority of households. In 1851, council assessed householders for the cost of putting in sewers throughout the rest of the city. It did nothing, however, until the 1854 cholera epidemic killed 1,500 people, 5 percent of the population. The public asked the province to pressure council to create an integrated public system for fresh piped water and waste disposal and to create a Board of Health. Despite improvements, the Board of Health in 1857 reported that 548 households in Saint John and Portland still disposed of excrement by spreading it on the streets. The city did not complete the system until 1860.

Delays and prevarication also shaped developments in Charlottetown, Prince Edward Island. Incorporated in 1855, Charlottetown had the power to develop a waterworks system to provide clean water and protect public health. It did not act, however, until 1887. Citizens dumped human excrement into bogs, the harbour, or an underground reservoir that sunk down to the water table. The city was characterized by filth and foul odours: poorly drained roads, outdoor privies, bogs, cesspools, slaughter-houses, and farm animals. A smallpox outbreak, however, inspired the city to develop municipal services. As in Saint John, however, a more pressing concern was making sure that fire fighters had an adequate supply of water so businesses could be insured. (The concerns of business leaders also led to the introduction of municipal services in Kingston, Ontario.) By 1893, over 1,500 houses in Charlottetown had running water. The system was self-sustaining financially, and the poor received free service so they would not use polluted well water. The city constructed a sewer system in 1898, but not all citizens were linked to it until 1917.

In Ontario, cities likewise delayed action despite pressure from reformers. Had they acted sooner, they could have prevented cholera outbreaks and the ravages of prevalent diseases, including typhoid fever, infant diarrhea, and tuberculosis. Hamilton installed water services in response to a cholera outbreak in 1854, as did Kingston in 1881. London did not purchase its own waterworks system until 1887. Most towns and cities had sewers by the end of the nineteenth century, but some resource towns remained without until the twentieth century. For instance, in 1914, Cobalt, which had sprung up in 1906 in response to a silver boom, had a main sewer that disgorged waste into a ditch.

Western Canadian cities developed later than those in central and eastern Canada but more quickly, as hundreds of thousands of settlers arrived on the Prairies, some settling in cities. The successful development of infrastructure depended not only on links to railways and markets but also on commercial and economic growth. Edmonton, for

example, built its infrastructure comprehensively rather than in the piecemeal fashion common in Ontario and the Maritimes. When the city became the capital of Alberta in 1906, its active civic administration ensured it had modern streets and sidewalks, electricity, telephones, water and sewage systems, a street railway, parks, and public health officials. Through property taxes, it increased the number of arc streetlights, extended the water and sewage pipelines, replaced mains with larger pipes, and installed an 11-million-litre electrically driven pump. It built a garbage incinerator in the east end's working-class area and operated a small street railway by 1908. The city, however, was slower to act on public health issues. Its street-cleaning department comprised a few horses and a "scavenging outfit," and it wasn't until a typhoid epidemic ravaged the city in 1906 that frightened officials agreed to build an isolation hospital.

Vancouver, British Columbia, in its early years was perhaps a model for other cities. From its founding in 1886, it provided extensive services, including a city hospital, a waste-disposal and drainage system, a clean water supply, and inspectors to preserve public health. Leading citizens and city council saw the provision of good services as attractions, along with the city's beautiful natural setting and mild climate, that would draw businesses and people. Nevertheless, Vancouver developed pollution problems because its waste-disposal systems used the city's waterways as "sinks." Engineers believed they could exploit "water's 'assimilative capacity' or its ability through chemical and biological processes to neutralize harmful pollutants" by dispersing, diluting, and absorbing them in sewage

(Keeling 2004, 70). A regional plan passed in 1913 involved new technologies and infrastructure. It lasted thirty-five years, but it did not end pollution.

In general, municipal services throughout Canada developed slowly and exposed citizens to pollution and disease. Fiscally conservative and cautious city councils were more likely to respond to insurance companies' demands for good water systems than a concern for citizens or the environment. When cities did build water and sewer systems, councillors tended to care more about presenting a modern image of their city to investors and tourists than about health and hygiene. And when they did respond to pressure from reformers, their policies were sometimes inconsistent. Local governments enacted rigid plumbing bylaws to safeguard against gas and sewer leaks, but they poured raw sewage into waterways that supplied drinking water. Sarnia, Ontario, installed its public drinking water intake pipe only 45 metres away from its untreated sewage outfall pipes. As sewerage issues became more complicated and specialized, however, the construction of waterworks and sewage systems required long-range planning and shifted from politicians to experts. Civil engineers created methods of sewage treatment and administered public works departments. Once built, these systems reduced illness and mortality rates, particularly after cities introduced the use of chlorine, but officials did not reduce the source of urban pollution if it interfered with business. Companies continued to dump industrial waste into urban waterways. Reform removed the public health issue from municipal politics, but public health officers continued to monitor the urban environment for problems.

Urban Design and Green Spaces

Reformers not only pressured governments to clean up cities, they also sought to improve them aesthetically by lobbying for more green spaces, playgrounds, and parks. Municipalities had showed foresight in acquiring parklands early, including the Halifax Common (1763), Place-d'Armes Square in Montreal (1840) (see Figure 3.8), Garrison Reserve in Toronto (1848), and Gore Park in Hamilton (1852). After Confederation, they converted land retained originally for defence purposes into urban parks, such as the Toronto Islands (1867), Stanley Park in Vancouver (1886), and Point Pleasant Park in Halifax (1875). With public pressure and the expertise of engineers and urban designers, city councils also made parks, playgrounds, and recreational spaces for urban families. In addition, they hired architects and landscapers to improve city centres, particularly around legislative buildings, and they erected monuments to evoke civic pride or, more often, to commemorate soldiers' wartime sacrifices. But the aesthetic vision remained only partially fulfilled because municipal councils focused pragmatically on reforming their own administrative structures and procedures and on improving utilities and basic amenities.

Public urban green spaces had no ancient precedent. In Europe, the great gardens at Kew or Versailles were royal or private estates of the landed aristocracy. But with urban industrial growth in North America, the idea emerged that parks could be breathing spaces or the "lungs of the city" and should be public and accessible to all. This vision represented a sea change in attitudes toward

FIGURE 3.8 Place-d'Armes, Montreal, 1886. The municipality acquired this green space early for an urban park. When completed, the park set off the building and created an aesthetically pleasing urban space, as some urban reformers advocated.
McCord Museum, William Notman Collection, M932.8.1.271

nature and the natural environment. Confronted with filthy, smoky, and gloomy cities, reformers, poets, and social observers began to idealize country living. In 1884, a Canadian journalist exalted rural life and remarked with distaste that, in the city, one lived in a distressing, unpleasant environment characterized by "the busy hum of machinery, the regal mansion of the capitalist, and a background of squalid tenements where vice, and penury, and dirt, produce a diseased and vicious population" (Smith 1990, 73). Early Canadian poets such as Archibald Lampman, Charles G.D. Roberts, and Louis-Honoré Fréchette likewise sought solace in nature, away from the noise, overcrowded conditions, and mechanization of the city. Their aversion was partly romantic, but changes in attitudes toward the natural world became common as cities grew larger. Early European pioneers and settlers had hated and feared "the wilderness," which they sought to clear and conquer to make farms, but as the countryside became settled, urbanites appreciated and were rejuvenated by manicured rural landscapes. At the same time, as cities became a permanent feature of industrial society, reformers pushed for improved urban environments by increasing the number of parks and green spaces.

Although municipal politicians viewed parks as expensive time-consuming projects,

BURIAL GROUNDS: THE FIRST GREEN SPACES

City parks were unnecessary when the countryside surrounded small urban communities and could be accessed easily. But as cities grew, the idea of green spaces emerged. The first spaces landscaped and maintained for public use were small rural burial grounds, which towns and cities consolidated into larger urban cemeteries. In 1874, for instance, the City of Toronto turned farmland into Mount Pleasant Cemetery, designed by landscape architect Henry Engelhardt. It opened in 1876 and today is the burial place of famous Canadians such as Prime Minister Mackenzie King. It also contains an arboretum of trees and shrubs from around the world.

they nevertheless developed administrative infrastructures to oversee their development. Toronto had a Committee on Public Walks and Gardens as early as 1860, and between 1888 and 1890 Vancouver's park committee became an elected Board of Parks Commissioners, the first in Canada. As Canadians embraced the idea of public city parks, the provinces passed enabling legislation for their establishment and management. The idea that nature had a salutary, rejuvenating effect on people's spiritual life and character, that it created beauty and was civilizing, led urban planners to incorporate more parks into their designs so citizens would have places to relax. Thus, Toronto's High Park, Montreal's Mount Royal Park, Winnipeg's Assiniboine Park, and Vancouver's Stanley Park were among those created as part of the urban parks movement in the last half of the nineteenth century.

The most famous city park at the time, and a model for other cities, was New York's Central Park, designed in the 1860s by Frederick Law Olmstead. Olmstead, famous for working in and with nature to achieve naturalistic effects, believed the environment influenced character, that people's inner convictions expressed themselves in their outward surroundings, and conversely, that the environment helped sustain inner beliefs. Olmstead and his clients – businessmen, politicians, and the social elite – wanted New York to be a "civilized" city, so he invented the distinctive public American park, one in which all citizens, from the upper class to the working class, could "find the feeling of relief ... from the cramped, confined, and controlling circumstances of the streets of the town; in other words, a sense of enlarged freedom" (Delbanco 2000, 56). In 1877, Montreal hired Olmstead to design Mount Royal Park, an experience he found frustrating. He urged council members to keep the park natural, to view its development as a work of art, to retain the "wildness," and to give due regard to the natural mountain environment, but he was skeptical about the council's commitment.

Early in the twentieth century, urban beautification got a boost from professionals who believed in progressive conservation. The Civic Art Guild wanted to beautify Toronto, and the City Improvement League in Montreal held its first convention in 1910 to discuss city planning, street and square design, and building regulations. In 1909, the Commission of Conservation had examined urban design to promote public health and hired Thomas Adams, an advocate of the beautification and planning goals of the garden city movement in England. America's city beautiful movement also influenced town planners in Canada, who adopted its vision of an ideal city, of "tomorrow's metropolis," as their own. Planning city parks

THE GARDEN CITY MOVEMENT AND THE CITY BEAUTIFUL MOVEMENT

The garden city movement originated in England in the 1890s and was a model for town planning. Garden cities, as planned communities, had designated areas for residences, industry, and agriculture, all surrounded by greenbelts. Following a concentric pattern composed of open spaces, public parks, and six radial boulevards, these communities were to be small, self-sufficient, and possibly built in clusters. Although only two garden cities were built – Letchworth and Welwyn, both in Hertfordshire, England – the idea affected regional planning and suburbs in England and spread to other countries, including Canada and the United States.

The city beautiful movement emerged at about the same time in the United States. Members, mostly middle-class reformers, sought to beautify urban areas by erecting grand monuments to encourage civic virtue in citizens and to ensure social order. The movement was a reaction to the rapid growth of appalling slums populated by immigrants from abroad and from the countryside. Its members were inspired by the garden city movement, and for several decades they influenced urban planning and some housing projects. The movement resulted in monumental buildings and formal gardens in some US cities, including the capital, Washington, DC. Canadian urban planners, aware of both movements, applied their ideas to the planning of Canadian cities, particularly capitals.

for public use often also coincided with the construction of early suburbs such as Rosedale in Toronto, which had curved streets, large grassy lots, and boulevards.

Ottawa, the nation's capital, and the provincial capitals developed plans for city centres surrounded by parkland. The designers who created these green spaces hoped to stimulate civic pride. Their parks included imposing monuments to reflect or inflate a city's power and status. Yet city parks, which varied in size and function, were also sites of friction. Larger parks, used by all social groups in the city, became contested terrain at the administrative level and the subject of public debate. Debates about the purpose of Stanley Park in Vancouver and about Victoria Park in London, Ontario, reflected clashing attitudes toward the natural world rooted in class and culture. Wealthier people were interested in natural spaces, whereas working-class people favoured built recreation areas for families. Despite these differences, urban environments in Canada gradually became cleaner, healthier, and more liveable.

THE RISE AND growth of urban industrial centres transformed Canada's environment. The problems that accompanied rapid urbanization and industrialism – slums, disease, filth, and pollution – gave rise to an urban reform movement that resulted in municipal services such as water and sewage systems, garbage removal, and city parks and green spaces. Despite these advances, the interests of business and industrial "progress" continued to hold sway over city councils and policy makers. As cities got larger, however, they did change people's attitudes toward nature and caused many to look to the countryside as a source of inspiration and renewal. This shift in mentality added fuel to Canada's conservation movement and its tourism industry.

Works Cited

Ames, Herbert. 1972 [1897]. *The City Below the Hill*. Toronto: University of Toronto Press.

Baldwin, Douglas. 1988. "Sewerage." In *Building Canada: A History of Public Works*, edited by Norman R. Ball, 221-44. Toronto: University of Toronto Press.

Blaise, Clark. 2001. *Time Lord*. Toronto: Vintage Canada.

Bradbury, Bettina. 1984. "Pigs, Cows, and Borders: Non-Wage Forms of Survival among Montreal Families, 1861-91." *Labour/Le Travail* 14 (Fall): 9-46.

Coheen, Peter G. 1970. *Victorian Toronto, 1850-1900: Pattern and Process of Growth*. Chicago: University of Chicago Press.

Delbanco, Andrew. 2000. "Sunday in the Park with Fred." *New York Review of Books,* 20 January, 55-57.

Gad, Gunter. 1988. "The Suburbanization of Manufacturing in Toronto, 1881-1951." In *Patterns of the Past: Reinterpreting Ontario's History,* edited by William Westfall, Roger Hall, and L.S. MacDowell, 143-77. Toronto: Dundurn Press.

Gowans, Alan. 1984. "The Evolution of Architectural Styles in Toronto." In *The Canadian City: Essays in Urban and Social History,* edited by Gilbert A. Stelter and Alan F. J. Artibise, 210-22. Ottawa: Carleton University Press.

Keeling, Arn. 2004. "'Sink or Swim': Water Pollution and Environmental Politics in Vancouver, 1889-1975." *BC Studies* 142-43: 69-104.

Kostal, R.W. 1988. "Legal Justice, Social Justice: An Incursion into the Social History of Work-Related Accident Law in Ontario, 1860-86." *Law and History Review* 6, 1: 1-24.

Lewis, Robert. 2004. "A City Transformed: Manufacturing Districts and Suburban Growth in Montreal, 1850-1929." In *Manufacturing Suburbs: Building Work and Home on the Metropolitan Fringe,* edited by Robert Lewis, 76-91. Philadelphia: Temple University Press.

Ontario. 1888, 1894. Factory Inspector's Reports. Department of Labour.

Smith, Allan. 1990. "Farms, Forests and Cities: The Image of the Land and the Rise of the Metropolis in Ontario, 1860-1914." In *Old Ontario: Essays in Honour of J.M.S. Careless,* edited by David Keane and Colin Read, 71-91. Toronto: Dundurn Press.

Steinberg, Theodore. 1986. "An Ecological Perspective on the Origins of Industrialization." *Environmental History Review* 10: 261-76.

Stelter, Gilbert A., and Alan F.J. Artibise, eds. 1984. *The Canadian City: Essays in Urban and Social History.* Ottawa: Carleton University Press.

Williams, Michael. 2006. *Deforesting the Earth: From Prehistory to Global Crisis.* Chicago: University of Chicago Press.

For Further Reading

The Growth of Cities

Careless, J.M.S. 1954. "Frontierism, Metropolitanism, and Canadian History." *Canadian Historical Review* 35, 1: 1-21.

Lundell, Liz. 1997. *The Estates of Old Toronto.* Erin: Boston Mills Press.

Stelter, Gilbert A., and Alan F.J. Artibise, eds. 1984. *The Canadian City: Essays in Urban and Social History.* Ottawa: Carleton University Press.

Tarr, Joel A. 1984. "The Evolution of the Urban Infrastructure in the Nineteenth and Twentieth Centuries." In *Perspectives on Urban Infrastructure,* edited by Royce Hanson, 4-66. Washington, DC: National Academy Press.

Voisey, Paul. 1975. "The Urbanization of the Canadian Prairies, 1871-1916." *Histoire sociale/Social History* 8, 15: 77-101.

Railways and Industrial Development

Clapp, B.W. 1994. *An Environmental History of Britain since the Industrial Revolution.* London: Longman Group.

Cruikshank, Ken, and Nancy B. Bouchier. 2004. "Blighted Areas and Obnoxious Industries: Constructing Environmental Inequality on an Industrial Waterfront, Hamilton, Ontario, 1890-1960." *Environmental History* 9, 3: 464-96.

Gad, Gunter. 1988. "The Suburbanization of Manufacturing in Toronto, 1881-1951." In *Patterns of the Past: Reinterpreting Ontario's History,* edited by William Westfall, Roger Hall, and L.S. MacDowell, 143-77. Toronto: Dundurn Press.

Thompson, E.P. 1967. "Time, Work-Discipline, and Industrial Capitalism." *Past and Present* 38, 1: 56-97.

Infrastructure and Spatial Development

Acheson, T.W. 1985. *Saint John: The Making of a Colonial Urban Community.* Toronto: University of Toronto Press.

Coheen, Peter G. 1970. *Victorian Toronto, 1850-1900: Pattern and Process of Growth.* Chicago: University of Chicago Press.

Lewis, Robert. 2004. "A City Transformed: Manufacturing Districts and Suburban Growth in Montreal, 1850-1929." In *Manufacturing Suburbs: Building Work and Home on the Metropolitan Fringe,* edited by Robert Lewis, 76-91. Philadelphia: Temple University Press.

Melosi, Martin V. 1993. "The Place of the City in Environmental History." *Environmental History Review* 17, 1: 1-23.

Urban Living and Pollution

Baldwin, Douglas. 1988. "Sewerage." In *Building Canada: A History of Public Works,* edited by Norman R. Ball, 221-44. Toronto: University of Toronto Press.

Blaise, Clark. 2001. *Time Lord.* Toronto: Vintage Canada.

Bradbury, Bettina. 1984. "Pigs, Cows, and Borders: Non-Wage Forms of Survival among Montreal Families, 1861-91." *Labour/Le Travail* 14 (Fall): 9-46.

Cronon, William. 1991. *Nature's Metropolis: Chicago and the Great West.* New York: W.W. Norton.

Kostal, R.W. 1988. "Legal Justice, Social Justice: An Incursion into the Social History of Work-Related Accident Law in Ontario, 1860-86." *Law and History Review* 6, 1: 1-24.

Melosi, Martin. 2001. *Effluent America: Cities, Industry, Energy, and the Environment.* Pittsburgh: University of Pittsburgh Press.

Spencer, Stephen. 1975. "The Good Queen of Hogs: Toronto 1850-1914." *Urban History Review* 75, 1: 42-53.

Stradling, David, and Peter Thorsheim. 1999. "The Smoke of Great Cities: British and American Efforts to Control Air Pollution, 1860-1914." *Environmental History* 4, 1: 6-31.

The Public Health Movement

Ames, Herbert. 1972 [1897]. *The City Below the Hill.* Toronto: University of Toronto Press.

Atkinson, Logan. 2002. "The Impact of Cholera on the Design and Implementation of Toronto's First Municipal By-Laws, 1834." *Urban History Review* 30, 2: 3-15.

Baldwin, Douglas. 1986. "The Campaign against Odors: Sanitarians and the Genesis of Public Health in Charlottetown, Prince Edward Island (1855-1900)." *Scientia Canadensis* 10, 1: 72-82.

Corbin, Alain. 1986. *The Foul and the Fragrant: Odor and the French Social Imagination.* Cambridge, MA: Harvard University Press.

Water and Waste Disposal Systems

Bloomfield, Elizabeth, Gerald Bloomfield, and Peter McCaskell. 1983. "Waterworks and Sewage Systems." In *Urban Growth and Local Services in the Development of Ontario Municipalities to 1981,* edited by Elizabeth and Gerald Bloomfield, 102-21. Guelph: Department of Geography, Guelph University.

Gillis, Peter. 1986. "Rivers of Sawdust: The Battle over Industrial Pollution in Canada, 1865-1903." *Journal of Canadian Studies* 21, 1: 84-102.

Hagopian, John S. 2003. "The Municipalization of the City of Kingston Water Works Company." *Ontario History* 95, 1: 66-94.

Keeling, Arn. 2004. "'Sink or Swim': Water Pollution and Environmental Politics in Vancouver, 1889-1975." *BC Studies* 142-43: 69-104.

MacNaughton, Colleen. 2000. "Promoting Clean Water in Nineteenth-Century Public Policy: Professors, Preachers, and Polliwogs in Kingston, Ontario." *Histoire sociale/Social History* 32, 63: 49-61.

Melosi, Martin. 1993. "Hazardous Waste and Environmental Liability: An Historical Perspective." In *Major Problems in American Environmental History,* edited by Carolyn Merchant, 427-34. Lexington, MA: D.C. Heath.

Murray, T. Aird. 1912. *The Prevention of Pollution of Canadian Surface Waters.* Ottawa: Lowe-Martin Company.

Rome, Adam. 1996. "Coming to Terms with Pollution: The Language of Environmental Reform, 1865-1915." *Environmental History* 1, 3: 6-28.

Tarr, Joel. 1996. *Search for the Ultimate Sink.* Akron, OH: University of Akron Press.

Urban Design and Green Spaces

Andrews, Margaret W. 1984. "The Best Advertisement a City Can Have: Public Health Services in Vancouver, 1886-1888." *Urban History Review* 12, 3: 19-27.

Armstrong, Alan H. 1968. "Thomas Adams and the Commission of Conservation." In *Planning the Canadian Environment,* edited by L.O. Gertler, 1-10. Montreal: Harvest House.

Delbanco, Andrew. 2000. "Sunday in the Park with Fred." *New York Review of Books,* 20 January, 55-57.

Kossuth, Robert S. 2005. "Spaces and Places to Play: The Formation of a Municipal Parks System in London Ontario, 1867-1914." *Ontario History* 97, 2: 160-90.

McDonald, Robert A.J. 1984. "'Holy Retreat' or 'Practical Breathing Spot'? Class Perceptions of Vancouver's Stanley Park, 1910-1913." *Canadian Historical Review* 65, 2: 127-53.

McFarland, E. 1982. "The Beginning of Municipal Parks Systems." In *Recreational Land Use: Perspectives on Its Evolution in Canada,* edited by Geoff Wall and John S. Marsh, 257-71. Ottawa: Carleton University Press.

Rosenzweig, Roy, and Elizabeth Blackmar. 1992. *The Park and the People: A History of Central Park.* Ithaca, NY: Cornell University Press.

Smith, Allan. 1990. "Farms, Forests and Cities: The Image of the Land and the Rise of the Metropolis in Ontario, 1860-1914." In *Old Ontario: Essays in Honour of J.M.S. Careless,* edited by David Keane and Colin Read, 71-94. Toronto: Dundurn Press.

4

The Conservation Movement

The laws of nature are the same everywhere. Whoever violates them any-where must always pay the penalty. No country ever so great and rich, no nation ever so powerful, inventive and enterprising can violate them with impunity. We most grievously delude ourselves if we think we can form an exception to the rule.

— CARL SCHURZ, LEGISLATOR AND REFORMER, SPEECH TO THE
AMERICAN FORESTRY ASSOCIATION, 15 OCTOBER 1889

THE MODERN ENVIRONMENTAL movement seeks to protect ecosystems and biodiversity and to create a sustainable society to slow down climate change. In contrast, the North American conservation movement, which began in the United States in the mid-nineteenth century, focused on the un-restrained exploitation of timber, fish, and wildlife resources. Its members sought regulations to limit and manage natural resource exploitation. Only a minority, the preserva-tionists, favoured the protection of resources and the environment. The conservation movement took time to catch on in Canada because the idea of Canada as an abundant wilderness persisted long after the fur trade, agriculture, forestry, and the fishing industry had begun to deplete natural resources and wildlife. In addition, the commercial exploita-tion of resources created wealth and economic growth, which Canadian policy makers equat-ed with the creation of a strong industrial

nation. Influenced in part by the American conservation movement and changing ideas about nature brought on by the growth of cities, Canadian conservationists – who were largely male middle-class scientists, foresters, farmers, urban planners, and civil servants concerned about the overuse of resources – amended this outlook. They counselled moderation and pressed for the efficient man-agement of forest resources and the establish-ment of national parks. The preservation of wildlife was less emphasized, but when it became clear that many species faced extinc-tion, conservationists – from within and without government circles – pressured gov-ernments for hunting regulations, sanctuaries, and the professional management of wildlife.

Conservationists and Preservationists

Explorers, fur traders, farmers, and loggers sought to civilize and cultivate. They believed that the vast resources of the New World were virtually inexhaustible and that no amount of use could deplete them. Even when landscapes changed beyond recognition – manicured agricultural countryside replacing lush old-growth forests – this attitude persisted. As early as the 1830s, however, preservationists such as American painter George Catlin began to suggest that "wild America" – its landscape, wildlife, and Aboriginal peoples – should be preserved in reserved areas. In 1865, George Marsh, an American diplomat, outlined the conservation idea in his book *Man and Nature; Or Physical Geography as Modified by Human Action.* In it, Marsh challenges the assumption that resources are inexhaustible, demonstrates the interdependence of man and nature, and outlines the deleterious effects of the overuse of resources on nature's ecological balance. Marsh's ideas inspired other conservationists to re-examine America's relationship to the natural world. When the Civil War ended, some feared future timber scarcity, others lamented the massive destruction of trees from wasteful practices, and still others encouraged citizens, lumber companies, and governments to place greater value on woodlands. Conservations also called for limits on forest clearing. The American Forestry Association, founded in 1875, included a small group of Canadian members who believed in conservation.

Early Canadian conservationists included individuals with close ties to the lumber industry, people who understood that resources had limits and that excessive waste harmed both business and the environment. James and William Little were lumbermen, and Henri-Gustave Joly, the seigneur of

FIGURE 4.1 Henri-Gustave Joly was the fourth premier of Quebec and active in federal politics. As a founder of the Canadian Forestry Association, he expressed concern about the future use of Canada's forests and favoured the "wise use" of its renewable resources. In 1900, Prime Minister Laurier appointed Joly lieutenant-governor of British Columbia.
Library and Archives Canada, Topley Studio fonds, PA-026311

Lotbinière, was prominent in both business and politics (see Figure 4.1). He published pamphlets on forest conservation in the 1870s. Concerned about a sharp reduction in the number of trees, Joly became Canada's leading forest conservationist and an advocate of European forest management techniques. In 1875, he published *The State of the Forests,* a survey for the Canadian government. The report warned that Canada's spruce and pine forests faced depletion and laid out a conservation program based on a number of premises: timberlands should be classified, there should be limits on leases and cuts, the size of logs that could be cut should be regulated, and action should be taken to prevent forest fires.

In addition to the Littles and Joly, early Canadian conservationists included the farmers who formed the Ontario Fruit Growers' Association in 1882. Their mandate was to improve the rural environment, "which had suffered greatly by deforestation through the settlement process" (Gillis and Roach 1995, 132). The association joined with some influential lumbermen interested in setting aside forest reserves to organize an 1882 session of the American Forestry Congress. When the members, including those of the American Forestry Association, convened in Montreal to discuss reforestation, three delegates from the Ontario Fruit Growers' Association told the meeting that southern Ontario "had been stripped by generations of settlement and lumbering so that fifty townships had been left with only

five percent of their forest cover" (Mackay 1985, 33). The congress adopted a number of resolutions – including regulations to prevent forest fires and officers to enforce them, regulations to limit settlers from burning brush, and the reservation of lands unfit for settlement for lumbering. Several governments in Canada later transformed these resolutions into law.

Support for the conservation of resources grew fitfully in Canada and the United States throughout the 1880s and 1890s, but the movement gained prominent adherents such as President Theodore Roosevelt, and the closing of the American "frontier" added fuel to the fire. In 1890, the director of the US Census announced that the end of free land for settlement in the United States. The announcement enhanced awareness of the finite nature of land and resources in North America. In addition, members of the progressive movement, an urban movement that sought managerial solutions to socioeconomic problems from the 1890s to the 1920s, argued that the conservation of renewable natural resources could be achieved only

TEDDY ROOSEVELT: ARDENT CONSERVATIONIST

Theodore Roosevelt – big game hunter, naturalist, military imperialist, and president of the United States (1901-9) – was an ardent conservationist. In 1888, he founded the Boone and Crockett Club, dedicated to saving big game animals. During his presidency, the Newlands Act (1902) allowed the federal government to fund irrigation projects and to establish farms for relief of urban congestion. With the support and encouragement of Gifford Pinchot, chief forester, Roosevelt also worked to preserve more than 170 million acres of land (69 million hectares) as national parks and monuments. Near the end of his presidency, he hosted the first national conference on conservation, which several Canadians attended as observers. Although the conference had few practical results, it helped make the conservation movement respectable and politically credible.

through government regulation. Americans increasingly demanded reliable sources of water in the arid western states, and visible evidence of deteriorating rangelands and forests throughout the United States led to a nationwide movement to "preserve watersheds, build dams, replant trees, and reseed grasslands" (Merchant 1993, 338).

The conservation movement eroded the driving sense of individualism that had dominated resource development and resulted in waste and exploitation. The conservationist movement's emphasis on management also reflected the progressives' faith in science, technology, and the bureaucratic method of administration. The emergence of new professional groups such as foresters, landscape architects, and town planners also coincided with the movement, which comprised disparate activities ranging from the building of dams and irrigation systems and the creation of national parks to campaigns to save endangered bird species and programs to replant trees.

The conservation movement broke into two branches that represented different approaches to the environment: utilitarian conservation, associated with Gifford Pinchot, and wilderness preservation, promoted by John Muir (whose ideas environmentalists would revisit in the 1970s). Pinchot, a professional forester, replaced Bernhard Fernow as chief of the US Forestry Division (later the US Forest Service) in 1898. Pinchot used his new position and friendship with President Roosevelt to promote conservation, which he defined narrowly as development in the public interest, "the greatest good for the greatest number," and opposition to wasteful exploitation. His utilitarian, managerial

BERNHARD FERNOW: FIRST DEAN OF FORESTRY

Bernhard Fernow, the third chief of the US Forestry Division (1886-98), laid the groundwork for the establishment of the US Forest Service. He sought to create a national forest system based on scientific management techniques. He left the position to become the first dean of the New York College of Forestry at Cornell University. In 1907, he became the founding dean of the University of Toronto's Faculty of Forestry. Born in Prussia, Fernow educated both American and Canadian foresters about German forestry and conservation methods.

FIGURE 4.2
Bernhard Fernow
With permission of the University of Toronto Archives

approach became the main ideological thrust in the American conservation movement, and Pinchot had a profound influence on conservationists concerned about forests in Canada.

The concept of preservation advocated by John Muir remained a minority viewpoint in the early conservation movement. A naturalist, explorer, mountaineer, and mystic, Muir too became an advisor to President Roosevelt. Described as a "wild-bearded, baggy-trousered individualist," Muir believed intuitively that harmony existed in the natural world, that the creator arranged and loved everything equally (Arden 1973, 433). His insight was that the earth did not spin at the whim of human beings: creation was not the result of a manlike Christian God but rather the impartial force of nature. Muir did not distinguish between the animate and inanimate, between higher and lower creatures – he valued everything equally. An instinctive pacifist, Muir escaped to Canada during the American Civil War, later popularized Yosemite in California, and enthralled North Americans with his articles on nature and pleas for forest protection.

Muir helped to make the wilderness part of America's identity. He invested nature with moral power and considered it the basis of a society and culture distinct from "old world" Europe. Muir and fellow preservationists wanted to protect natural landscapes and believed in their power for spiritual rejuvenation. Muir helped found Yosemite National Park and the Sierra Club, became the saviour of the sequoia, and served as a leader in the American national park movement. He is a spiritual ancestor of modern environmentalists.

In Canada, some conservationists, such as C. Gordon Hewitt, Dominion entomologist, linked scientific research and the conservation of natural resources to the broader goal of protecting nature, which Hewitt saw as an ethical as well as practical issue. He told the Ottawa Field-Naturalists' Club in 1911, "Nature is not ours to squander, to amass wealth at her expense and enjoy a transient prosperity; it is ours to protect, and the protection of Nature is nothing more or less than the ensuring of national happiness" (Hewitt 1911, 209-10). Hewitt's expertise and reputation in scientific and political circles, both in Ottawa and in Washington, had a

CONSERVATIONISTS: MIDDLE-CLASS ELITISTS?

Some historians in Canada and the United States, influenced by social history, criticize the conservationists for their elitism. The conservationists, they argue, like members of the broader reform movement (1880s-1920s), were predominantly middle-class and narrowly reformist. Utilitarian conservationists focused on institutional reform and were elitist in that they promoted their own professional interests and those of their colleagues in business and government. They were not ecologists sensitive to nature's complexity. They believed in stamping out forest fires, which destroyed property, but they did not understand the role fires sometimes played in preserving healthy forests. Most did not seek to preserve the wilderness: they believed proper harvesting and replanting would lead to manageable second-growth forests. They did not value old-growth forests because they did not understand the interdependent relationship among old trees, other plants, insects, and wildlife in ecosystems.

The conservation movement was reformist in that it favoured regulation and expertise to protect natural resources in the public interest and opposed their unlimited exploitation by private interests. Its members' moderate approach did, nevertheless, support industry and the larger goal of economic prosperity. By the standards of the day, conservationists were innovative. Their ideas and approaches differed from the exploitive practices of early industry and government and constituted a clear break from the past.

vital effect on policy, particularly concerning wildlife protection. He and other officials not only influenced policy makers but also public sentiment, to which politicians stayed attuned.

Both conservationists and preservationists worked to dispel the assumption that North America contained a superabundance of resources. Because conservationists outnumbered preservationists, however, a practical approach to the environment, one geared toward the efficient management of natural resources and toward development moderated by regulatory control, became the norm in both the United States and Canada and among the general public and policy makers. The different national identities of the two countries, however, led to slightly different emphases in forest conservation, parks policies, and wildlife preservation. Wilderness protection in Canada was less prominent than in the United States, probably because the idea of Canada as a huge northern nation with plenty of space and a large hinterland persisted. Canadians also largely remained unaware of the extent of resource extraction taking place in their own backyard "wilderness."

Forest Conservation

Following the 1882 session of the American Forestry Congress in Montreal, Canadian conservationists pressured the federal and provincial governments to adopt its resolutions on forest conservation. At the time, Conservative prime minister John A. Macdonald's national policy for economic development – building a transcontinental railway, settling the West, and protecting

---

FOREST RESERVES AND CONSERVATION

Forest reserves were pieces of land leased to lumber companies for finite periods of time. Early conservationists feared a future shortage of trees. They argued that a forest, once cut, was nonrenewable, capable of sustaining nothing more than weeds. The lumber industry's excessive waste and pollution also alarmed conservationists. Over time and with education, conservationists began to understand that forests were limited but renewable resources. If properly managed by trained foresters who applied scientific methods, they could be harvested indefinitely. Once forests were seen as renewable, forest reserves became one approach to conservation, an approach that suited governments and lumber interests alike. Governments could classify land as a forest reserve to exclude settlers and ensure future timber stands and a steady source of government revenue. Managed reserves increased the need to protect forests from fire and contributed to the professionalization of forestry.

Canadian industry with high tariffs – defined the priorities of both politicians and businessmen. The following year, however, the provincial government in Quebec hired the first forest rangers and established the first forest reserve, an area of wooded land preserved from settlement and managed for forestry or conservation. The government cancelled the reserve, however, in response to protests from the colonization movement, an organized movement that sought to prevent Quebecers from immigrating to the United States by opening up new lands for settlement in Quebec. Ontario responded to the congress's recommendations by hiring a forestry publicist for its Department of Agriculture in 1883. The publicist wrote pamphlets on woodlot management and the reforestation of abandoned farms, but he had no influence on the office that administered timber limits and collected timber dues.

The federal government put its own spin on the congress's resolutions. Interested in attracting settlers to the West, where it controlled land and natural resources, it researched tree planting and set aside some forests on the Prairies. It did not limit settlers from burning brush or disrupting the federal system of leasing timber berths in British Columbia, but in 1884 it did amend the Dominion Lands Act to provide for the preservation of trees on Rocky Mountain slopes. This was the government's first step in creating a forest reserve system, which would help conserve watersheds to make the settlement of dry areas possible. Conservation as a political issue led to surveys of forest reserves and the creation in 1894 of Moose Mountain Reserve in the Northwest.

Change was slow, however, because the lumber industry fell into recession in the 1880s and 1890s, and enthusiasm for conservation waned with it. In 1885, Alexander Kirkwood, a conservationist with the Ontario Department of Crown Lands, proposed the creation of a park to protect the headwaters of the Muskoka, Petawawa, Bonnechere, and Madawaska Rivers on the fringes of the Canadian Shield. Nearly a decade passed, however, before conservationists could exert enough pressure to convince the Ontario government to act on the proposal. Established in 1893, Algonquin Park comprised eighteen townships (3,797 square kilometres) set aside for "a public park and forest reservation, fish and game preserve, health resort and pleasure ground for the benefit, advantage and enjoyment of the people of the province" (Reynolds 1968, 74). From the beginning, the park held special meaning for Ontarians, partly because its location close to southern Ontario made it accessible to tourists. Its park rangers protected wildlife,

prevented poaching, and preserved timber. Hunting, fishing, and logging occurred only with government permission. Conservationists, supported by some lumbermen, persuaded Ontario to establish a forest reserve in the new park.

With the passage of the Forest Reserves Act in 1898, Ontario set aside other large forest reserves, including Temagami and Quetico. Reformers hoped this legislation would inaugurate scientific forestry management to ensure a perpetual source of timber through proper harvesting. The government of Quebec developed more extensive forest reserves than Ontario. It located some of them in two parks established in 1894, Laurentides and Mont Tremblant. But the province eventually eliminated large reserves in favour of smaller areas that suited local patterns of resource exploitation. In both provinces, the forest reserve policy failed to conserve public woodlands adequately on a sustained-yield basis because of lack of political will. Governments allocated insufficient resources to administer the reserves and bowed to competing pressures, such as mining in northern Ontario and the colonization movement and the pulp-and-paper industry in Quebec.

Pressure from conservationists did, however, lead to the first forest management programs and the professionalization of forestry. In 1899, Wilfrid Laurier's Liberal government hired Elihu Stewart to serve as chief inspector of the Timber and Grazing Branch of the Department of the Interior. Under his leadership, the government amended its leasing regulations to establish a minimum diameter limit (25 centimetres) on cut timber and required lumber operators to pay half the cost of fire prevention and suppression on their berths. Stewart created a judicious system of forestry in Canada by encouraging tree planting in Manitoba and the North-West Territories, by establishing forest reserves, and by helping to found the Canadian Forestry Association in 1900. The organization began to hold conferences in 1906.

Stewart developed an independent Forestry Branch within the Department of the Interior. With the support of lumbermen, he used the US Bureau of Forestry's programs as models to expand the scope of his department. Guided by the advice of Gifford Pinchot, Stewart tried to consolidate the management of reserves and extend them to all forested land in the West. By 1906, federal reserves comprised 1,173,588 hectares, including the eastern slopes of the Rocky Mountains, prairie parklands, and the northern tree belt. Unfortunately, Stewart underestimated the regional impulse in Canada. Clifford Sifton, an advocate of centralized planning and development of the Northwest, had resigned as minister of the interior in 1905. His replacement, Frank Oliver, did not want the East dictating to the West.

The conservationists who formed the Canadian Forestry Association, however, had an expansive vision for forestry management. The association's first convention in 1906 united the older leadership of the American Forestry Congress with a newer group of provincial and federal officials and politicians who wanted to advance the conservation cause in Canada by direct government intervention. Pinchot was the keynote speaker. The delegates focused on forestry problems, supported forest reserves, and discussed the relationships between forestry and agriculture, and between forest conservation and the maintenance of water resources. They advocated regulated exploitation of natural resources and new forest management practices that required their expertise. One leader, F.J. Thorpe, spoke of "the desirability of holding the forests under Crown ownership, of taking measures to protect the forests from fire and insects, of greater forestry education at the professional level, of the adoption of professionally acceptable forestry practices by timber operators, of an extensive program of tree planting, on both private and public lands, including the afforestation of denuded areas around the sources of river systems" (Mackay 1985, 26).

Although the federal government supported a national forestry policy, it responded with the Dominion Forestry Reserve Act in 1906, which Oliver interpreted as exempting timber berth leaseholders from control by the Forestry Branch. The act placed control of federal forest reserves under the purview of the superintendent of forestry but did not expand their size greatly. Stewart resigned in 1907. His successor, Robert Henry Campbell, carried on his commitment to a progressive forest policy. Provincial governments, in response to the conference's recommendations, also expanded their forest reserves and created forest services, and the Universities of Toronto and New Brunswick established schools of forestry.

Laurier's Liberals had wanted Canadians to associate their party with conservation, but the party's rhetoric proved stronger than its actions. The federal government created the Forestry Branch, which strengthened its authority over fire regulations and regulated access to and logging on reserves. It also expanded forest reserves and created the Commission of Conservation in 1909 to provide governments with scientific information and advice on the conservation of human and natural resources. In its twelve-year history, the commission produced hundreds of books, articles, and studies. Governments, however, were slow to accept the commission's advice, and they continued to permit politically influential groups to engage in poor logging practices on valuable forestlands.

The Commission of Conservation

The Commission of Conservation came into being in 1909, when President Theodore Roosevelt invited Canada and Mexico to send representatives to the North American Conservation Conference to discuss international conservation issues. The group concluded the conference with a declaration of principles. By regulating private resource development and opposing private monopolies in any resource field, governments, they argued, could protect the public interest by conserving forests, waterways, lands, and minerals. The declaration advocated protecting public health by passing legislation to control pollution, protect headwaters, and ensure public control of inland waterways essential for navigation, irrigation, and power. The conference attendees also supported public education and agricultural research. In mining, they sought the prevention of waste, the separation of surface ground rights and subsurface mineral rights to permit public control over mineral exploitation, and enforcement of mine safety regulations. They actively favoured wildlife protection and the establishment of game preserves.

The conference attendees agreed to co-ordinate natural resource policies among the three countries, but each country would first have to establish a permanent conservation commission to facilitate cooperation and exchange information. Although the agreement came to nothing, Canada, unlike the other two countries, did establish the non-partisan Commission of Conservation, which completed over two hundred studies by 1919. Composed of an executive committee (with prominent representatives of the federal and provincial governments), it involved universities for scientific and technical expertise and had seven working committees (forestry, lands, fisheries, game and wildlife, water and waterpower, minerals, and public health). Sir Clifford Sifton, who had been the powerful minister of the interior in Laurier's government between 1896 and 1905 and who favoured the administration of forest resources along lines implemented by Pinchot in the United States, chaired the commission (see Figure 4.3). Sifton was an able, experienced, and energetic administrator, knowledgable about resources and an advocate of conservation. The commission

ONTARIO'S FOREST FIRES PREVENTION ACT

Before the conservation movement, few laws safeguarded forests, and those that did exist, such as Nova Scotia's 1761 fire-prevention law, were ineffectual. Lumbermen, however, viewed forest fires as a waste and a threat to timber stocks. The conservation movement in Canada took up the cause to protect forests from fires. After the Matheson fire in 1916 killed 224 people and burned 340,000 hectares, Ontario passed the 1917 Forest Fires Prevention Act, which had a forester administer the legislation, practice reforestation, and research tree diseases.

had a mandate to consider all questions "relating to the conservation and better utilization of natural resources of Canada," to make inventories, do research, disseminate information, and frame recommendations "conducive to the accomplishment of that end" (Hall 1985, 240).

Sifton believed that conservation would protect land and resources for future prosperity and that Canada could learn from the United States and avoid its wasteful, unregulated, unscientific exploitation, which served the interests of large private monopolies rather than those of the public. The public interest, Sifton believed, would be best served through the development of hydroelectricity – a valuable, cheap, and clean source of power – and regulations against agricultural methods and mining practices that led to water pollution. He opposed deforestation without conservation and the export of unprocessed pulpwood, and he favoured limited timber leases.

In addition to promoting the idea of national parks and wildlife preservation, the commission made a number of prescient conclusions and recommendations:

- It linked problems in cities such as disease to the lack of town planning and poor housing.
- It opposed the overcutting of forests.
- It recommended the use of organic rather than chemical fertilizers in agriculture.
- It supported small hydroelectric dams rather than large ones, which flooded and destroyed large areas of land.
- It recommended filters on smokestacks and introduced affordable technology to improve air quality.

FIGURE 4.3 **Sir Clifford Sifton. As minister of the interior in Laurier's Liberal government, Sifton oversaw the large wave** of immigration to the Canadian West. As chair of the Commission of Conservation, he influenced public policy on conservation and the exploitation of natural resources.
Library and Archives Canada, Topley Studio fonds, PA-027942

- It favoured the large-scale composting of organic waste, and its pilot project recycled used newspapers, wood products, glass, iron, and manufactured goods.

Some of these recommendations resulted in further study – for example, the National Conference on City Planning in 1914 – and some planning legislation. But the war interrupted action in other areas. As the commission began to exert some influence, politicians and civil servants also challenged it. Sifton insisted on independence, but ministers complained of lack of control. No minister was responsible for the commission, they argued, and it duplicated the work of government departments. They claimed that the commission's costs were too high and that it had no legislative capacity. Sifton resigned in frustration in 1918, following a dispute over staff salaries. The commission was dissolved in 1921, in the midst of a recession. It later served as a model for the National Research Council.

National Parks

Conservationists supported the establishment of parks, beginning with Banff National Park in 1885. Their advocacy challenged older assumptions about the superabundance of resources in Canada and led to the doctrine of usefulness, the federal government's practical approach to the management of natural resources. "Development moderated by regulatory control" became their mantra, and they extended it to parks administration. In the 1890s, the public also began to respond negatively to unregulated development. A consensus started to form among urbanites seeking relief from industrialization, experts involved in the Commission of Conservation, scientists and naturalists, some business leaders, and government officials. They all agreed that Canada needed national parks. Three aims motivated the government's establishment of parks: economic development, a desire to create areas for recreation and leisure, and lastly, wilderness and wild-

life protection. The Canadian government viewed parks as useful places with exploitable resources that it could regulate in partnership with private enterprise. Policy makers viewed parks as a potential source of revenue from tourism, mining and logging, and hunting and fishing licences.

Motivated by potential profits, the Canadian government established Canada's first national park at Banff in 1885 at the urging of the Canadian Pacific Railway (CPR). The CPR wanted to increase the number of passengers on its trains; the government wanted to enhance tourism and promote Banff's newly discovered hot springs. The park became a showpiece for Canada, of the nation's bountiful wilderness, even though it excluded Aboriginal people and was a planned community for the wealthy, similar to a European spa, with roads, bridges, and tourist facilities (see Figure 4.4). The CPR got into the hotel business by launching the magnificent Banff Springs Hotel. It hired photographers to portray the grandeur of the mountains and actively encouraged travellers with scenic postcards (see Figure 4.5). Policy makers did not prohibit animal grazing, lumbering, or mining because they believed these activities enhanced the park's usefulness in the nation's interest. At the earliest national parks – Glacier National and Yoho (1886, British Columbia) and Waterton Lakes and Jasper (1895 and 1907, Alberta) – tourists interested in mountain climbing, wildlife, and outdoor pursuits could be found alongside hunters, loggers, and miners.

Attitudes toward parks changed gradually. As urbanization created a new appreciation for nature and its powers of rejuvenation, the

FIGURE 4.4 View of Banff from Tunnel Mountain, 1929. Over time, Canadians embraced national parks as their own, as an integral part of their national identity. They travelled to early parks by train, and the invention and spread of the automobile allowed Canadians of all classes to enjoy their vistas and facilities.

William J. Oliver, photographer, Library and Archives Canada, PA-057241

FIGURE 4.5 With the mountains and the Banff Springs Hotel in the background, this tourist enjoys a game on the hotel's famous golf course. The poster markets a luxurious recreational experience in Canada's first national park.

Canadian Pacific Archives, BR92

federal government's focus shifted to recreation. Inspiration and pressure for more parks came not only from developments in the United States and the Commission of Conservation but also from the Canadian National Parks Association, an outgrowth of the Alpine Club of Canada, a mountaineering association formed in 1906. The association considered national parks an inviolable public domain. In response, the federal government prepared to regulate commercial activity, protect some wildlife and landscapes, and keep small businesses out of recreational areas. It established the Dominion Parks Branch in 1911. Under James B. Harkin, the Dominion parks commissioner from 1911 to 1936, the Parks Branch focused on recreation, fire control, restoring damaged landscapes, and wildlife management, particularly the protection of nonpredators. The branch hired game wardens and foresters and favoured multiple-use parks with controlled tree cutting and moderate harvesting of resources. The Commission of Conservation recommended that the government establish forest reserves in parks to protect forests from fires and to improve watershed management and reduce floods and soil erosion, especially in the West. The Dominion Forest Reserves and Parks Act (1911) increased federal reserves from twenty-one to thirty-six areas and to 6,717,782 hectares. The legislation was not a wholly positive development, however. The act also increased timber leaseholders' security of tenure and equated forest reserves with parks so that the act allowed lumbermen to exploit timber resources in parks without fulfilling the conservationists' goals of implementing modern resource management and land classification policies.

As the public embraced the idea, the federal government established new national parks, including Elk Island (1913, Alberta), St. Lawrence Islands (1914, Ontario), and Mt. Revelstoke and Kootenay (1914 and 1920, British Columbia). Although the idea of parks as preserves and recreational areas strengthened over time, motivations for their establishment remained mixed, even in the late 1920s. Prince Albert National Park, created in 1927 as Saskatchewan's first national park, largely served political ends. It included three large lakes and a forest reserve. The province, supported by a public that wanted to enhance tourism, had persistently pressured the federal government for a national park. Harkin reluctantly agreed, but only because the idea had the prime minister's support. At the opening ceremonies, Prime Minister Mackenzie King spoke of the importance of national parks in building national character and contributing to Canadian life. But the park was also a political reward: the riding in which it was located had provided King with a safe seat in 1926, when he so desperately needed it.

Between 1885 and 1927, motivations for parks and their administration became increasingly complex. Early parks offered visitors space and scenery for hiking and canoeing, and over time the Parks Branch developed camping grounds and more varied educational programs and park facilities, including golf courses, swimming facilities and lessons, and guided nature walks. Stressed urban dwellers were drawn to the parks by the early back-to-the-land movement, particularly after naturalist Ernest Thompson Seton founded his Woodcraft Indians camps to educate urban children about nature. The

ARCHIBALD BELANEY, GREY OWL

Although he claimed his father was Scots American and his mother Apache, Grey Owl was really an Englishman, born in 1888 in Hastings. As a child, Archie Belaney enjoyed reading about North American Indians and, as an adult, travelled to Canada, where he worked in the North as a canoeist, packer, fire ranger, and guide. He fought during the Great War but then returned to Canada, where he began to take on the persona of Grey Owl. He dyed his hair and adopted Aboriginal dress.

Belaney became famous as a naturalist and writer. His books included *The Men of the Last Frontier* (1931), *Pilgrims of the Wild* (1934), and *Sajo and Her Beaver People* (1935). At first, Belaney told publishers and audiences that he had lived among Aboriginal people; he then claimed that he had been adopted by them. By 1931, Belaney *was* an Indian. As a conservationist, Grey Owl cut a striking figure and went on speaking tours to England and the United States, where he educated people about shrinking forests and the need to conserve resources and wildlife. He worked to eliminate cruel trapping practices and opposed trophy hunting by wealthy sportsmen. He at first campaigned to save the beaver, but after 1928 broadened his campaign to include all animals, particularly buffalo, muskox, and caribou. In 1931, James Harkin of the National Parks Service hired Grey Owl as a conservationist. He lived in cabins in Riding Mountain and Prince Albert National Parks.

Grey Owl's real identity was not disclosed to the public until after his death in 1938, even though dozens of people knew the truth. At the time of his death, he was one of the most famous Canadians of his day. When a new generation of Canadians rediscovered his books in the 1960s and 1970s, he became an important link between the early conservation movement and the modern environmental movement. His message – that Canadians belonged to nature, not nature to Canadians – was timeless.

FIGURE 4.6 Grey Owl holding a young beaver, probably one that lived in a beaver house attached to his dwelling in the park.
Archives of Ontario, AO514232

movement's scouting lore was absorbed and amended by the more popular Boy Scouts, who used the parks for camps. The publication of better field guides for birding also led more people to national parks in the 1920s and 1930s, as did the cottage boom, which began in the 1880s, and the proliferation of automobiles in the 1920s.

As citizens' experience and appreciation of nature and the landscape deepened, they became entwined with Canadian nationalism, which was being expressed by artists such as the Group of Seven, who depicted the landscape and national parks in exciting new ways. In the difficult years of the Depression, Grey Owl, a naturalist who lived and worked at Prince Albert National Park, likewise captured the national imagination through his public appearances and writings. He celebrated the forests and educated the public about wildlife protection.

Wildlife Conservation

Conservationists worked to prevent the further destruction of wildlife in Canada and to undermine the myth of superabundance. With plentiful flora and fauna and a huge

THE DESTRUCTION OF WILDLIFE

Numerous species were hunted to extinction or near extinction before governments passed protective legislation. For instance, the elk *(wapiti)* was nearly extirpated in Ontario by 1850, as was the wild turkey by the end of the century. On Cape Breton Island, settlers hunted moose for their hides until 1856, when they were nearly extirpated. At that time, the colonial government in Nova Scotia introduced a closed season during which moose hunting was punishable by fines.

Animals defined as predators fell outside of protective legislation, and ranchers, farmers, and game managers singled them out for annihilation. Ranchers in Alberta used guns, poison, and traps to destroy wolves and coyotes that preyed on livestock, and farmers everywhere shot "pests" such as hawks, eagles, and magpies. The latter had nearly disappeared by 1911. Provincial governments frequently offered bounties for kills, and the death counts were huge: nearly 100,000 coyotes were killed in 1926-27 alone. In Saskatchewan, which held its notorious "Gopher Day" on the first day of May of each year, schoolchildren killed 2 million gophers in 1920 and earned one cent per carcass.

FIGURE 4.7 Deer carcasses at Grand Trunk Rail Station, Haliburton, Ontario, 1897. Hunting season, then as now, was part of rural culture in Canada. Canadians viewed hunting as an individual right, as a leisure activity, as a source of food, and, before there were regulations, as a commercial business. Wealthy sports hunters engaged in such recreations to project an image of rugged masculinity, to fit the ideal of the great northern hunter.
Archives of Ontario, AO991217

frontier, Canadians had unquestioningly embraced the idea that no amount of harvesting could deplete the nation's wildlife. This myth of superabundance led to waste and the extinction of some species. In addition to the early commercial slaughter of species such as beaver and buffalo, the process of settlement and hunting game for food or sport rapidly depleted species throughout the nineteenth and early twentieth centuries. For instance, although billions of passenger pigeons inhabited North America in the 1870s, they were reduced to only dozens by the 1890s. Settlers shot them for food, hunters bagged them for sport, market-hunters sold them as game, and farmers killed them for destroying crops. The last captive bird died in the Cincinnati Zoo in 1914. Disease and loss of habitat also contributed to their extinction and the depletion of other species. Fuelled by anthropocentricism, the view that humans are the most significant element in the universe and that other species are ours do with as we please, farmers also destroyed habitats and killed noxious predators such as bears, wild cats, and wolves to protect their livestock.

Unlike the United States, Canada had no Sierra Club or National Audubon Society to influence public opinion and push for the preservation of wildlife. Although the number of field naturalist clubs increased in the early 1900s, all but a few focused on local natural history rather than preservation. In the Canadian conservation movement itself, the preservation of wildlife took second place to the protection of forests. The Canadian government was more concerned with developing the West and industrializing the nation than preserving wildlife. The loss of wildlife and changing sensibilities toward animals, however, caused some conservationists to take up the cause of wildlife preservation. Between 1885 and the 1920s, the impetus for change came from a small group of sportsmen, naturalists, and civil servants who managed to turn the goal of wildlife preservation into government policy.

Sportsmen in fish and game clubs – of which the Game and Inland Fishery Protection Society of Halifax was the oldest – were among the earliest proponents of wildlife conservation. Their hunting ethic had developed to ensure game for gentlemen hunters who did not believe that hunting and fishing were wanton but rather that the government should put an end to "ungentlemanly slaughter." They lobbied governments and worked closely with game wardens to sustain, if not increase, species they wished to hunt. They argued that game conservation would help promote tourism, and they developed various programs, including feeding wild birds, introducing new species, killing off species considered vermin, such as crows, and re-stocking depleted areas. Sportsmen pushed for what they considered a fair and ethical code of hunting, one backed up by legislation to ban hunting during certain seasons so

species could reproduce and a ban on the sale of wild meat to restaurants and work camps. Even individuals who hunted fish and game for their families' consumption would require a licence.

Naturalists were collectors who, before the invention of binoculars and cameras, hunted to identify, study, record, and document species. They had inconsistent ideas about hunting and wildlife. Most opposed the killing of birds for women's hats and thought "useful" birds such as those that ate insects that preyed on agricultural crops should be protected. But most felt crows that ate corn should be shot. Only a minority believed in preservation, and none were ecologists. William Wood, a retired historian who pressed for a bird sanctuary in Labrador, stood apart from the crowd when he declared in 1911, "every animal is essentially the same as myself in kind, whatever the vast distinctions" (Wood 1911, n.p.).

Naturalists conveyed their concerns to governments and supported parks and forest reserves to protect wildlife habitats. Henry Hind noted the loss of salmon in virtually all streams and connected it to the construction of milldams. Bernard Gilpin decried the slaughter of walruses in the Bay of Chaleur. William Wood reviled commercial egg collectors in Newfoundland and the Gulf Islands. And Percy Taverner, ornithologist at the National Museum from 1911, pressed for the creation of bird sanctuaries. Despite their scientific approach to conservation, naturalists such as Taverner frequently distinguished between good and bad species in terms of their value to human activities, a view that many wildlife managers held for decades.

Because the national and provincial governments shared responsibility for wildlife management, regulations occurred simultaneously at both levels. Developments in what would become Ontario followed a pattern repeated in other regions throughout the nation. Until the nineteenth century, governments took measures to protect wildlife only in response to overhunting or to protect specific species. For instance, the military governor of Upper Canada declared a closed season on ruffed grouse in 1762. To protect deer and livestock, the government placed a bounty on wolves in 1793 and offered rewards for pelts. In 1821, it introduced a closed season on hunting deer. It extended this legislation to several other game species in 1839, to all fur-bearing animals in 1856, and to all "beneficial" insectivorous (insect-eating) animals and small birds in 1864. In the 1880s, the Royal Commission on Fish and Game reported on the "sickening tale of merciless, ruthless and remorseless slaughter" and warned that game could become extinct. Its 1892 report concluded, "The clearing of the land, the cutting down of the forests, the introduction of railways, the ravages of wolves, and the indiscriminate hunting of the human assassin, and the use of dynamite and nets have all contributed to the general decrease of game and fish of this land. This is indeed a deplorable state of affairs" (Foster 1978, 10).

Ontario responded by strengthening its Game and Fish Act, setting up a new Game and Fisheries Board, and hiring 392 full-time game wardens. In 1894, one year after it established Algonquin Park, it created Rondeau Park, which had designated wildlife preserves. Despite local resistance to game wardens and hunting regulations, behaviour gradually changed. Before 1900, for instance, trappers used decoys to catch large numbers of live birds in nets during migration season. They then sold the birds to gun clubs, which released them from traps so hunters could shoot them. As the province recognized the passing of its wilderness frontier, and as public pressure mounted, it enacted legislation to put an end to these types of practices, as

POACHING

Because governments shaped early wildlife protection legislation to meet the needs of elite sportsmen rather than ordinary people, the legislation often led to resentment and resistance in the form of poaching. Some poachers ignored the law and hunted as a matter of individual rights. Magistrate Charles Fothergill complained to R.B. Sullivan, the mayor of Toronto in 1835, about "a most incorrigible poacher of this neighbourhood, John Sparks, who bids utter defiance both to the laws and the Magistrates" (Fothergill, 21 September 1835). Early in the history of Algonquin Park, staffers repeatedly caught poachers and confiscated their gear, even though the public could obtain licences to fish in the park and could hunt in similar terrain outside of it. In the case of some Aboriginal groups, so-called poaching was in effect an assertion of Aboriginal hunting and fishing rights. For instance, Aboriginal people displaced from their homeland by the creation of Algonquin Park were supposed to be exempt from provincial game laws if they were hunting for food. The exemption, however, did not extend to the park.

Poaching persisted until wildlife managers and park officials gained the trust of local people and educated them about the need for hunting regulations. Relationships of trust took years to develop. In Newfoundland, wildlife officers were still trying to enforce regulations in the 1940s to save the Atlantic puffin.

did other provinces and regions throughout Canada.

As the idea of wildlife conservation took hold, the federal government responded with legislation, studies, and initiatives. Civil servants, game wardens, and wildlife managers, in turn, took up the cause from within. Before the creation of timber reserves and national parks, the federal government had passed a fishery act in 1868 that included an environmental management plan, a hatchery program, and anti-pollution measures to rehabilitate degraded rivers and protect Atlantic salmon. The legislation, however, favoured wealthy, influential American and Canadian sportsmen whose organizations participated in framing the regulations. The act prevented salmon harvesting by local settlers and farmers, which disrupted their cultural patterns of many years. In 1887, the federal government established North America's first waterfowl refuge at Long Lake (now Last Mountain Lake, Saskatchewan). The Northwest Game Act, passed in 1906, established wildlife administration in areas under federal jurisdiction, and the creation of the Commission of Conservation in 1909 set the stage for systematic research on wildlife.

The commission held a conference in 1915 and released a report titled *Conservation of Fish, Birds, and Game* the following year. The commission favoured protecting wildlife, "the common heritage of all people," and opposed the sale of game. It concluded, "The time has passed when wild game was a legitimate part of our food supply, excepting in a very few very remote sections" (Vreeland 1916, 93). In one sense a step forward, the recommendations also reflected pressure from sportsmen who resented competition for game from rural dwellers who hunted for food or extra income. The report therefore supported conservation through the regulation of hunting as envisaged by sportsmen.

That same year, the federal government created the Advisory Board on Wildlife Protection. James Harkin was a member, as was C.G. Hewitt, the Dominion biologist. The advisory board signed the Migratory Bird Convention with the United States, which led, in 1917, to the first federal legislation to establish a national framework to protect wildlife, the Migratory Birds Convention Act. One year later, on the recommendation of the Commission of Conservation, the federal government established a new national park – Point Pelee, in southeastern Ontario – to protect migratory birds. Three years previously, Percy Taverner had advised the commission that the buildup of mining residue on the bottom of Lake Erie was endangering the area. Jack Miner, a naturalist, organized Leamington's business community and Essex County's wildlife conservation association to put pressure on the government. The government established Point Pelee National Park to preserve the flyway at the southernmost tip of Canada, where migrating birds stop each spring to rest (see Figure 4.8).

That same year, the revised Northwest Game Act (1918) placed wildlife administration in Northwest Territories under the Parks Branch and forbade the hunting of buffalo, muskox, wapiti (elk), white pelicans, swans, and eider ducks. For other species, the act established hunting seasons and banned poisons. The government did not always protect Aboriginal people's right to hunt and subjected it periodically to negotiation.

FIGURE 4.8 In 1904, Jack Miner created a sanctuary in Leamington for migrating ducks and geese, who arrived in great numbers. His life-long banding, research, and habitat preservation methods encouraged wildlife conservation education and policy.
Library and Archives Canada, 1914/P. 134-135

Non-Aboriginal hunters sometimes used Aboriginal people to circumvent legislation that required licences.

In 1919, Arthur Meighen, the minister of the interior, opened the first National Conference on Wildlife Protection to conserve game, fur-bearing animals, and other wildlife. Parks Commissioner James Harkin spoke about the need for sanctuaries to protect certain animals, but not predators. The conference reflected a change in attitude within the federal government, which began to promote the study, conservation, and management of wildlife. Professional wildlife managers inside and outside of national parks amended their views over time. At first, without a concept of a balanced environment, they focused on decreasing or increasing individual species, depending on whether they were classified as good or bad. For years, the Parks Branch encouraged park wardens to manage wildlife so sportsmen could fish or even hunt in the parks or just outside of

sanctuaries. Managers administered regulations such as hunting seasons, bag limits, and licences, and they educated the public about hunting regulations and tried to control poachers. They viewed wildlife preservation from a commercial perspective. They placed bounties on predators, and park managers sometimes gave sportsmen permission to hunt them for a fee. As limited as the system was from an ecological perspective, it did, in certain cases, lead to a better understanding of species and their habitats. For instance, at Elk Island National Park in Alberta, located east of Edmonton, park workers had to deal with rising numbers of elk and buffalo. They fenced them, culled them, and even marketed their meat commercially. Although their approach was rooted in agricultural science rather than wildlife biology, it did enhance knowledge about the species and their habitats.

Those game wardens, park officials, and hunters who came to recognize the paradox of conserving wildlife so it could be hunted ceased to hunt predators and tried to change ingrained attitudes. Howard Douglas, superintendent of Banff National Park, believed in both wildlife preservation and educating the public about wild animals. In 1897, he started an early program of ecotourism by building a refuge for indigenous species and a zoo. His actions were unusual at a time when park managers facilitated hunting and shot, trapped, or poisoned predators to protect harmless animals that appealed to tourists. In 1928, armed with more scientific knowledge, Harkin finally reined in the killing of predators so "wild life conditions in the National Parks remain as nearly as possible in a natural condition to preserve a balance in nature" (Burnett 2003, 7). Wildlife managers, in general, however, were slow to embrace an ecological perspective. Some parks officers resisted polices to protect predators well into the 1940s.

Conservation after the Commission of Conservation

Conservation as a policy approach tended to have less influence once the Commission of Conservation ended in 1921. The pro-business mood of the 1920s did not lend itself to innovative policies or approaches to administration. The 1920s, a time of economic boom, included expanded hydroelectric development, increased agricultural acreage, and intense exploitation of timber, pulpwood, minerals, and fish without conservation measures. In 1924, however, the federal Royal Commission on Pulpwood did reiterate the need to conserve forest resources and to introduce forest management practices. It revealed

that the lumber and pulp-and-paper industries earned $500 million a year, $12 million of which went to the federal government. The federal government, however, spent only $35,000 a year researching silviculture, the practice of controlling the growth and quality of forests to meet diverse needs and values. Because the government lacked knowledge about the extent of timber supplies, the lumber industry destroyed more timber than it regenerated. The commission reported that the government's focus on short-term economic gain had made forest renewal a major problem. Two conferences held that same year stressed public education about fire prevention, which led to advertisements warning scouts and tourists to put out their campfires.

Even when the economic boom burst in 1929, ushering in the Great Depression, conservationism had only a feeble influence on public policy and practice. On the Prairies, where economic depression was compounded by disastrous drought, farmers began to diversify their crops, and they explored new irrigation and soil conservation techniques as they wrestled with insects, massive soil erosion, and dust storms. The federal government created the Prairie Farm Rehabilitation Administration (PFRA) in 1935 to assist destitute people in prairie communities. Before the PFRA, the government had actively encouraged people to abandon their farms and leave the Prairies. The PFRA, however, addressed the problems of soil erosion, irrigation, and other soil conservation matters. Emergency measures included on-farm dugouts to conserve water for livestock, community pastures converted from abandoned land, tree planting to protect the soil from wind erosion, and strip farming to prevent soil drift, the cause of the great dust bowl. Strip farming, the practice of growing crops in strips alternated with summerfallow, diminished erosion by reducing the wind speed on the surface of the soil and the distance the wind travelled across exposed summerfallow.

In general, however, the Canadian government was not committed to conservation during the Depression. In 1937, a Canadian Wildlife Conference passed resolutions for legislation to prevent the pollution of inland waters by oil, which harmed birds. The government took no action until the 1970s. During the Depression, some parks also hosted work projects for unemployed men, who built facilities and roads for future recreational needs. Unlike the American Civilian Conservation Corps, however, which educated unemployed men about conservation, Canadian camp projects had little funding. They were pragmatic relief enterprises with few creative educational programs.

THE CONSERVATION MOVEMENT in Canada had few members, was of short duration, and was oriented more toward utilitarian goals that accommodated the "national policy" than to the ideas of preservationists. The elitist movement – directed by middle-class male civil servants, scientists, foresters, urban planners, and farmers – focused on the overuse of resources and concentrated on applying science to policy and the bureaucratic method to government. Its members believed the new professions could modernize society. Sportsmen took up the cause of wildlife conservation to serve their own

needs. The movement, however, did constitute the first attempt to counsel moderation and restraint in development to protect the environment, an idea inherent in modern environmentalism but new at the turn of the century. The introduction of forest management techniques and the national parks movement set a precedent for measured development and conservation. Effective measures to protect Canada's forests and wildlife would not come, however, until the 1970s.

The close relationship between business and government meant politicians had economic motives in mind when they implemented legislation, such as for national parks, and business leaders used the state to stabilize, extend, and legitimize their economic power. This relationship meant that governments did not often attend to other groups' issues – or, indeed, to the public interest – even when the Crown owned natural resources. The capitalistic rhetoric of free enterprise prevailed, even though businesses relied on the state's cooperation as they expanded and consolidated. The conservation movement waned because the consistent central theme of business ideology was economic growth to maximize profits, an approach that favoured all-out development and exploitation rather than conservation or protection. Insufficient political support for controls to protect the environment, public health, and the public interest persisted throughout the twentieth century, despite the resurgence of conservationist values and environmental concerns in the 1970s.

Works Cited

Arden, Harvey. 1973. "John Muir's Wild America." *National Geographic* 143, 4 (April): 433-57.

Burnett, Alexander J. 2003. *A Passion for Wildlife: The History of the Canadian Wildlife Service.* Vancouver: UBC Press.

Foster, Janet. 1978. *Working for Wildlife: The Beginning of Preservation in Canada.* Toronto: University of Toronto Press.

Fothergill, Charles, to R.B. Sullivan. 21 September 1835. Charles Fothergill papers, 1795-1875. Thomas Fisher Rare Book Library, University of Toronto.

Gillis, Peter, and Thomas Roach. 1995. "The Beginnings of a Movement: The Montreal Congress and Its Aftermath, 1880-1896." In *Consuming Canada: Readings in Environmental History,* edited by Chad Gaffield and Pam Gaffield, 131-51. Toronto: Copp Clark.

Hall, David J. 1985. *Clifford Sifton: The Lonely Eminence, 1901-1929.* Vol. 2. Vancouver: UBC Press.

Hewitt, C. Gordon. 1911. "Conservation or the Protection of Nature." *Ottawa Naturalist* 24, 12 (March): 209-10.

Mackay, Donald. 1985. *Heritage Lost: The Crisis in Canada's Forests.* Toronto: Macmillan of Canada.

Merchant, Carolyn. 1993. *Major Problems in American Environmental History.* Lexington, MA: D.C. Heath.

Reynolds, Nila. 1968. *In Quest of Yesterday: Haliburton Highlands: Provisional County.* Haliburton: Provisional County of Haliburton.

Vreeland, Frederick. 1916. "Prohibition of the Sale of Game." In *Conservation of Fish, Birds, and Game,* 93-99. Commission of Conservation, Canada. Toronto: Methodist Book and Publishing House.

Wood, William. 1911. *Animal Sanctuaries in Labrador: Address to the Second Annual Meeting of the Commission of Conservation, Quebec, January.* Ottawa: Capital Press. http://www.gutenberg.org/.

Brinkley, Douglas. 2009. *The Wilderness Warrior: Theodore Roosevelt and the Crusade for America.* New York: HarperCollins.

Gillis, Peter, and Thomas Roach. 1995. "The Beginnings of a Movement: The Montreal Congress and Its Aftermath, 1880-1896." In *Consuming Canada: Readings in Environmental History,* edited by Chad Gaffield and Pam Gaffield, 131-51. Toronto: Copp Clark.

Harris, Cole. 1966. "The Myth of the Land in Canadian Nationalism." In *Nationalism in Canada,* edited by Peter Russell, 27-41. Toronto: McGraw-Hill.

Hewitt, C. Gordon. 1911. "Conservation or the Protection of Nature." *Ottawa Naturalist* 24, 12 (March): 209-10.

Kline, Marcia. 1970. *Beyond the Land Itself: Views of Nature in Canada and the United States.* Cambridge, MA: Harvard University Press.

Mackay, Donald. 1985. *Heritage Lost: The Crisis in Canada's Forests.* Toronto: Macmillan of Canada.

Nash, Roderick. 2001. *Wilderness and the American Mind.* 4th ed. New Haven: Yale University Press.

Worster, Donald. 2008. *A Passion for Nature. The Life of John Muir.* New York: Oxford University Press.

Wynn, Graeme. 2009. "Travels with George Perkins Marsh: Notes on a Journey into Environmental History." In *Method and Meaning in Canadian Environmental History,* edited by Alan MacEachern and William J. Turkel, 2-23. Toronto: Nelson.

For Further Reading

Conservationists and Preservationists

Balogh, Brian. 2002. "Scientific Forestry and the Roots of the Modern American State: Gifford Pinchot's Path to Progressive Reform." *Environmental History* 7, 2: 198-225.

Berger, Carl. 1966. "The True North Strong and Free." In *Nationalism in Canada,* edited by Peter Russell, 4-14. Toronto: McGraw-Hill.

Forest Conservation

Gillis, R. Peter, and Thomas R. Roach. 1986. "The American Influence on Conservation in Canada: 1899-1911." *Journal of Forest History* 30 (October): 160-74.

Gillis, Robert Peter. 1974. "The Ottawa Lumber Barons and the Conservation Movement." *Journal of Canadian Studies* 9, 1: 14-31.

Hodgins, Bruce W., Jamie Benidickson, and Peter Gillis. 1982. "The Ontario and Quebec Experiments in Forest Reserves, 1883-1930." *Journal of Forest History* 26 (January): 20-32.

Mackay, Donald. 1985. *Heritage Lost: The Crisis in Canada's Forests.* Toronto: Macmillan of Canada.

McLaren, John P.S. 1984. "'The Tribulations of Antoine Ratté': A Case Study of the Environmental Regulation of the Canadian Lumbering Industry in the Nineteenth Century." *University of New Brunswick Law Journal* 33: 203-59.

Pisani, Donald J. 1985. "Forests and Conservation, 1865-1890." *Journal of American History* 72, 2: 340-59.

Pyne, Stephen J. 2007. *Awful Splendour: A Fire History of Canada.* Vancouver: UBC Press.

Twight, B.W. 1990. "Bernhard Fernow and Prussian Forestry in America." *Journal of Forestry* (US) 88, 2: 21-25.

The Commission of Conservation

Armstrong, Alan H. 1972. "Thomas Adams and the Commission of Conservation." In *Planning the Canadian Environment,* edited by L.O. Gertler. Montreal: Harvest House.

Artibise, Alan F.J., and Gilbert A. Stelter. 1981. "Conservation Planning and Urban Planning: The Canadian Commission on Conservation in Historical Perspective." In *Planning for Conservation: An International Perspective,* edited by R.J.P. Kain, 17-36. London: Mansell.

Girard, Michel. 1991. "The Commission of Conservation as a Forerunner to the National Research Council, 1909-1921." *Scientia Canadensis* 15, 41: 19-40.

—. 2003. "The Canadian Commission of Conservation: Urban Planning." In *The Atlas of US and Canadian Environmental History,* edited by Char Miller, 108-9. New York: Routledge.

Hall, David J. 1985. *Clifford Sifton: The Lonely Eminence, 1901-1929.* Vol. 2. Vancouver: UBC Press.

Simpson, Michael. 1982. "Thomas Adams in Canada, 1914-1930." *Urban History Review* 11, 2: 1-15.

National Parks

Binnema, Ted, and Melanie Niemi. 2006. "'Let the Line Be Drawn Now': Wilderness Conservation, and the Exclusion of Aboriginal People from Banff National Park in Canada." *Environmental History* 11 (October): 724-50.

Brown, R.C. 1970. "The Doctrine of Usefulness: Natural Resources and National Park Policy in Canada, 1887-1914." In *Canadian Parks in Perspective,* edited by J.G. Nelson, 46-62. Montreal: Harvest House.

Jasen, Patricia. 1995. *Wild Things: Nature, Culture, and Tourism in Ontario 1790-1914.* Toronto: University of Toronto Press.

MacDonald, Graham A. 1994. "Science and History at Elk Island National Park: Conservation and Its Contradictions." Paper presented at the annual meeting of the Canadian Historical Association, Calgary, March.

MacEachern, Alan. 1996. "Rationality and Rationalization in Canadian National Parks' Predator Policy." *Canadian Papers in Rural History* 10: 149-64.

—. 2001. *Natural Selections: National Parks in Atlantic Canada, 1935-1970.* Montreal and Kingston: McGill-Queen's University Press.

MacLaren, Ian. 2007. *Culturing Wilderness in Jasper National Park: Studies in Two Centuries of Human History in the Upper Athabasca River Watershed.* Edmonton: University of Alberta Press.

Nelson, J.G. 1978. "Canada's National Parks: Past, Present and Future." In *Man's Impact on the Western Canadian Landscape,* edited by J.G. Nelson, 78-101. Toronto: McClelland and Stewart.

Reichwein, Pearlann. 1995. "'Hands Off Our National Parks': The Alpine Club of Canada and Hydro-Development Controversies in the Canadian Rockies, 1922-1930." *Journal of the Canadian Historical Association* 6, 1: 129-55.

Waiser, William. 1995. *Park Prisoners: The Untold Story of Western Canada's National Parks, 1915-1946.* Saskatoon: Fifth House Publishers.

—. 1998. "The Political Art of Park Making: Mackenzie King and the Creation of Prince Albert National Park." Paper presented to the Themes and Issues in North American Environmental History Conference, University of Toronto, April.

Wolfe, Roy I. 1962. "The Summer Resorts of Ontario in the 19th Century." *Ontario History* 54 (September): 149-61.

Wildlife Conservation

Burnett, Alexander J. 2003. *A Passion for Wildlife: The History of the Canadian Wildlife Service.* Vancouver: UBC Press.

Colpitts, George. 2002. *Game in the Garden: A Human History of Wildlife in Western Canada to 1940.* Vancouver: UBC Press.

Dowie, Mark. 2009. *Conservation Refugees: The Hundred-Year Conflict between Global Conservation and Native Peoples.* Cambridge, MA: MIT Press.

Foster, Janet. 1978. *Working for Wildlife: The Beginning of Preservation in Canada.* Toronto: University of Toronto Press.

Loo, Tina. 2006. *States of Nature: Conserving Canada's Wildlife in the Twentieth Century.* Vancouver: UBC Press.

Manore, Jean L. 2001. "Modernity's Contested Terrains of Space and Place: Hunting and the Landscape Known as Algonquin Park, 1890-1950." Paper presented to the annual meeting of the Canadian Historical Association, Laval, May.

Parenteau, Bill. 2004. "A 'Very Determined Opposition to the Law': Conservation, Angling Leases and Social Conflict in the Canadian Atlantic Salmon Fishery, 1867-1914." *Environmental History* 9, 3: 436-63.

Sandlos, John. 2008. *Hunters at the Margins: Native People and Wildlife Conservation in the Northwest Territories.* Vancouver: UBC Press.

Vreeland, Frederick. 1916. "Prohibition of the Sale of Game." In *Conservation of Fish, Birds, and Game,* 93-99. Commission of Conservation, Canada. Toronto: Methodist Book and Publishing House.

Conservation after the Commission of Conservation

Lambert, R.S., with R. Pross. 1967. *Renewing Nature's Wealth: A Centennial History of the Public Management of Lands, Forests, and Wildlife in Ontario, 1763-1967.* Toronto: Department of Lands and Forests.

Nelles, H.V. 1974. *The Politics of Development: Forests, Mines and Hydro-Electric Power in Ontario, 1849-1941.* Toronto: Macmillan of Canada.

5

Mining Resources

Mining, whether surface or underground, disturbs the topography of the locality, affects water flows and produces wastes that have to be disposed of. It may also produce damaging acids.

– FRANK ANTON, MINING CONSULTANT, *THE CANADIAN COAL INDUSTRY,* 1981

PRESSURE FROM CONSERVATIONISTS convinced Canadian policy makers to manage national parks and wildlife in the late nineteenth and early twentieth centuries. They proved less willing to intervene in resources development because they shared the mining industry's priorities and concern for profit. As historian Morris Zaslow observes, "governments sometimes treated the resources under their stewardship as if they were inexhaustible and completely valueless in their natural state; and they disposed of them as though they were their personal property, heedless of developmental priorities, or in line with every fleeting wind of public opinion" (Zaslow 1971, 284). The remoteness of the mining "frontier" and the close relationship between government and industry fostered this disregard, which was evident in the early work of the Geological Survey of Canada and extended into mining operations in the late nineteenth and twentieth centuries.

Railway construction and breakthroughs in hard rock mining techniques in the 1890s opened up the Canadian Shield to resource development. This early period of exploration and development continued until the First World War. After the war, in the 1920s, prospectors used airplanes to explore farther north, and they found significant new sites in the hinterlands of Hudson Bay and Great Slave Lake. Innovations in aeronautics during and after the Second World War moved the mining frontier still northward. As Canadian mining companies developed more advanced technologies and expertise, they expanded their investments in the Far North and around the world, and they responded to new demands – driven by postwar consumerism and car culture – for mining products, including metals. Mining disrupted the landscape, produced hazardous waste piles, and created extensive pollution, which had a detrimental effect not only on water, air, and soil quality but also on the health of miners, mining towns, and northern communities. On the international stage, Canada distinguished itself, not by pushing for more stringent regulations to prevent pollution and health problems, but by taking a pro-business stance on issues such as asbestos mining.

The Geological Survey of Canada

The federal government established the Geological Survey of Canada (GSC) in 1842 as its scientific arm. Policy makers and politicians had pushed for the survey because they realized that if Canada was to develop an industrial economy that could compete with those in Europe and the United States, it would need to develop a viable mining industry. A thorough geological assessment of the landmass was in order. Members of the agency were in the forefront of geology – the science that deals with the physical matter and energy that constitute the earth, its history, and the processes that act upon it – and other scientific fields and were associated with universities and professional science societies. In its first fifty years, the agency mapped Canada's terrain and studied its geology and geography. Its pioneering studies expanded knowledge in the earth sciences, and its topographers became authorities on the soils, forests, waters, wildlife, climate, minerals, and Aboriginal peoples of regions that had yet to be settled.

In 1902, Robert Bell, the GSC's acting director, published a map to celebrate the agency's diamond jubilee. The map displayed the routes and districts surveyed, work that had helped to open up the Northwest to settlement. The agency's employees had also collected artifacts that reflected their personal interests. To justify their work and ensure continued funding, the GSC stressed its

practical objectives. In the nineteenth century, for instance, it showcased its efforts to advance agricultural settlement on the Prairies. In the twentieth century, it emphasized its assistance to a mining frontier expanding into the Canadian Shield. The agency advertised that its staff searched for mineral deposits by "reading the rocks," and at international science events, it published reports on likely places to find ore bodies. The GSC therefore "played an important role in introducing the Canadian Shield to the public imagination: as a scientific phenomenon, a continental geological formation (an appealing concept to imperialists dreaming of national expansion *ad mare usque mare*), and a potential treasure of mineral ore for a country on the brink of industrialization" (Campbell 2005, 40). The Arctic was the final frontier. Building on the work of British naval explorers in the nineteenth century, agency staff used bush planes in the 1930s for aerial surveying. This technique provided the information necessary for mining companies to conquer a vast territory characterized by rocky hills, muskeg bogs, and lakes, rivers, and creeks. All of Canada was surveyed and mapped by the 1950s.

The surveys, maps, and annual reports produced by the Geological Survey of Canada helped guide generations of prospectors to mineral-bearing rock and exploitable deposits. As geological science grew more exact, the GSC could locate mineral deposits with precision and studied ways to extract minerals from the earth. At established mines, the agency's geologists advised mine operators on the possible behaviour of mineral-bearing formations at certain depths and helped

THE NATIONAL MUSEUM OF CANADA

The Geological Survey of Canada's work in remote districts stimulated curiosity about all aspects of the environment. Among staff members, tension developed between "practical" and "pure" science. In addition to mapping and searching for mineral deposits, agency personnel collected rock samples, fossils, flora and fauna, fishes, and Aboriginal artifacts. Some studied Aboriginal languages, legends, and cultures. Their growing botanical, zoological, and anthropological collections resulted in the establishment of the national Victoria Memorial Museum, which opened in 1912. It was renamed the National Museum of Canada in 1927 and became the present-day Canadian Museum of Civilization.

them solve problems, such as underground rock bursts.

Coal Mining

Early mining activity in Canada centred on coal, a carbon product used to heat homes, generate electricity, produce steel, and power railway locomotives. Coal deposits form when the organic remains of plants and animals decompose under anaerobic conditions (in the absence of free oxygen). Over time, the remains compact and undergo gradual lithification, to create peat, lignite, bituminous coal, anthracite coal, graphite, and diamonds. Coal was first discovered on Cape Breton Island in the early eighteenth century. During the War of 1812, John McKay, in Pictou County, Nova Scotia, was licensed to extract coal and "commenced with fresh vigour to drain off the water from the Pits ... made roads and bridges – brought wagons for the carriage of coal – built lighters – and erected buildings necessary for his purposes" (Martell 1980, 45). As this description suggests, from its beginnings, coal mining in

Canada transformed, and damaged, the environment.

As coal-mining companies emerged and consolidated in Nova Scotia, British (and later American and Canadian) investors brought in skilled workers, built row housing for them, and developed iron foundries, steam engines, and transportation infrastructure. Located near the water, the industry included surface, slope, and strip mining (processes that remove the soil and rock above the mineral) and underground mining (a process that leaves soil and rock in place and removes the mineral through shafts or tunnels, which, depending on the location, can extend under the ocean) (see Figure 5.1). The latter type of mining predominated in Cape Breton. Miners sunk the first shaft in the Sydney coal field in 1830. By the 1880s, coal mines "ringed the magnificent expanse of Sydney harbour and were strung along the coast on either side of its headlands" (Muise 1980, 77). The industry boomed in the 1890s, and in 1901 investors from the United States formed the Dominion Iron and Steel Company and opened a major steel works on Sydney Harbour. The town became the focal point of the Cape Breton coal mines, which included smaller communities such as Glace Bay, New Waterford, and Reserve. Workers sorted and cleaned the coal in ancillary buildings that included machine shops and, later, generators for electricity to light, drain, and ventilate mines. Sydney's integrated coal and steel industry inhabited three square kilometres of downtown waterfront property. Coke ovens, equipped with Bessamer-type blast furnaces, converted coal into steel. The final product went by railway to piers and was shipped to other parts of the Atlantic

FIGURE 5.1 **This photograph of a coal-mining operation in Nova Scotia in the 1860s depicts both the rudimentary technology and structures of early coal-mining developments and the extreme disruption to the environment caused by the miners' digging.**

G.W. MacKay, Nova Scotia Archives and Records Management, Album 55 no. 4/negative no. N-2109

region, Quebec, and New England. By 1912, the Sydney mill turned out nearly half of Canada's steel production.

The Nova Scotia mining industry provided substantial energy but plundered the natural landscape and polluted the water. The under-ground mines produced a relatively small amount of waste from water discharges and from blasting agents and therefore had a smaller environmental impact than open pits. The high sulphur content of eastern coal, however, proved to be a challenge, and the

THE SYDNEY TAR PONDS

In the early 1980s, the Department of Fisheries and Oceans conducted a survey of Sydney Harbour and discovered high levels of mercury, PCB, lead, and polynuclear aromatic hydrocarbons (a family of chemicals produced by the incomplete combustion of organic material) in lobster. It traced the contamination to the Sydney Tar Ponds, an estuary at the mouth of the Muggah Creek, a freshwater stream that empties into the harbour. The ponds contain waste runoff from the Sydney coke ovens, built in the nineteenth century.

The discovery of contaminants forced the closure of the coke ovens in 1988. In 1986, the federal and provincial governments also signed a $34-million agreement to dredge the ponds and pump the sediments through a pipeline to an incinerator. The sludge, however, proved to be too thick to handle, and the project ended in 1995. Delays, disagreements, and countless public meetings and scientific reports followed. In 2004, the federal and provincial governments announced another plan to clean up the ponds by incinerating PCB-contaminated sediments. The site, however, continues to be surrounded by controversy. Whereas some locals support moves to dig up and destroy all contaminants, others advocate leaving the site undisturbed. The Sierra Club of Canada opposes plans to incinerate materials and favours novel destruction technologies such as hydrogen reduction and soil washing. In 2007, the two governments announced a new plan to solidify and bury, not burn, the contents of the ponds.

FIGURE 5.2 This view of the hardscrabble coal-mining community in Rosedale, Alberta (ca. 1912), shows the close proximity of the mine to workers' housing.
Glenbow Archives, NA-2389-34

techniques developed to remove it were inadequate. The process of cleaning the coal created solid wastes discharged as tailings – the refuse or dross that remains after ore is processed – and as dust emissions. Depending on the type of ore and the process of extraction, tailings can also contain arsenic and cyanide. The coal mines wrought lasting environmental destruction, evidenced by the Sydney Tar Ponds, the worst toxic waste site in Canada and the second worst in North America.

Coal was also discovered and exploited in British Columbia and the Prairies. In 1832, William Fraser Tolmie – a Canadian surgeon, politician, and officer of the Hudson's Bay Company – learned from local people that coal deposits existed on Vancouver Island. The company started mining at Nanaimo twenty years later. The British government required individuals or companies who established mines to obtain a licence and collected royalties on the tonnage. Nanaimo was a booming mining town by the 1870s, when the Hudson's Bay Company sold its mining interests and entrepreneurs such as

Robert Dunsmuir moved in to make their fortunes. British Columbia's coal-mining frontier expanded to other one-industry towns such as Ladysmith, and in 1879 the coal field at Crowsnest Pass started production. The Prairies likewise contained vast coal reserves. Coal-bearing formations underlie most of the southern half of Alberta, whose coal fields employed over seven thousand miners and labourers by 1931 (see Figure 5.2). The lignite mines near Estevan, Saskatchewan, employed over four hundred men that same year. Most of the coal in the region was extracted by underground mining until 1927, when open pit or strip mining, a process that leaves an indelible imprint on the environment, became more typical.

In all regions, dangerous mining processes led to fires, accidents, occupational diseases, pollution, and devastation of the landscape. The Vancouver Island mines were plagued by industrial conflicts and were among the most dangerous in the world. Miners experienced roof falls, coal dust and gas fumes, and explosions. Throughout the West, the extensive use of surface mining caused drainage problems, particularly in mountainous regions, where mining undermined slope stability and led to soil erosion. In the 1970s, the results of a satellite survey of twenty-six sites on the Prairies revealed that coal mining had disturbed on average 335 hectares of land at each site. On the positive side, although open pit mines covered more area than underground mines, the coal deposits were shallow, and 40 percent of the sites surveyed had vegetative cover. Beginning in the 1960s, legislation was passed to regulate strip mining and reclaim lands when mines closed.

Governments across Canada have learned that land reclamation following the closure of a mine is possible, but it is expensive and can be ineffective, especially in mountainous areas. At the lignite mines in Estevan, for example, new regulations passed in 1984 made it mandatory for operators to reclaim the land for agriculture or wildlife by stabilizing the soils and growing self-sustaining vegetative cover. Because the open pits were shallow and the terrain flat, reclamation efforts were successful. Coal mining at Hinton, Alberta, had likewise destroyed the land – a forest of spruce, fir, and lodgepole pine – but forages were introduced to create a habitat for bighorn sheep, and an exhausted pit was transformed into a mountain lake for sports fishermen. At Byron Creek Collieries in southeast British Columbia, runoff sediment from the mine contained small particles of mudstones, shale, and coal that were used to amend the high salinity of the soil and thereby increase revegetation. In 1979, the Science Council of Canada recommended that the costs of reclamation should be determined by testing small integrated programs that combined environmental protection, land-use planning, and mining reclamation. In the deficit-cutting years of the 1980s and 1990s, however, these projects were not a high government priority.

Waste from coal mining continues to be an environmental problem, particularly the quality of water discharged into the environment, the most famous example being the Sydney Tar Ponds. In the early 1980s, the National Coal Wastewater Survey, undertaken by Environment Canada, recorded trace elements of contaminants and concluded that wastewater needed to be treated before discharge. In addition, the quality of stream water in the coal-mining areas of the upper foothills of western Alberta indicated that mine sediment had moved into drainage systems, as had oil contaminants and odours. Springs and streams on the eastern slopes of the Rocky Mountains near Grand Cache, Alberta, had also been adversely affected. Scientists discovered that the release of mine sediments into the stream ecosystems of British Columbia had harmed salmon and other fishes by reducing the number of fish eggs and hatching rates and by lowering aquatic organisms' resistance to disease. Although regulations to stop the drainage of acid and sulphur dioxide are increasingly stringent, sulphur residue remains an issue in both the water and air because methods of removal are either very expensive or not fully developed. With increased demand for energy and without a major breakthrough in renewable energy technology or conservation, coal production for hydroelectricity generation may continue, making research and development to ease the environmental damage of coal mining essential.

British Columbia and Yukon

Mining played an important role in British Columbia's history after gold was discovered in the Fraser River. In 1858, British writer Kinahan Cornwallis published *The New Eldorado; or, British Columbia* to encourage immigration. In it, he praised the region's "salubrious climate," agricultural potential, lumber and mineral resources, and beauty. He expressed surprise "that a region so palpably auriferous [gold-filled] should have remained so long unproclaimed and hidden from the gaze of civilization" (Sterne 1998, 76). He did, however, recognize that its isolation and the Hudson's Bay Company's desire to protect the fur trade had helped maintain its ecological integrity by delaying resources exploitation, outside of fur.

Once the news of gold got out, however, over thirty thousand men rushed to the Mainland, and gold mining replaced the fur trade as the main economic activity there. The British government established the colony of British Columbia on the Mainland in 1858 to impose legal and administrative order on the sudden influx of people. Steamers took miners from Victoria up the Fraser River to Yale, where the river became nearly impassable. To reach the upper river through the mountain barrier, the miners themselves built the first road through which mule trains could pass to reach Lillooet.

The arrival of thousands of miners had an immediate impact on the environment. At Victoria, 225 new buildings sprang up in six weeks. The British government encouraged settlement and the establishment of businesses. It planned a post office and sent in the Royal Engineers to survey and plan the roads and townsites of Fort Langley, Fort Hope, Fort Yale, and, later, Point Douglas. The Hudson's Bay Company opened a land office. As the mining frontier expanded over the next seventy years, it stimulated the growth or emergence of commercial supply centres on the coast, whose stable populations contrasted with the mobile, mostly male residents of mining towns.

In the early days, miners wielded basic tools: hand picks, hammers, shovels, gold pans, cases of dynamite sticks, blasting machines that could ignite fifty caps of dynamite in a series of blasts, and blasting wires that connected the caps to the machine. Using placer mining, which involved washing or dredging, the miners quickly found gold in the beds, tributaries, and streams and on the shores of the Fraser River. Further inland, in the valleys, miners constructed terraces or benches and used high-pressure hoses to spray them with water. As the soil disintegrated, the miners captured the gold in sluices, artificial water troughs controlled at their head by a gate. Hydraulic mining killed trees and damaged soil and watercourses (see Figure 5.3). A contemporary summarized the environmental impact: "The first gold diggings were upon the bank of the river; upon this bank grew giant trees – all these, and acres of soil, have been swept away to the depth of some ten or twelve feet. It is now found that the higher banks, or flats, still further from the river, are auriferous. These are now being worked" (Hazlitt 1974, 110). Aboriginal people, also involved in gold removal, feared that the mining process would drive away salmon, their main source of food and trade.

FIGURE 5.3 The devastating effects of hydraulic mining are apparent in this photograph of a hydraulic mine near Horsefly in the Cariboo region of British Columbia. The soil was completely eroded and denuded by water under pressure being sprayed from large industrial hoses, which created large breaks in the ground. Horsefly was the focus of a second gold rush in 1887, when Thaddeus Harper opened a hydraulic mine in the Horsefly River area. John B. Hobson took it over in 1893, but mining gold remained a costly process in Horsefly. The gold that the Horsefly Hydraulic Mining Company recovered from 1894 to 1896 was worth only about $150,000.

BC Archives, I-55131

The mining frontier expanded inland into the mountainous, sparsely populated areas of the southeast, which had a natural entrance through the Crowsnest Pass. Aboriginal peoples in the region laboured as miners and industrial workers in the coal and gold mines. They suffered population decreases from disease and were subject to the miners' racism and land hunger, but they remained the majority in the area as the mining frontier moved northward. Important mineral discoveries in the Cariboo during the 1860s created the heart of the mining community. In 1862, five thousand miners built permanent settlements at Williams Creek, Richfield, Barkerville, Van Winkle, and Lightning, places "where churches and brothels could be found side by side" (Barry Gough, introduction in Hazlitt 1974, 5). Prospectors continued to tap British Columbia's immense mineral wealth throughout the 1880s and 1890s. They opened up the Kootenay and Boundary areas with discoveries of gold, silver, copper, lead, and zinc.

Mining development spread to Yukon when placer gold was discovered on Rabbit Creek, a tributary of the Klondike River, in 1896. American and Canadian miners and others from around the world rushed to the Klondike through the gateways of Seattle, Vancouver, and Victoria. Memorable photographs captured their journeys through the White and Chilkoot Passes. In 1900, James MacIntosh Bell and Charles Camsell discovered cobalt and silver near Great Bear Lake and traces of gold near Great Slave Lake. Mining connected this isolated hinterland to industrial America, which shipped up consumer goods and permanently changed the landscape and culture of the region, even after the miners left. Surface, streamside, and placer mining resulted in dirt and gravel piles that transformed creeks. Miners literally tore apart the ecosystem by chopping down trees for firewood and to make boats, cabins, and sluices; by stripping vegetation from the earth; and by altering streams and valleys with ditches, dams, and reservoirs. The changed topography precipitated floods, dry waterbeds, and the loss of previously abundant fish and large mammals. The heavily mined areas ceased to be living ecosystems, at least temporarily. Aboriginal people worked as packers and boat pilots, and they sold food such as salmon, moose, and caribou to miners. Some communities faced starvation as wildlife in the area was depleted, and many succumbed to diseases brought to the region by miners.

Between 1895 and 1902, American investment also led to a mining and smelting boom in the Kootenays. Smelting, the extraction of metal from ore by a process that involves heating and melting, was hailed as the "epitome of industrialization, the promise of prosperity, the hallmark of the modern age"

THE MINING LANDSCAPE: ROADS AND RAILWAYS

The Cariboo Wagon Road, completed in 1865, opened up travel to the Cariboo gold fields. A central artery, the road connected Yale to Barkerville and oriented transportation through Quesnel. Following the early years of the gold rush, older roads, trails, and settlements were reworked and redesigned to meet the needs of the shifting mining frontier and with no regard for their environmental impact. Miners used pack trains, wagons, and horse-drawn rawhide sleds to get ore to waterways, where paddle wheelers transferred the ore to smelters. Rail connections made the cumbersome process easier. Between 1881 and 1898, the Canadian Pacific Railway built the Crowsnest Pass line, which extended from its main line in southern Alberta through the coal-mining area and the mountain pass to the Kootenays and Boundary areas in the Interior.

CANADIAN COMPANIES AND TRANSBOUNDARY POLLUTION

From 1906 to 1995, Cominco's smelter at Trail, British Columbia, discharged up to 145,000 tons (131,542 tonnes) of waste annually into the Canadian portion of the Columbia River. In 2003, Cominco's successor company, Teck Cominco, responded slowly to an order from the US Environmental Protection Agency to investigate its alleged contamination of the river. In 2008, however, the tide began to turn when the Confederated Tribes of the Colville Reservation in Washington State launched a citizen lawsuit in the state courts against the Vancouver-based company *(Pakootas v Teck Cominco Minerals)*. The US Supreme Court refused to hear Teck Cominco's appeal that it could not be tried in a US court. The case suggested that US environmental standards could be imposed for corporate conduct on foreign soil in the future and thus dealt a blow to the old tradition of dealing with cross-border pollution ineffectively through diplomatic channels. Given that the Trail smelter operation is regulated by British Columbia's Environmental Management Act, which is similar to US environmental laws, the extraterritorial aspect of the case is unlikely to create international discord. In 2008, when Teck's refinery in Trail spilled lead into the Columbia River, the BC government took no action.

(Mouat 1995, 25). At rough mining towns such as Nelson, Rossland, Slocan, and Trail, smelters reduced ores and shipped them to markets. In 1898, the Canadian Pacific Railway purchased US entrepreneur F.A. Heinze's smelter at Trail, the BC Copper Company, and in 1906 it consolidated its mining interests into a larger corporation called Cominco. The company's refining technologies and modern plant helped it to dominate Canadian mining by the 1920s and become a world leader in lead-zinc technology.

Smelters, however, ruined the wild beauty of the region. At Trail, smelter smoke – which contained arsenic, lead dust, and sulphur dioxide – killed trees, withered plants, and devastated crops. Air quality quickly became a matter of controversy in the community as Cominco's tall smokestack spewed huge amounts of sulphur dioxide into the town and into farmlands across the border in the United States. "To live in Trail, was literally to be an eater of smoke, a consumer of the relentless emissions that poured from the stacks of the local smelter" (Allum 1995, 1).

American farmers sued in 1926, but a joint American-Canadian investigation ruled in favour of the company. Although the commission did require Cominco to make compensation payments to US farmers, the company escaped regulation, its main concern. The farmers' continued distress resulted in further negotiations, an arbitration tribunal (1937), and additional compensation but no emission standards. "Air pollution became an accepted, culturally sanctioned consequence of industrial capitalism, and 'smoke eating' became a normal part of everyday life" (Allum 1995, 5). The mining company's powerful political allies considered Cominco's interests more important than the farmers' businesses or environmental quality. The case set a precedent for using joint commissions to deal with international environmental disputes and allowing companies to voluntarily invest in upgrades to reduce emissions. The relative lack of concern for the environment or the adverse health effects on individuals and communities persisted until the 1970s.

Northern Ontario and Quebec

Mineral discoveries by prospectors and the building of railways in the late nineteenth century helped to extend the mining frontier into the Canadian Shield of northern Ontario and Quebec. When labourers dynamited rocks to make way for rails, they sometimes discovered resources. Railways opened up the country and serviced mining claims and towns in a complex network of tracks that included main lines such as the Canadian Pacific Railway and branch lines such as the Temiskaming and Northern Ontario Railway, completed in 1902. In the early twentieth century, mining transformed the Canadian Shield "from a largely undeveloped territory into a resource hinterland for Central Canada (and to some extent the United States)" (Kerr and Holdsworth 1990, plate 16).

Prospectors discovered copper and nickel at Sudbury, Ontario, in the 1880s. The Canadian Copper Company quickly acquired rights to the ore bodies and built a mine. The discovery in 1892 of two processes to separate copper and nickel fuelled exploration and mining in the region. In 1893, Sudbury had 1,400 citizens, including French Canadians and European immigrants who worked as miners. In 1902, the Canadian Copper Company and the Orford Copper Company in Copper Cliff, Ontario, formed the International Nickel Company (Inco). Inco's production skyrocketed, and it became the largest nickel company in the world. The discovery of nickel deposits at Falconbridge near Sudbury led to the creation of Falconbridge Nickel Mines in 1926. Early mining efforts took place close to the surface, but over time the main shaft of the Sudbury mine extended 183 metres beneath the earth's surface, where seven mines operated. Mining companies used either cyanide or mercury or roasting to extract copper and nickel. Both processes created vast amounts of pollution: sulphur dioxide emissions, tailings, and slag heaps of waste. Sulphuric acid polluted

CLEANING UP THE SUDBURY BASIN

Although years of scientific research demonstrated the damage caused by sulphur dioxide emissions, the Ontario government maintained its commitment to the nickel-smelting industry and refused to act to reduce emissions. Because reducing pollution was feasible, "solving the Sudbury tragedy was never a matter of closing the smelters to protect the forests" (Munton 2002, 155). In 1969, after intense pressure from the Steelworkers' Union and environmentalists, and out of concern for public health rather than the environment or the forests, the government finally issued control orders on Sudbury's smelter operations to improve air quality. Thereafter, labour-intensive reclamation efforts at existing and abandoned mining sites involved spreading lime on charred soil and planting wild grasses and millions of trees to renew plant and tree vegetation. Other improvements introduced in the 1970s included the installation of a superstack to disperse pollution (1972), two plant shutdowns, and emissions controls. In the 1980s, with fewer emissions, the region's lakes had declining sulphate concentrations and increased levels of algae, invertebrates, and fish. Surface water and soil, which received acids or metals directly, were slower to improve. In 1992, Sudbury was one of twelve cities in the world given the Local Government Honours Award at the United Nations Earth Summit to honour community-based environmental reclamation strategies. By 2010, Greater Sudbury had rehabilitated 3,350 hectares of land and was working on 30,000 more.

surface and groundwater and damaged thousands of hectares of forests. Released particulate matter such as arsenic and mercury destroyed soil, vegetation, and fish in ecosystems within a thirty-kilometre circumference of the mines. By the 1980s, Inco's Copper Cliff tailings disposal area included more than a thousand hectares in various stages of reclamation and revegetation, though the reclaimed land remained unsuitable for growing food because of metal uptake by plants.

Ontario's northern mining frontier expanded further when the Temiskaming and Northern Ontario Railway extended beyond North Bay. Workers revealed rich silver veins at Cobalt in 1906 and at Gowganda in 1908. When prospectors discovered gold at Porcupine the following year and at Kirkland Lake in 1911, Ontario replaced Yukon as Canada's leading gold-producing region. The discovery of precious minerals and the arrival of railways lessened northern Ontario's isolation but changed the physical landscape. To reach Porcupine, railway workers filled in marshes to cover a sinkhole and prepare the way for track. The mining town of Cobalt sprang up overnight and reached a population of eight thousand within two years.

Unlike in British Columbia or Yukon, where gold could be accessed by placer mining, bedrock-mining techniques had to be developed to extract gold in Ontario. Companies dug deep mineshafts, and miners descended into the bowels of the earth in elevators. Twelve mines were in operation at Kirkland Lake by the Second World War. Mills crushed ore to release minerals, a process that resulted in tonnes of waste that companies either piled near the mills or dumped in lakes. The companies dumped

so many mine tailings into Kirkland Lake that it disappeared. At Cobalt, the transformation of lake water from tolerably clear to tainted or a yellow green was "due largely or wholly to the powerful water hydrant of the Nipissing Mine clearing away the earth and clay from the surface of the Nipissing Hill" (Baldwin and Dunn 1976, 16). The south end of the lake also filled with slimes and mill tailings.

Developments in Quebec's northern mining frontier, at towns such as Rouyn-Noranda, followed a pattern similar to those in Ontario. The region, however, also contained chrysotile, or white asbestos. Mining began in 1879 at the Thetford Mines, a town that rapidly became the hub of one of the largest asbestos-producing regions in the world. Asbestos was increasingly used as a building material in the late nineteenth century because it could be woven into cloth, could absorb sound, and was resistant to fire, heat, and electrical and chemical damage. Manufacturers used it as electrical insulation for hotplate wiring, in building insulation, and to make heat-resistant clothing for metal workers and firefighters. Asbestos deposits lie underground, and miners use conventional practices to bring the ore to the surface for processing. Chrysotile asbestos lies near the surface and can be accessed through open pit mining (see Figure 5.4).

The Far North

By the outbreak of the First World War, a major period of mining expansion in several regions of Canada had come to an end. In the war and interwar years, new processes allowed companies to mine low-grade or

FIGURE 5.4 An open pit asbestos mine in Quebec, 1944. Asbestos mining gouged huge holes in the landscape, polluting the air with dust particles and local waterways with waste.
Harry Rowed, photographer, National Film Board of Canada/Library and Archives Canada, R1196-14-7-E

complex ores profitably. Some areas with precious metals were mined out, but the Canadian Shield remained a major source of nickel, copper, gold, and silver well into the decades following the Second World War. Bush planes made the Far North more accessible and resulted in new discoveries. In 1935, C.J. "Johnny" Baker and H. Muir staked twenty-one claims along Great Slave Lake's Back Bay for the Bear Exploration Company. The site eventually produced over 7 million ounces of gold and became one of the longest-operating gold mines in Canada. Mining operations did falter, however, before the war and came to a complete halt during it, when gold mining was not deemed a strategic priority and when there was a shortage of men to work the site. The Giant Yellowknife Gold Mines, owned by Falconbridge, and the Con Mine, owned by Cominco, resumed mining in the Yellowknife area in 1948.

Ore in the Yellowknife area contained more arsenic than gold and had to be roasted at high temperatures to release the gold. The process released toxic arsenic-rich gas directly into the environment. In 1949, two men were hospitalized with arsenic poisoning after drinking contaminated snow water. A herd of cattle died of arsenic poisoning that same year. After an Aboriginal child died from ingesting snow laced with arsenic, checkups for arsenic began and were repeated every ten years. It was already known in 1940 that arsenic exposure led to cancer and cardiovascular problems. In 1951, Giant Mine installed a Cold Cottrell Electrostatic Precipitator to remove arsenic trioxide dust, which resulted when roaster gas combined with oxygen.

The new technology reduced emissions only gradually. Over the next two decades, scientists developed technologies to reduce arsenic emissions by 80 percent, but these

CANADA'S CONTRARY STANCE ON ASBESTOS

When inhaled in significant quantities, asbestos fibres can cause asbestosis (a scarring of the lungs that makes breathing difficult), mesothelioma (a rare cancer of the lining of the chest or abdominal cavity), and lung cancer. Environmental and health problems associated with exposure to airborne asbestos particles had been noted since the early 1900s and resulted in the passage of the Asbestos Industry Regulations of 1931 in England. In Canada, miners walked off the job at four asbestos mines in the Eastern Townships, near Asbestos, Quebec, and the Thetford Mines in 1949. Premier Maurice Duplessis supported business owners and opposed the union and the strike. Workers demanded not only union recognition and better wages but also the elimination of asbestos dust inside and outside the mills. In the mid-1960s, health problems began to surface among shipyard workers who had handled asbestos insulation during the Second World War. In the United States, the problem reached the crisis stage in the 1970s, when the Environmental Protection Agency (EPA) was forced to place severe restrictions on the use of asbestos.

In 1970, the British standard of two asbestos fibres per cubic centimetre of air was extended to all parts of Canada except British Columbia, Newfoundland, and Quebec, the provinces where asbestos was mined. Between 1970 and 1974, over 250 workers in Quebec received compensation, but many more died of cancer. In 1975, their union collected its own air samples, which demonstrated the existence of high levels of asbestos dust and fibres in the air. Three thousand workers went on strike for eight months. A commission of inquiry into working conditions in chrysotile mines disclosed the health and environmental risks associated with asbestos. Massive grey piles of asbestos tailings towered over the town of Thetford Mines. On top of the piles, swivel pilers sprayed clouds of asbestos waste that spilled into the yards of nearby homes, a process that was illegal in the United States. A federal report in 1976 criticized the industry for not improving working conditions and for spending money on legal battles to "prevent the payment of compensation more than the prevention of the disease." It accused the provincial government of collaborating with the industry to cover up dangerous conditions at Thetford Mines (Tataryn 1979, 18). In the 1980s, an American medical researcher commented, "The government's general attitude is to balance the cost to industry and their profits with the risk to exposed populations. The standards are set to permit an acceptable number of cancer deaths in exposed populations and to allow industry to make profits at the same time. It's the maximum number of people we get away with murdering without a public uproar" (Tataryn 1979, 42).

As awareness grew, the transportation and construction industries began to use asbestos less, and it was removed from older buildings throughout Canada. But Quebec continued to produce and export it to poor countries. When a study in 2007 found that asbestos fibre levels at the Thetford Mines were higher than would be tolerated under US guidelines, the industry, with the support of the provincial government, accused the researchers of exaggeration. Critics responded by arguing that Canada was out of step with the world, exporting asbestos to underdeveloped countries when many European countries had banned its use. Canadian businesses, with the support of the federal and Quebec governments, challenged the World Trade Organization's ban on the grounds that that it violated their rights under international trade rules. The industry, with government support, continues to put profit before occupational and environmental health. In 2011, Canada opposed listing chrysotile asbestos as a hazardous chemical under the Rotterdam Convention, a UN treaty that covers banned or restricted pesticides and industrial chemicals, but there were signs that the industry was closing down either temporarily or permanently.

innovations were not used. Emissions from mines – including arsenic, lead, copper, zinc, and cadmium – polluted the soil, water, fish, and the entire food chain near Yellowknife. Cancer rates in the mining community were high, as were deaths from heart disease. However, because Giant Mine destroyed its personnel records from before 1969, it was impossible to scientifically assess the cancer rate among workers. In addition, workers and members of the local community could not access government studies on the arsenic hazard. Out of concern, the federal government built a pipeline in 1969 to provide the town with clean water from the Yellowknife River. Aboriginal communities, however, relied on water from Yellowknife Bay, where the mines dumped effluent. Warning signs were not posted in English until 1974 and in the local Aboriginal language until some time later. Bottled water was made available, but many Aboriginal people could not afford it. As with asbestos mining in Quebec, the federal government conducted poor research, consistently minimized the risks of arsenic exposure, withheld information from the public, and generally lagged behind the United States in the area of occupational and environmental health. When the National Indian Brotherhood and the United Steelworkers reported on hazardous practices in the mines in 1977, the federal government did not order a cleanup – it ordered another study. In 1978, the government recommended reducing arsenic levels and monitoring the work environment, but it accepted an exposure standard for arsenic much higher than was allowed in the United States under the Occupational Safety and Health Act.

As the technology and expertise of companies increased in the twentieth century, mining areas expanded in the North. Zinc mines opened at Flin Flon, Manitoba, and iron-ore production began in Labrador, northern Ontario, and Baffin Island. In communities such as Elliot Lake, Ontario, and Uranium City on the north shore of Lake Athabasca in northern Saskatchewan, uranium mines developed mid-century to fuel the nuclear industry, and nickel mines opened at Thompson in northern Manitoba. Most recently, two companies began to mine diamonds in open pit mines in Northwest Territories.

Mining Towns

Mining in Canada transformed the environment not only through the mining process itself but also by promoting the growth of haphazard but distinctive boomtowns, some of which developed into industrial cities – "hard places" characterized by environmental abuse, aggressive pragmatism, and economic exploitation. Mining towns are concrete expressions of the mining industry's cavalier attitude toward the environment. In most regions, rough camps with bunkhouses evolved into booming company towns, which later evolved into settled communities of families whose breadwinners worked for large mining conglomerates. Cobalt and Elliott Lake in Ontario and Nelson and Trail in British Columbia followed this pattern.

Early mining towns had a frontier character. They catered to all-male workforces and were serviced by boarding houses, bars, brothels, and gambling dens. In some company towns, such as Copper Cliff, Ontario,

mining companies had enormous power. They often built the communities, leased houses to workers' families, provided recreation and medical facilities, and sometimes ran the municipal councils, if such civic institutions existed. Canadians viewed company towns simultaneously as symbols of progress, technology, wealth, and risk and as places characterized by dirty work, danger, and illness. The towns' mining culture reflected the intense individualism and fierce independence of both the mine owners and the miners.

A number of factors shaped the distinctive physical appearance and spatial arrangement of mining towns. In the early years, the location of prospectors' claims determined the location of mines. Towns therefore sprang up haphazardly and without regard for the terrain. Streets rarely conformed to a grid, as they did in most urban communities. Because mining towns emerged around mine-

shafts or pits, they had no clear boundaries between residential and industrial areas. Although they grew sporadically, mining towns had highly stratified social groups. Miners and company owners or managers lived in completely separate spheres and sometimes in different towns. Haileybury, Ontario, for example, emerged as a manager's town with large residences along "millionaires' row." The workers, by contrast, struggled for higher wages and unionization, protested against dangerous working conditions, and suffered substandard living conditions in communities such as Kirkland Lake and Cobalt.

In the twentieth century, mining towns were a visible representation of the conflict between culture and nature. When a boom ended, towns declined. Although companies usually dismantled mineshaft buildings, the mines themselves formed deep scars on the landscape. In some areas, citizens attempted

FIGURE 5.5 A group of men assemble on the main street of Barkerville, BC, in 1865 to escort a shipment of gold out of town. Mining towns were rough places inhabited by tough men who laboured at dangerous mining jobs in rapidly changing social and physical environments.
Charles Gentile, photographer, Library and Archives Canada, C-088917

to preserve them, both physically and in the popular imagination, through novels, films, theme parks, museums, and historic sites. People wanted to keep alive memories of these lively places where the effects of human activity were visible. This romanticized view of the past, however, could not disguise that once the resource was removed and the mines shut down, the industry left behind damaged environments and communities.

Mines and Miners: The Interior Environment

Mining was, and remains, one of the most dangerous jobs. It generally took place in interior environments that were poorly lit by candles, oil, and acetylene lamps before hydroelectricity became common. In addition to smoke, miners had to deal with gases and clouds of dust created by pneumatic drills, and compressed air systems further rendered their workplace deficient in oxygen. Mining was like few other jobs in the industrialized world. It caused illness, physical injuries, and deformities. Miners often laboured in a bent-over position in damp, dirty, and cramped quarters. Devoid of natural light, fresh air, and physical space, mines were unnatural places. In the 1940s and 1950s, workers who laboured in uranium mines were exposed to radioactive waste, a yellow powder strewn around both the workplace and residential areas. Pollutants – whether from uranium or asbestos mining – caused a wide range of lung diseases, including silicosis, asbestosis, emphysema, pneumoconiosis, and cancer.

When miners were forced to consult apathetic doctors recruited by mining companies, they turned to unions and pressed for more stringent regulations and compensation for diseases and injuries acquired on the job. Unions occasionally initiated community medical clinics that specialized in occupational health and represented miners at workers' compensation boards or at pertinent inquiries. In 1974, uranium miners at Elliot Lake, Ontario, went on a wildcat strike after learning their cancer rates were unusually high, their exposure to radiation levels was over the permitted level, and that governments had known this and done nothing to inform or protect them. As a result of pressure from politicians and the labour movement, the Ontario government established a Royal Commission on the Health and Safety of Workers in Mines, known as the Ham Commission. The commission's investigation led to the introduction of occupational health and safety acts in Ontario and throughout the country. The legislation included joint occupational health and safety committees on all job sites and the right of workers to refuse unsafe work.

Unions also negotiated strong occupational health and safety provisions in collective agreements. At Elliot Lake, for example, contracts with Denison Mines and Rio Algom stipulated that worker inspectors could shut down workplaces they judged unsafe. The union pushed for this clause because uranium miners were exposed to "significantly higher amounts of silica dust than in other mines, as well as several types of radiation and potentially cancer-causing uranium dust" (Moses 1981, 4). Awareness of occupational health issues in mining communities has increased sensitivity to the wider issue of mining's impact on the environment.

THE ENVIRONMENTAL EFFECTS of mining in Canada can be seen on the ground and in the air: railways, open pit mines, mills and smelters, and vast tailing ponds. These visible scars on the landscape reflect a political environment that has consistently favoured industry and opposed regulation. The federal and provincial governments encouraged and assisted mining development because it created enormous wealth, increased expertise, provided employment, and resulted in government income and substantial Canadian exports. But when it became clear that mining companies produced toxic waste and pollution and contributed to occupational and environmental health issues, politicians were slow to act. Despite some successful reclamation efforts, the mining industry's effect on the environment has been severe, and Canadian mining companies have exported their practices to other countries. One response to governments' and the industry's failure to protect the public and environment from destructive mining practices was the founding of Mining Watch Canada in 1999, which monitors and analyzes the Canadian mining industry's activities. Reversing these trends has been a slow process, dependent on the struggles and legal battles of miners and labour organizations, farmers and Aboriginal communities, and members of the modern environmental movement. More often than not, taxpayers bear the burden of paying for cleanups.

Works Cited

Allum, James. 1995. "Smoke across the Border: The Environmental Politics of the Trail Smelter Investigation." PhD thesis, Queen's University.

Anton, Frank R. 1981. *The Canadian Coal Industry: Challenge in the Years Ahead.* Calgary: Detselig Enterprises Ltd.

Baldwin, Doug, and John Dunn. 1976. *Cobalt: A Pictorial History.* Cobalt: Highway Book Shop.

Campbell, Claire Elizabeth. 2005. *Shaped by the West Wind: Nature and History in Georgian Bay.* Vancouver: UBC Press.

Hazlitt, William Carew. 1974. *The Great Gold Fields of Cariboo.* Victoria: Klanak Press.

Kerr, Donald, and Deryck Holdsworth. 1990. *Historical Atlas of Canada.* Vol. 3, *Addressing the Twentieth Century.* Toronto: University of Toronto Press.

Martell, J.S. 1980. "Early Coal Mining in Nova Scotia." In *Cape Breton Historical Essays,* edited by Don MacGillivray, 41-53. Sydney: College of Cape Breton Press.

Moses, Arthur. 1981. "Union-Picked Inspectors Will Have the Authority to Close Uranium Mines." *Globe and Mail,* 7 September, 4.

Mouat, Jeremy. 1995. *Roaring Days: Rossland's Mines and the History of British Columbia.* Vancouver: UBC Press.

Muise, Del. 1980. "The Making of an Industrial Community: Cape Breton Coal Towns, 1867-1900." In *Cape Breton Historical Essays,* edited by Don MacGillivray, 76-94. Sydney: College of Cape Breton Press.

Munton, Don. 2002. "Fumes, Forests and Further Studies: Environmental Science and Policy Inaction in Ontario." *Journal of Canadian Studies* 37, 2: 130-63.

Sterne, Netta. 1998. *Fraser Gold 1858: The Founding of British Columbia.* Pullman: Washington State University Press.

Tataryn, Lloyd. 1979. *Dying for a Living.* Montreal: Deneau and Greenberg Publishers.

Zaslow, Morris. 1971. *The Opening of the Canadian North, 1870-1914.* Toronto: McClelland and Stewart.

For Further Reading

The Geological Survey of Canada

Campbell, Claire Elizabeth. 2005. *Shaped By the West Wind: Nature and History in Georgian Bay.* Vancouver: UBC Press.

Cronin, Marionne. 2007. "Northern Visions: Aerial Surveying and the Canadian Mining Industry, 1919-1928." *Technology and Culture* 48, 2: 303-30.

Zaslow, Morris. 1975. *Reading the Rocks: The Story of the Geological Survey of Canada, 1842-1972.* Ottawa: Macmillan of Canada.

Zeller, Suzanne. 1991. "Mapping the Canadian Mind: Reports of the Geological Survey of Canada, 1842-1863." *Canadian Literature* 131 (Winter): 156-67.

Coal Mining

Cameron, Silver Donald. 1999. "Last Call for Cape Breton Coal." *Canadian Geographic,* November-December, 32-40.

Frank, David. 1980. "The Cape Breton Coal Industry and the Rise and Fall of the British Empire Steel Corporation." In *Cape Breton Historical Essays,* edited by Don MacGillivray, 110-28. Sydney: College of Cape Breton Press.

Martell, J.S. 1980. "Early Coal Mining in Nova Scotia." In *Cape Breton Historical Essays,* edited by Don MacGillivray, 441-53. Sydney: College of Cape Breton Press.

Muise, Del. 1980. "The Making of an Industrial Community: Cape Breton Coal Towns, 1867-1900." In *Cape Breton Historical Essays,* edited by Don MacGillivray, 76-94. Sydney: College of Cape Breton Press.

Newsome, Eric. 1989. *The Coal Coast: A History of Coal Mining in British Columbia, 1835-1900.* Victoria: Orca.

Ripley, Earle A., Robert E. Redman, and Adele A. Lowder. 1996. *Environmental Effects of Mining.* Delroy Beach, FL: St. Lucie Press.

Roderick, John. 2003. *When Coal Was King: Ladysmith and the Coal-Mining Industry on Vancouver Island.* Vancouver: UBC Press.

British Columbia and Yukon

Allum, James. 1995. "Smoke across the Border: The Environmental Politics of the Trail Smelter Investigation." PhD thesis, Queen's University.

Fisher, Robin A. 1992. *Contact and Conflict: Indian-European Relations in British Columbia, 1774-1890.* Vancouver: UBC Press.

Hazlitt, William Carew. 1974. *The Great Gold Fields of Cariboo.* Victoria: Klanak Press.

Morse, Kathryn. 2003. *The Nature of Gold: An Environmental History of the Klondike Gold Rush.* Seattle: University of Washington Press.

Mouat, Jeremy. 1995. *Roaring Days: Rossland's Mines and the History of British Columbia.* Vancouver: UBC Press.

Sterne, Netta. 1998. *Fraser Gold 1858: The Founding of British Columbia.* Pullman: Washington State University Press.

Wirth, John D. 1996. "The Trail Smelter Dispute: Canadians and Americans Confront Transboundary Pollution, 1927-1941." *Environmental History* 1, 2: 34-51.

Northern Ontario and Quebec

Baldwin, Doug, and John Dunn. 1976. *Cobalt: A Pictorial History.* Cobalt: Highway Book Shop.

MacDowell, Laurel Sefton. 2001. *"Remember Kirkland Lake": The Gold Miners' Strike of 1941-42.* Toronto: Canadian Scholars' Press.

Munton, Don. 2002. "Fumes, Forests and Further Studies: Environmental Science and Policy Inaction in Ontario." *Journal of Canadian Studies* 37, 2: 130-63.

Nelles, H.V. 1975. *The Politics of Development: Forests, Mines and Hydro-Electric Power in Ontario 1849-1941.* Toronto: Macmillan of Canada.

Tataryn, Lloyd. 1979. *Dying for a Living.* Montreal: Deneau and Greenberg Publishers.

Trudeau, Pierre. 1974. *The Asbestos Strike.* Toronto: James, Lewis and Samuel.

The Far North

Hamilton, John David. 1994. *Arctic Revolution: Social Change in the Northwest Territories, 1935-1994.* Toronto: Dundurn.

Jenkins, Robert G. 1999. *The Port Radium Story.* Summerland, BC: Valley.

Piper, Liza. 2009. *The Industrial Transformation of Subarctic Canada.* Vancouver: UBC Press.

Zaslow, Morris. 1988. *The Northward Expansion of Canada, 1914-1967.* Toronto: McClelland and Stewart.

Mining Towns

Angus, Charlie, and Susan Meurer. 1997. *Carved from the Rock.* Toronto: Miners' History Project, USW.

Barlow, Maude, and Elizabeth May. 2000. *Frederick Street: Life and Death on Canada's Love Canal.* Toronto: Harper Collins.

Fancaviglia, Richard V. 1991. *Hard Places: Reading the Landscape of America's Historic Mining Districts.* Iowa City: University of Iowa Press.

Lucas, Rex. 1971. *Minetown, Milltown, Railtown: Life in Canadian Communities of Single Industry.* Toronto: University of Toronto Press.

Tait, D.T. 1963. "Haileybury: The Early Years." *Ontario History* 55, 4: 192-204.

Mines and Miners: The Interior Environment
Brophy, James T., Margaret M. Keith, and Jenny Schieman. 2007. "Canada's Asbestos Legacy at Home and Abroad." *International Journal of Occupational and Environmental Health* 13, 2: 236-43.

Marvin Shaffer and Associates. 1982. *Impacts of Canada's Uranium Mining Industry.* Study 14. Calgary: Canadian Energy Research Institute.

Storey, Robert. 2004. "From the Environment to the Workplace ... and Back Again?" *Canadian Review of Sociology and Anthropology* 41, 4: 419-47.

6

Cars, Consumerism, and Suburbs

The car has become an article of dress without which we feel uncertain,
unclad, and incomplete in the urban compound.

— MARSHALL MCLUHAN, MEDIA GURU, *UNDERSTANDING MEDIA*, 1964

JUST AS INDUSTRIALISM and the transition from country living to the city changed people's sense of time, automobiles changed their use of space and put new pressures on the environment. Cars, like the bicycles that came before them, enhanced individual freedom, mobility, and comfort (see Figure 6.1). They democratized mobility and leisure, enabling more Canadians to travel to their cottages, visit and camp in national parks, and take cross-country road trips. But car dependency and auto manufacturing also desensitized people to the natural world and polluted the environment. The early supremacy of gasoline-driven cars over other alternatives, such as electric cars, had profound implications for the environment, and Canadians did not realize the consequences until the late twentieth century. Love of cars fuelled the expansion of vast road networks and suburbs, increased demand for metals and fossil fuels, and made the auto industry the centrepiece of the new consumer-driven economy of the postwar era. After the Second World War, Canada took its place among developed nations, which were characterized by industrialism, rising standards of living, and the baby boom. Policy makers and citizens alike viewed the production and consumption of new material goods such as cars and household appliances as the embodiment of progress. They "promised the cachet of the modern and the practicality of easy maintenance and durability" (Owram 1996, 77). Consumerism had such a profound influence on attitudes, lifestyles, and work habits that the promotion of sustainable practices and lifestyles in the current era of climate change is a tough sell.

The Auto Industry and Car Ownership

Transportation and travel before the invention of the gasoline-driven internal combustion engine were defined by their limitations. Because travel by foot, water, or horse-drawn carriage was slow, difficult, and often uncomfortable, life centred on local communities that, by modern standards, had infrequent interactions and communications with the outside world. Railways connected communities and became symbols of

THE BICYCLE

In 1869, Henry Poole in Glace Bay, Nova Scotia, and John Kerr in Perth, Ontario, imported the first "boneshakers" from Europe and became dedicated cyclists. Cycling became a craze over the next thirty years, and every town had a bike club by the 1890s. In 1897, when the owners of Toronto's streetcars wanted to run them on Sundays to make more money, outraged churchgoers who opposed doing business on the Sabbath encouraged citizens to ride bikes, some of which were sold by the Methodist Bicycle Company. The bicycle craze died as cars became more affordable and popular. Canadians did not again embrace cycling as a form of transportation until the 1980s, when environmental concerns and health issues rather than religion proved to be the primary motivations.

FIGURE 6.1 Norman and Adam Ballantyne with their bicycles in Ottawa, 1897. The cycling craze swept North America in the late nineteenth century, and with improvements such as pneumatic tires, it became a speedy, pleasant way to travel.

May Ballantyne, photogapher, Library and Archives Canada, James Ballantyne fonds, PA-132226

industrialism and nation building in Western countries, but they represented only one short stage in the transportation revolution. In 1841, Thomas Roy, a Canadian surveyor and civil engineer, predicted in a pamphlet on roads that "steam carriages" operating on adequately planned roads would compete with railways. His observations were prescient: within a few short decades, the invention and mass production of the bicycle and automobile revolutionized personal and commercial travel.

American companies and gasoline-driven cars eventually dominated the North American auto industry, but Canadian mechanics, engineers, and companies participated in the rush to invent the "horseless carriage" – run on steam, electricity, or gasoline – a process that continued until mass production by large companies dominated. Watchmaker Henry Seth Taylor, inspired by steam loco-

motives, made the first Canadian car in 1867 when he mounted a steam engine on the back of a carriage. The car was hot, dangerous, and had no brakes. In 1893, only seven years after Karl Benz of Germany had patented the world's first practical gasoline-fired internal combustion engine, Frederick Featherstonhaugh, working with William Still, built Toronto's first electric car. Although steam power was at its peak, Featherstonhaugh thought steam engines were dangerous, and he wanted to avoid the noise of gasoline-powered cars. In 1897, Still set up the Canadian Motor Syndicate to sell vehicles that ran on batteries, but the syndicate went out of business for lack of capital. Early electric cars were smooth and silent, but they were not fast. George Foots Ross of Sherbrooke, Quebec, built Canada's first gasoline-driven car, the Crestmobile, in 1897, the same year that John Moodie, the

EARLY ELECTRIC CARS

Before gasoline-powered cars became standard, mechanics and engineers experimented with electric cars, which became a niche market directed at women in the early years of mass production. From the beginning, women enjoyed driving cars as much as men did, and several manufactories made electric cars for a niche market of wealthy ladies, who disliked trolley cars and the grease from early gasoline cars. The cars had no cranks or gears, lacked speed, could be driven on sidewalks, and needed to be recharged every 35 kilometres. Electric cars continued to be produced until the First World War, but gasoline-fuelled cars eventually triumphed as power tests and auto races publicized their superior performance. Most families could afford only one vehicle, and the electric car could not easily manage bad roads. One area where electric cars had some success was public transportation. New York City, for instance, ran up to a thousand electric taxicabs between 1897 and 1907.

founder of Canada's first automobile club, bought his first gas car, a one-cylinder Winton, which resembled a horse-drawn carriage but had a motor under the seat. Montreal's first car, a steam-driven Waltham, built in 1899, used kerosene to produce steam to turn the wheels.

The first truly successful Canadian automobile was the Russell, which appeared in 1905 (see Figure 6.2). Built in Toronto by Tom Russell, the owner of the Canada Cycle and Motor Company (CC&M), a large bicycle company, the Russell car revived the company's declining fortunes as the bicycle craze waned. It featured right-hand drive and a column-mounted gearshift, an innovation not adopted by other manufacturers until the late 1930s. The Russell Motor Company was formed in 1911 to build and distribute the cars, which sold for thirteen hundred dollars. The company was sold to the US manufacturer Willys-Overland in 1915.

A number of developments contributed to the triumph of gasoline-run vehicles over other options, the most important being their speed, the discovery of large oil fields in Texas in 1901, and the development in 1913 of a quicker method to refine "motor spirits" from crude oil. North American companies became leaders in the science of mass production. In 1899, some thirty American companies produced about six hundred vehicles each year. In 1901, however, Ransom E. Olds began to use the assembly line to manufacture cars in Detroit. His factory's output leaped from 425 cars in 1901 to 2,500 in 1902. In 1903, Henry Ford, a bicycle mechanic, also began producing cars by assembly line in Michigan. The first Model T rolled off the assembly line in 1908. In 1913, Ford introduced a conveyor belt to the assembly line, thereby converting a pleasure vehicle for the elite into a product for mass consumption. Mass production made the diffusion of the automobile in North America possible. As the costs of production fell, the price of cars dropped and became affordable to most families. As the industry became more competitive, offering consumers more choice, car prices dropped 38 percent between 1920 and 1924.

The Model T was touted as the "people's car": it was priced reasonably, was produced on schedule, had a twenty-horsepower engine that was easy to repair, and went 60 kilometres an hour. It was not easy to start, but it ran well and in 1912 was upgraded with an electric self-starter to replace the hand crank. People loved the Model T, and within a few years Ford was producing half the automobiles in North America. With competition from Chrysler and General

FIGURE 6.2   A line of Russell cars sits outside Toronto City Hall in 1909. The builder, Tom Russell, sits beside the driver in the first car.
Toronto Reference Library, 966-1-6

Motors, however, sales began to decline. Ford discontinued the Model T in 1926 and introduced the Model A one year later. The model sold half a million vehicles in two weeks in North America but had to compete with the La Salle and the Chevrolet from General Motors and with luxury cars such as the Dousenberg Model A and E.L. Cord's Model J.

When Canada failed to develop a home-grown auto industry, it became the home of branch plants of American companies. The Ford Motor Company of Canada was established in 1904 to manufacture and sell Fords in Canada and the British Empire. Canadian investors held a 49 percent interest. General Motors of Canada came about when the McLaughlin brothers, sons of the dean of Canadian carriage builders, decided to build automobiles. In 1915, the two men signed a contract to manufacture Chevrolets in Canada. In 1918, General Motors bought Chevrolet, and the Canadian company

became a subsidiary of the American company. Between 1918 and 1923, Canada became the second-largest carmaker in the world. Locating plants in Canada allowed US auto companies to skirt around Canada's high tariff on imported manufactured products. Canadian-produced automobiles were also eligible for the low tariff advantage known as British Preference when they were shipped to other countries in the Empire. Cities such as Oshawa and Windsor in southern Ontario came to be defined by their large car factories and large industrial workforces.

Automobile ownership spread quickly in Canada. In 1920, there were approximately 400,000 cars and trucks registered in the country – one-third in Ontario and as many in the West. A decade later, there was one car for every ten Canadians, except in British Columbia, where the ratio was one for every seven. Although city people were the first to buy cars, the Model T appealed to farmers because cars saved them time. Ford, born in the countryside, understood the isolation and toil associated with rural life. Going to town by horse and buggy could take a day. Farmers drove into town to get groceries or visit friends, and they adapted their cars for different chores, such as sawing wood, grinding grain, or hauling newborn calves. In 1931, 42 percent of Canadian farmers owned a car. Even though car sales waned during the Great Depression, one in nine Canadians owned a car in 1939.

On the eve of the Second World War, automakers envisaged a future in which the car would remake society, both physically and culturally. At the 1939 New York World's Fair, attended by 50 million visitors, General Motors featured a Super City composed of networks of throughways and countless cars. The industry experimented with futuristic streamlined designs. During the war, however, the 1941 car models were the last produced for civilian use. The car industry employed its mass production techniques to produce for the war effort. Canadian factories turned out 4 million military vehicles a year, as well as airplanes, parts, and tanks. Ford Canada produced twenty-one bombers a day. Jeeps, built at a rate of thirty an hour, served as a general-purpose vehicle – nicknamed "the G.I. mule" by soldiers.

In the postwar era of the baby boom and mass consumption, North Americans who had endured the Depression and war were bursting to spend. Those with wartime jobs had saved a little money, and war veterans quickly found jobs. A "golden age" of prosperity opened and lasted until the early 1970s. Among the first items purchased was a family car, and the number of automobiles in

TABLE 6.1 Cars in Canada, 1920-2011	
Year	Number registered
1920	402,999
1945	1,497,000
1950	2,600,000
1954	3,644,589
1963	6,074,655
1980	12,000,000
2011	26,000,000

Sources: Davies (1989, 200); Morton (1998, 29, 51, 61, 81); Transport Canada, http://www.tc.gc.ca/.

Canada more than doubled between 1945 and 1954 (see Table 6.1). The 1950s ushered in unprecedented consumerism, and the North American car industry reflected the prevailing mood of optimism and increased wealth. The automobiles of the decade were large, colourful, and had extravagant details such as fins. These huge behemoths stimulated the car culture of the modern era, a culture enhanced by advertising and an expanding automobile industry. In the 1960s, when the first baby boomers turned sixteen, car ownership surged to one car for every three Canadians. By 1980, there was one car for every two Canadians.

Roads and Infrastructure

The revolution in transportation had immediate and long-term consequences for the environment. Car factories and steel-manufacturing companies transformed the landscape of southern Ontario, the "Golden Horseshoe," into the industrial heartland of the nation, complete with traffic congestion and smog. The burgeoning automobile industry also fuelled demand for parts, tires, and fuel. By 1923, 2,500 service stations dotted intersections and roadsides throughout the country. With more cars, Canada needed more and better roads, which also resulted in dramatic environmental changes in a spatial sense. In the United States, the National Highway Movement demanded more roads, and in 1913 the Canadian Good Roads Association and the Canadian Automobile Association followed its lead and campaigned for improved roads to better link Canadian cities, Canada and the United States, and urban and rural communities.

The federal government passed the Highway Act in 1919 and offered $20 million in funding for roads. Over the next decade, the provinces put gravel on the surface of 130,000 kilometres – about a quarter – of the nation's roads. By 1937, Canada had 160,000 kilometres of surfaced roads, many built by unemployed men on public works projects during the Depression. In 1939, Ontario opened its first highway, the Queen Elizabeth Way. The highway linked cities in the Golden Horseshoe but destroyed fruit farms throughout the Niagara Peninsula. During the 1940s and 1950s, the government expanded the highway to four and then six lanes to deal with traffic congestion in the region. In the 1950s and 1960s, provincial governments spent billions to build, pave, and widen highways to accommodate millions of cars. W.A.C. Bennett's government in British Columbia spent more money paving existing roads and expanding the road system than had been spent in the history of the province.

In 1949, the federal government announced its plan to build a Trans-Canada Highway. The highway, one of the longest in the world, took twenty years to build and one billion dollars to complete (see Figure 6.3). Like the national railway before it, it

AIR TRAVEL

The airline industry supplemented the expansion of traffic networks on the ground. After the Second World War, Canada's aeronautics industry converted over to peacetime purposes, including mapping the North, transporting mail and goods, and providing growing numbers of business and vacationing travellers a quick, safe form of travel. In 1961, Canada's two major airlines, Air Canada and Canadian Airlines, began jet service. Like automobiles, planes create enormous amounts of pollution. They are a major source of greenhouse gas emissions and a significant contributor to global climate change. In a voluntary agreement with the federal government, the airline industry promised to improve its energy use by 24 percent between 1990 and 2012.

fulfilled a dream to link regions of the country. Completed in 1971, the highway also symbolized the transition from railways to cars, trucks, and planes as the main means of transportation. In the North, the United States built the Alaska Highway through British Columbia and Yukon during the Second World War to connect its ground transport to the state of Alaska. After the war, the highway became a thoroughfare for commercial purposes, facilitated mineral exploration, and serviced adventurous tourists. In the late 1950s, Prime Minister Diefenbaker's Roads to Resources policy expanded the number of northern highways to enhance access to northern minerals and resources. Inexpensive fuel and the automobile industry's close relationship with the oil and gas industry hastened the spread of service stations, which by the mid-1990s numbered over thirteen thousand. Both industries, as powerful lobbyists, put pressure on governments to protect and promote their interests and profits and resisted attempts to regulate cars to protect the environment.

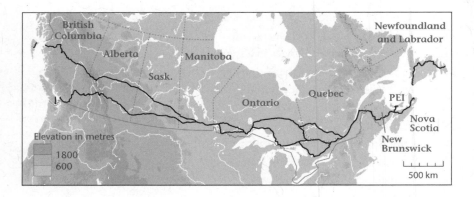

FIGURE 6.3 Today, the Trans-Canada Highway links citizens and provinces in a vast, expansive landscape. One of the longest highways in the world, it is recognizable by its distinctive white-on-green maple leaf route markers. Building the highway transformed the immediate physical landscape and also fuelled the automobile craze in Canada, which increased pressures on the environment in the form of air pollution and urban sprawl.

The Environmental Effects of Car Culture

The development of a road system for a country as vast as Canada was a technical and political achievement. But cars wreak havoc on people's everyday lives, communities, and ecosystems. Canadians, particularly in cities, had to accustom themselves to new sights, sounds, and smells. The odour of horse manure gave way to smells of car exhaust and gasoline. The clatter of horses' hooves and the rumbling of carriages were replaced with the sounds of cars starting, honking, stopping, and crashing. To prevent accidents,

cities put regulations in place to control drivers, cars, and pedestrians. Colourful traffic signs dotted cities and highways, and both pedestrians and drivers had to learn new, more regimented ways of navigating streets. Ontario's 1903 Motor Vehicles Act defined a speed limit for cars, warned drivers not to frighten horses, and forced them to equip their vehicles with lights and horns. Over the next forty years, speed limits increased from a low of 13 kilometres an hour to 50 kilometres an hour after 1945. As Canada became more car dependent, traffic laws favoured automobile use and marginalized mass transit

ON THE ROAD

As Canada's road network expanded and became more comfortable, people began to view driving as a form of leisure and entertainment. In a period when one-third of homes had no washrooms, stops along the road advertised public toilets. "Mom 'n' Pop" restaurants sprouted up overnight and motor hotels (motels), which

offered parking spots in front of rooms, were invented as a cheaper option to hotels. In the 1950s, people went to drive-in movies and flocked to drive-in restaurants where carhops brought fast food such as burgers or chicken directly to their cars. McDonald's opened in California, and its golden arches eventually spread around the

world. Convenience became a marketable commodity as car culture transformed North American lifestyles. By the end of the twentieth century, the drive-in or drive-through concept extended to gas stations, car washes, restaurants, and even banking machines. Writer Heather Robertson (1995, 334) notes that "the European tends

to regard the vehicle as an immediate extension of the person. By comparison, North Americans have tended to use the motor car as a container, an enclosed space." Recently, the tendency to do jobs while driving, such as conversing on a cellphone, has led to accidents and more regulations.

and bicycle use, two environmentally friendly means of transportation.

There was little public awareness of the car's environmentally destructive effects, even though automobile exhaust became a serious problem in Los Angeles, New York, and other large cities in the 1950s. In London, car emissions – which contain chemicals such as fine particulate matter, nitrogen oxides, carbon monoxide, and volatile organic compounds – surpassed factory smoke and gases as the greatest contributor to air pollution. Pollutants emitted from tailpipes contributed to both smog (a mixture of pollutants and ground-level ozone formed when nitrogen oxide and volatile organic compounds interact in sunlight) and acid rain (precipitation that contains elevated levels of hydrogen ions [low pH], which have adverse effects on forests, lakes and rivers, and soils). Acid rain kills insect and aquatic life forms and causes damage to buildings.

Profit motives outweighed environmental considerations. Low gasoline prices and higher profit margins encouraged car manufacturers to produce larger, less fuel-efficient cars, and the new, improved road infrastructure made faster, more powerful vehicles attractive. By 1968, the average car emitted more than twice the nitrogen oxide exhaust of the average car in 1946. The automobile industry took no responsibility for air pollution or automobile energy inefficiency. In 1953, the president of Ford Motor Company, when asked if the company planned to reduce auto exhaust vapours, denied any problem. Only in 1961 did General Motors introduce pollution control devices on cars sold in California – an innovation that cut carbon emissions by 25 percent. By 1966,

GRIDLOCK

Although automobiles represented freedom, by the end of the twentieth century, drivers, particularly in southern Ontario and Quebec, experienced gridlock – road congestion so severe that traffic comes to a standstill, resulting in more emissions and excess fuel consumption. At the turn of the twenty-first century, 90 percent of commuters chose to drive rather than take public transportation. Nationwide, the average time spent commuting to and from work increased from fifty-four minutes in 1992 to sixty-three minutes in 2005. The typical Canadian thus spends thirty-two working days a year sitting in traffic. The personal costs are high, but the environmental consequences are even higher. The cost of rebuilding comprehensive rail systems for commuters and travellers will be expensive, but they are more energy efficient, release fewer greenhouse gas emissions, and hold the promise of decreasing traffic congestion.

US Congress was pressuring the industry to put exhaust control devices on all new cars. In 1969, the antitrust division of the American Justice Department filed a civil complaint against the four major automakers for conspiring to delay the development of anti-pollution devices. The case was settled out of court, and the companies agreed not to cause future delays.

Postwar consumer culture and advertising by the auto industry, which emphasized the positive attributes of automobiles, made changing public awareness and attitudes about cars a slow process. In 1967, Ralph Nader, a progressive American political activist, published *Unsafe at Any Speed,* in which he charged that North American cars killed or injured millions. The book made waves because car companies were seldom criticized. It drew attention to safety standards, which eventually led to seatbelts and their mandatory use in most Canadian jurisdictions. In Canada, consumer advocate Phil Edmonston

SPORT UTILITY VEHICLES: DEFIANT CONSUMPTION

When the United States passed laws to regulate the fuel economy and emissions of passenger vehicles in the 1970s, the auto industry responded by producing four-wheel drive sport utility vehicles (SUVs), which were classified as light trucks, or work vehicles with lower fuel-efficiency standards than passenger vehicles. By law, they could burn more gas and emit enormous quantities of carbon dioxide and other smog-producing pollutants. Studies indicated that SUVs were more likely to kill people in the cars they hit and were more likely to roll. Despite flaws in design, SUVs grew in popularity in both the United States and Canada. By 2003, they made up 17 percent of the Canadian market. Skilled advertising partly accounted for their popularity. "The SUV represents the height of conspicuous energy consumption. The extra size, weight, and power of the vehicles are rarely justified by the way their owners drive them" (Roberts 2004, 154). Ninety percent of SUV drivers use them for short city drives.

Historian William Rollins argues that the popularity of SUVs reflects "postmodern aspirations and anxieties" and embodies "a profoundly contradictory set of desires having to do with nature" (Rollins 2006, 686). If the advertisements are any guide, these desires range from a drive to control nature to a wish to be closer to it. In the age of climate change, these vehicles seem like a perverse example of consumerism and have been condemned by environmental protection organizations such as the American Sierra Club. The Toronto Environmental Alliance called SUV ads misleading "ecobunk."

---

criticized the car industry for producing defective products. He founded the Automobile Protective Association in 1968 and successfully pressured car companies to implement recalls. In the 1970s, he began to publish an annual car guide in his series *Lemon-Aid,* and he led class actions to get compensation for injury from the automotive industry. He was less "green" than Nader, whose *Unsafe at Any Speed* also included a chapter titled "The Power to Pollute," which documented the automobile's impact on air pollution and its contribution to smog. People only really began to understand the consequences of hydrocarbon emissions in the 1970s, when the environmental movement drew attention to the issue. Yet it was the price of gasoline, more so than environmental awareness, that changed people's attitudes toward their cars.

After the 1973 OPEC oil crisis, during which Arab oil-producing countries proclaimed an embargo that quadrupled the price of oil, some Canadians bought smaller imported cars because they were more fuel-efficient. The crisis heightened awareness of North America's oil dependence and led to experiments in oil conservation and the development of alternative technologies.

The United States lowered the speed limit to 55 miles (88.5 kilometres) per hour, an option Canada did not pursue; it imposed price controls on domestic oil; and it rushed approval of a 1,287-kilometre pipeline to carry oil from northern Alaska to the port of Valdez on the southern coast. The global energy situation aggravated tensions among provincial, federal and industry leaders in Canada over the domestic price of oil, which climaxed in 1980 with Prime Minister Trudeau's controversial National Energy Program. But in 1974, for the first time since the invention of the car, Americans and Canadians reduced their gasoline use. In the 1980s and 1990s, however, when lower gas prices resumed, governments failed to introduce tougher fuel and emission standards, and auto companies refused to improve their product's energy use. In 1981, for example, Parliament passed a bill to increase fuel efficiency in all vehicles. The car industry, however, lobbied furiously against it and eventually undermined the legislation. Fuel efficiency actually worsened. The average new car got 9.4 kilometres per litre in 1988 and only 8.8 kilometres per litre in 2004.

Car companies and politicians acted more quickly to deal with lead pollution, which increased as cars became more numerous and powerful. In 1921, Thomas Midgley, a chemical engineer at General Motors, had discovered that adding lead to gasoline prevented engine knocks. Leaded gasoline soon became the norm throughout North America. Medical researchers, however, almost immediately noted higher lead levels in human bodies, a development that posed numerous health risks, particularly among children. The US government made low-lead gasoline available in 1971 and switched to unleaded gasoline for cars at the end of the decade, despite lawsuits by "interested" manufacturers. Canada followed suit. Between 1987 and 1994, ambient lead concentrations in the United States declined by 95 percent. The same reduction was apparent in a study of lead levels in Toronto's air between 1990 and 2005. Lead reduction has been described as "one of the most significant national-scale air-pollution-abatement stories over the last 30 years" (Di Menna 2005, 37).

In 1991, Pollution Probe estimated that over $4.5 billion in public funds were spent annually on the automobile in Ontario alone, including the costs for highway construction and maintenance, auto-related interest on the public debt, health care costs, and car-related policing. Road maintenance in Canada's extreme weather conditions meant expenditures on snowplowing, sand, and salt, which cause polluted runoff. The Toronto Board of Health estimated that about 1,500 people each year die during smog alerts, and Pollution Probe estimated that 6 percent of respiratory ailments in Canada were smog-related. In Ontario alone, respiratory diseases cost more than one billion dollars annually in health care costs and

absenteeism from work. Pollution Probe also calculated an additional $3.75 billion spent on indirect costs, including the loss of farmland caused by expanding roads and suburbs; crop damage from ground-level ozone; lost productivity due to delays, injury, and death; and environmental damage from acid rain. Although governments collect revenue from auto corporations, provincial and federal gas taxes, and registration fees, the net loss annually is in the billions. The costs to the environment are incalculable.

Efforts to reduce emissions in the twenty-first century have developed slowly. In 2000, Toyota and Honda introduced hybrid cars into Canada. Sales were slow – there were only 2,000 in 2005 – until concerns about climate change and higher gas prices raised interest. Toronto introduced a few hybrid buses, and in 2000 Vancouver introduced the first hybrid taxi. In 2007, the BC government pledged to cut greenhouse gas emissions by at least 33 percent by 2020. All new taxi companies or additions to taxi companies were to be highly energy-efficient vehicles or hybrids. Canada also had two electric car companies, which produced Dynasty and Zenn vehicles, but the regulatory process

THE ENVIRONMENTAL IMPACT OF ONE CAR

In the mid-1990s, the Umwelt-und Prognose-Institut in Germany calculated the environmental impact of one car. Each car produces 28.4 tonnes of waste and pollutes over 442 million cubic metres of air. In its lifetime, a car will pollute over 2 billion cubic metres of air; it will emit 66.9 tonnes of carbon dioxide; and it will produce 29.7 tonnes of solid waste. The average car, over an average life span, produces enough emissions to sicken ten trees and kill three others. It costs society US$3,752 a year in pollution, general physical damage, injury, and noise – *after* deducting vehicle and fuel taxes.

raised roadblocks. Dynasty sold a few cars in British Columbia before the company moved overseas, but Zenn could sell cars only in the United States. Although GM developed the experimental EV1 electric car, which it displayed at car shows until 1999, it destroyed the model. It promised to develop hybrids, but its interest remained "muscle cars" until the financial crisis in 2008. Ford produced a hybrid truck, and Mercedes Benz introduced the small Smart car. The Smart car caught on in Europe but less so in North America.

The technology to make energy-efficient cars exists, but the auto industry and consumers have in general proved resistant. After Canada ratified the Kyoto Protocol on Climate Change in 2002, the auto industry exerted pressure on the federal government, which granted it exemptions from obligations to cut emissions. The auto industry then sought further concessions on the contributions it would make to fight global warming, seeking to avoid a proposal that it improve vehicle fuel efficiency by 25 percent by 2010. The Sierra Club supported holding the car industry to the 25-percent target, which would result in 5.2 million tonnes of carbon reductions by 2010. The government passed no regulations to implement the target. Only after a steep rise in gasoline prices did consumers reluctantly begin to trade in SUVs for more efficient, cleaner vehicles. As with the earlier oil crisis in 1973, environmentally friendly options became more popular because they were economically convenient. Only in 2009, in an economic crisis that reduced car sales drastically, did GM and Chrysler, with promises of billions of dollars in public bailout funds in the United States and Canada, display electric and hybrid cars at the annual car show in Detroit and think seriously about the production of smaller hybrid or electric cars. Even with support from automobile companies, however, North America still lacks the infrastructure for electric cars, such as stations to recharge or exchange batteries.

Urban Design and the Suburbs

Efforts to reduce Canadians' dependency on cars ran up against a car culture that had developed over a century. Cars appealed to Canadians because they offered freedom, flexibility, convenience, speed, and privacy. The automobile enabled longer commutes between home and work and allowed urban dwellers to travel easily between the city and recreational retreats in the countryside. The tourist industry expanded and became more inclusive. Thousands visited parks or "wonders of the world" such as Niagara Falls each year, and an estimated 2 to 4 million American tourists visited Canada each summer in the 1920s. For those women who could afford a car, life became less circumscribed. For teenagers, the automobile in the 1960s came to be associated with a new youth culture symbolized by drive-ins, cruising, and rock 'n' roll.

The irony was that the regulation of public spaces and social dislocation accompanied this newfound freedom. The automobile "generated a host of social, spatial and administrative developments that sharply altered the pattern of urban life" (Tarr 1984, 35). Whereas urban streets in the nineteenth century had been planned to serve the needs of communities (for play, processions, weddings, funerals, and commerce), in the twentieth century they were redesigned and planned to accommodate the automobile. Green spaces and local businesses in towns gave way to parking lots and gas stations. As streets ceased to be public spaces, house designs featured large back decks rather than front porches. As one or two cars became the norm for Canadian families, houses also expanded to include driveways, carports, and garages, and neighbourhoods gained wider streets. As the disconnect between Canadians and the physical environment grew, and as their neighbourhoods became less personalized, concerns about public safety and feelings of insecurity increased.

Changes brought on by the automobile, consumerism, and the persistent idea that city living was unhealthy helped fuel urban and suburban expansion across Canada. Originally, wealthy Canadians who sought distance from industrialized centres and more spacious natural landscapes occupied the earliest suburbs, which were countrified urban environments. But suburbs were adjuncts to cities and fundamentally urban in character, with residents who made their living from non-agricultural pursuits. Streetcar systems allowed some working-class families to move farther from their workplaces to modest suburbs that reduced congestion. They sometimes settled in suburbs located close to businesses that had chosen to move outside of city centres. In general, however, rapid economic expansion and population growth after each world war fuelled a middle-class exodus to the suburbs and centralized municipal development. Between 1883 and 1918, for example, Montreal absorbed twenty suburban municipalities and increased its geographical area twenty-five times.

From an environmental perspective, the creation and proliferation of suburbs led to low-density urban sprawl, which, in turn, either disrupted the countryside or erased it. Geographer James Lemon (1996, 4) describes the spatial pattern of commercial development that accompanied suburbanization: "Before 1900, commercial strips emerged along tramlines, then later with branch banks at main intersections. The suburban trend accelerated when department stores and insurance companies moved outward from downtowns in the 1920s, followed after 1945 by shopping malls and outlying office clusters, some adjacent to airports." Suburbs built after the advent of the automobile accommodated the car. As early as 1911, when the suburb of Lawrence Park was built in Toronto, the development was advertised in the *Canadian Motorist*. Suburban society became a "visual blight" of pole lines, shopping centres, neon signs, and gas stations that reflected a battle "of grey and green, artificial and real, authentic natural landscapes against modern consumer paradises" (Penfold 2004, 10).

The postwar era also saw the rise of large corporate suburbs, designed, financed, built, and marketed by large land developers and construction companies who were more concerned about profiting from the population boom than preserving the environment. These suburban developments restructured the landscape with unique urban designs that sometimes included industrial parks but always included a new type of retail centre, the suburban mall or shopping plaza, which had enormous asphalt parking lots geared, like the neighbourhood, to the automobile (see Figure 6.4). These companies followed

FIGURE 6.4 Aerial view
of Don Mills, Ontario,
1955. Don Mills, a mixed-
use neighbourhood in
the North York district of
Toronto, used to be farm-
land. Private enterprise
developed the area
between 1952 and 1965,
and it became a blue-
print for postwar sub-
urban developments in
Canada.
York University Libraries, Clara
Thomas Archives and Special
Collections, ASC00853

new housing standards set by the federal
government and had government funding
through the Central (later Canadian) Mort-
gage and Housing Corporation. Housing
starts increased from 40,000 in 1945 to
150,000 in the mid-1950s. Between 1951 and
1961, over 70 percent of new dwellings were
low-density, single-family homes, typically
bungalows with picture windows, modern
kitchens, front driveways, front- and backyards, and garages. Gradually, the houses
expanded in size, came to include double or
triple garages, and were constructed according to building codes that focused on economic and social but not environmental
standards. The ideal lifestyle associated with
the suburbs centred on the car, conspicuous

consumption, social conformity, the nuclear
family, and a gendered division of labour.
Men went to work in the city, women
shopped at the local mall, and family outings
with children usually involved a drive.

Few people understood that suburbanization on prime agricultural land contributed
to environmental pollution. In Ontario's
Golden Horseshoe, suburban expansion in
the 1950s ate up 6,000 to 8,000 acres (2,438
to 3,237 hectares) of forests in the Mixed-
wood Plains Ecozone per year, destroying
wildlife habitats and reducing biodiversity.
Environmental degradation came not only
from an expanding urban ecological footprint but also from the postwar revolution in
construction, which introduced destructive

mass-production techniques. Construction crews used heavy machinery to raze and level the ground and mount new developments, often in environmentally sensitive areas, such as wetlands, hillsides, and floodplains. As Ontario politicians learned during Hurricane Hazel in 1954, some areas were inappropriate for houses. People who lived on a floodplain in western Toronto died. Other developments, devoid of trees and with large tracts of pavement, destroyed wildlife and suffered from floods and soil erosion. Essential services – including water, power, and waste disposal in many suburbs – were often inadequate, contributed to water pollution, and raised sewage contamination issues. Because builders in the 1940s and 1950s built without concern for the environmental consequences, the increase in home building intensified the environmental impact of suburbs.

Consumer Culture

Life in the suburbs reflected a new urban postwar culture that revolved around consumerism, the fostering of a social and economic culture based on promoting a systemic desire to purchase goods and services in ever-greater amounts. The population explosion between 1945 and 1961 from the baby boom and immigration led to an expanding economy, higher wages and salaries, new technologies, and the increased consumption of goods, a central feature of life in the suburbs. The suburbs embodied the core values of Canadian society in the postwar era: "the primacy of laissez-faire development, individualism, the right to property, and the virtue of private domesticity" (Harris 2004, 31). In the new economy, the consumption of goods was linked to economic growth, which encouraged manufacturers to produce disposable products and engage in planned obsolescence. Postwar Canadians bought and wasted as never before.

Homeownership of a single-family dwelling in the suburbs was considered the ideal and was encouraged by all levels of government. In the typical family, the purchase of a house and car fuelled a whole host of expenditures and purchases that were seen as signs of progress and rising standards of living but vastly increased the ecological footprint of households (see Figure 6.5). In 1941, 80 percent of Canadian households depended on iceboxes; 90 percent used coal or wood for heating; only 60 percent had piped water; and only 50 percent had flush toilets. In 1961, by contrast, new homes came with central heating, fuelled either by oil, gas, or electricity; hot and cold water; flush toilets; and baths and showers. Once ensconced in their new homes, Canadians bought the latest, most modern appliances – refrigerators, ovens, automatic washers, dryers, and dishwashers – marketed as labour-saving devices. Television sets, once a luxury good, became a necessity in the late 1950s: 70 percent of Canadian households owned one by 1959. As millions of televisions sold, their prices dropped, as had car prices in the 1920s. Televisions, in turn, became an important vehicle for promoting new products, particularly to the so-called children's market. In 1960, Canada had fifty-nine television stations that reached 90 percent of the population.

Marketers also exploited postwar optimism about science and technology to feed

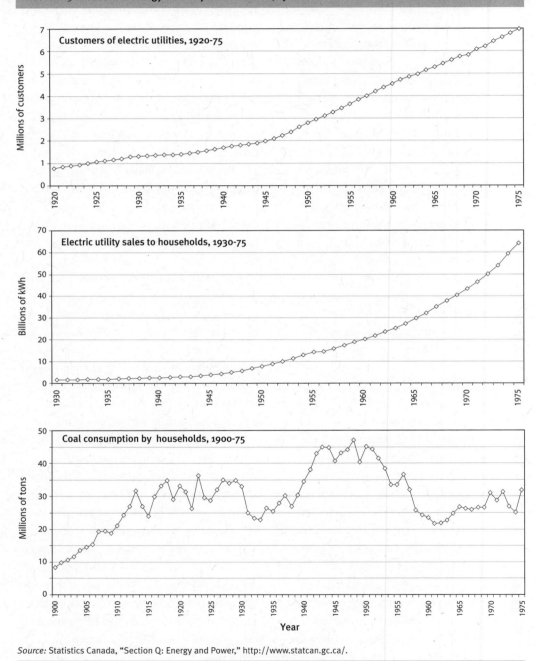

FIGURE 6.5   Household energy consumption in Canada, 1900s

Source: Statistics Canada, "Section Q: Energy and Power," http://www.statcan.gc.ca/.

the new consumerism. The chemical industry, for instance, celebrated and promoted "wartime miracles" such as DDT, a synthetic pesticide. Many so-called miracle products replaced older materials in the postwar decades: soap gave way to detergent; plastics replaced rubber, wood, and glass; and artificial fibres such as nylon and polyester took the place of wool and cotton. Linoleum flooring, made originally of seed oil and cork, was manufactured in the 1950s from cheaper polyvinyl chloride (PVC), a substance found to be toxic in the 1970s. As old linoleum deteriorated in landfills, it leached carcinogenic vinyl chloride into the soil and groundwater. Advertised as wondrous byproducts of an affluent modern society, chemically processed synthetics and plastics actually contributed to urban pollution and environmental degradation. Many synthetic materials were byproducts of petroleum and other nonrenewable resources and used energy-intensive manufacturing processes. In addition, the elaborate packaging that came with the new consumer products was often not biodegradable and was sometimes toxic. Synthetic materials and disposable goods filled up rapidly expanding landfill sites.

The undifferentiated suburban landscape and conformist lifestyle of the 1950s and 1960s changed people, the environment, and the relationship between the two. Contemporary observers and later critics pointed out that the gendered division of labour (with men as producers and women as consumers) isolated women and children in the domestic sphere. Women broke the monotony of their lifestyles by shopping, which for some became

an expressive but addictive habit. The suburban mall or shopping plaza was marketed as convenient one-stop shopping. The first Canadian mall appeared in Winnipeg in 1947, and forty-six others popped up throughout the country over the next four years. In 1962, Park Royal in Vancouver became the first Canadian shopping centre to be anchored by two department stores (see Figure 6.6). The malls promised a "new" shopping experience but were designed as "sites of consumption geared to maximize profits" in an environment that encouraged "liberal spending for better living" (Harris 2004, 131; Strong-Boag 1991, 494).

The culture of consumption, which promised that happiness was only a shopping trip away, created a society that encouraged people to define and identify themselves as consumers of goods, to view the environment simply as the source of exploitable resources, and to use disposable goods made increasingly from artificial materials that filled up landfill sites and took years to break down. Consumerism pushed environmental concerns to the background so that even Canadians concerned about the environment did not necessarily want to alter their affluent, comfortable lifestyles. Consumer society separated Canadians from the natural environment and replaced it with fast-paced city life – distinctive, convenient, and bursting with technology but also stressful. The experience of living in a developed country also separated Canadians from other peoples in the world, from places where the pace of industrialization was slower and levels of poverty greater. Consumer culture did

FIGURE 6.6 Park Royal Shopping Centre, West Vancouver, 1975. This photograph shows the prominence of the large department stores, the four-lane highway leading from the sub-urban area on the hill to the plaza, and ample parking spaces for ease of shopping.

BC Archives, I-21655

give rise, however, to an alternative counter-culture in the 1960s and 1970s that favoured whole foods over processed food, natural fabrics over synthetics, and environmentalism over materialism.

ECONOMIC TRENDS, SOCIAL conditions, and public policy supported the birth and growth of modern car culture, which reshaped the urban landscape just as Canadians sought to reshape their lives to fit the ideal of the nuclear family nestled in the suburbs. Urbanized consumers were not always aware that their very well-being depended on a

healthy environment. In the twenty-first century, however, it is general knowledge that cars cause traffic congestion and more pollution than industry, that fossil fuels will not last forever, and that the cumulative effect of modern life has been environmental damage resulting in climate change. North America's car culture is not sustainable, and some believe it is "an environmental, fiscal and social disaster" (Zielinski and Laird 1995, 69). We have become dependent economically and culturally on the auto industry and on oil and gas for energy. Although corporations and politicians have not actively advocated changes to create a more sustainable society, environmentally friendly hybrid cars are available, and modern cars could become as eclectic as those that cruised the streets of early towns and cities. Lifestyles involving more walking, bicycling, and public transit are also an option. Substantive changes in transportation policy will facilitate a healthier environment and adaptations to climate change.

Works Cited

Davies, Stephen. 1989. "'Reckless Walking Must Be Discouraged': The Automobile Revolution and the Shaping of Modern Urban Canada to 1930." *Urban History Review* 18, 2: 199-212.

Di Menna, Jodi. 2005. "Unleaded Leaves." *Canadian Geographic,* May-June.

Harris, Richard. 2004. *Creeping Conformity: How Canada Became Suburban, 1900-1960.* Toronto: University of Toronto Press.

Lemon, James T. 1996. *Liberal Dreams and Nature's Limits: Great Cities of North America since 1600.* Toronto: Oxford University Press.

McLuhan, Marshall. 1964. *Understanding Media: The Extensions of Man.* Toronto: Signet Books.

Morton, Desmond. 1998. *Wheels: The Car in Canada.* Toronto: Umbrella Press.

Owram, Doug. 1996. *Born at the Right Time: A History of the Baby Boom Generation.* Toronto: University of Toronto Press.

Penfold, Steve. 2004. "'Are We Literally Going to the Hot Dogs?' Parking Lots, Drive-Ins and the Critique of Progress in Toronto's Suburbs, 1965-75." *Urban History Review* 33, 1: 8-23.

Roberts, Paul. 2004. *The End of Oil: On the Edge of a Perilous New World.* New York: Houghton Mifflin.

Robertson, Heather. 1995. *Driving Force: The McLaughlin Family and the Age of the Car.* Toronto: McClelland and Stewart.

Rollins, William. 2006. "Reflections on a Spare Tire: SUVs and Postmodern Environmental Consciousness." *Environmental History* 11, 4: 684-723.

Strong-Boag, Veronica. 1991. "Home Dreams: Women and the Suburban Experience in Canada, 1945-1960." *Canadian Historical Review* 72, 4: 470-504.

Tarr, Joel A. 1984. "The Evolution of Urban Infrastructure in the Nineteenth and Twentieth Centuries." In *Perspectives on Urban Infrastructure,* edited by Royce Hanson, 4-60. Washington, DC: National Academy Press.

Zielinski, Sue, and Gordon Laird, eds. 1995. *Beyond the Car.* Toronto: Steel Rail Publishing.

For Further Reading

Melosi, Martin. 1993. "The Place of the City in Environmental History." *Environmental History Review* 17 (Spring): 1-23.

Rosen, Christine Meisner, and Joel Arthur Tarr. 1994. "The Importance of an Urban Perspective in Environmental History." *Journal of Urban History* 20, 3: 299-310.

The Auto Industry and Car Ownership

Armstrong, Christopher, and H.V. Nelles. 1977. *The Revenge of the Methodist Bicycle Company: Sunday Streetcars and Municipal Reform in Toronto, 1888-1897.* Toronto: Peter Martin Associates.

Duquet, Denis. 1984. "Automakers in Canada." *Horizon Canada* 1, 1: 44-48.

Flink, James J. 1988. *The Automobile Age.* Cambridge, MA: MIT Press.

Norcliffe, Glen. 2001. *The Ride to Modernity: The Bicycle in Canada, 1869-1900.* Toronto: University of Toronto Press.

White, Richard. 2007. *Making Cars in Canada: A Brief History of the Canadian Automobile Industry, 1900-1980.* Ottawa: Canada Science and Technology Museum.

Roads and Infrastructure

Kalbach, Warren E. 1999. "Spatial Growth." In *Special Places: The Changing Ecosystems of the Toronto Region,* edited by Betty I. Roots, Donald A. Chant, and Conrad E. Heidenreich, 77-89. Vancouver: UBC Press.

Laird, George. 1995. "Manufacturing Value: The Modern Auto Corporation." In *Beyond the Car,* edited by Sue Zielinski and Gordon Laird, 67-84. Toronto: Steel Rail Publishing.

Lewis, Tom. 1997. *Divided Highways: Building the Interstate Highways, Transforming American Life.* New York: Viking.

Pigott, Peter. 1997. *Flying Colours: A History of Commercial Aviation in Canada.* Vancouver: Douglas and McIntyre.

Robertson, Heather. 1995. *Driving Force: The McLaughlin Family and the Age of the Car.* Toronto: McClelland and Stewart.

The Environmental Effects of Car Culture

Carpenter, Tom. 2005. "Guzzler Growth." *Canadian Geographic,* May-June.

Davis, Donald F. 1986. "Dependent Motorization: Canada and the Automobile to the 1930s." *Journal of Canadian Studies* 21, 3: 106-20.

Di Menna, Jodi. 2005. "Unleaded Leaves." *Canadian Geographic,* May-June.

Engwicht, David. 1993. *Reclaiming Our Cities and Towns: Better Living with Less Traffic.* Philadelphia: New Society Publishers.

McCarthy, Tom. 2007. *Auto Mania: Cars, Consumers and the Environment.* New Haven: Yale University Press.

Roberts, Paul. 2004. *The End of Oil: On the Edge of a Perilous New World.* New York: Houghton Mifflin.

Rollins, William. 2006. "Reflections on a Spare Tire: SUVs and Postmodern Environmental Consciousness." *Environmental History* 11, 4: 684-723.

Sutter, Paul. 2002. *Driven Wild: How the Fight against Automobiles Launched a Modern Wilderness Movement.* Seattle: University of Washington Press.

Urban Design and the Suburbs

Baldwin, Douglas. 1988. "Sewerage." In *Building Canada: A History of Public Works,* edited by Norman R. Ball, 221-44. Toronto: University of Toronto Press.

Gad, Gunter. 1988. "The Suburbanization of Manufacturing in Toronto, 1881-1951." In *Patterns of the Past: Reinterpreting Ontario's History,* edited by William Westfall, Roger Hall, and L.S. MacDowell, 143-77. Toronto: Dundurn Press.

Guillet, Edwin C. 1966. *The Story of Canadian Roads.* Toronto: University of Toronto Press.

Lemon, James T. 1996. *Liberal Dreams and Nature's Limits: Great Cities of North America since 1600.* Toronto: Oxford University Press.

Penfold, Steve. 2004. "'Are We Literally Going to the Hot Dogs?' Parking Lots, Drive-Ins and the Critique of Progress in Toronto's Suburbs, 1965-75." *Urban History Review* 33, 1: 8-23.

Roberts, Wayne. 1995. "Blazing Saddles and Appropriate Technology: The Bike Path to a Green Economy." In *Beyond the Car,* edited by Sue Zielinski and Gordon Laird, 102-7. Toronto: Steel Rail Publishing,

Rome, Adam. 1994. "Building on the Land: Toward an Environmental History of Residential Development in American Cities and Suburbs, 1870-1990." *Journal of Urban History* 20, 3: 407-34.

–. 2001. *The Bulldozer in the Countryside: Suburban Sprawl and the Rise of American Environmentalism.* Cambridge: Cambridge University Press.

Spelt, Jacob. 1972. *Urban Development in South-Central Ontario.* Toronto: McClelland and Stewart.

Tarr, Joel A. 1984. "The Evolution of Urban Infrastructure in the Nineteenth and Twentieth Centuries." In *Perspectives on Urban Infrastructure,* edited by Royce Hanson, 4-60. Washington, DC: National Academy Press.

Consumer Culture

Belisle, Donica. 2003. "Toward a Canadian Consumer Society." *Labour/Le Travail* 52 (Fall): 181-206.

Cohen, Lizabeth. 2003. *A Consumer's Republic: The Politics of Mass Consumption in Post-War America.* New York: Knopf.

–. 2003. "Is There an Urban History of Consumption?" *Journal of Urban History* 29, 2: 87-106.

Crooks, Harold. 1993. *Giants of Garbage: The Rise of the Global Waste Industry and the Politics of Pollution Control.* Toronto: James Lorimer and Co.

Harris, Richard. 2004. *Creeping Conformity: How Canada Became Suburban, 1900-1960.* Toronto: University of Toronto Press.

Munton, Don. 1996. *Siting by Choice: Waste Facilities, NIMBY, and Volunteer Communities.* Washington, DC: Georgetown University Press.

Parr, Joy. 1993. "Household Choices as Politics and Pleasure in 1950s Canada." *International Labor and Working-Class History* 55 (Spring): 112-28.

–. 1997. "What Makes Washday Less Blue? Gender and Nation and Technology Choice in Postwar Canada." *Technology and Culture* 38, 1: 153-86.

–. 2000. "Reinventing Consumption." *The Beaver* 80, 1: 66-73.

Rutherford, Paul. 1990. *When Television Was Young.* Toronto: University of Toronto Press.

Strong-Boag, Veronica. 1991. "Home Dreams: Women and the Suburban Experience in Canada, 1945-1960." *Canadian Historical Review* 72, 4: 470-504.

–. 1995. "'Their Side of the Story': Women's Voices from Ontario Suburbs." In *A Diversity of Women: Ontario, 1945-1980,* edited by Joy Parr, 46-74. Toronto: University of Toronto Press.

–. 2002. "Home Dreams: Women and the Suburban Experiment in Canada, 1945-60." In *Rethinking Canada: The Promise of Women's History,* 4th ed., edited by Veronica Strong-Boag, Mona Gleason, and Adele Perry. Toronto: Oxford University Press.

PART 3

Harnessing Nature, Harming Nature

7

Changing Energy Regimes

*From the moment humans sought to control their environment, success
and material progress have been intimately bound up with the ability to
find and exploit greater, more concentrated sources of energy.*

— PAUL ROBERTS, JOURNALIST, *THE END OF OIL:
ON THE EDGE OF A PERILOUS NEW WORLD*, 2005

ENERGY IS BASIC to human life, and the inhabitants of North America have experienced a number of energy regimes, for the "history of energy utilization is one of substitution" (Deming 2000, 9). Aboriginal peoples relied on muscle power, burned wood for cooking and for warmth, and set fire to brush to attract the wildlife they hunted. Pioneer settlers relied on wood for heating and cooking and water to power mills. Steam drove early factories, boats, and trains, and some settlers used windmills. As settlers cleared land for agriculture and cities, forests declined. Industrialism demanded better heating and transportation systems and required large amounts of concentrated energy. By 1900, coal was also used to power machinery, railways, and the iron and steel industries. Although Canadians continued to use coal for heating and electricity generation after the Second World War, hydroelectric companies expanded their markets as consumption increased. Whether provinces depended on coal or reservoir hydropower

for their electricity, they were dependent on their energy source base. When gasoline-driven automobiles came to dominate the auto industry, fossil fuels became *the* energy source. Oil continues to be the largest source of energy consumption in Canada, but Canada is also the largest producer of hydroelectricity in the world. Its dams produce 60 percent of the nation's electricity. Hydroelectricity is a relatively clean source of energy compared to fossil fuels, but the damage dams do to landscapes and habitats is extensive and has contributed to the search for more renewable and sustainable forms of energy. This search is complicated by the fact that, since the 1960s, Canada's energy infrastructure has become increasingly interconnected with that of the United States.

Coal and Hydroelectricity

Canadians relied on coal because it was cheap, available in large amounts throughout the country, and well understood as an energy

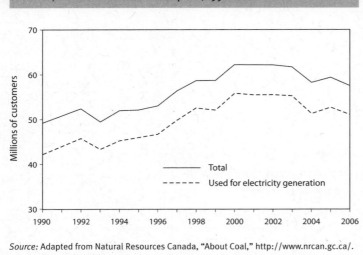

FIGURE 7.1   Canadian coal consumption, 1990-2006

Source: Adapted from Natural Resources Canada, "About Coal," http://www.nrcan.gc.ca/.

source. Mass consumption of coal required a production and distribution system, a corporate business model, a financial structure to build large capital projects, and the fostering of political relationships to protect investments (see Chapter 5). Coal was the first energy source to fuel a public culture of energy consumption – people understood that energy created wealth and rising standards of living. Although Nova Scotia dominated the coal industry in the mid-nineteenth century, western Canadian mines – particularly in Alberta – dominated production by the eve of the First World War. When oil and gas were discovered at Leduc, Alberta, in 1947, coal supplied 50 percent of Canada's energy needs. Over the next decade, petroleum products and natural gas almost replaced all coal used for domestic heating, industrial energy, and transportation energy. In the 1960s, however, a number of provinces began to use coal dust to produce thermal electricity. During the 1970s, when oil and gas

prices skyrocketed, attention turned to coal as an alternative energy source. In 2006, Canada consumed 58 million tonnes of coal. Most of it, was used to generate electricity in Alberta (74 percent), Saskatchewan (63 percent), Nova Scotia (60 percent), and Ontario (18 percent). In total, coal now supplies about one-tenth of Canada's energy needs (see Figure 7.1).

In the nineteenth century, people contrasted coal with hydroelectricity, dubbed "white coal" because it was considered a renewable and fairly clean source of power. In the 1850s, waterwheels and turbines drove machinery such as gristmills and sawmills. In 1882, Thomas Edison commissioned the first hydropower-generating station in the United States, and Canada followed suit three years later, building a station at Montmorency Falls to provide lighting for the city of Quebec. Over the next fifteen years, private electrical companies built stations in Sherbrooke, Trois-Rivières, Montreal, and Shawinigan. In Ontario, by contrast, the government entrusted the industry to state-controlled provincial and municipal agencies, such as the Canadian Niagara Power Company, to develop hydroelectricity at Niagara Falls and to keep it in Canadian hands (see Figure 7.2). Demand increased as individual electric motors replaced water- and steam-driven factory machines.

Combined demand for cheap hydroelectricity from industry, householders, and farms led to dam building on all major waterways (see Chapter 8). Using an inventory of viable waterways completed by the Commission of Conservation, entrepreneurs began to harness waterways to run small mills. In 1910, Clifford Sifton, head of the commission,

COAL AS AN "ALTERNATIVE" ENERGY SOURCE

After oil and gas, coal is the most abundant hydrocarbon in Canada. Environmentalists consider it problematic, because burning coal harms the environment and human health (see Chapter 5). Coal produces sulphur dioxide and fifty-three other trace elements – including particulate matter, carbon monoxide, hydrocarbons, and nitrogen oxides – into the air. It also contributes to greenhouse gases and climate change. Technological advances such as flue gas desulphurization units and particulate scrubbers make coal emissions cleaner, but the industry does not consider them economical, and politicians do not insist on their implementation.

Some environmentalists assert that even with the best available control technology, pollution from coal combustion remains unacceptably high and releases too much carbon into the atmosphere. Unlike incineration, in which coal is burned under high temperatures to produce heat energy, gasification converts the hydrocarbons in solid fuels such as coal or oil into syngas. Under intense heat and pressure, the syngas is then cleaned of sulphur and other pollutants. Gasification remains expensive, but it is cheaper than oil. Supporters claim that if gasification becomes commonplace, it will minimize emissions of sulphur oxide, nitrogen oxide, and harmful particulates. Opponents argue that gasification may be cleaner, but it still depends on coal mining, which has its own adverse environmental effects (Chapter 5). In addition, gasification produces carbon dioxide. Although scientists have experimented with carbon capture, a geoengineering technique to capture carbon dioxide in underground storage systems, the carbon dioxide could leak into the atmosphere. At this time, countries continue to experiment with the technology.

FIGURE 7.2 The hydroelectric industry began harnessing water for cheap electricity to spur nineteenth-century industrial production and to power electric light systems near local waterpower works. The process was most obvious at Niagara Falls, where "the potential for reaping power from the vast waters tumbling over the escarpment transfixed governments and developers alike" (Dempsey 2004, 65). The development of energy resources on the Canadian side of Niagara Falls also served to keep the industry Canadian. The three men pictured here worked on the early power plant at Niagara Falls around 1903. A. Lavigne *(on the left)* lost his life when he fell off the coffer dam. John McGee *(centre)* went on to work on many big construction projects. The man on the right is unknown.

Niagara Falls Public Library, OPG Collection, D421910

FIGURE 7.3
Hydroelectric power plants in Canada, 2009
Source: Canadian Centre for Energy Information.

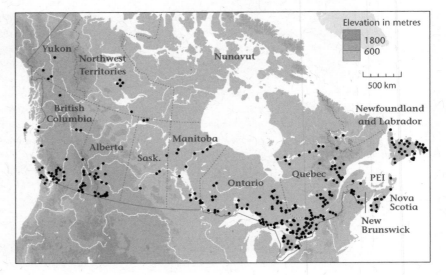

noted "a perfect epidemic of water-power legislation" and tried to influence policy so that "no perpetual franchise on waterpower should ever be given by a Government. Limited franchise might be granted, but the rate to be charged for power should be under public control" and by public utilities regulated in the public interest (Sifton 1910).

The system that evolved – public or private ownership – depended on the province. Private ownership prevailed in Quebec until

the provincial government established Hydro-Québec. Founded in 1944, the company became a major force during the 1960s, when the provincial government, as part of Quebec's Quiet Revolution, nationalized electrical utilities. In Manitoba, the hydroelectric industry supported both public ownership and private interests such as the Winnipeg Electric Company. Because Manitoba did not control its hydroelectric resources until 1930, the "federal government

---

A SURVEY OF CANADA'S WATER POWER

In the early twentieth century, the Commission of Conservation inventoried Canada's water power and published the results of its research in three volumes: *The Water Powers of Canada* (1911), *The Water Powers of Manitoba, Saskatchewan, and Alberta* (1916), and *The Water*

Powers of British Columbia (1918). The reports detailed, region by region, how the reshaping of the environment should be undertaken to tap Canada's most bountiful natural resource. For instance, in the chapter on Quebec, in Volume 1, the commission divided the

province into ten districts, listed their major rivers, and evaluated them in terms of the hydroelectric power they could generate. It pictured existing dams and new plants that would use the resulting electricity. Chapters on other regions took the same approach.

directly controlled entry into the industry and subtly influenced competition" in its system, which benefitted the consumer (Nelles 1976, 473). Later in the century, Manitoba consolidated its system, which became increasingly public. In 1960, the government established Manitoba Hydro. British Columbia's integrated utility, BC Hydro, was public until 2000.

Ontario's system resulted from pressure from the public power movement, led by Sir Adam Beck, businessman, politician, and hydroelectricity advocate. Beck wanted the province to nationalize electrical power resources so all users could have equal access to "this natural monopoly" and cheap power. Private interests, he argued, had failed to deliver inexpensive power to all businesses, including ones in marginal areas. Although the public power movement generated debate about "people's power" versus private power, the Conservative government, influenced by progressivism, decided in 1906 to establish the Hydro-Electric Power Commission of Ontario to develop, transmit, and distribute cheap power. The company built transmission lines to supply cities with electricity generated at Niagara Falls and other waterways, and it moved into power generation by buying up private companies. The provincial government's involvement in the industry was not unusual since "nearly one hundred Ontario municipalities operated a variety of municipally owned utilities: waterworks, electric street-lighting services, or gas works" (Humphries 1985, 77). By 1930, having absorbed its competitors, the Hydro-Electric Power Commission of Ontario had become the world's largest hydroelectric company. It operated generating stations that produced 75 percent of the province's electrical energy. A power unto itself, the company worked closely with successive provincial Conservative governments.

Both public and private utilities fuelled the expansion of Canada's hydroelectricity infrastructure. After the Second World War, hydroelectric companies grew by encouraging Canadians to "live better electrically." As electricity use exploded in the 1950s and 1960s, it unquestionably improved Canadians' standard of living, but it also contributed to consumer culture. The technology to "wire" large northern generating facilities into a national power network became available in the 1960s, but attempts to do so fell apart because the provinces wanted to control their own energy policies, which they linked to industrial development. Provincial policy makers preferred to develop an infrastructure that supported the export of surplus electricity to the United States. This approach led the provinces to become interconnected with US regional markets to such a degree that Canada would eventually accept deregulation and "the US neo-liberal agenda of free trade in energy, including electricity" (Froschauer 1999, 11). In the process, politicians increasingly viewed electricity as a commodity rather than a public service.

In 1974, the Ontario government reorganized the Hydro-Electric Power Commission into a Crown corporation and renamed it Ontario Hydro. As Canada's economy became more integrated with that of the United States over the next two decades, however, the provincial government embraced deregulation and privatization. In 1998, Ontario's energy minister introduced the Ontario Electricity Act and exclaimed,

FREE TRADE AND CONSERVATION

Canada and the United States signed the Free Trade Agreement (FTA) in 1988. The agreement removed trade restrictions in stages over the next ten years, and electricity was put on the table in the mid-1980s. In 1992, the United States deregulated its wholesale electricity market. Although Canadian electricity exports to the United States amounted to only 10 percent of overall production, provincial utilities responded by separating their transmission and generating systems. They joined US regional transmission groups and power pools; thereafter, the provinces had to follow US and FTA rules and open up their transmission systems to competition from both Canadian and American suppliers. Canada's mostly publicly owned provincial hydro systems were competitive with US power marketers because they supplied lower-priced hydroelectricity. These structural changes, however, limited Canada's ability to control prices or initiate serious conservation policies if their policies conflicted with the FTA's rules.

"The Adam Beck vision is at an end. There is a new vision for Hydro in Ontario" (Frame 2004, 25). In 1999, despite protest, the government replaced Ontario Hydro with five successor companies, two of which were commercial entities. One of the companies, Ontario Hydro Services Company, is responsible for transmission and retail services. Before the restructuring process was complete, increased prices, alienated municipal public utilities (which took Ontario Hydro to court and won a huge settlement in rate rebates), and the opposition of the public and hydro employees' unions to further privatization halted the process and resulted in a change of government. The new government tried to balance public leadership with private investment and gradually increased power supplies, but Ontario's public power tradition had been reversed. British Columbia, in 2000, also embraced privatization when it broke BC Hydro into private companies. Environmentalists in both provinces had pushed for conservation and renewable energy alternatives. In Ontario, environmentalists had also opposed Ontario Hydro's emphasis on nuclear power. Politicians were unresponsive, however, because they had embraced the neoliberal political agenda and free trade. Electricity had become but one commodity among many.

Electricity and the Environment

Electricity companies urged Canadians to live better electrically, and Canadians responded. Even though environmentalists began in the 1970s to urge Canadians to turn down their thermostats and use energy-efficient appliances and lighting, energy consumption increased as Canadians bought into the consumer culture. By 1997, 60 percent of Ontario households had air conditioners, which they used for half the summer. A third of Canadian households had a second refrigerator; three of five households had a dishwasher; three-quarters of households had an aging freezer (on average, over fifteen years old); and nearly a quarter had over three television sets. Only about a quarter of households used energy-efficient light bulbs. Thus, electricity consumption increased, despite the manufacturing of energy-efficient appliances and the use of more insulation in homes. These statistics do not take into account energy use by personal computers and home-security technologies.

As the electricity industry expanded, and in certain jurisdictions moved from the public to the private sector, it affected the environment in other ways. As the emphasis shifted from electricity as a service to electricity as a commodity that could be exported, companies and governments began massive hydroelectric development projects that required the construction of huge dams (see Chapter 8). These dams flooded large tracts of land, reconstructed major river systems, destroyed ecosystems, and had an incalculable effect on Aboriginal communities. Canada's dam building coincided with similar developments in other countries, and the total global construction of dams after the First World War contributed to a minute shift in the earth's rotation.

The provincial and federal governments were also guilty of overestimating demand, which led to surpluses that could not be utilized in other parts of the country because the industry's infrastructure was overbuilt. The result was waste. For example, Robert Bourassa, the premier of Quebec, had predicted that the province would suffer an

energy shortfall if the James Bay Hydroelectricity Project did not go ahead. In 1984, however, Hydro-Québec reported that half the James Bay plants were not needed during the winter and that all plants were available for electricity export during the summer because eastern US utilities had cancelled $32 billion worth of future contracts. Provincial utilities then claimed that surplus capacity would eventually be needed for the Canadian market and predicted hydro shortages in Ontario. Although Quebec and Manitoba had surpluses, Ontario could not use them because the infrastructure followed a north-south rather than an east-west trajectory. Regions with energy shortfalls had to purchase electricity from the United States, and prices increased. The underlying assumption that expansion would lead to further industrial development was not borne out. Instead, the projects fuelled primary industries and the creation of semi-manufactured products, such as pulp for export.

OPPOSITION TO MEGAPROJECTS AND THE NATIONAL ENERGY BOARD

The federal government created the National Energy Board (NEB) in 1959. In addition to its regulatory function – for instance, on the import and export of electricity – it serves an advisory function to the federal government, Parliament, and the general public. Because megaprojects such as the James Bay Hydroelectricity Project (see Chapter 8) had a disruptive impact on Aboriginal lands and ecosystems, Aboriginal groups and environmentalists spoke out against overbuilding and urged companies and governments to engage in environmental impact assessments *before* construction. These two groups were not given a voice in public hearings, however, because the hydroelectricity industry had shifted its emphasis to exports. The NEB's public hearings on various projects from the 1970s resulted in decisions that supported export licences and international power lines. Amendments to the National Energy Board Act in 1990 further weighted the regulatory process toward continental interests and often made hearings unlikely. Even when hearings did occur, they were controlled so the government did not mediate between opposing interests. Instead, the process favoured private hydroelectric businesses and neglected public groups who opposed developments for social, environmental, or economic reasons. The public received a one-sided view of the options. Thereafter, the only option for Aboriginal and environmental groups was the courts.

Oil and Gas

By the time Canada developed its oil and gas resources, the worldwide oil regime was well established. John D. Rockefeller had founded Standard Oil Trust, the largest oil company in the world, in 1870. The company, which integrated production, transportation, refining, and marketing, sought to profit as households switched from whale oil to kerosene for lighting. The rise and spread of the automobile and its use of gasoline – up to that time considered a nearly worthless byproduct of oil refining – brought untold profits. The passing of anti-monopoly legislation in the United States in 1911, however, broke the company into smaller companies. Mergers resulted in the creation of eight "majors," which came to control most of the international oil business.

Enlarged by war demands, oil company research led to the invention of oil-based products such as plastics and synthetic rubber, which flooded the market. The oil industry therefore became closely linked to consumer society as it supplied fuel for transport and materials for many products. As demand began to outstrip supply, the large companies became involved in exploration and development in new areas such as Canada, where reliable sources of oil and gas were found in Ontario and on the Prairies, and they became major players in geopolitics because the largest supplies were in the Middle East. With the formation of OPEC in 1961, global politics became more complicated and intricately connected to oil supply.

Fossil fuels were known to exist in northern North America in the fur trade era. A Cree merchant reported on the Athabasca oil sands to Europeans. He had sampled "that gum or pitch that flows out of the banks of that river" (MacGregor 1972, 35). Peter Fidler, explorer and fur trader, likewise noticed the oil sands in 1791, when he surveyed rivers for the North West Company. Canada's resources were not used until the nineteenth century, however, when crude oil was discovered at Petrolia, Ontario, in the 1860s and refined to make fuel products such as kerosene. Small refineries quickly sprang up and consolidated around London, Ontario, in the 1880s. Imperial Oil, the dominant producer, centralized its refinery operations at Sarnia, but Alberta became the main source of oil and gas.

In 1911, William S. Herron, a rancher, noticed oil seepages on Sheep Creek near Calgary. He purchased the land and formed Calgary Petroleum Products. The company studded three wells in 1913 and the following year struck a substantial flow of wet gas saturated with light oil, "the first successful well in the first major oil and gas field" (Taylor and Baskerville 1994, 413). In the 1930s, despite a global oil glut, companies made a number of oil strikes at Turner Valley, southwest of Calgary. The industry's investment of $150 million on exploration and development increased production in the 1940s. In 1946, Imperial Oil studded Leduc Oil Well No. 1, located near the old fur traders' trail from Edmonton to Rocky Mountain House, where, in 1799, the North West and Hudson's Bay Companies had set up rival posts at the end of the fur trade line on the North Saskatchewan River. When the Leduc well erupted in 1947, it ushered in a new era of prosperity for Alberta (see Figure 7.4). The Leduc field, twice the size of Turner Valley, expanded to include 1,278 wells and produced millions of barrels of oil. In the 1970s, estimates placed Alberta's oil reserves at 8 billion barrels.

The rapid expansion of oil exploration and discovery punctured the landscape with wells: "The land was dotted with oil pumps [sixteen wells for every 2.6 square kilometres] resembling prehistoric monsters in neatly fenced plots the size of a backyard garden" (MacGregor 1972, 294). When the Atlantic No. 3 Well, located near Leduc No. 1, first struck, oil and gas flowed so fast that craters formed in the surrounding soil. The oil and gas flowed into streams until workers put up dikes and laid pipes to collect and transport it. The well caught fire, drawing spectators and the media to celebrate the find. Oil wells also came with gas flares, or flare stacks, which burned natural gas that could neither be used nor transported. Flares not only wasted a valuable clean energy source, they emitted carbon dioxide, a greenhouse gas, into the air.

Canada has natural gas in abundance. Fur traders knew about seepages along the Peace and Athabasca Rivers, and they used gas to boil water in their kettles. Natural gas, at first viewed by the oil industry as a useless byproduct, was developed from the 1960s as

FIGURE 7.4 When Leduc Well No. 1 opened in 1947, it attracted spectators and the media, who celebrated the resource. This picture shows some of the bystanders and their cars on opening day. Harry Pollard, photographer, Glenbow Archives, IP-6f-18

GAS FLARES

In the 1990s, the environmental and social costs of gas flares grabbed headlines when Alberta ranchers, who owned their farms but not the resources beneath them, raised their voices in protest. The provincial government had allowed companies to increase the number of gas flares even though their emissions caused serious health problems, including miscarriages in farmwomen and in livestock. Gas companies took precedence, and the government failed to address the ranchers' complaints. In 1998, a respected rancher named Wayne Roberts killed oilman Patrick Kent out of frustration. Rancher Wiebo Ludwig, an infamous protester, was suspected of sabotaging oil and gas wells. The government responded by increasing security against ecoterrorism rather than regulating the industry to protect ranchers.

an important commodity in its own right. In 1970, it was estimated that Canada's reserves consisted of about 1,359 billion cubic metres. Like oil exploration, gas exploration ushered in a new era of surveyors and crews who perforated valleys, muskeg, and hilltops. In open areas, men with light trucks and drills made holes a few feet deep to set off dynamite charges. They then used seismographs to record the shock waves as they penetrated the strata to help them identify potential reservoirs. In Alberta, the surveyors moved north and west of Waterton Lakes, through Clear Hills and the Caribou Mountains, westward along the Chinchaga River, and then into Northwest Territories. When the crews entered northern forests and marshes, they used bulldozers to clear trails for the surveyors' trucks. Clusters of oil wells and long strips of gas wells sprouted in their wake. The "hitherto silent forests became a crisscross of seismic lines" (MacGregor 1972, 291).

Growing demand and the commercial value of oil and gas drove further exploration and development. By 1971, thousands of workers were heading west to take up jobs in Alberta's booming cities. Calgary became the headquarters of the oil industry, joining oil towns such as Devon, Redwater, and Swan Hills, which had been set up by oil companies and with government financing. The Redwater field had reached 926 wells in 1952, and in 1953 the Pembina field, southwest of Edmonton, contained 1,700 wells. American capital flooded the industry, enhancing Canada's foreign exchange position and contributing to unprecedented prosperity.

To market oil and gas, the industry built pipelines to Calgary and Edmonton, a major refining centre. Beginning with a short pipeline built from the Turner Valley field in 1947, other lines were superimposed on the landscape (see Figure 7.5). In 1950, when Alberta's refineries could not handle the huge supply, Interprovincial Pipeline completed an eastern line to Lake Superior, in Superior, Wisconsin. Trans Mountain Pipeline constructed a line to the West Coast three years later, and other lines connected to the Interprovincial line. Some carried oil or gas from northern Alberta south to Montana in the United States. The Alberta Gas Trunk Line delivered gas to TransCanada PipeLines for transport to Ontario, British Columbia, or California. In 1971, Alberta's pipeline network consisted of over 49,000 kilometres of oil pipelines, two-thirds of which also carried gas. Along the lines, processing plants sprouted up to treat oil, scrub the gas, and produce propane, butane, and sulphur. Petrochemical and fertilizer plants also appeared as offshoots of the oil industry, creating new consumer products in Canada that broadened the base of Alberta's economy.

The oil and gas industry brought not only prosperity but also boom-and-bust cycles and controversy regarding Canada's energy policy as the price of oil hit US$40 a barrel in the 1970s following the OPEC oil crisis (see Chapter 6), dipped in the 1980s, rose again to US$90 in the 1990s, and continued to climb until 2008. Between 1973 and 1979, rising oil prices created turmoil in the markets, to which North American consumers responded by conserving energy and switching to alternative energy sources. While governments researched new energy sources, companies began to explore new, remote oil sources such as Hibernia off the coast of

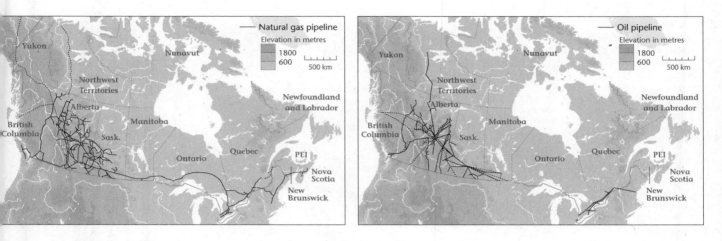

FIGURE 7.5 Major natural gas and crude oil pipelines, 2011
Canadian Centre for Energy Information

Newfoundland and the Athabasca oil sands. When oil prices fell in the 1980s and 1990s, interest in alternative sources decreased, and consumers resumed high-consumption patterns, including the purchase of gas-guzzling SUVs. This price shift was good for the oil and gas industry but not for the environment.

As with hydroelectricity, the Canadian government adopted a free market approach to the oil patch, beginning in the mid-1980s with repeal of the National Energy Program (NEP). The NEP had been introduced in 1980 by Pierre Trudeau's Liberal government to break a stalemate between Alberta and the federal government over energy prices and revenue sharing. Assuming that oil prices would continue to rise, the program designers believed it would ensure a secure supply throughout the country, redistribute wealth from oil companies to the federal government and consumers, and guarantee greater Canadian ownership of the industry. The Progressive Conservative Party dismantled

the NEP when it came to power in 1984. It scrapped reserve requirements for natural gas exports, and the energy-security provisions of the North American Free Trade Agreement guaranteed the United States equal access to Canadian resources.

In this free market context, companies began to develop crude oil in the Athabasca oil sands. Crude oil, an unconventional hydrocarbon resource, is harder to extract than petroleum from more accessible wells. The oil sands' development became viable, however, with technological advances in production and as oil prices rose in the late twentieth century. The Great Canadian Oil Sands (now Suncor) opened an oil sands plant in 1967. In the 1970s, the Alberta government established the Alberta Oil Sands Technology and Research Authority. The authority's researchers reduced production costs substantially, and Suncor began to produce oil profitably in the 1990s. As more big players entered oil sands development, Fort McMurray, the nearest town, received

FIGURE 7.6 Suncor Upgrader Facility and Millennium Mine Site along the Athabasca River, north of Fort McMurray, Alberta. Note the proximity of the Athabasca River to the huge fossil fuels development. Water is essential for processing oil sands, but crude oil comes at the price of polluted water systems, scarred riverbanks, open pits, dead fish, and low water levels.
Peter Essick, photographer, GetStock.com

an influx of workers. Housing pushed back the forest, and huge earth-moving equipment began to dominate the landscape. In 2008, Alberta's oil sands plants produced more than a million barrels of crude every day, and it is estimated that 300 billion barrels of oil could be recovered from the tar sands. This is enough oil to service North America for fifty years, and it constitutes the world's largest known reserve of oil.

From an environmental perspective, the Athabasca oil sands are an ecological disaster (see Figure 7.6). Extracting oil from concessions that cover 50,000 square kilometres is "the single largest contributor to Canada's greenhouse gas emissions" (Woynillowicz, Severson-Baker, and Reynolds 2005, 3.1). Because large amounts of water are required

to produce a single barrel of bitumen, the oil sands will probably lead to a crisis in the quantity and quality of Alberta's water. Companies also dump effluents into the Athabasca River, and there are now reports of higher incidences of cancer in nearby Aboriginal communities. In addition, vast tar ponds filled with waste from the industrial process are killing birds that accidentally land in them. The destruction of wildlife will continue as the project expands: "Researchers calculate that the mining of 300,000 hectares of forest, already scheduled by the oil companies, will destroy the habitat of between 480,000 and 3.6 million adult birds ... the loss of some 4.8 million to 36 million young over twenty years, climbing to between 9.6 million and 72 million by 2050" (Vincent 2009, 32).

Although the environmental effects of the Alberta oil sands are well known, the Canadian government supports the project and sees its development as a source of wealth. Oil companies influence government priorities and have stalled policies to combat climate change. The project is a good example of the new energy regime: we expend more labour and money to extract smaller quantities of fossil fuels because modern society remains dependent on oil. Oil predominates over other energy sources because, with its massive infrastructure, it can be delivered anywhere. High oil prices also mean maximum profits. Although oil and gas supplies are finite, they are in increasing demand in the twenty-first century. And even though the climate change issue and criticisms of the oil sands project have increased calls for a moratorium on oil production, the government continues to support the industry. Since 2006, Stephen Harper, prime minister and son of an Imperial Oil executive, has proclaimed Canada an emerging energy superpower. Canada signed the Kyoto Protocol, an international agreement that sets targets to reduce greenhouse gas emissions, on February 2005. But the Canadian government then announced that it would not even try to meet the targets, and in December 2011, it formally withdrew from the Kyoto Protocol. It was a drop in the price of oil in 2009 and the dismal state of the world economy that slowed production, not concern for the environment.

Nuclear Energy

Although oil and gas were Canada's major energy sources in the twentieth century, "harnessing nuclear energy for war and peace was arguably the most momentous event in the twentieth century" (Engels 2005, 2). During the Second World War, large amounts of Canadian uranium ore were sent to the Manhattan Project in the United States, which made the first atomic bomb. The United States built weapons either by enriching natural uranium or by making plutonium from the spent fuel of a controlled nuclear reaction. The Eldorado refinery in Port Hope, Ontario, which had good rail connections to uranium sources in the North, was crucial to the industry and processed 2,032 tonnes of uranium oxide between 1942 and 1946.

PEAK OIL

Although global demand for oil is increasing, supply has decreased since the end of the twentieth century, rendering exploration and development ever more difficult. M. King Hubbert, a geoscientist, became famous in 1956 when he formulated the theory of peak oil and speculated, "If a single oil well has a predictable life cycle of discovery, production and depletion, so too must the planet" (McKenna 2005, B15). Hubbert estimated that US oil production would peak in about 1970 and then decline. Hubbert's prediction that the fossil fuel era would be short was dismissed at the time but has since proven accurate in that *conventional* oil resources have moved beyond the peak and declined. However, the discovery of new extraction technologies and new sources of supply – such as Alberta's oil sands – has expanded oil resources in the last fifty years. Although Canada has large reserves such as the oil sands, output is unlikely to offset growing world demand. The processing of unconventional resources is also unsustainable from an environmental perspective.

England established its own wartime nuclear research project in Montreal and competed with the United States for Canadian uranium refined at Port Hope. The two countries did, however, exchange information about nuclear power. The Chalk River Laboratories, a collaborative wartime research project set up by England and Canada in 1942, launched the first nuclear reactor outside of the United States in 1945. The reactor used heavy water to control a nuclear chain reaction, and the new technology became the basis of Canada's military and civilian nuclear energy programs.

From the beginning, the nuclear industry had close ties to the federal and provincial governments. The Canadian government bought shares in Eldorado and then converted the company into a Crown corporation in 1944. Although Canada sold plutonium to the US nuclear weapons program, it studied peacetime uses for uranium. It established the Atomic Energy Control Board in 1946 to regulate atomic energy in Canada, and it set up Atomic Energy of Canada in 1952 to design, build, market, and manage reactors, do nuclear research, oversee nuclear waste management, and develop nuclear energy for peaceful purposes. Chalk River gained government approval in 1955 to develop nuclear energy for civilian use.

In 1951, the Atomic Energy Control Board opened negotiations with Ontario Hydro to build a nuclear power plant. When the world market for uranium collapsed in 1963, the Ontario government stockpiled the ore, and Ontario Hydro used it to produce nuclear power at the country's first nuclear power plant, which had opened at Rolphton in 1962 and had the first CANDU reactor. At the time, the province had no remaining untapped hydroelectricity sites and no oil, gas, or coal. It did, however, have plenty of uranium. The provincial government developed its nuclear energy capacity to service growing communities. Taxpayers subsidized the massive costs, and the government's partnership with the nuclear industry provided Ontario Hydro's personnel with training and status. In 1968, Ontario Hydro and Atomic Energy of Canada collaborated to build the second CANDU reactor, which operated at Kincardine until 1984. Quebec purchased two reactors, New Brunswick one, and Ontario expanded its nuclear output until it had nineteen reactors. In 1976, 5 percent of Canada's electricity came from nuclear power. In 1992, nuclear energy produced 48 percent of Ontario's electricity and 15 percent of the country's as a whole.

When climate change became an issue around 2006, the nuclear power industry promoted itself as a "green industry" on the grounds that nuclear energy does not release carbon dioxide into the atmosphere. In reality, generating nuclear energy creates

THE CANDU REACTOR

The federal government spent billions promoting nuclear energy in Canada and selling CANDU reactors abroad to India, Pakistan, Argentina, South Korea, and Romania. After India misused its Canadian nuclear reactor to develop a bomb, which it detonated in 1974, Canada renegotiated its contracts to include tougher but not necessarily more effective nonproliferation requirements. Sales dropped off after 1978, but in the 1990s, as the number of nuclear nations increased, Atomic Energy of Canada used aggressive marketing to introduce the next generation of CANDUs. It delivered nuclear plants to South Korea and China, sold a CANDU-6 reactor to China in 2003, and produced the compact ACR-700s, which use light-water cooling and increase power and safety at a reduced cost.

DRINKING-WATER CONTAMINATION AND THE SERPENT RIVER FIRST NATION

When the Serpent River First Nation learned in the late 1950s that uranium mining and milling had contaminated its water supply, Health and Welfare Canada assured local people they could use the water without facing health risks. Radiation levels were 6.2 picocuries per litre, well below the federal standard for reserves, which was 10 picocuries per litre. When the radiation levels became public, the Ontario government built water treatment facilities for the town of Serpent River alone. The water standard for Ontario in general was 3 picocuries per litre. The governments' response suggested that though the water was safe for Aboriginal people, it was unsafe for whites (Tataryn 1979, 102). Between 1957 and 1970, the Ontario Water Resources Commission repeatedly reported high levels of radioactive contamination in the Elliot Lake region and that radium concentrations in the Serpent River system were above the safe drinking-water level.

In 1971, the commission finally recommended using other water supplies. The province's Ministry of the Environment confirmed that radium levels were more than double the amount allowed by the province, and it warned people not to drink the water or eat the fish. By the mid-1970s, illnesses such as thyroid disorders and lung, stomach, and lymphatic cancers were prevalent among Aboriginal people in the area. Rosalie Bertell, an activist and scientist, documented the high incidence of illness among the Serpent River First Nation in a federal government report. In 1980, the Ontario government recommended that the band be compensated for environmental damage, and a lengthy but inadequate cleanup followed.

pollution at every stage of the production process, and the industry has frequently been insensitive toward the environment, its employees' health, and Aboriginal communities in Ontario, Saskatchewan, and Northwest Territories. Uranium mining involves the same hard work, dangers, and environmental disruptions as other types of mining, but it also exposes miners, communities, and the environment to radiation, which can be carcinogenic unless handled carefully.

After the ore is mined, it is milled to separate uranium from other elements in a chemical treatment process. At the uranium mills, the crushed ore is turned into a powder called yellowcake (urania). The yellowcake is then shipped to refineries and converted into uranium fuel pellets and fuel bundles to power CANDU reactors. The refining process produces mine tailings in the form of fine yellow gravel and mill wastes from acid leaching that contain elements such as thorium. Thorium remains in the environment for 250,000 years and has health impacts that are not well understood.

In the early 1950s, the federal government entered into an agreement with the Serpent River First Nation near Elliot Lake, Ontario, to build a plant on its reserve to produce sulphuric acid for its uranium mills located upstream at Elliot Lake. The government promised the community jobs and that it would return the land in its original condition. When the plant shut down in 1962, however, the land was contaminated. In the 1960s, hunters noticed changes in fish and game and found dead animals around tailings ponds. The uranium mines and mills contaminated the watershed with radiation, heavy metals, and acids. The International Joint Commission identified the Serpent River system, which included dozens of lakes, as the largest contributor to radium contamination in the Great Lakes.

After two decades of complaints and pressure from activists, scientists, and First Nations, the federal government cleaned up the abandoned sulphuric acid plant. However, neither the Atomic Energy Control Board nor the mining companies dealt with the waste, even though the environment was covered with yellow dust and massive tailings containment structures. At environmental assessment hearings in 1976, the committee ignored Serpent River leaders' testimony about environmental and radiation contamination, and government officials and mining company executives denied that the problems had resulted from mining activities. In a classic case of blaming the victim, they claimed Aboriginal peoples' health problems had resulted from smoking, drinking, improper diet, and the abandonment of their traditional culture. After the mines closed, the government set up a decommission process to maintain safer conditions around the tailing sites, but damage to the lakes and ecosystems would be a perpetual environmental hazard. Mining companies relocated to northern Saskatchewan in 1992 and the last mine at Elliott Lake closed in 1996, but nearly 200 million tonnes of radioactive acidic uranium mill tailings continued to be stored behind earthen dams, which periodically leak. In 1993, a dammed tailing site leaked and spilled contaminated water into a nearby lake.

At the uranium mines in Northwest Territories, Eldorado Mining Company dumped 2 million tonnes of radioactive tailings into Great Bear Lake and failed to inform Dene and Inuit of the hazards associated with nuclear facilities. The Inuit of Déline, whom the industry recruited to mine uranium in the 1940s, "were carelessly, even criminally, exposed to excessive radiation from uranium ore," often working without protective clothing (Barlow and May 2000, 184). The interior of the Port Radium mines was hazardous to miners' health despite ventilation improvements made after the war. Activist scientist Rosalie Bertell reported that northern uranium-mining communities were disaster zones. Underground, in rock form, uranium ore is not hazardous, but on the surface its waste can blow and land on "vegetation,

enter the food chain, and contaminate distant rivers and lakes" (Engels 2005, 109).

Provinces are responsible for occupational health and safety within mines, but in 1960 the Atomic Energy Control Board enacted its own radiological regulations. From 1959, the International Committee on Radiological Protection set standards for acceptable levels of exposure, which it lowered as it learned more about the effects of radiation. In 1967, the United States established its own higher radiation exposure standard, and Canada accepted the US level in the 1970s. The Canadian board, however, allowed the Ontario provincial government to measure its own silica dust and radiation levels – to essentially police itself. Mining companies consistently violated existing standards. In the 1960s and 1970s, working conditions at Elliot Lake's uranium mines were a scandal: workers suffered high levels of silica dust and radiation and soaring rates of cancer and silicosis. In 1974, unionized miners went on a wildcat strike to draw public attention to their plight. Two years later, the Ontario government appointed James Ham, dean of the University of Toronto's Engineering Faculty, to head a royal commission on the health and safety of workers in Ontario mines. It discovered that the results of health studies went to the government but were not made available to miners. Ham commented, "one of the shocking things to me ... is the fact that workers have not known the levels of dust, radiation and noise in which they've been working" (Jefferson 1976).

Ham's report, which came out in 1976, made 117 recommendations and concluded that there really was no safe level of radiation. Twenty-three recommendations dealt with lung cancer and radiation levels and called for better research, stricter regulations to protect miners, and improved on-site monitoring systems. The report criticized the lack of government regulation, the confused jurisdiction over health and safety in the uranium industry, and unclear policies at both the federal and provincial levels. It recommended a drastic overhaul of the Atomic Energy Control Board and the province's health and safety policies and the development of a provincial occupational health and safety framework to facilitate cooperation between management and labour. Ham stated publicly that it was "immoral for there not to be statutory regulations which govern the exposure of workers to toxic substances fifty years *after* a disease like silicosis has been discovered" (Webster 1976). The report influenced the passage of the Occupational Health and Safety Act (1978) in Ontario and similar legislation in other provinces.

The Atomic Energy Control Board had its Mine Safety Advisory Committee investigate health and safety matters, but it waited until 1984 to pass the Uranium (Ontario) Occupational Health and Safety Regulations, which made uranium mines comply with the Ontario Occupational Health and Safety Act. Despite its earlier casual approach to occupational and environmental health and other regulations, the board instituted more inspections, introduced more stringent regulations on transporting and packaging radioactive substances, and required uranium-mining companies to report on all accidents.

A combination of public outrage and government investigations also led to changes at the Port Hope refinery, where Eldorado was also careless with radioactive waste. The Ganaraska River contained low levels of radioactivity as soon as the company began to dump waste into the town harbour in the 1930s. The highly radioactive sediment was not cleaned up because a federal investigation concluded that the contamination was not dangerous. Port Hope and a dump located outside of the town in the 1950s became heavily polluted with radioactive and toxic wastes, such as arsenic and lead. Nearby farmers sued Eldorado when their cows began to die, but the dispute was settled out of court. In the 1970s, the public learned that an Eldorado contractor had dumped 200,000 tonnes of radioactive waste around the town during the Second World War. Some of the waste was used as landfill in over one hundred sites, including two schools. The buildings were emitting radon gas and had unacceptably high radiation levels. The Atomic Energy Control Board had taken a hands-off approach because its mandate was to encourage prospecting and mining with a minimum of controls. Following the investigation, however, St. Mary's School was evacuated in 1975, and in 1979 the Atomic Energy Control Board ordered a multi-million-dollar cleanup. Radioactive debris persists, however, and in 2007 the Ontario Environmental Department urged Eldorado Nuclear to complete the cleanup.

Inside the Port Hope refinery, employees continued to be exposed to hazardous radiation levels, but the levels declined as public knowledge about the dangers grew and as more money was spent on security and training. In 1979, however, the Atomic Energy Control Board approved Eldorado's plan to expand the refinery, even though there were no provisions for waste disposal or an accompanying study of health effects. Doctors reported unusually high cancer rates, and concerned residents pressed for a community health study to track cancer, asthma, emphysema, thyroid problems, learning disabilities, and other ailments possibly linked to radioactive contamination.

The public will always be concerned with nuclear energy because there is no solution to the long-term management of nuclear waste, either nationally or internationally. The nuclear industry produces deadly waste products at every stage, from mining to decommissioning. The life of a CANDU reactor is only about forty years or less, and about a million bundles of nuclear fuel waste from Canada's twenty-two reactors and Atomic Energy of Canada prototype and research reactors are stored on local sites that increase

TABLE 7.1   Canada's nuclear power reactors, 2011

Reactor	MWe (net)*	Status	Operator	First power	Planned closure
Pickering A1	515	Operating	Ontario Power Generation	1971/2005[†]	2022
Pickering A4	515	Operating	Ontario Power Generation	1972/2003[†]	2018
Pickering B5	516	Operating	Ontario Power Generation	1982	2014
Pickering B6	516	Operating	Ontario Power Generation	1983	2015
Pickering B7	516	Operating	Ontario Power Generation	1984	2016
Pickering B8	516	Operating	Ontario Power Generation	1986	2017
Bruce A1	(750)	Refurbishing	Bruce Power	1977 (2011)[†]	2035
Bruce A2	(750)	Refurbishing	Bruce Power	1976 (2012)[†]	2035
Bruce A3	750	Operating	Bruce Power	1977/2004[†]	2036
Bruce A4	750	Operating	Bruce Power	1978/2003[†]	2036
Bruce B5	822	Operating	Bruce Power	1984	2014
Bruce B6	822	Operating	Bruce Power	1984	2014
Bruce B7	822	Operating	Bruce Power	1986	2016
Bruce B8	822	Operating	Bruce Power	1987	2017
Darlington 1	881	Operating	Ontario Power Generation	1990	2020
Darlington 2	881	Operating	Ontario Power Generation	1990	2020
Darlington 3	881	Operating	Ontario Power Generation	1992	2022
Darlington 4	881	Operating	Ontario Power Generation	1993	2023
Gentilly 2	638	Operating	Hydro-Québec	1982	2016
Point Lepreau 1	(635)	Refurbishing	New Brunswick Power	1982 (2012)	2034

Totals for:

17 operating reactors	12,044
3 refurbished reactors	2,135

*   MWe = megawatt electric

†   The four Pickering A reactors were laid up in 1997. Pickering A4 was restarted in 2003 and Pickering A1 in 2005. There are no plans to bring Pickering A2 and A3 back into service, and these are not listed in the table. Bruce A2 was taken out of service in 1995, A1 followed in 1997, and Bruce A3 and A4 in 1998. Bruce A3 and A4 were restarted in 2004 and 2003, respectively. Bruce A1 and A2 are being refurbished and are now due to restart in 2011-12.

Source: Adapted from World Nuclear Association, http://world -nuclear.org/

by about sixty thousand bundles each year. The system is aging and requires constant monitoring for security (see Table 7.1).

In the late 1970s, when a report titled *The Management of Canada's Nuclear Wastes* recommended burying nuclear waste in the Canadian Shield, the public reacted with fear. The study estimated that the process would cost between $10 billion and $30 billion over more than seven decades. The concept development itself cost $700 million, most of it federal money. In 1996, the federal government announced its Policy Framework for Radioactive Waste. When public hearings revealed insufficient public acceptance for the framework, the government took no action. Although technical experts supported the viability of the "geological solution" – burying the waste in the Canadian Shield – the government recognized that if the plan failed, it would need a feasible reversal strategy. Water seepage could be a problem, and long-term storage leaves a dubious legacy for future generations.

Nuclear plants also emit small quantities of radioactive effluent into the atmosphere and adjoining water bodies. An Ontario Hydro/Ministry of the Environment study conducted between 1986 and 1989 found samples of tritium, a carcinogen, in grass near the Pickering plants and in nearby fruits and vegetables. The Atomic Energy Control Board sets maximum limits for radioactive emissions and monitors them to keep them low. But the hidden costs of environmental degradation and damage to health from both radiation and radioactive waste-disposal sites remain an issue: "Until the modern nuclear power era, the costs of exposure to radiation were paid by a limited number of people,

such as the victims of nuclear warfare. Now, in the context of worldwide power expansion, radiation exposure is a potential threat to a large part of the population; as radioactive materials proliferate, so do the dangers associated with them" (Estrin and Swaigen 1993, 674). Neither scientists nor doctors know the threshold exposure level below which there is no risk for any exposed individual. They know that exposure to a high level of radiation causes death and that low-level exposure over time may lead to cancer, leukemia, and genetic mutation. The more scientists know, the lower the recommended permissible levels of radiation exposure.

A combination of developments adversely affected public opinion and caused the nuclear industry to contract in the 1990s. These ranged from unmarked radioactive nuclear dumps to frequent malfunctions at the Douglas Point reactor, and from high-profile hearings to international incidents such as the Three Mile Island meltdown in the United States in 1979 and the Chernobyl disaster in Russia in 1986. By 1983, Canadians favoured phasing out nuclear power completely. Anti-nuclear sentiment was reinforced in 1992, when it was discovered that a crack in the cooling device at the aging reactor at Pickering had caused 3,000 litres of radioactive water to spill into Lake Ontario. Citizens also worried about the industry's huge capital expenses and cost over-runs, which contributed to enormous public debts. The generation of nuclear power peaked in the 1990s and then declined as one-third of Ontario's nuclear generators shut down. In 1990, Premier Bob Rae announced a moratorium on nuclear energy facilities in response to public concerns about cost and safety, a policy later reversed by his successor, Mike Harris. In 1993, Ontario Hydro rates rose 7.9 percent when the province was forced to repair the Darlington nuclear plant. In 2000, the federal government overhauled its nuclear regulatory system and replaced the Atomic Energy Control Board with the more transparent Canadian Nuclear Safety Commission, which many critics considered too close to the hydro industry.

Despite its lax record in terms of health, safety, and environmental standards, the nuclear energy industry in an era of global climate change and excessive emissions from fossil fuels continues to present itself as a green industry. Industry officials claim that the full use of Canada's twenty-two reactors could reduce carbon emissions by 15 to 20 percent. In 1999, Canada proposed that countries that export nuclear reactors should receive emissions credits under the Kyoto Protocol. Germany, however, whose coalition government included Green Party members, opposed the suggestion as incompatible with sustainable development and the Kyoto process. The following year, Germany announced it would phase out nuclear reactors over the next twenty years in favour of alternative energy sources.

In the twenty-first century, poor air quality and hydro blackouts have renewed interest in nuclear energy in Canada. In 2003 and 2004, Bruce Power, with new private owners, restarted two reactors. Some energy experts reject the nuclear industry's viability, as nuclear energy remains expensive, potentially dangerous in the post-9/11 era of global terrorism, and unsustainable without a solution to the waste problem. Most environmentalists want policies in favour of energy conservation

and the development of alternative fuels. American journalist Paul Roberts concludes that "nuclear energy has so many technical, economic and political problems that its future is in doubt, while *fusion* energy – the so-called good nuclear power – is by most accounts probably a century away from being feasible on a large scale" (Roberts 2005, 190).

Getting Off the Grid: Alternative Energy Sources

Perhaps the concern about depleting energy sources will seem strange to future generations. With intense heat coming from the sun and trapped inside the earth's core, the need for companies to attack the earth's surface and waters to find fossil fuels or uranium to provide electricity may seem bizarre in the future if alternative energy sources become the norm. The transition from fossil fuels to alternative, clean energy sources, if it happens, will be long and difficult according to Vaclav Smil – a distinguished Canadian expert on energy and the author of interdisciplinary books on the environment, food, population, the economy, and public policy. The modern energy regime is massive and resistant to change. Among high-use countries such as Canada, a short-term transition to lower energy use through conservation may be relatively easy to accomplish. In the long term, however, the creation of a sustainable society (as yet undefined) must be based on a new energy regime that does not emit carbon. This larger transition will be difficult because it will depend on lower levels of energy consumption, which imply a low-growth economy. Such changes will challenge the ideological underpinnings of current industrial society, which link energy to material progress and posit that continuous economic growth fuelled by energy consumption is good. Substantial adaptations to the new global reality of environmental degradation will require a commitment to change. It is conceivable, Smil cautions, that, leaving aside the possibility of nuclear war, "the global, high-energy civilization may collapse long before approaching the limits of its resources." Such dissipation would result from "degradation of the biosphere beyond sustainable habitability" (Smil 1994, 254).

In the meantime, Canadians and Americans could cut back on their consumption. North Americans consume more energy per person than any other people in the world and double that of western Europeans. They could consume half the energy and still live affluent lifestyles in energy-efficient buildings, cities, and cars. But in 2011, Canada continues to lag behind Europe in investing in new alternative energy sources, even though the country has seen breakthroughs in research.

In the 1980s, for instance, Ballard Power Systems, a Vancouver-based company, developed the hydrogen fuel cell, which mixes hydrogen and oxygen to produce electricity and water. The process produces no pollution, and the water is good enough to drink. The company, which was founded by Geoffrey Ballard in 1979, has since reduced the size of the fuel cell and increased its power so it can be used in appliances or electric cars. The oil and gas and automobile industries' reaction to the discovery has been uneven. Although there was some hostility, based on fears that the hydrogen fuel cells could upset the gaso-

line monopoly in the transportation sector, German automaker Daimler-Benz formed a partnership with Ballard, and the Detroit auto show in 2003 displayed an advanced model of Ballard's fuel cell, a more compact, powerful, and lighter cell that could run on hydrogen or methanol. The company announced that it was testing the cells in cars, that it planned to set up its own manufacturing facility, and that it had gone into partnership with three car companies, three oil companies, and the State of California. In 2007, however, Ballard pulled out of the hydrogen vehicle sector, sold its automotive fuel cell assets to Daimler AG and Ford Motor, and focused on fuel cells for forklifts and stationary electrical generation.

The hydrogen car died for a number of reasons: the high cost of fuel cells, technical problems with their use in cars, the lack of an infrastructure to service the vehicles, and the lack of consumer knowledge. But interest in hydrogen and other cheap, clean alternatives or additives to gasoline such as ethanol or methanol persists. Biofuels made from biomass such as fermented grain, crop waste, poplar trees, or other organic matter are one option. Government departments and research organizations such as Energy for the Forest (ENFOR) and National Resources Canada are studying the potential and pitfalls of biomass energy. Canada is also a signatory to the International Energy Agency's Bioenergy Agreement, which provides for collaboration among sixteen countries. Although biomass energy has potential in Canada, which has access to large and diverse biomass sources, more research is needed to ensure the sustainability of land, soil, and forests. The use of crops to fuel cars when people are suffering

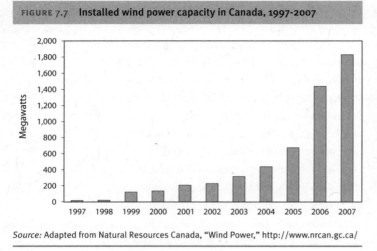

FIGURE 7.7   Installed wind power capacity in Canada, 1997-2007

Source: Adapted from Natural Resources Canada, "Wind Power," http://www.nrcan.gc.ca/

from hunger in developing countries also raises ethical issues. In 2009, bioenergy was the second most important form of renewable energy in Canada, representing about 5 percent of its total primary energy.

Solar energy is electromagnetic radiation released by thermonuclear reactors in the core of the sun. Solar energy can be harnessed using passive solar technologies such as the strategic use of windows. Active solar technologies that use electrical or mechanical equipment – such as solar collectors or panels – have also been developed extensively, especially in Germany and Japan. In Canada, however, they constitute but a tiny fraction of energy use. Large companies have the potential and knowledge to be major producers in the field but are invested in the oil energy regime. Solar power prices will remain high as long as production in the sector remains small. In 2009, environmentalists criticized Shell Oil when it decided to leave the solar business and increase its investment in biofuels, and the World Bank criticized the company for leaving its solar customers in poor countries in the lurch.

Wind power is an old form of energy that French settlers brought to Canada in the seventeenth century and used to grind grain. Before rural electrification, wind turbines generated electricity on prairie farms. Today, several small Canadian companies are producing small windmills for this same purpose and are marketing them globally. The need for new energy sources has driven the revival of modern large windmills, which are expanding with wind farms in Europe, China, and North America. Canada's growing wind farms produce a small percentage of the nation's electricity, which is likely to increase (see Figure 7.7). Some critics are opposed to them, however, for their noise, appearance, and potential threat to migrating birds.

CANADA HAS EXPERIENCED a number of energy regimes, and the country will eventually have to break its dependence on fossil fuels. Unlike European countries, which have developed long-term energy policies to create alternative energy sources and reduce their dependence on fossil fuels, Canada does not have extensive programs to promote the use and development of alternative energy sources. Governments do not talk much about fuel efficiency or solar power or our future energy needs; instead, they focus on keeping the economy growing and oil and gas flowing, steadily and cheaply. The only federal initiative to date has been in carbon capture and storage – a technology that gathers carbon dioxide released in power generation and stores it beneath the earth's surface. The technology has not yet been used successfully anywhere in the world, and some see it as a subsidy for the oil industry. The energy issue for many Canadian politicians has been reduced to the question of whether their government will get a share of Alberta's oil and gas revenues.

In the current era, which is characterized by declining energy sources and rapid climate change, there is no obvious single replacement for oil and gas and no readily available energy source that produces low carbon emissions. The next energy regime will probably be a blend of technologies in different regions, a system flexible enough to adapt to changing conditions. This transition will be difficult because the modern era's core ideology links economic growth with energy consumption and because our energy infrastructure is unwieldy. The evolution to a new sustainable society will probably depend on both policy makers and average citizens accepting the idea of lower levels of energy consumption, which would mean a lower-growth economy. The consumption of fossil fuels has contributed to growth and prosperity, but it has also resulted in widespread industrial pollution, automobile emissions, resources depletion, and environmental degradation. Getting to a sustainable energy regime will be an expensive, difficult transition process, one as significant as the shift from a preindustrial to an industrial society. Either voluntarily or under duress, we will need to be creative to find alternative energy sources and develop new lifestyles less destructive to the planet.

Works Cited

Barlow, Maude, and Elizabeth May. 2000. *Frederick Street: Life and Death on Canada's Love Canal.* Toronto: Harper Collins.

Deming, David. 2000. "Oil: Are We Running Out?" Paper presented to the Second Wallace E. Pratt Memorial Conference, "Petroleum Provinces in the 21st Century," San Diego, 12-15 January.

Dempsey, Dave. 2004. *On the Brink: The Great Lakes in the Twenty-First Century.* East Lansing: Michigan State University Press.

Engels, Mary-Louise. 2005. *Rosalie Bertell: Scientist, Eco-Feminist, Visionary.* Toronto: Women's Press.

Estrin, David, and John Swaigen. 1993. *Environment on Trial: A Guide to Ontario Environmental Law and Policy.* Toronto: Edmond Montgomery Publications.

Frame, Andy. 2004. "Requiem for a Fallen Giant: The Unlamented Demise of Ontario Hydro." *Literary Review of Canada,* November, 24-26.

Froschauer, Karl. 1999. *White Gold: Hydroelectric Power in Canada.* Vancouver: UBC Press.

Humphries, Charles. 1985. *"Honest Enough to Be Bold": The Life and Times of Sir James Pliny Whitney.* Toronto: University of Toronto Press.

Jefferson, James. 1976. "Mining Report Author Quiet but Not Meek." *Globe and Mail,* 24 August.

MacGregor, James G. 1972. *A History of Alberta.* Edmonton: Hurtig.

McKenna, Barrie. 2005. "Welcome to the Age of Scarcity." *Globe and Mail,* 21 May.

Nelles, H.V. 1976. "Public Ownership of Electrical Utilities in Manitoba and Ontario, 1906-1930." *Canadian Historical Review* 57, 4: 461-84.

Roberts, Paul. 2005. *The End of Oil: On the Edge of a Perilous New World.* New York: Mariner Books.

Sifton, Clifford. 1910. The Empire Club of Canada Addresses, 20 October. http://speeches.empireclub.org/.

Smil, Vaclav. 1994. *Energy in World History.* San Francisco: Westview Press.

Tataryn, Lloyd. 1979. *Dying for a Living.* Montreal: Deneau and Greenberg Publishers.

Taylor, Graham D., and Peter A. Baskerville. 1994. *A Concise History of Business in Canada.* Toronto: Oxford University Press.

Vincent, Catherine. 2009. "Tar Sand Extraction Threatens Birdlife of North America." *Guardian Weekly,* 16 January.

Webster, Norman. 1976. "Dandy Issue for Polls." *Globe and Mail,* 26 August.

Woynillowicz, Dan, Chris Severson-Baker, and Marlo Reynolds. 2005. *Oil Sands Fever: The Environmental Implications of Canada's Oil Sands Rush.* Drayton Valley, AB: Pembina Institute.

For Further Reading

Nye, David. 1998. *Consuming Power: A Social History of American Energies.* Cambridge, MA: MIT Press.

Sessions, George, ed. 1995. *Deep Ecology for the 21st Century: Readings on the Philosophy and Practice of the New Environmentalism.* Boston: Shambhala.

Yergin, Daniel. 1992. *The Prize: The Epic Quest for Oil, Money and Power.* New York: Free Press.

Coal and Hydroelectricity

Anton, Frank R. 1981. *The Canadian Coal Industry: Challenge in the Years Ahead.* Calgary: Detselig Enterprises Ltd.

Dempsey, Dave. 2004. *On the Brink: The Great Lakes in the Twenty-First Century.* East Lansing: Michigan State University Press.

Frame, Andy. 2004. "Requiem for a Fallen Giant: The Unlamented Demise of Ontario Hydro." *Literary Review of Canada,* November, 24-26.

Froschauer, Karl. 1999. *White Gold: Hydroelectric Power in Canada.* Vancouver: UBC Press.

Hampton, Howard. 2003. *Public Power: The Fight for Publicly Owned Electricity.* Toronto: Insomniac Press.

Humphries, Charles. 1985. *"Honest Enough to Be Bold": The Life and Times of Sir James Pliny Whitney.* Toronto: University of Toronto Press.

Nelles, H.V. 1976. "Public Ownership of Electrical Utilities in Manitoba and Ontario, 1906-1930." *Canadian Historical Review* 57, 4: 461-84.

Sifton, Clifford. 1910. The Empire Club of Canada Addresses, 20 October. http://speeches.empireclub.org/.

Swift, Jamie, and Keith Stewart. 2004. *Hydro: The Decline and Fall of Ontario's Electric Empire.* Toronto: Between the Lines.

Electricity and the Environment

Cohen, Marjorie Griffin. 2001. *From Public Good to Private Exploitation: GATS and the Restructuring of Canadian Electrical Utilities.* Orono, ME: Canadian-American Center.

–. 2003. "Gutting a Power House: BC Hydro and the New Energy Plan." Centre for Policy Alternatives, BC office, April.

Hampton, Howard. 2003. *Public Power: The Fight for Publicly Owned Electricity.* Toronto: Insomniac Press.

Mahon, Rianne. 1977. "Canadian Public Policy: Unequal Structure of Representation." In *The Canadian State,* edited by Leo Panitch, 165-98. Toronto: University of Toronto Press.

Massell, David. 2004-5. "Power and the Peribonka, a Prehistory: 1900-1930s." *Quebec Studies* 38 (Fall): 87-104.

–. 2011. "A Question of Power: A Brief History of Hydroelectricity in Quebec." In *Quebec Questions: Quebec Studies for the Twenty-First Century,* edited by Stéphan Gervais, Christopher Kirkey, and Jarrett Rudy, 338-56. Oxford: Oxford University Press.

Swift, Jamie, and Keith Stewart. 2004. *Hydro: The Decline and Fall of Ontario's Electric Empire.* Toronto: Between the Lines.

Oil and Gas

Brethour, Patrick. 2005. "Oil Patch Heresy: An Albertan Petro-History Makes the Case for a New National Energy Program." *Literary Review of Canada,* October, 13-15.

Gillespie, Curtis. 2008. "Scar Sands." *Canadian Geographic,* June, 64-78.

MacGregor, James G. 1972. *A History of Alberta.* Edmonton: Hurtig.

McKenna, Barrie. 2005. "Welcome to the Age of Scarcity." *Globe and Mail,* 21 May.

Nikiforuk, Andrew. 2002. *Saboteurs: Wiebo Ludwig's War against Big Oil.* Toronto: Macfarlane, Walter, and Ross.

–. 2008. *Tar Sands: Dirty Oil and the Future of a Continent.* Vancouver: Greystone Books.

Taylor, Graham D., and Peter A. Baskerville. 1994. *A Concise History of Business in Canada.* Toronto: Oxford University Press.

Vincent, Catherine. 2009. "Tar Sand Extraction Threatens Birdlife of North America." *Guardian Weekly,* 16 January.

Woynillowicz, Dan, Chris Severson-Baker, and Marlo Reynolds. 2005. *Oil Sands Fever: The Environmental Implications of Canada's Oil Sands Rush.* Drayton Valley, AB: Pembina Institute.

Nuclear Energy

Babin, Ronald. 1985. *The Nuclear Power Game.* Montreal: Black Rose Books.

Bothwell, Robert. 1984. *Eldorado: Canada's National Uranium Company*. Toronto: University of Toronto Press.

–. 1988. *Nucleus: The History of Atomic Energy of Canada Limited*. Toronto: University of Toronto Press.

Dewar, Elaine. 2005. "Nuclear Reaction." *Canadian Geographic*, May-June, 69-84.

Doern, G. Bruce, Arslan Dorman, and Robert W. Morrison, eds. 2001. *Canadian Nuclear Energy Policy: Changing Ideas, Institutions, and Interests*. Toronto: University of Toronto Press.

Durant, Darrin. 2007. "Burying Globally, Acting Locally: Control and Co-option in Nuclear Waste Management." *Science and Public Policy* 34, 7: 515-28.

Giangrande, Carol. 1983. *The Nuclear North: The People, the Regions and the Arms Race*. Toronto: Anansi.

Ontario. 1976. *Report of the Royal Commission on the Health and Safety of Workers in Mines*. Toronto: Ministry of the Attorney General, Province of Ontario.

Stanley, Anna. 2008a. "Citizenship and the Production of Landscape and Knowledge in Contemporary Canadian Nuclear Fuel Waste Management." *Canadian Geographer* 52, 1: 64-82.

–. 2008b. "Risk, Scale and Exclusion in Canadian Nuclear Fuel Waste Management." *ACME: An International E-Journal for Critical Geographies* 4, 2: 194-227.

Getting Off the Grid

Mittelstadt, Martin. 2009. "A Revolution in the Air." *Globe and Mail*, 6 January.

Walton, Dawn. 2000. "Ballard Powers Ahead with Fuel Cell." *Globe and Mail*, 10 January.

Webb, Tim. 2009. "Shell Dumps Wind, Solar Hydro Power in Favour of Biofuels." *Guardian*, 17 March.

8
Water

The flowing waters of Canada are, at the moment, apart from the soil, our greatest and most valuable undeveloped natural resource.

— SIR CLIFFORD SIFTON, CHAIR, CONSERVATION COMMISSION OF CANADA, 1909

CANADA HAS FRESH water in abundance. Streams, rivers, and lakes, including the world's largest, cover an estimated area of 1,325,704 square kilometres. Water scarcity has not been an issue in Canada's history, but settlement, industrialism, public policy, and modernity have altered the country's waterways. The story of water in Canada has been one of manipulation (for agricultural, energy, or industrial purposes) and abuse (as water became a convenient dumping ground for waste from agricultural and industrial processes and expanding cities). Many of the problems of today – for instance, preserving wetlands and reversing the effects of overfishing and pollution in the Great Lakes – have their origins in the early desire to transform the Canadian landscape either into a European-style agrarian economy or to make way for industrial "progress." Fisheries, canals, and dams were attempts to harness nature to serve human goals in a modern society. In the process of draining, damming, and diverting water, Canadians changed hydrological cycles, urban contours, and vast ecosystems. In 1971, a scientist wrote, "the creation of man-made lakes and the control of natural water bodies has reached such a scale that it can now be said these huge engineering works are modifying and changing the landscape of the earth more than either agricultural or urban expansion" (Ehrenfeld 1971, 30). The repercussions of these transformations have become apparent in the last fifty years. Pollution and environmental disruption have, in turn, created ongoing social conflicts among environmentalists, First Nations, big business, and government.

The Great Lakes

As the world's largest bodies of fresh water, the Great Lakes are one of the wonders of the natural world. Lake Superior alone contains over 10 percent of the world's total supply of fresh water. Humans, however, have consistently taken the lakes and their fish for granted. A pattern of so-called progress and consumption without conservation set in early, and the Great Lakes serve as an example, or microcosm, of water issues in Canada and around the world.

Aboriginal peoples used the Great Lakes for transportation, water, and fish. In 1670, when the explorer and missionary René de Bréhant de Galinée travelled the St. Mary's River, which linked Lake Superior to the lower Great Lakes, he exclaimed that the rapids so teemed with white fish, "the Indians could easily catch enough to feed 10,000 men" (Dempsey 2004, 37). But because Aboriginal populations were small, their environmental impact was slight. The Great Lakes had abundant fish, but there were only a few species, and these species held an integral place in simple food chains that spread throughout twenty diverse but easily disrupted ecoregions. Aboriginal people used spears, hooks and lines, and weirs in the upper lakes and nets in the lower lakes to catch fish to supplement their diet of game and plants. Animism, the attribution of souls to plants and animals, ensured that overfishing would be limited and that surpluses would be bartered in trade. The Great Lakes, however, provided a route for fur traders, who exhausted their wildlife, including beavers. As beaver dams collapsed, water flow increased, disrupting fish spawning beds and depriving waterfowl of wetlands and nesting areas.

In the eighteenth and nineteenth centuries, British and American settlers and businessmen began to "develop" the eastern Great Lakes Basin, altering the area around Lakes Ontario and Erie. The nature of development was shaped by the drawing of international boundaries. In 1783, Britain

THE GREAT LAKES: AN UNLIMITED RESOURCE?

In 1999 and 2001, the International Joint Commission, an agency that deals with problems associated with rivers and lakes along the Canada-US border, raised an alarm when it suggested that water levels in the Great Lakes were likely to fall with global warming and that the diversion of water from the lakes was an issue. Chicago had been diverting water from the Great Lakes to serve its needs, but the joint commission had ensured that an equal amount had been put back into the lakes from another source. In 1985, provinces and states in the Great Lakes Basin had also drafted the Great Lakes Charter, which prevents harmful water diversions and exports. In 2001, to maintain current water levels, the joint commission recommended that governments resist pressure and *not* allow corporations to remove water from the lakes for sale elsewhere. Climate change will make future water conservation measures essential.

and the United States settled the international boundary through the lakes, and conventions on river boundaries were concluded in the nineteenth century. Newcomers viewed the New World's water and fish as commodities to be exploited; their mindset resulted in an altered landscape, water pollution, and drastically reduced fish resources. The commercial lumber industry decimated the region's old-growth boreal, transitional, and hardwood forests. As elsewhere, logging involved the removal of bankside soil and vegetation, caused soil erosion, and increased flooding, which raised silt levels and water temperatures, endangering fish. Sawmill operators and workers used the banks of rivers to store boards, and their dams blocked fish from moving upstream. The mills polluted the lakes with bark and sawdust, further depleting fish populations. Lumber interests ignored early laws against industrial pollution entering the water, and governments failed to enforce them.

Control over the Great Lakes fisheries was divided among eight US states, the British or Canadian governments, and the Province of Ontario, which held title to the water and the lakebeds in its territory. Too many authorities and no uniform law made enforcing regulations difficult. British colonial authorities believed that fishery resources should be regulated, that conservation of this valuable food source was essential, and that commercial fishing was important to wealth creation. These ideals of value and protection for long-term use persisted in the laws of both British North America and Canada and in the United States; however, no systematic protective legislation was passed or enforced. Fish protection laws with some enforcement powers were passed in Canada West (Ontario) in 1857 and 1858, but fish conservation was not a priority compared to the interests of commercial anglers and industrial entrepreneurs. A lacklustre track record in fish and water conservation resulted.

The long history of water pollution in the Great Lakes was also linked to settlement, population growth (see Figure 8.1), and industrialism (auto making, iron ore and copper mining, steel smelting, and chemical and nuclear plants). As towns and cities such as Hamilton, Toronto, Goderich, Windsor, and Sarnia grew around the Great Lakes to service the countryside and industries, their construction required the removal of groundcover and trees to make way for the roads, railways, and canals that facilitated travel and commerce. The Great Lakes shorelines changed beyond recognition. City planning involved filling in wetlands, dredging sand-

FIGURE 8.1 Population growth in the Great Lakes Basin since 1900

The rapid growth of communities around many of the Great Lakes resulted in increased agricultural production, a thriving commercial fishery, and expanding industries. As population growth soared (particularly around Lakes Michigan, Erie, and Ontario), the inevitable result was soil erosion, overfishing, higher pollution levels, and the loss of groundcover and trees.

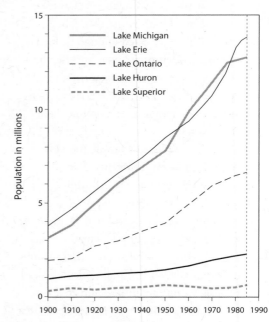

Source: Adapted from the Environmental Protection Agency, "Great Lakes," http://www.epa.gov/

bars, and paving over lake banks. Hamilton, Ontario, for example, "lost much of its natural beauty" as "industry after industry located along the shore of Hamilton Bay" (Storey 1982, 124). Huckleberry Point, given to the Hamilton Steel and Iron Company in 1893, was "a beauty spot," known by boaters and outdoorsmen for its oak and walnut woods. As industries expanded and filled in "the many inlets where Hamiltonians fished and bathed in the summer and skated and played hockey in the winter," the bay became a wasteland. By 1926, a quarter of it had been filled (Storey 1982, 12).

As the population of cities such as Hamilton grew, they produced both organic and industrial wastes that entered the Great Lakes. They dumped dust, dirt, ashes, and horse manure from the town's streets directly into the lakes. Human waste – which was deposited into pits, outhouses, and eventually, indoor plumbing systems – entered sewage systems and likewise ended up in the water. Among the many "hotspots" created by industrial pollution was the Windermere Basin in Hamilton Harbour, an entry point for sewage, detergents, sludges, chemicals, and oil. Although North Americans and people from around the world viewed the Great Lakes as a natural wonder, they also perceived them as giant "sinks" for waste, a view enhanced by the misconception that water had enormous assimilative capacities and could neutralize harmful pollutants.

The idea of unlimited resources also fuelled the commercial fishery. Fishing required relatively little capital and enriched company owners, whose mantra was "exploitation for quick profit." Aggressive entrepreneurship and poaching by Americans in Canadian waters not only created tensions between the two countries but also resulted in expanded markets and more jobs as large companies and processing plants replaced independent fishermen. In 1872, nine firms handled 3.8 million kilograms of fish annually. They controlled markets, prices, and the quality of fish, and they planned extensive and intensive harvests. Production peaked in 1889, and then a long-term but irregular decline set in

as larger operations developed more efficient technology such as gill-net steamships, which caught millions of fish at a time (see Table 8.1). Advancements in fishing gear and techniques and in preserving and transporting fish to markets (such as refrigerated railway cars) contributed to overharvesting. Unique landlocked Atlantic salmon, which spawned in the rivers entering Lake Ontario, disappeared by 1890. Disturbed by their disappearance, legislators passed the first conservation regulations, but they were ineffective. Whitefish disappeared from the lower lakes, trout and herring populations declined, and only one of seven species of chub survived. In 1901, it was estimated that Canadian and American fisheries had reduced

TABLE 8.1 **Production of Great Lakes fisheries in Canada and the United States, 1879-1930 (thousands of kilograms)**

Year	All species	Commercial species				All other species	Major commercial species as % of catch
		Whitefish	Trout	Herring	Sturgeon		
1879	79,027	24,336	7,997	18,040	7,841	20,813	74
1885	121,290	22,178	17,673	33,679	8,578	39,182	68
1890	143,406	19,098	18,473	59,820	5,207	40,808	72
1893	134,211	12,977	21,727	55,623	2,742	41,142	69
1899	146,617	9,002	17,898	72,723	1,772	45,222	69
1903	114,050	7,653	22,656	40,523	687	42,531	63
1908	139,266	10,931	19,123	56,089	375	52,748	63
1913	107,854	4,329	16,989	47,653	138	38,745	64
1918	146,347	9,802	17,218	76,712	161	42,454	71
1923	113,313	9,358	16,073	43,179	136	44,567	61
1924	113,412	8,472	17,668	46,757	128	40,387	65
1925	100,671	8,721	17,962	25,874	106	48,008	52
1926	98,530	9,544	17,973	22,322	124	48,567	51
1927	107,869	9,940	17,546	30,264	107	50,012	54
1928	89,547	10,547	15,823	20,922	107	42,148	52
1929	98,712	11,857	16,561	25,571	70	44,653	54
1930	116,246	13,567	14,512	28,904	115	59,148	49

Source: Bogue (2001, 256, 257). Copyright 2001 by the Board of Regents of the University of Wisconsin System. Reprinted with permission of the University of Wisconsin Press.

Lake Erie's sturgeon population by 80 percent. The blue pike lake trout disappeared from Lake Erie in the 1950s, a decade marked by the collapse of the Great Lakes fishing industry.

Throughout the history of the Great Lakes fisheries, governments preferred to operate fish hatcheries and restock the lakes rather than pass regulations that limited catches. In 1866, Samuel Wilmot built a government-funded hatchery, and his success "helped popularize government-sponsored fish hatcheries and stocking throughout the United States and Canada" (Taylor 1999, 69). Governments boosted fish stocks to address nature's "inefficiencies" rather than moderating human actions. As fish numbers dropped, hatcheries attempted to manage the resource by stocking alien fish species to support sport and commercial anglers. From an economic perspective, this manipulation of the Great Lakes environment worked; from an environmental perspective, many of these initiatives failed. The new species harmed indigenous fish populations and constituted artificial incursions into the ecosystem. Alien species such as carp, alewives, and smelt continue to affect the mix of species in the lakes. More recently, aquaculture facilities and the bait-fish industry have also accidentally added new alien species. The state's pattern of neglect and mismanagement resulted in over-fishing and the introduction of new species. When combined with the adverse effects of industrial pollution, the result has been destruction of the most abundant freshwater fish region in the world. Despite scientific research and changing public attitudes, fish populations have continued to decline.

The Lake Erie Crisis

The problem of environmental degradation in the Great Lakes did not become a matter

THE CLASS DIMENSION OF WATER POLLUTION: HAMILTON HARBOUR

Industrialization and urbanization led to pollution of water-ways, which requires elaborate systems to reverse. As early as the 1860s, a fishery inspector at Hamilton Harbour discovered that fish found along the shore tasted of coal oil and that dead ducks and muskrats were coated with oil from two refineries. Although the inspector was authorized to prevent industries from dumping waste, he had little support from political or business elites and could only ameliorate the problem by encouraging companies to either dilute their waste or improve their waste-storage systems. This pattern – reliance on corporate voluntarism combined with the state's unwillingness to regulate industrial wastes – was ineffective in preventing water pollution.

The problem of maintaining clean water and preserving habitats became increasingly complex over time as waste changed from biological filth to toxic wastes, pharmaceuticals, and hormones. In 1917, Noulan Cauchon, influenced by the city beautiful movement, created an ambitious design for Hamilton that involved transforming the city's north end into an industrial district and filling in parts of the harbour for industrial purposes. His plan "sacrificed north-end waterfront recreational areas to industry," limited working-class families' access to the waterfront, and put an end to swimming in Hamilton Bay when polluted waters forced the city to close beaches. By the 1950s, industrial and residential wastes had rendered Hamilton Harbour unfit for recreation.

Developments in Hamilton fit a pattern repeated throughout the country. City planners associated industry and polluted land with poorer neighbourhoods; therefore, the distribution of hazardous wastes, industrial pollutants, and environmental risks disproportionately became a burden for the less affluent.

of grave public concern until the 1960s, when the press exposed Lake Erie as a "dying sinkhole." People had been aware of the problem since the mid-nineteenth century, and the United States and Canada had established the International Joint Commission to deal with Great Lakes issues in 1909. The commission studied the source, location, and extent of pollution and, in 1918, reported that the "situation along the frontier ... is generally chaotic, everywhere perilous and in some cases disgraceful" (Dempsey 2004, 98). The Detroit and Niagara Rivers, which had been fouled by sewage from Detroit, posed the biggest concern, but the commission also reported that all channels connecting the Great Lakes were contaminated. Municipalities had developed waste management systems and sewers and had hired professional sanitary engineers to manage water treatment systems for drinking water, yet they did little about the source of pollution – dumping by municipalities and industries. Rather than developing programs to eliminate pollution, which would involve regulating businesses, policy makers opted to chlorinate and filter drinking water to reduce waterborne diseases and to implement limited sewage treatment. As a result, industrial pollution increased, particularly in the lower lakes, where ducks died and mutations appeared in other species.

When the Lake Erie Crisis erupted nearly a half century later, it sparked a widespread public outcry and attention from environmentalists. Pressures from population growth, fisheries, and industrial waste had changed the water chemistry of the Great Lakes. According to Dave Dempsey, Lake Erie, the shallowest Great Lake, "was destined to become a global poster child for environmental disgrace on a developed continent" (Dempsey 2004, 106). Pollution from agricultural runoff, toxic materials, sewage, and detergents had combined to create phosphorus, which in turn had stimulated masses of decaying algae, which exuded odours and consumed oxygen needed by fish and aquatic life. The lake was experiencing cultural eutrophication, the process by which humans speed up the natural decaying process in algae by allowing excessive amounts of nutrients to enter an ecosystem. Scientists sparked public debates about the crisis when they reported that they had discovered a huge oxygen-free area on the bottom of Lake Erie (see Figure 8.2). Algae blooms interfered with boating, swimming, and fishing and served as a visible reminder that Lake Erie had become a dump.

Population growth around the lake had increased phosphorus and other organic wastes, but a new ingredient had also contributed to the eutrophication problem. In 1947, Proctor and Gamble added phosphates to a new detergent, called Tide, and conquered the mass market for laundry and dishwashing soap. Within fifteen years, detergents accounted for 40 to 70 percent of the phosphorus discharged by sewage treatment plants. The problem of algae and foam in the Great Lakes, first noticed in the 1930s, finally turned the public against phosphates in detergents in the 1960s. Scientists in the Public Health Service in the United States and in the Ontario Water Resources Commission (formed in 1956) investigated but did not state the obvious – that Lake Erie had a problem with eutrophication – until the 1960s. Instead, they tried to eradicate excessive algae

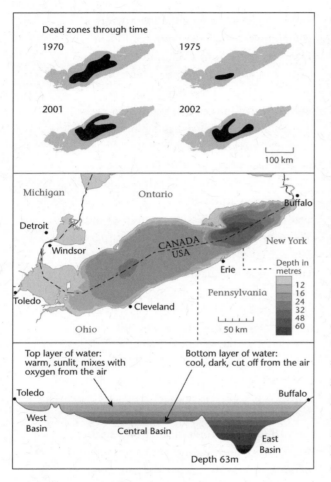

Dead zones through time

1970   1975

2001   2002

100 km

Michigan   Ontario

Detroit

Windsor

CANADA
USA

Toledo

Cleveland

Ohio

Buffalo

New York

Erie

Pennsylvania

Depth in
metres

12
16
24
32
48
60

50 km

Top layer of water:
warm, sunlit, mixes with
oxygen from the air

Bottom layer of water:
cool, dark, cut off from the air

Toledo   Buffalo

West
Basin

Central Basin

East
Basin

Depth 63m

FIGURE 8.2 Lake Erie's dead zones, 1970-2002. Recent rainfall increases caused by climate change and the continued use of phosphorus in such things as dishwasher detergents will probably expand the lake's dead zones.

Source: Adapted from *Canadian Geographic,* http://www.canadiangeographic.ca/

which citizens demanded that the government "Save Lake Erie Now." That year, detergent makers switched to biodegradable ingredients to reduce suds, but they resisted eliminating phosphorus. In response, grassroots groups such as the League of Women Voters and Housewives against Phosphates in the United States and Pollution Probe in Canada lobbied politicians. Pollution Probe's brief to the commission called for a ban on the manufacture, sale, and use of high-phosphate detergents. The anti-phosphate campaign was effective. The Canadian government limited the phosphorus content in detergents in 1970 and further reduced the allowable limit two years later.

The joint commission's recommendation of a broad legal framework to protect the Great Lakes led to the US Clean Water Act and Canada's Water Act (1972), which set out guidelines, standards, and penalties against polluters. The two countries signed the International Great Lakes Water Quality Agreement, a framework agreement to protect the lakes by monitoring pollution levels and by taking a cooperative approach to cleaning them up. The framework set water quality objectives but left enforcement to the two nations' governments. The initial focus was combatting eutrophication by reducing phosphorus in municipal and industrial wastewaters. The Ontario Water Resources Commission assisted municipalities in building or modernizing their sewage treatment plants. After years of disputes among governments over who would pay for sewage infrastructure and monitor sewage levels, local governments agreed to set standards for sewage effluent. These overdue improvements in sewage treatment eliminated most phosphates

with chemical treatments and even mechanical removal.

In 1964, when the International Joint Commission again studied pollution in the Great Lakes, it recommended the immediate reduction of phosphates in detergents. The commission had been influenced by public hearings about the crisis, during

Mercury, a heavy metal, is produced naturally by volcanoes, forest fires, sediment erosion, and evaporation from bodies of water. In Canada, mercury was released into the environment from mercury-based fungicides and by the pulp-and-paper industry. Scientists believed mercury was a stable, inactive element until 1953, when hundreds of people in Japan suffered severe brain damage, birth defects, and blindness from fish contaminated by mercury dumped into Minimata Bay. In 1969, Norvald Fimreite, a Norwegian doctoral student at the University of Western Ontario, revealed that fish in many lakes along the US-Canada border were contaminated with mercury from the Dow Chemical Plant. Fimreite's discovery prompted researchers around the world to test mercury levels in fish and led to the discovery that big fish – fresh and saltwater – contained dangerous levels of the heavy metal.

In 1970, the Ontario Water Resources Commission took action to reduce Dow's output. That same year, however, it was discovered that a chemical plant operated by Reed Paper had been dumping mercury into the Wabigoon River in northwestern Ontario for nearly a decade. An alarming number of people from two Ojibwa bands, the Grassy Narrows and the Islington, displayed symptoms of mercury poisoning. The government closed down the bands' commercial fishery in communities already devastated by unemployment and health problems. Although it ordered Reed Paper to cut its disposal of mercury, the company continued dumping the heavy metal until 1975. The communities received no offer of compensation until 1985 because the government did not want to set a precedent of making compensation payments for industrial pollution or of collecting payment from the company for its environmental damage. The resulting agreement established a mercury disability board and a fund to pay benefits, and it abolished any future claims. In 1994, Canada and Ontario's agreement on the Great Lakes Basin ecosystem monitored mercury emissions, which had decreased 83 percent since 1988. Because mercury was used less in paint, household batteries, and fungicides, sewage and medical waste contained fewer traces of it. A new agreement in 2002 set a new goal of a 90 percent reduction by 2010.

and nitrates. A revised Great Lakes Water Quality Agreement (1978) set broader control targets for reducing phosphorus in the lower lakes and for preventing eutrophication in the upper lakes. By the 1990s, comprehensive policies were being implemented.

The campaign to save Lake Erie stimulated the modern environmental movement by providing an early success story. With reduced phosphorus levels and improved sewage treatments, the lake improved noticeably in the 1970s: there was no new algae, and stench and scum disappeared from the surface. Cities reopened beaches, the lake's colour changed from green to blue, ducks returned to previously lethal areas, and fish populations rose with oxygen levels. An unprecedented cooperative effort by Canada and the United States had rehabilitated the lake, but some ecological changes could not be reversed. The victory over eutrophication was incomplete – for example, phosphorus continued to contaminate the waters. People, however, came to realize "that they themselves were an integral part of the Great Lakes ecosystem" and paid more attention to their behaviour (Dempsey 2004, 276).

Toxic Pollutants

Another problem – toxic pollutants – also came to public attention in the same period through a number of high-profile scandals and events. In 1969, a fire broke out in Cleveland, Ohio, on the Cuyahoga River, a tributary of Lake Erie. The fire was five storeys high, lasted twenty-four minutes, caused US$50,000 in damages, gained international attention, angered Canadians and Americans, and became a rallying point for the passage of the US Clean Water Act (1972). The toxic pollution that had caused the fire was invisible and consisted of hazardous man-made substances such as PCBs (polychlorinated biphenyls), pesticides, dioxin, and nuclear discharges. Invented in 1929, PCBs were used to make plastics, pesticides, solvents, and hydraulic fluids. In 1977, governments banned them because of their adverse environmental and health effects on aquatic environments and on human immune systems, motor skills, and memory. Although they were never manufactured in Canada, they were used widely until the ban, when they were put in storage and still persist in the environment.

Toxic waste again received public attention in 1978, when the Love Canal scandal broke out. The scandal had roots nearly a century in the past. In 1892, businessman William T. Love, hoping to tap the Niagara River in New York State for hydroelectricity, had developed a plan to connect the upper and lower rivers with a canal. Never completed, the trench was used from 1920 onward as a garbage and chemical disposal site and in the 1940s by the Hooker Chemical Company as a dumping site for approximately twenty-one thousand tons of chemicals. Hooker sold the property to the Niagara Falls Board of Education for a dollar in 1953. The deed of sale disclosed the nature and extent of the waste and prohibited construction on the area. The school board, however,

ignored the agreement and built a school. New housing developments followed. By the 1970s, construction activities and heavy rainstorms had released the chemicals, and residents began to complain of odours and fumes. Although a consulting company recommended measures to seal the site, the city ignored its advice. When a state agency investigated the site in 1978, it discovered four hundred chemicals with unsafe levels. Residents had become so ill that they could no longer live in the area. In 1978, President Jimmy Carter announced a federal health emergency and ordered the Federal Disaster Assistance Agency to help remedy the situation. The publicity surrounding the health crisis helped to raise public awareness and concern about toxic wastes in the nearby Great Lakes.

In 1978, the International Joint Commission, through the revised Great Lakes Water Quality Agreement, sought to control the entry of toxic substances into the Great Lakes and ensure that Canada and the United States would share the costs of restoring the ecosystem. Its recommendations, however, were nonbinding, and both governments had a poor record of enacting the commission's recommendations. But as the watchdog of the agreement, the commission developed programs and technologies to eliminate or reduce the discharge of pollutants. Between 1978 and 1992, it stimulated citizen groups to clean up the Great Lakes and provided public forums at its biennial water-quality meetings. The result was new knowledge, an ecosystem approach to action on pollution, and a dispute resolution mechanism aimed at preventing further pollution crises.

WARNING SIGNS

The Great Lakes provide drinking water for millions of Canadians and Americans, yet they routinely carry signs in the summer that read "Unfit for Swimming." In 1993, two-thirds of North American fish advisories covered the Great Lakes region, most of them because of excessive amounts of mercury, PCBs, dioxins, and DDT. Ontario fish advisories caution the public not to eat fish caught in the Great Lakes more than a few times each month, and not at if they are young children or pregnant. In 1998, the International Joint Commission reported that the Great Lakes were cleaner, but it also reported on the accumulation of noxious chemicals in "trouble spots" and found a "buildup of radioactive contaminants in the lakes from nuclear power plant discharges" (Dempsey 2004, 181).

ACID RAIN

In the 1980s, acid rain – rain or precipitation that possesses high levels of hydrogen ions – also began to threaten the Great Lakes. Caused by fossil fuels such as coal, oil, and natural gases being burned to fuel industry, power plants, and motor vehicles, acid rain is a significant hazard to human health and causes widespread destruction of forests, lakes, fish, soils, and food crops. Acid rain is a particular problem in the Great Lakes region since the area contains the bulk of industry in North America. The Coalition for the Prevention of Acid Rain and the Canadian government worked together to get the US government to sign the US-Canada Air Quality Agreement (1991). The two countries agreed to reduce acid rain emissions by 50 percent and to establish a research and monitoring network to assess improvements. In 2011, it was reported that emissions causing acid rain had been cut in half and that emissions causing smog had been cut by one-third.

Increasingly, Canada has been forced to depend on the United States to support initiatives since it is the origin of most of the pollutants dumped into the Great Lakes and most of the sulphur and nitrogen oxides that contribute to acid rain. Although Canada gained US cooperation on pollution issues, resolution of the problem and enforcement continues to be an issue. But Canada's own record in eliminating water pollution has not been good, as it consistently puts private economic growth before environmental rehabilitation and public health.

In the United States, state governors agreed to the Great Lakes Toxic Substances Control Agreement in 1986 and a $100 million Great Lakes Protection Fund in 1989. Although citizens also raised funds and lobbied for protection and restoration of the Great Lakes ecosystem, local action was inadequate. Governments banned DDT and PCBs, but toxic chemical levels remained the same, and deformed fish and birds continued to appear in the Great Lakes. In 1986, when he published *The Late, Great Lakes: An Environmental History,* William Ashworth reported that the Great Lakes had a number of problems, including carcinogenity (the ability to cause cancer), mutagenity (the ability to cause birth defects), and bioaccumulation (the tendency of toxic compounds to concentrate in increasing amounts as they move up the food chain): "small amounts in the water lead to larger amounts in plankton, still larger amounts in small fish that eat the plankton and, potentially, dangerous amounts in big fish that eat the small fish" (Ashworth 1986, 162). In 2004, scientists discovered that herring gull eggs had large concentrations of chemicals known as brominated diphenyl ethers, unregulated substances used as flame retardants in polyurethane foam in furniture upholstery. Concentrations of these chemicals had doubled about every three years from the early 1980s, and toxic fallout from elsewhere had blown into the area.

In Canada, enforcement of the agreement lagged as governments took a conciliatory approach to industrial polluters. In the 1980s, for instance, in Ontario's chemical valley near Sarnia, Dow Chemical and other companies reported 275 chemical spills. From the mid-1980s, the province's Ministry of the Environment spent $280 million on local advisory bodies that developed cleanup plans to rehabilitate only badly polluted hot spots in the Great Lakes. Between 1989 and 1992, the public pressured the joint commission for systematic action. It responded with a set goal of zero discharges of persistent toxic chemicals. It also called for a policy of "reverse onus" by which chemical manufacturers had to prove new chemicals were *not* harmful to public health or the environment before getting approval for their manufacture. In addition, given that over half of the 362 harmful toxic chemicals in the Great Lakes system were chlorinated organic compounds, the joint commission recommended that governments develop timetables to "sunset the use of chlorine and chlorine-containing

THE WALKERTON TRAGEDY

Canada's need to develop local stewardship of smaller waterways became apparent in May 2000 when seven people died after consuming polluted drinking water in Walkerton, Ontario. A torrential downpour had washed bacteria from cattle manure at an industrial farm into a shallow town well. Residents became ill with *E. coli* poisoning. Although tests revealed that the water had been contaminated, the water utilities manager did not inform either the public health office or the public. By the time the public health unit had completed its own tests and ordered a boiled-water alert, 2,300 people had taken ill.

The provincial government denied any responsibility, but under pressure from the Opposition, it ordered a public inquiry. After two and a half years, the commission made ninety-three recommendations and placed the blame not only on local authorities but also on the provincial government's budget cuts, which had resulted in ineffective monitoring. The province promised to pass a Safe Water Drinking Act, to offer better training to local utilities officials, and to monitor the laboratories that test water samples. In 2002, an Ontario study found that half the province's water plants violated safety regulations implemented after Walkerton. Since then, municipalities have become more vigilant about water quality, and Ontario has upgraded regulations for water systems. Communities in provinces such as Saskatchewan and in the Maritimes, however, continue to face recurring problems with contaminated water.

compounds as industrial feedstocks" (Dempsey 2004, 186).

The commission's policies delighted environmentalists but aroused organized opposition from industry. Conservative governments in both Canada and the United States in the 1990s retained the policies and gave rhetorical support to cleaning up the Great Lakes, but they increasingly bypassed the International Joint Commission. They reduced environmental expenditures, lessened public input, made information less accessible, and failed to monitor chemical discharges or enforce environmental violations. In 1994, for the first time, the joint commission's report suggested that pollution-related illnesses in other species could also affect people; in other words, it linked water pollution in the Great Lakes to public health. In 1997, the Ontario government cancelled funding to local groups and justified its decision on the grounds that the private sector should finance pollution programs. Environmentalists accused the provincial government of violating a 1994 agreement with the federal government, in which both governments had pledged to cooperate to eliminate 60 percent of the pollution in hot spots by 2000.

Ongoing lax government enforcement of water quality standards persisted: pulp, chemical, and power-generating companies committed over three thousand violations in Ontario in 1998 alone, many on the Great Lakes. To acquire this information, the Sierra Legal Defence Fund was obliged to use the Freedom of Information Act because, after 1995, Ontario stopped releasing pollution reports to the public. Water problems in Lake Erie persisted. Once again the lake was in crisis in 2000. Scientists discovered a large, central oxygen-free zone (Figure 8.2); botulism, which was killing off birds and fish; dead puppy salamanders on the beach; and abundant new algae blooms. The state of the lake reflected the damaging effects of chemical waste and government inaction.

Problems in the Great Lakes remain because, "for nearly two hundred years, governments have been failing" them in defiance of public wants and needs and in deference to industry (Dempsey 2004, 276). And all of Canada's waterways suffer the same problems as the Great Lakes. Despite the importance of ensuring a safe supply of drinking water, many waterways in Canada have disrupted ecosystems and degraded water quality. Their preservation and improvement remains essential both for public health and the economy. Yet, as the twenty-first century dawned, public trust in the present system has only declined with incidents such as the outbreak of *E. coli* poisoning at Walkerton, Ontario, in 2000. Government cutbacks have caused policy makers and politicians to take a cavalier attitude toward water, as has the constant power struggle between provincial and federal politicians. In 2001, environmental commissioner Johanne Gélinas noted that Canada's approach to protecting the amount and quality of its water was inadequate and hampered by too little funding and slipshod environmental monitoring and research.

Wetlands

When waterways served as important transportation routes, people thought of their environment as a world of watersheds. That worldview changed, however, with the development of agriculture and the forestry industry and as Canada shifted to an urban industrial economy. Along the St. Lawrence Estuary, for instance, Aboriginal hunters and gatherers appreciated the wetlands for their abundant fish, birds, and wildlife, and settlers tilled their rich soils and used their grasses for hay. Across the country, Canada's wetlands account for 127 million hectares, or 14 percent of the country's land (see Figure 8.3). Wetlands include bogs, fens, swamps, and marshes that were protected by their remote location and marginal utility for agricultural and economic development. In southern areas, however, they sat in the way of agricultural development and were increasingly viewed as unproductive, useless,

and insect-ridden wastelands. With little understanding that wetlands play an important role in the ecological cycle by purifying water, containing soil erosion and floods, and increasing biodiversity, agriculturalists and planners began to either fill them in or pave over them to make way for farms and roads. In late nineteenth-century Ontario, pioneer Catharine Parr Traill noted that "the government is going to drain all the marshes and small lakes and swamps and survey all unclaimed lots" (Ballstadt, Hopkins, and Peterman 1996, 182).

Destruction of wetlands, combined with the damage wrought by the demise of the beaver during the fur trade, led to concern about their disappearance. In 1967, naturalist Fred Bosworth warned that wooded swamps and open cattail marshes had once been widespread features in Canada's natural scene but were being destroyed (Litteljohn and Pimlott 1971, 9). From the 1970s, preservation of wetlands has been linked to global environmental issues such as soil and water conservation, biodiversity, and wildlife protection. Although Canada has no general protection policy, the federal government has mapped wetlands, signed international agreements relating to wetland preservation, and designated a few protected areas. The provinces have also developed guidelines to classify and protect significant wetlands. For example, in 1992, Ontario required municipalities to protect wetlands within their boundaries, and the Ministry of Natural Resources has formed partnerships with nongovernmental organizations such as Wildlife Habitat Canada and Ducks Unlimited to encourage the stewardship and enhancement of private lands. Reclamation efforts often fall to private local

FIGURE 8.3 Canada's wetland inventory. Ducks Unlimited, founded in 1938, was in the forefront of restoring and protecting habitats and is Canada's leading wetland conservation organization. Its valuable work restores and creates wetlands for migrating birds. In cooperation with Environment Canada and other agencies, it produces an inventory of Canada's wetlands to better enable decision making in wetlands conservation, management, and land-use planning.

Source: Adapted from Ducks Unlimited Canada, http://www.ducks.ca/. Copyright Ducks Unlimited Canada

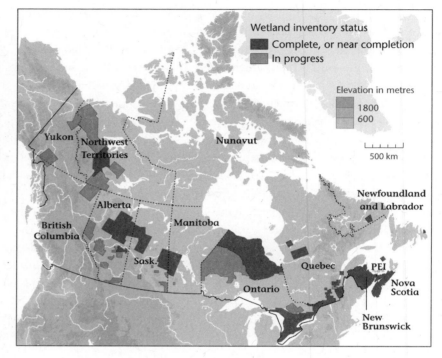

groups such as the Bring Back the Don movement in Toronto, the Cootes Paradise project in Hamilton, Ontario, and Ducks Unlimited's efforts in western Canada. All wetland projects help to combat water pollution, increase wildlife, and educate the public about the interconnectedness of nature and the importance of healthy water systems to maintaining life.

Canals and Waterways

The drive to manipulate and control waterways for human needs included the construction of vast canal and waterway systems in central Canada to transport goods and natural resources to market. As with wetlands destruction, these projects proceeded with little concern for their short- or long-term effect on the environment. These large megaprojects, particularly the building of dams, were part of a global phenomenon to control nature to fulfill economic and

THE COOTES PARADISE PROJECT

Cootes Paradise, the largest wetland at the western end of Lake Ontario, is bordered by Burlington and Hamilton, Ontario, and owned and managed by the Royal Botanical Gardens, a charitable organization. The wetland began to decline in the late nineteenth century because of pollution and the introduction of carp. In 1985, a study showed that the area had lost 85 percent of its plant cover and that the remainder consisted of non-native species. In 1993, Project Paradise, part of the larger Hamilton Harbour Remedial Plan, was founded to restore the wetland. The project is the largest undertaken in the Great Lakes Basin and a model for others across North America. The project concentrates on addressing the major stressors that led to the wetland's decline to create the underlying conditions for ecosystem recovery. Its short-term strategy focused on building a carp barrier called the Fishway to control non-native carp.

political purposes. Leaders and policy makers of all stripes projected powerful visions of tamed rivers that would benefit nations and their economies by providing new navigation routes, electricity, flood control, irrigation, and water for human use. In Canada, as elsewhere, their rhetoric often incorporated the language of heroic masculinity. Large dams were held up as technological achievements that embodied modernity and progress. The tourism industry focused on the grandeur of projects such as in Niagara Falls and made no mention of the impact their construction would have on local communities and ecosystems.

The Lachine Canal (see Figure 8.4), which allows ships to pass the rapids of St. Louis above Montreal, for instance, was completed by the colonial government in 1825-26. Fourteen kilometres long, the canal cut a swath through the land and included seven single locks. Between 1842 and 1848, the Canadian government created a deeper twin-lock canal system, and it enlarged the canal in the 1870s to enable bigger ships to reach Lakes Ontario and Erie. Repeated dredging of the St. Lawrence River downstream from Montreal

created a depth, by 1880, of 6.9 metres, and the increased number of ocean-going vessels allowed Montreal to compete for shipping with New York and Baltimore. In addition to the damage that construction did to the landscape, the canal helped make Montreal a major port, which, in turn, attracted more industry to the region. Other canals built in central Canada, including the Welland Canal (between Lake Ontario and Lake Erie, 1829), the Rideau Canal (between Ottawa and Kingston, 1832), and the Trent-Severn Waterway (between Lake Ontario at Trenton and Lake Huron at Port Severn, 1833), had a similar effect on the land and the environment. The Trent-Severn system was complex and consisted of locks, bridges, a lift-lock in Peterborough, and dams on forty Ontario lakes to regulate water levels and flow.

The St. Lawrence Seaway (see Figure 8.5), a joint Canada-US project built between 1954 and 1959, illustrates the lack of foresight and attention paid to environmental effects that accompanied the building of Canadian megaprojects in the twentieth century. Before the seaway, the river provided an insurmountable obstacle in the form of a bottleneck that

FIGURE 8.4 This panoramic view of the Montreal portion of the Lachine Canal, 1896, shows the factories that sprang up around the canal. Their emissions led the canal to be nicknamed Smokey Valley.
Montreal from Street Railway Power House chimney, 1896, Wm. Notman & Son – McCord Museum, View-2942, View-2943, View-2944

FIGURE 8.5 The Canadian icebreaker *D'Iberville* leads the first four ships going through the St. Lambert lock during the opening of the St. Lawrence Seaway in 1959.
Bettman/Corbis

narrowed to fast-moving rapids. The seaway, a deep-draft inland waterway, now extends 3,700 kilometres. Policy makers had long discussed the project as a potential way to expand trade by enabling huge ocean-going ships to penetrate the North American interior as far as the western freshwater shores of Lake Superior. The seaway, as envisaged, would also include hydro dams and generating stations to produce energy. The power stations required a head pond, which required the creation of Lake St. Lawrence. The seaway created enormous environmental changes and unforeseen problems that are expensive, if not impossible, to fix.

Building the St. Lawrence Seaway changed the St. Lawrence River–Great Lakes system

forever. The project employed fifteen thousand men who dug, dredged, and blasted the terrain to "tame" the river. Engineers and crews widened the Welland Canal for the fourth time. They also widened and deepened channels; built dams, locks, powerhouse structures, and navigation facilities; modified highways and railway tracks; and constructed new bridges or elevated existing ones (see Figure 8.6). In the International Rapids Section, they either removed, flooded, or sliced islands into fragments to clear a path for large ships. The project flooded 17,806 hectares on both sides of the border and ten villages on the Canadian side, including the old village of Iroquois (part of the Aboriginal community of Caughnawaga) and farm communities that dated back to the Loyalist migration. Approximately 6,500 Canadians were forced to relocate, a development that had long-term social and cultural effects. The historic buildings that were rescued were moved to the newly created Upper Canada Village near Morrisburg, Ontario.

Building the seaway's locks and canals led to the destruction, removal, and relocation of thousands of fish and the contamination of spawning grounds with polluted water. Some species (sturgeon) disappeared, others (muskellunge, pike, pickerel) declined, and still others (bass) migrated to new habitats. The seaway caused the American eel population to decline, and it disrupted bird migrations as ancient trees were felled and as plant cover either disappeared or changed with the introduction of new species.

The St. Lawrence Seaway opened up the region to new, alien species of plants and animals. Before the seaway, sea lampreys had entered Lake Ontario, probably through the

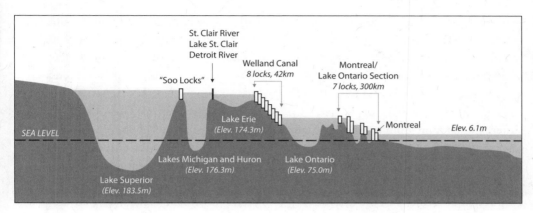

FIGURE 8.6 **This diagram shows the scale of the Great Lakes–St. Lawrence Seaway system, ranked by many as one of the outstanding engineering feats of the twentieth century.**
Source: Adapted from Marine Buzz, http://www.marinebuzz.com/

Welland Canal, and spread to the upper lakes. Alewives, a northwestern Atlantic fish of the herring family, were found in Lake Huron in 1933 and had spread to Lake Superior by 1954. To control the alewives population (and service the sports fishery industry), the States of Michigan and Ohio introduced Pacific salmon species into the lakes to prey on them. This intervention, environmentalists complained, undermined the restoration of indigenous lake trout. Other alien species followed alewives into the St. Lawrence system. In 1988, for instance, zebra mussels began to appear in the Great Lakes in large numbers: they reproduced rapidly and spread through all the lakes and their tributaries, where they wreaked havoc. The mussels clung to boat hulls, spread over beaches, covered screens on water intake systems at five Canadian power plants, and clogged the intake pipe at an Ontario drinking-water plant. Fish species such as the ruffe (from northern Europe), the tubenose goby (from eastern Europe), and bighead and silver carp (from Asia) likewise threatened the aquatic food chain.

In 1993, it was estimated that alien species accounted for 30 percent of all aquatic life in the Great Lakes. Legislators were slow to implement effective controls. In 1989 and 1990, respectively, Canada and the United States passed voluntary regulations that advised ships entering the Great Lakes to change their ballast water to prevent alien species from entering the lakes. Even though 89 percent of ships complied, it only requires one ship to introduce a new alien species. Without strict law enforcement, new species continue to disrupt the ecosystems of interior waterways. Despite investigations of other water control technologies – for instance, microfiltration and thermal, ultraviolet, and chemical treatments – the persistent influx of alien species in 2007 caused frustrated environmentalists and scientists to advocate closing the seaway to ocean-going ships.

The St. Lawrence Seaway's environmental impact has been extensive and has undermined the project's economic potential. For instance, the cost of transferring freight from ocean liners to trains at Montreal would be less than dealing with the effects of alien species. Although the St. Lawrence Seaway Authority and the shipping industry insist that they can "manage" the problem of continuing infestations, their track record has been poor. Whatever the outcome of the issue, an International Joint Commission report noted in 2000 that the "construction of power and navigation projects on the St. Lawrence River in the late 1950s forever changed the characteristics of the river" (International Joint Commission 2000, 18). Overconfident faith in technology on the part of governments and the shipping and hydroelectricity industries resulted in the destruction of ecosystems, the disruption of people's lives, and ongoing expensive environmental problems.

Hydroelectric Megaprojects

The spread of dams across the country after the Second World War likewise required deep restructuring of the land to harness water resources. When Canada and the United States decided to use Niagara Falls to generate hydroelectricity (see Chapter 7), for instance, they agreed to divert large amounts of water to "tame the falls." A treaty signed by the two countries in 1950 held that all water "in excess of that required for domestic and sanitary purposes, navigation and the falls may be diverted for power generation" (Dempsey 2004, 66). The project would adjust flow rates to ensure a scenic view of the falls during the tourist season but would otherwise reduce them. Thus, the development of the Niagara River "transmuted the character of the falling water into a controlled and focused force" to be exploited for human purposes (Dempsey 2004, 66).

Between 1945 and 1975, 613 large dams were completed in Canada. Nearly 60 percent of them were built to generate hydroelectricity. Dam building in Canada coincided

with a wave of projects around the globe. More than one large dam was completed per day in the 1960s. By the 1970s, the world's largest artificial lakes together covered 300,000 square kilometres, an area 20 percent larger than the Great Lakes. By the 1990s, approximately one-third of the world's stream flow passed over or through dams. Projects diverted or dammed virtually all major and many smaller rivers, but the largest projects in Canada were on the Peace, Columbia, St. Lawrence, and South Saskatchewan Rivers and included the Churchill Falls and James Bay Projects. Contemporary decision makers viewed these massive transformations of the environment positively, as developments for "the common good." But the projects were characterized by arbitrary decision making by elites, the sacrifice of local and minority interests, and environmental destruction, sometimes from unforeseen consequences. "Dams and irrigation held great appeal for those who make decisions. The benefits were tangible and immediate," and the state, large landowners, and powerful industries could capture "a tantalizing share." The costs could be "shunted onto the poor, the powerless, foreigners – or the future" (McNeill 2000, 179). Manipulation of water resources in one region led to manipulation in others, because "the lessons of manipulating the Great Lakes system without adequate predictive capacity and caution by governments still did not take hold" (Dempsey 2004, 147).

The Columbia River Project, situated in the Pacific Northwest region of Canada and the United States and built in the 1960s, had the same effects as the St. Lawrence Seaway Project, including flooding, environmental disruption, and the relocation of residents. The Columbia River has the largest volume of all the rivers that flow into the Pacific Ocean from North America, and it is the second largest river in America (its head-waters begin in the Canadian Rockies, and it flows 2,044 kilometres). The hydroelectric project was the largest completed in North America, and the river in general has been "dammed into submission," particularly in the United States, to provide cheap electricity to millions; to control flooding; to provide irrigation to dry, fertile lands south of the border; to open the river to shipping; and to provide water to cool nuclear reactors. Its dams "to improve nature" were seen as engines of economic progress and sources of renewable energy, which was in demand. The dams drastically altered the landscape and the river's ecosystem as their construction "raced ahead of knowledge of the consequences" (White 1995, 95).

Canada and the United States negotiated the Columbia River Treaty in 1961, which led to the construction of three storage dams – the Duncan (1967), the High Arrow (1968), and the Mica (1973) – on the upper Columbia River (see Figure 8.7). In the treaty, Canada and the International Joint Commission agreed that the United States would build the Libby Dam on the Kootenay River in Montana with an enormous storage project or reservoir that would extend north across the border. Together, the four "treaty dams" would double the storage capacity of the Columbia River Basin. The project would also increase the ability to control annual flooding downstream, which threatened damage to large areas of British Columbia, Washington, and Oregon. The two

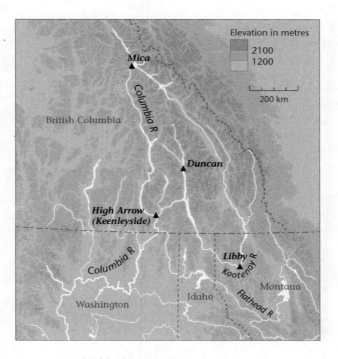

FIGURE 8.7 Columbia River Treaty storage projects

countries ratified the agreement in 1964, and the United States agreed to pay Canada $69 million in installments for flood control benefits as each dam was completed. British Columbia was also entitled to half the power generated in the United States in return for the operation of the Canadian storage sites. Because the province did not need power generated by the Columbia (it already had an energy-producing dam project on the Peace River), it sold the power back to American utility companies for thirty years for $275 million and used the revenue to fund construction of the three treaty dams.

From the earliest negotiations to the completion of the project, nationalists in Canada raised concerns. The disruption to people

THE PEACE RIVER PROJECT

The W.A.C. Bennett Dam, named after a BC premier, is a large hydroelectric earth-fill dam located on the Peace River in northern British Columbia. Completed in 1968, the dam required diverting and burying sections of the Peace River, created the largest artificial lake in western Canada (Williston Lake), and caused flooding in the Arrow Lakes. Capable of generating 2,730 megawatts of electricity at peak capacity, at the time, the Peace River Project was one of the largest of its kind in the world. Although the dam provided relatively inexpensive electricity to the Lower Mainland and Vancouver, building it destroyed Aboriginal sites and artifacts and early farm communities. The dam also altered water levels to such a degree that it created immense environmental disruption in the Peace-Athabasca Delta and in the Mackenzie Delta located hundreds of kilometres away.

FIGURE 8.8 Construction of the W.A.C. Bennett Dam, 1968
BC Archives, G-01514

and the environment, they argued, was unnecessary because the Columbia River Project would benefit only the United States. The Columbia River Treaty eliminated Canada's option to divert water for its own purposes and replaced the International Joint Commission with a new international board, which gave the United States more control. The treaty benefitted the United States in terms of power and water and integrated the smaller but vital Canadian part of the basin into the whole. When finished, the project

also flooded fertile farmland in the Kootenay Valley, land that was potentially worth more than the $344 million the United States transferred to Canada and British Columbia.

Hydroelectricity projects on the Columbia and Peace Rivers caused extensive environmental decline and disrupted communities (see Figure 8.8). Provincial fishery biologists predicted a 70 percent decline in the number of Kokanee salmon and Dolly Varden and rainbow trout, and they warned that all valuable game fish would be disrupted as water levels, temperatures, and flows were changed. The Columbia River had been one of the best for salmon. The effects of agricultural runoff, overfishing, and dams, however, reduced some wild species to the point of extinction. Their decline threatened jobs, cultural traditions, and communities dependent on the salmon fishery. Although BC Hydro in 1967 created the largest man-made spawning channel in the world at Meadow Creek, located near the Duncan dam site outside Revelstoke, the government did nothing about the High Arrow dam's disruptions to the habitats of beaver, muskrat, waterfowl, and upland game birds. The flooding caused concerns about the loss of beaches and docks along the lakeshore. When BC Hydro's engineers covered the shores with "huge pieces of jagged rock," ostensibly "on engineering and economic grounds," locals did not approve (Loo 2004, 185).

Opposition to Megaprojects

Before the emergence of the environmental movement in the 1970s, opponents of dam megaprojects did not have the language to express their opposition clearly. Many objected to the destruction of spacious, scattered, self-sufficient communities that had, they believed, grown in an integrated relationship with the surrounding environment. Early settlements had affected local rivers and landscapes, but the environment had also influenced local people – it was a reciprocal process. Faith in technology and the promotion of economic growth with little concern about their social and environmental effects characterized the postwar period, an era when politicians and engineers, the leaders

of the technopolitical regime, arrogantly asserted their power over local people and environments.

In the case of the St. Lawrence Seaway and Columbia River Projects, provincial governments favoured the hydroelectric industry over local farming, fishing, and tourism interests. The state took a bureaucratic, arbitrary approach to planning that rankled local citizens, who were accustomed to independence. Their protests were muted but extended to the new communities and towns created for displaced persons from flooded areas. Planners laid out new towns according to textbook plans. The towns looked like suburbs and were characterized by modern lighting, minimalist houses, community centres, and shopping plazas. Hydro and telephone companies could service them easily because planners bunched their facilities together. In Ontario, along the St. Lawrence Seaway, objectors' concerns revolved around the issue of compensation, the loss of historical buildings and places, and the construction of commonplace town layouts that did not "relate the towns to the river on which the inhabitants have always lived" (Parr 2010, 86). In British Columbia, citizens also criticized the new towns for their artificiality. They characterized the towns as soulless creations imposed on the landscape with little concern for space or re-creating a sense of connection to the environment. One resident of the Arrow Lakes remarked, "What hurts is that you are losing the land on which you worked, where you know every bit of it, where you got accustomed to it ... It becomes part of you" (Loo 2004, 193). Planners urged BC Hydro to include mature nursery-grown trees in the new towns to "hasten the mature appearance of the community," mask the residents' dislocation, and ease their transition to their new lives (Loo 2004, 193). But the trees only added to the controlled and artificial feeling of the towns. In both provinces, a few older buildings were preserved when citizens objected to the plans, but most were burned before the areas were flooded.

In all regions, hydroelectric projects big and small proceeded without assessments of their environmental impact. Negotiations with local residents in northern regions between the 1950s and the 1980s on the Saskatchewan, Churchill, and Nelson Rivers consistently resulted in the victimization of Aboriginal peoples. Projects took away their way of life by flooding reserves and traditional lands, eroding hunting and trapping areas, and blocking the use of waterways for fishing and transportation. Some Aboriginal groups, assisted by environmentalists, took legal action to obtain compensation for damages. The treatment of Aboriginal people by provincial governments was a replay of the western treaty-signing process in the nineteenth century and had the same result — a loss of land and livelihood.

The James Bay Hydroelectric Project

The James Bay Hydroelectric Project sparked the most controversy, particularly because of the Quebec government's insensitivity to Aboriginal peoples and their lands. Although the government emphasized the economic benefits of the project, its origins were less than altruistic. Six months after the 1970 October Crisis, during which the provincial government had appeared weak and indeci-

sive in its dealings with the Front de libération du Québec, Premier Robert Bourassa announced Hydro-Québec's intention to dam and harness the province's northern rivers for hydroelectric power. The "development of James Bay," he proclaimed, "is a project without precedent in the economic history of Quebec" (Richardson 1972, 9).

Built in two phases (1972-85 and 1989-94), the project was the second largest hydroelectric installation in the world after the Itaipu Dam in Brazil. Located in an enormous little-known subarctic area with a fragile terrain, it proceeded without sufficient planning or scientific study and no environmental assessment, for none was required at that time. The government did not consult Aboriginal people and viewed them as incidental. Policy makers and planners did not consider their traditional way of life viable, even though the Cree had maintained their language and culture for centuries. The project profoundly affected both Cree and Innu communities, their environment, which was their traditional hunting ground, and their health.

Phase 1 alone involved the creation of the La Grande Rivière Complex, which stretched over 800 kilometres along the main river and, when completed, included 5 powerhouse reservoirs, 9 dams, 206 dikes, 37 generating units, and thousands of kilometres of transmission lines (see Figure 8.9). Because La Grande Rivière dropped only 376 metres in its course, with no natural falls, Hydro-Québec built huge dams along the river and flooded low-lying areas to create reservoirs. Because the drop of other rivers in the area was also small, engineers, in the interest of efficiency, diverted their flows to La Grande Rivière. As a result, 87 percent of the water from the Rivière Eastmain's basin and 27 percent of the water from the Caniapiscau Basin went to the main river, doubling its flow potential. The builders used local morainic sands, gravels, and broken rock because they were cheaper than concrete. They moved and poured nearly 153 million cubic metres of fill and flooded 11,655 square kilometres of land. The Caniapiscau Reservoir, one of five, became the second largest water surface in Quebec.

Flooding the land had demonstrable ecological and social effects. Hydro-Québec literally assaulted the environment and destroyed wildlife. Building the complex involved at least one massive drowning of caribou, in 1984, deforestation, and community dislocation and relocation. In the newly flooded reservoirs, the appearance of elevated concentrations of mercury in fish after 1978 surprised the project's administrators, who informed the Cree after the fact about the hazards of methyl mercury. Planners later learned that the impoundment of hydroelectric reservoirs leads to the conversion of mercury already present in plants and flooded soil. It wasn't until 1986 that the project established the James Bay Mercury Committee to monitor mercury levels in fish and people, research the problem, and educate Aboriginal people on how best to modify their diet to avoid serious illness.

The project transformed an isolated area previously accessible only by helicopter and light aircraft to one with 1,500 kilometres of all-weather roads and five airports. Each major construction site had camps with

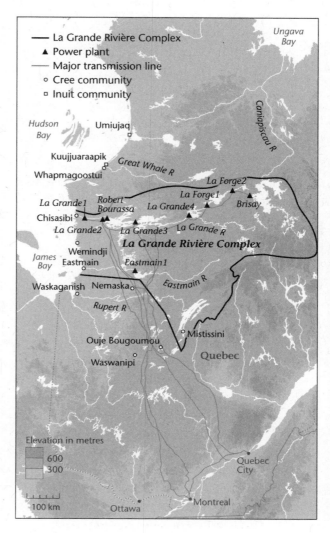

FIGURE 8.9 The James Bay Hydroelectric Project has a combined capacity of over 16,000 megawatts, almost half of Hydro-Québec's total output and capacity. The project stretches over 177,000 kilometres and covers approximately 11 percent of the total area of Quebec. The first phase alone cost $13.7 billion (1987 dollars).

HYDROELECTRICITY PROJECTS AND SMALL STREAMS

The effect of hydroelectricity projects on the environment extends even to the smallest streams. Shelter Valley Creek, for instance, empties into Lake Ontario east of Cobourg. In the nineteenth century, the creek was exceptionally beautiful and was dotted by sawmills, gristmills, wool factories, carding mills, and pump factories. The stream had well-wooded banks and many trout. When small dams were constructed to regulate its flow, however, the number of fish declined. Later, large-scale production of hydro-electricity in Ontario required forests to be cleared. Erosion washed soil into the stream, and neglected and broken milldams and flash floods ravaged the streambed and turned the creek into "a sorry sight, full of boulders, broken fences and refuse" (Guillet 1957, xxvii). The process of environmental degradation at Shelter Valley Creek exemplified "in a small way the waste of natural resources so evident almost everywhere in the Trent Valley and its environs on a much greater scale" (Guillet 1957, liv).

modern facilities and family villages to accommodate twenty-two thousand workers in the peak construction period. New connections to the south and the invasion of non-Aboriginal people facilitated the influx of consumer goods and intensified human pressure on the ecozone. Non-Aboriginal sports hunters also gained access to the territory and competed with local people for wildlife resources.

The Cree reacted to the James Bay Project by getting organized. After losing on appeal an injunction to stop the project, which was already under construction, they signed, under extreme pressure, the James Bay and Northern Quebec Agreement (JBNQA) in 1975. The Cree relinquished Aboriginal title to their land in return for benefits: an income security program, a fund for long-term economic security, a fund for community services, an environmental-monitoring framework (on wildlife populations and water flows), and $275 million from Hydro-Québec.

The JBNQA established a three-tiered land regime in which Aboriginal people retained a small area of land for their exclusive use and subsistence purposes. The agreement gave the Cree control over natural resources and traditional hunting territories, and they could use a second, larger portion for hunting, trapping, and fishing. Non-Aboriginal people, however, also had access to the area for economic development. The agreement left the vast majority of lands open to economic development and hunting, trapping, and fishing by both Aboriginal and non-Aboriginal people. Persistent hunting by both groups in the region was not sustainable.

Conflict between environmentalists, Aboriginal groups, and the government escalated during Phase 2 of the project, when construction centred on building five secondary power plants on the La Grande Rivière and its tributaries and three new reservoirs. The project would flood another 10,000 square kilometres of land and would require 138 dams and dikes. Hydro-Québec also proposed an additional project on the Great Whale River to the north. The goal of Phase 2 was to increase production of electricity for export. Unlike the first phase, Phase 2 proceeded with an environmental impact assessment after the Sierra Legal Defence Fund won a long, costly battle in the Supreme Court of Canada, which ordered the federal government to examine the project's environmental impact.

Environmental studies on Phase 1 concluded that "the overall effect of the project on the terrestrial ecosystem is negative because it will take some time for vegetative regeneration and for fauna to find new feed- ing and breeding grounds" (Hornig 1999, 4). Some experts, however, saw the creation of artificial lakes as a positive development on the grounds that they constituted a new aquatic ecosystem that could result in a new commercial fishing industry in Quebec. Opposition among Cree to the Great Whale extension, however, also raised awareness of the project's environmental impact. In 1990, Grand Chief Matthew Coon Come organ- ized a canoe trip from the Hudson River to Albany, New York, to bring international pressure to bear on the Quebec government. The Cree argued that the project had intro- duced poverty, social problems, and few jobs to their communities. Environmentally, the project had also had a profound impact on their traditional lands and way of life. Because the natural flow of the rivers had been modified, 4 percent of traditional Cree hunting and trapping territories had been lost to reservoirs, including 10 percent of the territories of the village of Chisasibi. In

response to opposition, the State of New York withdrew from a multi-million-dollar purchasing agreement in 1992. The Quebec government and Hydro-Québec abandoned the Great Whale extension in 1994 when the courts ordered them to respect their legal obligations in the JBNQA.

In 2002, the Cree negotiated a new deal, La Paix des Braves, in which they gave up efforts to prevent Phase 3 of the project, which would entail diverting the Rupert River into the Eastmain River and the con- struction of the Eastmain generating station and reservoir. In return, unlike in the old, poorly enforced agreement, the Cree received more representation in a new development corporation, an improved forestry manage- ment system that stipulated "mosaic cuts" instead of clear-cutting in Cree territory, and compensation of up to $3.5 billion over half a century.

After the Second World War, large dam projects took precedence over other busi- nesses, local peoples, healthy ecosystems, and

ARTIFICIAL LAKES

Artificial lakes formed from dam reservoirs have well-known environmental consequences, including flooding, the decom- position of organic matter and the release of greenhouse gas emissions, the fragmentation of river ecosystems, riverline and coastal erosion, and altered water temperatures. Yet in Canada, as elsewhere, artificial lakes were hailed as progress.

Before the Second World War, Canada had only one large man-made lake, the Gouin Reservoir on the St. Maurice River. Eight more were con- structed in the 1960s. The Manicouagan Dam and Reser- voir became a symbol of Quebec pride and popular culture during the Quiet Revolution when Georges Dor released the song "La Manic" in 1966. Because

North America had fewer natural- flowing large rivers than other continents, Canada, like the United States with its Hoover Dam, played up the mystique of dams by emphasizing their power, technological prowess, and modernity. They became objects worthy of visits by admiring tourists.

public health. The state's arbitrary approach to local communities dislodged people, ignored local interests, and imposed new living arrangements and new patterns of interaction with newly manipulated environments. Construction frequently went ahead without environmental assessments and, as historian Donald Worster notes in the case of the Hoover Dam, megaprojects not only reconfigured the face of the earth, they also altered "the distribution of social and economic power on it" (Worster 1992, 64).

WATER IS ESSENTIAL to human life, but Canadians have taken it for granted. The idea that waterways existed for human use, could absorb massive amounts of waste, and could survive manipulation by humans has meant that, for much of Canada's history, governments and industry felt free to do as they pleased – to subject bodies of water such as the Great Lakes to multiple forms of environmental degradation and to literally reshape the landscape to tap water resources. When this approach resulted in disaster – chemical fires, public health emergencies,

and acid rain – officials responded by passing protective legislation. But pressure from business has ensured that these measures are not strictly enforced. Since the 1960s, environmentalists, community groups, and nongovernmental organizations have made Canadians more aware that water is not an unlimited resource – but rather a scarce resource coveted by other nations – and they have raised the question of whether the benefits of vast megaprojects such as the St. Lawrence Seaway Project outweigh the risks, driving home the importance of environmental assessments and community participation. There is still much to be done. The necessity of cleaning up and protecting fresh water is evident to a more environmentally conscious public that urgently needs environmental laws enforced for a safe, clean, future water supply. In 2008, D.W. Schindler, an ecology professor and recipient of the Stockholm Water Prize in 1991, commented that "the lack of a water policy is an excellent example of a major shortcoming in Canadian environmental policy" (Schindler 2008, 25).

Works Cited

Ashworth, William. 1986. *The Late, Great Lakes: An Environmental History.* Toronto: Collins.

Ballstadt, C., E. Hopkins, and M.A. Peterman, eds. 1996. *I Bless You in My Heart: Selected Correspondence of Catharine Parr Traill.* Toronto: University of Toronto Press.

Bogue, Margaret Beattie. 2001. *Fishing on the Great Lakes: An Environmental History, 1783-1933.* Madison: University of Wisconsin Press.

Dempsey, Dave. 2004. *On the Brink: The Great Lakes in the 21st Century.* East Lansing: Michigan State University Press.

Ehrenfeld, David W. 1971. *Biological Conservation.* New York: Holt, Rinehart and Winston.

Guillet, E.C. 1957. *The Valley of the Trent.* Toronto: Champlain Society.

Hornig, James F. 1999. *Social and Environmental Impacts of the James Bay Hydroelectric Project.* Montreal and Kingston: McGill-Queen's University Press.

International Joint Commission. 2000. "Protection of the Waters of the Great Lakes: Final Report to the Governments of Canada and the United States." http://www.cglg.org/.

Litteljohn, Bruce M., and Douglas H. Pimlott. 1971. *Why Wilderness: A Report on Mismanagement in Lake Superior Park.* Toronto: New Press

Loo, Tina. 2004. "People in the Way: Modernity, Environment, and Society on the Arrow Lakes." *BC Studies* 142-43 (Summer-Autumn): 161-96.

McNeill, John R. 2000. *Something New under the Sun: An Environmental History of the Twentieth-Century World.* New York: W.W. Norton.

Parr, Joy. 2010. *Sensing Changes: Technologies, Environments, and the Everyday, 1953-2003.* Vancouver: UBC Press.

Richardson, Boyce. 1972. *James Bay: The Plot to Drown the North Woods.* San Francisco/Toronto: Sierra Club/Clarke Irwin.

Schindler, D.W. 2008. "The Role of Science in Making Sound Environmental Policy." Killam Annual Lecture, Edmonton, October.

Storey, Robert H. 1982. "Workers, Unions and Steel: The Shaping of the Hamilton Working Class, 1935-48." PhD diss., University of Toronto.

Taylor, Joseph E., III. 1999. *Making Salmon: An Environmental History of the Northwest Fisheries Crisis.* Seattle: University of Washington Press.

White, Richard. 1995. *The Organic Machine.* New York: Hill and Wang.

Worster, Donald. 1992. *Under Western Skies.* New York: Oxford University Press.

For Further Reading

Armstrong, C., M. Evenden, and H.V. Nelles. 2009. *The River Returns: An Environmental History of the Bow.* Montreal and Kingston: McGill-Queen's University Press.

Bocking, Richard C. 1972. *Canada's Water for Sale?* Toronto: James Lewis and Samuel.

Massell, David. 2000. *Amassing Power: J.B. Duke and the Saguenay River, 1897-1927.* Montreal and Kingston: McGill-Queen's University Press.

Worster, Donald. 1985. *Rivers of Empire: Water, Aridity, and the Growth of the American West.* New York: Oxford University Press.

The Great Lakes

Ashworth, William. 1986. *The Late, Great Lakes: An Environmental History.* Toronto: Collins.

Bogue, Margaret Beattie. 2001. *Fishing on the Great Lakes: An Environmental History, 1783-1933.* Madison: University of Wisconsin Press.

Campbell, Claire Elizabeth. 2005. *Shaped by the West Wind: Nature and History in Georgian Bay.* Vancouver: UBC Press.

Dempsey, Dave. 2004. *On the Brink: The Great Lakes in the 21st Century.* East Lansing: Michigan State University Press.

Globe and Mail. 1998. "Water-Pollution Violations Triple in Ontario." 2 May.

—. 2004. "Rising Levels of Contaminants in Gull Eggs Raising Alarm." 7 May.

Mittelstaedt, Martin. 1997. "Ontario Cuts Pollution Funds." *Globe and Mail,* 10 February, A1 and A6.

Storey, Robert H. 1982. "Workers, Unions and Steel: The Shaping of the Hamilton Working Class, 1935-48." PhD diss., University of Toronto.

The Lake Erie Crisis

Ashworth, William. 1986. *The Late, Great Lakes: An Environmental History.* Toronto: Collins.

Dempsey, Dave. 2004. *On the Brink: The Great Lakes in the 21st Century.* East Lansing: Michigan State University Press.

McGucken, William. 2000. *Lake Erie Rehabilitated: Controlling Cultural Eutrophication, 1960s-1990s.* Akron, OH: University of Akron Press.

Read, Jennifer. 1996. "'Let Us Heed the Voice of Youth': Laundry Detergents, Phosphates and the Emergence of the Environmental Movement of Ontario." *Journal of the Canadian Historical Association* 7, 1: 227-50.

—. 2000. "Managing Water Quality in the Great Lakes Basin: Sewage Pollution Control, 1951-1960." In *Ontario since Confederation,* edited by Edgar-Andre Montigny and Lori Chambers, 339-61. Toronto: University of Toronto Press.

Toxic Pollutants

Ashworth, William. 1986. *The Late, Great Lakes: An Environmental History.* Toronto: Collins.

Cruikshank, Ken, and Nancy B. Bouchier. 2004. "Blighted Areas and Obnoxious Industries: Constructing Environmental Inequality on an Industrial Waterfront, Hamilton, Ontario, 1890-1960." *Environmental History* 9, 3: 464-96.

Dempsey, Dave. 2004. *On the Brink: The Great Lakes in the 21st Century.* East Lansing: Michigan State University Press.

Findlay, Alan. 2002. "Premier Okays Water Reforms." *Sun Media,* 25 May.

Fletcher, Thomas H. 2003. *From Love Canal to Environmental Justice: The Politics of Hazardous Waste on the Canadian-American Border.* Peterborough, ON: Broadview Press.

Keeling, Arn. 2004. "'Sink or Swim': Water Pollution and Environmental Politics, 1889-1975." *BC Studies* 142-43 (Summer-Autumn): 85-99.

Kidd, Jim. 1993. "Mercury Alert: Grassy Narrows and White Dog Anti-Mercury Campaign." *The Archivist* 21, 1: 26-28.

Mackie, Richard. 2000. "Water Tragedy Could Happen Again, MD Says." *Globe and Mail,* 11 October.

Shkilnyk, Anastasia M. 1985. *A Poison Stronger Than Love: The Destruction of an Ojibway Community.* New Haven: Yale University Press.

Wetlands

Estrin, David, and John Swaigen. 1993. *Environment on Trial: A Guide to Environmental Law and Policy.* Toronto: Emond Montgomery Publications.

Hatvany, Matthew G. 2003. *Marshlands: Four Centuries of Environmental Change on the Shores of the St. Lawrence.* Sainte-Foy: Les Presses de l'Université Laval.

Litteljohn, Bruce M., and Douglas H. Pimlott. 1971. *Why Wilderness: A Report on Mismanagement in Lake Superior Park.* Toronto: New Press

Canals and Waterways

Angus, James T. 1988. *A Respectable Ditch: A History of the Trent-Severn Waterway, 1833-1920.* Montreal and Kingston: McGill-Queen's University Press.

Goumay, Isabelle, and France Vanlaethen. 1998. *Montreal Metropolis, 1880-1930.* Toronto: Stoddart Publishing.

International Joint Commission. 2000. "Protection of the Waters of the Great Lakes: Final Report to the Governments of Canada and the United States." http://www.cglg.org/.

Hydroelectric Megaprojects

Alexander, Jeff. 2009. *Pandora's Locks: The Opening of the Great Lakes–St. Lawrence Seaway.* East Lansing: Michigan State University Press.

Dempsey, Dave. 2004. *On the Brink: The Great Lakes in the 21st Century.* East Lansing: Michigan State University Press.

Higgins, Larratt T. 1995. "The Alienation of Canadian Resources: The Case of the Columbia River Treaty." In *Consuming Canada: Readings in Environmental History,* edited by Chad Gaffield and Pam Gaffield, 267-79. Mississauga: Copp Clark.

Loo, Tina. 2004. "People in the Way: Modernity, Environment, and Society on the Arrow Lakes." *BC Studies* 142-43 (Summer-Autumn): 161-96.

MacDowell, Laurel Sefton. 2008. "The Conquest of Nature, Environmental Destruction and the Failed St. Lawrence Seaway." Paper presented to the annual meeting of the Canadian Historical Association, Vancouver, June.

Massell, David. 2011. *Quebec Hydropolitics: The Peribonka Concessions of the Second World War.* Montreal and Kingston: McGill-Queen's University Press.

Mills, E.L., J.H. Leach, J.T. Carlton, and C.L. Secor. 1994. "Exotic Species and the Integrity of the Great Lakes: Lessons from the Past." *BioScience* 44, 10: 666-76.

Taylor, James E., III. 1999. *Making Salmon: An Environmental History of the Northwest Fisheries Crisis.* Seattle: University of Washington Press.

Waldran, James B. 1988. *As Long as the Rivers Run: Hydroelectric Development and Native Communities in Western Canada.* Winnipeg: University of Manitoba Press.

Opposition to Megaprojects

Loo, Tina. 2004. "People in the Way: Modernity, Environment, and Society on the Arrow Lakes." *BC Studies* 142-43 (Summer-Autumn): 161-96.

Parr, Joy. 2010. *Sensing Changes: Technologies, Environments, and the Everyday, 1953-2003.* Vancouver: UBC Press.

Wilson, J.W. 1973. *People in the Way: The Human Aspects of the Columbia River Project.* Toronto: University of Toronto Press.

The James Bay Hydroelectric Project

Carlson, Hans M. 2008. *Home Is the Hunter: The James Bay Cree and Their Land.* Vancouver: UBC Press.

Hamley, William. 1983. "Geographical Record: Hydroelectric Developments in the James Bay Region, Quebec." *Geographical Review* 73, 1: 110-12.

Hornig, James F. 1999. *Social and Environmental Impacts of the James Bay Hydroelectric Project.* Montreal and Kingston: McGill-Queen's University Press.

Richardson, Boyce. 1972. *James Bay: The Plot to Drown the North Woods.* San Francisco/Toronto: Sierra Club/Clarke Irwin and Co.

9

The Contested World of Food and Agriculture

Our ingenuity in feeding ourselves is prodigious, but at various points our
technologies come into conflict with nature's ways of doing things, as when
we seek to maximize efficiency by planting crops or raising animals in vast
monocultures. This is something nature never does, always and for good
reasons practicing diversity instead.

– MICHAEL POLLAN, AUTHOR, JOURNALIST, AND ACTIVIST,
THE OMNIVORE'S DILEMMA, 2006

FOOD IS BASIC to life, and throughout history the diet of Canadians has reflected their
cultural relationship to the environment.
During the settlement period, farmers were
limited not only by agriculture's rural basis
but also by climate and biology – by limited
growing times and animal gestation. Since
then, expanding transportation and distribution systems and corporate organization in
an international marketplace have fundamentally reorganized food production. New
methods to reduce the importance of nature
in agriculture such as mechanization and
monoculture (see Chapter 2), hybrid plants,
the use of chemical and nitrogen fertilizers,
and biotechnology have increased production and lowered consumer food costs but
have ignored ecosystems. Harnessing these
methods, agribusiness – agriculture conducted on commercial principles, using

advanced technology – rapidly gained
ground in the twentieth century, pushing
small farmers into debt or out of agriculture
entirely. As consumers grew less and bought
more mass-produced and processed products,
the quality and nature of the soil, food, and
consumption declined.

Recent debates about the application
of biotechnology to food production reflect
concerns about the transformation of agriculture, the control of nature, the loss of
biodiversity, and food security. Attacks on
the geographic and biological constraints of
agriculture have been so successful that more
natural forms of farming – organic, local,
and sustainable – are now deemed "alternative." Supporters of the alternative food
movement argue that the modern food system and farming economy are unsustainable
and pose grave health risks to Canadians.

The Revolution in Agriculture

Beginning in the late nineteenth century, government-sponsored research supported farmers, industrial agriculture, and the modern food industry. Just as the Canadian Geological Survey assisted the development of the mining industry, so too did government-run experimental farms contribute to the commercialization of agriculture by developing hardier grains, larger, more uniform fruit, and hybrid plants. Agricultural colleges trained farmers and horticulturalists in the most modern methods, and a regulatory framework emerged as governments set national and provincial nutritional standards and required labels.

Plant breeding, which had traditionally been carried out by farmers who collected seeds, was gradually replaced with a systematic scientific approach carried out by professionals. Farmers supported and sometimes initiated government programs, and the fruits of their research transformed agriculture in Canada. In 1884, the federal govern-ment considered the possibility of funding agricultural research when it established a select committee to investigate how to improve farming in Canada. The committee recommended the creation of an experimental farm, which would test grain varieties, trees, and fertilizers and distribute them throughout the country. In 1886, the Act Respecting Experimental Farm Stations passed, and William Saunders was appointed director of the Experimental Farms Service. The legislation authorized five farms – located in Ottawa (for Ontario and Quebec), Nappan (Nova Scotia), Brandon (Manitoba), Indian Head (North-West Territories, now Saskatchewan), and Agassiz (British Columbia) – with programs dedicated to the improvement of plant and livestock breeding. The experimental farm on the Prairies played an integral role in the settlement of the West and the development of wheat farming (see Chapter 2).

More farms followed in the twentieth century. Scientists at the stations tested crops and new techniques in animal management developed by farmers and researchers working in cooperation. They planted trial plots on hundreds of farms to develop and test new plant varieties, and farmers, in turn, used the research stations and discussed problems with their superintendents. The landscaped grounds of the stations themselves became showpieces for this collaborative research (see Figure 9.1). Staff at the farms also cooperated with parallel provincial agencies such as provincial experimental farms.

The Ontario Agricultural College and Experimental Farm, for instance, was established in the 1870s. It developed early trial programs, offered lectures on horticulture,

GREGOR MENDEL AND GENETICS

In addition to developing inorganic fertilizers, scientific advances in industrial agriculture extended to plants. In 1865, Gregor Mendel, an Austrian scientist and Augustinian friar, learned how certain characteristics passed from one generation to the next by experimenting with pea plants. He noticed that when he crossed a plant with a certain characteristic, such as a long stem, with a plant with the opposite characteristic, a short stem, the resulting hybrid plant did not have a medium stem but rather a long one. When he crossed the hybrid plants with each other, one type dominated the other: there were three times as many offspring that had long stems as short stems. Mendel attributed this three-to-one ratio to what he called dominant and recessive "particles" in the plants, what we now know as genes.

FIGURE 9.1 Barns at the Central Experimental Farm in Ottawa in the 1920s. The experimental farm, a 400 hectare national historic site, still conducts research with laboratories and research plots.
Library and Archives Canada, PA-034408

and did public outreach, including advising immigrants on how to farm in Canada. From the 1920s, its expanding plant-breeding program included ornamentals, strawberries, gooseberries, apples, and vegetables. In 1904, the Ontario Fruit Growers' Association and the Ontario Vegetable Growers' Association sought legislation, regulations, subsidies, and standards controls and pressured the provincial government for experimental stations to assist growers. The government established an experimental farm at Vineland in 1906, and stations at Simcoe and Brantford in the Holland Marsh (now a part of Guelph University) followed. The farms developed fruits, such as peaches, for commercial purposes. Their experiments with new breeds became the basis for a viable fruit-growing industry. Between 1916 and 1956, E.F. Palmer directed scientists at the Vineland station as they researched over one thousand varieties of fruits and vegetables and, after 1928, tested

them within a local network of farmers. Most Vineland breeds were given names that started with a "V," such as the Victor sweet cherry and Vedette, Valiant, and Veteran peaches. In the 1930s, the station began to research grapes for winemaking, and in 1936 and 1937 it developed mould-resistant tomatoes and vegetables for tomato growers in Leamington and for commercial growers in the Holland Marsh.

In the West, noted plant breeder Frank L. Skinner introduced over two hundred hybrids and was an advocate of patents for hybrids and for labelling plants by place of origin. In the Maritimes, Roscoe Fillmore hybridized shrubs such as rhododendrons and azaleas for hardiness and, after heading up the largest commercial orchard in New Brunswick, started the Valley Nursery in the Annapolis Valley. Over the next few decades, the selective breeding of plants for desirable or popular traits spread across the nation. In the 1960s, for instance, farmers and wine-growers used the process to improve the grape and wine industries of Ontario and British Columbia.

Regulatory legislation that set standards for commercial plants accompanied the development of new hybrid plants. Ontario, for instance, established the Fruit Branch in the Department of Agriculture in 1908. Ten years later, with the passage of the Ontario Fruit Pests Act, it began to inspect orchards. The Fruit Packaging Act (1922) set standards for cold storage and for packaging fruit to upgrade products. The Ontario government built a cold storage plant to help fruit farmers distribute and market their fruit. In 1929, it appointed its own horticulturalist to upgrade the fruit being marketed. Other provinces developed new varieties and products. British Columbia's Summerland station, for instance, raised Spartan apples and hardy berries and kiwi. Morden station in Manitoba grew trees suitable to the Prairies. Crop yields improved as the federal and provincial governments worked with farmers to encourage crop spraying and inspections. In 1912,

the Dominion Entomological Branch joined forces with the provinces to research pest control.

Agricultural and horticultural research – federal and provincial, public and private – changed the landscape. As monoculture and the use of hybrids increased, biodiversity decreased. Advances in agriculture and horticulture created jobs, more commercial products, and higher standards, but scientists increasingly used plant-breeding techniques to develop plant characteristics compatible with industrial agriculture, crop varieties that farmers could cultivate mechanically to meet the specific needs of the processing industries. These technologies therefore also changed what Canadians ate and how farmers approached the land.

Modern agribusiness integrated food growing and processing into an increasingly global market. These developments were part of the green revolution, which the United States set in motion in the 1940s and 1950s with policies designed to restructure production and consumption patterns outside of North America. Research, development, and

ISABELLA PRESTON: "DEAN OF HYBRIDISTS"

Isabella Preston was born in Lancaster, England, and immigrated to Canada in 1912. She began her career at the Ontario Agricultural College, where she worked to breed quick-ripening and disease- and insect-resistant fruit. She was hired by the Central Experimental Farm in Ottawa in 1920. She also worked on hybridizing flowers and became instrumental in the burgeoning science of breeding hardier hybrids. In 1916, she crossed two lilies, *Lilium regale* and *Lilium sargentiae,* and then developed the cross into the acclaimed George C. Creelman lily, which is often still used as a parent for contemporary hybrids.

During her career, Preston created nearly two hundred hybrids, including varieties of lilies, lilacs, roses, iris, columbines, and crabapples, which became the basis of later cultivars. Throughout North America, she won many horticultural society awards for her contributions to ornamental horticulture. She also wrote numerous articles and published *Garden Lilies* in 1929. When she retired in 1948, nurseries were selling many of her renowned cultivars. The North American Lily Society established a trophy in her name. When she died in 1965, her gardening and plant books were donated to the Royal Botanical Gardens Library in Hamilton, Ontario.

technology-transfer initiatives spread around the world as countries adopted industrialized farming techniques, including irrigation, pesticides, synthetic fertilizers, hybridized seeds, and high-yield varieties of cereal grains. The green revolution made farmers world-wide, including those in Canada, dependent consumers of agricultural implements, chemicals, and hybrid seeds circulated by US food aid organizations and technology programs. The green revolution is credited with saving millions of people from starving, but it also had a number of harmful effects. It decreased biodiversity by supporting mono-culture. The cultivation of grains on huge mechanized farms around the world ren-dered crops more vulnerable to pests (see Chapter 2), an "ecological prescription for trouble" (Fleming 1972, 54). The revolution also lowered the quality of people's diets as more farmers and nations focused on fewer crops. Finally, it introduced many toxic chem-icals into ecosystems and food chains. Some ecologists were ambivalent about the revolu-tion because it uprooted higher-yield varieties of grain from their natural environments.

Like mechanization and the development of hybrids, the application of chemicals to crops was another turning point in agricul-tural production. The use of pesticides, herbicides, and fertilizers constituted a cul-tural change from traditional farm practices such as incessant weeding, which farmers viewed as an inevitable part of nature. Farmers instead engaged in a veritable war on weeds to overcome an aspect of the nat-ural world inimical to their interests. In the Canadian West, following the Second World War, chemical use in agriculture rose to new heights as farmers began to apply substances originally developed for military purposes to their crops. In the 1940s, farmers used herbi-cides such as 2,4-D and insecticides such as DDT and HCH; in the 1950s, their arsenal included the pesticides dieldrin and aldrin and new nitrogen-based fertilizers to replace manure and "balance" soil nutrients. Farmers took to herbicides because they were a quick-fix solution to weeds. Herbicides freed up time to spend on other tasks but polluted the environment and changed the ecology of the land. Nitrogen-based fertilizers and indus-trial chemical additives treated soils, con-trolled weeds, destroyed insects, balanced nutrients, and increased productivity, but they did so at the expense of the health of the soil. Unlike natural enriching agents, chemical additives do not contribute to soil humus. The state, however, supported pesti-cide use. Agricultural departments across Canada tested 2,4-D and, after 1947, strongly advocated chemical weed control (see Figure 9.2). Companies marketed 2,4-D so aggres-sively that the western Canadian market had twenty-four brands in 1954. The number of herbicides registered under the federal Pest Control Act (1939) grew quickly.

Chemical treatments resulted in about 20 percent more crops for domestic and foreign markets. They enabled farmers to make a better living, and they advanced industrial agriculture. Pesticide production became an enormous global industry. Along with nitrogen fertilizers, herbicides, and hybrids, pesticides formed the basis of the green revolution and domestic agribusiness. In 1978, Environment Canada estimated that 6.3 tonnes of pesticides were used on field crops, fruits, vegetables, and roadsides in Ontario's Great Lakes drainage basin alone.

FIGURE 9.2 This employee displays the equipment used in aerial spray operations in Ontario in 1943.
Archives of Ontario, 10002754

Just as chemical use was an innovation in mechanized farm production, increased crop specialization proved to be another structural turning point in the agricultural revolution. Since monoculture exacerbates the problem of pests, the use of pesticides jumped, and farmers became more dependent on major chemical companies. Although chemicals also overcame weeds, their use supported monoculture and helped "preserve the ecologically unsound, weed-friendly state of farming that persists on the Prairies" (Evans 2002, x). As early as 1968, scientists noticed that weeds and pests developed resistance to chemical sprays. Governments and corporations responded by simply developing new products.

Scientists increasingly used plant-breeding techniques to develop plant characteristics compatible with industrial agriculture, crops that could be cultivated mechanically to meet "the specific needs of the processing industries" (Goodman, Sorj, and Wilkinson 1987, 34). Mechanization, chemical use, and increased crop specialization characterized agro-industrial development. New hybrids did not necessarily provide consumers with the best tasting or most nutritious food, and selectivity reduced biodiversity. In the case of tomatoes, for instance, certain breeds were favoured because they had thick skins and travelled well. By contrast, heirloom tomatoes and older varieties, though tasty, were not suitable for supermarkets. Today, vegetables must conform to an international code of nomenclature. Seed growers do not reveal the names of the parent plants of their new cultivars, and companies, to protect their intellectual property, now patent plant species

By the 1990s, over 60 percent of pesticides were applied to staple food crops such as cereals and vegetables, particularly corn. Fifty-five percent of the usage was concentrated in North America and western Europe. Government research on herbicides and pesticides and farmers' support of the products increased their use with little calculation of their potential environmental and public health effects.

as commercial commodities, a practice that restricts their use by growers.

Farmers and corporations also applied standardization to animal products such as poultry, pork, and beef. Industrialized agriculture focused on fewer breeds of livestock, propagated species by artificial insemination, and genetically manipulated them. Initially, Agriculture Canada's Animal Disease Research Institute developed vaccines and diagnostic materials for livestock. In the 1940s and 1950s, however, researchers in animal breeding at research stations in Alberta, Manitoba, Quebec, and Ontario learned more about using artificial insemination to transfer a male animal's "best" qualities. They then used embryo transfer to ensure that the best qualities on the female side of a pedigree were bred in new animals. These innovations in animal genetics and nutrition made the production of farm animals more efficient and promoted the industrial production of livestock, which could take place anywhere, not necessarily only in barns or on farms.

The basis of modern biotechnology – the exploitation of biological processes for industrial and commercial purposes – was laid in 1953, when James Watson, Francis Crick, and Maurice Wilkins discovered the structure of deoxyribonucleic acid (DNA), the molecule that is the basis of heredity. Scientists could now modify the DNA of host cells to produce a desired result. At the end of the twentieth century, scientists completed mapping the twenty-three pairs of chromosomes that make up the human genome. It was, arguably, the most significant discovery of the new century but raised scientific, ethical, and environmental questions.

THE POTATO AND BIODIVERSITY

Potatoes used to come in many varieties, and people ate them in their natural state – roasted or boiled. The fast food and processed food industries, however, created an insatiable demand for French fries, potato chips, and dehydrated and frozen alternatives. Fast food companies demanded a year-round consistent product – potatoes of the same size, shape, and colour to fit machinery for chopping and dicing. To meet this demand for absolute consistency, researchers have developed new ways to grow a few varieties of uniform potatoes. The result has been reduced choice for Canadian consumers, who now have only four types (white, gold, red, and baking), out of the thousands of known varieties worldwide, to choose from at major supermarkets.

Biotechnology took the scientific manipulation of animals to a new level. The turkey industry, for example, is now controlled by three multinational corporations that own all "elite" genetic stocks. "The turkey has been so tampered with genetically," writes a former president of Seeds of Diversity Canada, "that, because of its size and huge breast (people eat more white meat than dark), the commercial turkey can no longer breed naturally" (Wildfong 2000, 146). Manipulation on this scale, which was motivated by short-term gain, required a complete transformation in animal husbandry. For instance, cattle, once raised on the open range and fed grass, are now often raised in large, intensive factory farms and fed products from the expanding livestock feed industry (see Figure 9.3). As animal husbandry has become more industrialized and divorced from natural processes, the food chain has become more susceptible to contamination.

The appearance of modern farms – prefabricated buildings, uniform fields, and large machines – reflects the widening gulf

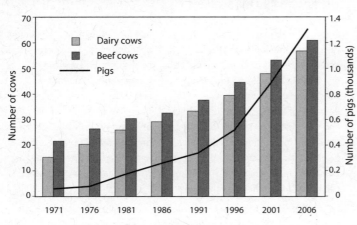

FIGURE 9.3 **Average herd sizes, 1971-2006**

Source: Adapted from Agriculture and Agri-Food Canada, "Special Features: Census of Agriculture Summary," http://www4.agr.gc.ca/; Statistics Canada, Census of Agriculture, various years. Reproduced with permission of the Minister of Public Works and Government Services Canada, 2012.

between agriculture and nature. Barns, which were once places to house farm animals and store feed and equipment are now "controlled environments in which light, heat, feeding and reproduction" are carefully regulated (Rees 1988, 169). They have become "confinement facilities for the production of eggs, meat, milk" (Goodman, Sorj, and Wilkinson 1987, 49). Land is no longer a significant material element in farming, and cattle are mere commodities: farmers speak of animal husbandry as a process of growing cows or producing "livestock units" (Boyens 2003, 9).

Although federal and provincial agricultural research supported the chemical and food industries, the Canadian government did pass some legislation to regulate food products, set marketing standards, prevent fraud, and control the safety, composition, nutritional content, and labelling requirements for food. In 1920, for example, the

Food and Drugs Act (1920) introduced regulations to prevent companies from providing consumers with false information. Subsequent amendments to the act reflected changes occurring in the agricultural and food industries. In the 1960s, for instance, the government passed regulations to control the use of additives such as monosodium glutamate in food. Although some regulations regarding the addition of preservatives and colouring to food already existed, these new changes, which were discussed beforehand with industry, defined the term *food additives* and their permissible uses broadly. They established procedures for companies to secure permission to use additives and for labelling and testing products to ensure their safety. Vitamin additives were permitted in some products for nutritional reasons. When companies began to add vitamins to enhance sales rather than for nutritional purposes, the government again amended the act to control the vitamins, minerals, and amino acids added to foods. Reflecting the increasingly global nature of food production and agriculture, Canadian amendments often followed US precedents.

What began as a partnership among government scientists, farmers, and food companies to educate one another, improve crops and yields, set standards, and protect public health became, over time, more commercial. The Canadian Food Inspection Agency, for instance, was formed in 1997 to combine and integrate the inspection services of three federal government departments: Agriculture and Agri-Food Canada, Fisheries and Oceans Canada, and Health Canada. The agency views agribusiness as a partner, and its critics argue that it has become the dominant

MAD COW DISEASE

In 1986, the first case of bovine spongiform encephalopathy (BSE) was reported in England. The country reported 181,376 cases by 2002. Mad cow disease is a fatal disease in cattle that causes degeneration in the brain and spinal cord. It can be transferred to humans as a variant of the deadly Creutzfeldt-Jakob disease (vCJD). Between 1996 and 2003, 129 cases of vCJD were reported in France, other European countries, and the United States. Canada reported one case. Investigations into the outbreak revealed that cows, normally herbivores, were being fed the remains of other cattle in the form of meat and bone meal, which caused the disease to spread (see Figure 9.4).

Neither BSE in cattle nor vCJD in humans were epidemics, but these diseases raised questions about the quality and safety of food. The World Health Organization sponsored several scientific consultations on the public health implications and in 1999 recommended that all countries prohibit the use of "ruminant tissues" in animal feed and exclude all tissues likely to contain the BSE agent from the human food chain. Public concern about "Frankenfoods" led environmentalists to support the recommendation, which had the backing of the European Union. The Canadian Food Inspection Agency's response to the crisis, however, was slow, partial, and ineffective. In 1997, it banned beef but not other animal protein in feed, and it did not ensure that all existing supplies were destroyed. The total elimination of beef offal from cattle feed was, therefore, unlikely. The agency was lax in enforcing regulations, and its surveillance system for animal disease control was minimal and took few precautions (it tested only animals that showed signs of illness). The beef industry rejected the use of vegetable protein on the grounds that it was too expensive. Before 2003, Canada, along with the United States, treated BSE as a trade issue and merely banned beef or beef products from countries with BSE cases. In 2003, after the discovery of four cases of BSE in Canadian cows, other countries banned Canada's beef, and the United States closed its market, a serious economic blow to the Canadian beef industry.

In response, Canada banned "specific risk material" in 2003, but feed still contained animal components, and calves in both Canada and the United States routinely received "milk replacer" made from bovine blood. Thus, Canada, like the United States, refused to "impose a total ban on recycling ruminant protein in animal feed" (Leiss 2004, 252). The divergence between responses in Europe and North America, from both a public health and environmental perspective, resulted partly from the European experience of the BSE scare and partly from greater public surveillance and activism in Europe.

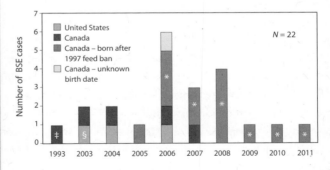

FIGURE 9.4   BSE cases in North America, by year and country, 1993, 2003-11

Notes:
‡   Imported from UK into Canada
§   Imported from Canada into the United States
*   Canada – Born after 1 March 1999

Source: Adapted from Center for Disease Control, "Overview of BSE in North America, 2011," http://www.cdc.gov/

partner, a development not in the public interest. As the number of commercial products has proliferated, for instance, the government has set guidelines and standards, but it does little independent testing and instead relies on studies completed by industry scientists.

Conflicts concerning food issues increased criticism of the government's approach to regulation and the impact of new food products on public health and on the environment. These conflicts reveal the changing nature of agriculture and food as environmentalists challenge the methods and values of agribusiness. Modern food wars reflect the growing disconnect between modern society and the natural world.

The Altered Landscape of Farming

The changes wrought by the revolution in agriculture bore an indelible imprint on the Canadian landscape and the struggles of small farmers across the land. Paved roads and automobiles linked the countryside to cities and to distant markets, and trucks increasingly replaced railways as the preferred method for moving food and specialized crops. On the Prairies, in particular, monoculture transformed the landscape's appearance as mixed perennial grasses and flowers gave way to quarter-section and half-section farms and then to larger corporate-owned fields of hybridized wheat worked by combine and tractor and interspersed with dugouts, irrigation ditches, fallow pastures, and feedlots for livestock (see Figure 9.5). By 1969, western wheat was Canada's top foreign exchange earner and its second largest export, and Canada provided 6 percent of the world's

wheat. The new spatial reality of the Prairies is consistent with the mechanistic spirit of the original settlement plan, and experimental research stations continue to assist the consolidation process by helping owners of large farms turn a profit.

The postwar agricultural environment caused ecological changes on the Canadian Prairies that further reduced biodiversity as fewer species, valued "for the commercial profits they generated," replaced indigenous plants and mixed crops. In 2005, the president of Seeds of Diversity Canada noted, "It is worrisome that so many farmers – presumably because of compelling business reasons – choose to grow a very small number of patented crop varieties," which displace other crops and lead to "the further decline in genetic diversity on Canadian farms" (Canadian Organic Growers 2002). Farmers are now less like stewards of the land and more like engineers who use technology and biotechnology to manipulate the environment. In the 1970s, for example, as wheat prices fluctuated and led to surpluses, the federal government instituted a wheat-growing reduction plan and encouraged crop diversification. Farmers were encouraged to grow barley and canola, not for environmental reasons but for commercial ones.

In the Prairies and throughout Canada, small and independent farmers saw their lives and livelihoods disrupted as the gradual expansion of agribusiness forced them to operate in an increasingly competitive market. Many failed. Mechanization, increased land and production costs, and declining prices for farm goods caught many in a cost-price squeeze, a situation that bore similarities to the Highland Clearances of the eighteenth

FIGURE 9.5 This aerial view of the landscape near Gray, Saskatchewan, reflects not only the pattern of the prairie land survey but also the effects of industrial agriculture in Canada. Since the 1950s, the traditional family farm has given way to larger farms run by fewer farmers and corporations.

George Hunter, photographer, from Don W. Thomson, *Men and Meridians: The History of Surveying and Mapping in Canada*, vol. 2 (Ottawa: Queen's Printer, 1967)

and nineteenth centuries. In the 1980s on the Prairies, farm costs rose 16.3 percent while the price of wheat dropped 22.0 percent. Farm incomes dropped, even though production rose. Greater use of mechanized farm equipment, chemical sprays, hybrids, and genetically engineered seeds boosted not only yields but also overhead costs. Although many farmers used the new products to increase production, others dropped out. In 1941, the number of farms on the Prairies was 732,832; by 1986, that number had dropped to 293,087, a decline of 67 percent. In the Maritimes, the number of farms declined by 85 percent. In the country as a whole, the number of farms dropped 7 percent between 2001 and 2006. At the same time, the size of farms increased (see Figure 9.6). The family farm, once the centrepiece of Canada's agricultural policy, is slowly disappearing. Since 2001, the number of larger farms with gross farm receipts of $250,000 or more (at 2005 constant prices) has increased by 13.8 percent, whereas those with less than $250,000 in receipts have declined by 10.5 percent.

Farmers under financial pressure developed different strategies to stay on the land. Some bought more land to produce more crops; others tried to get by with less or got off-farm work to supplement their incomes. Some smaller farmers tried to survive by adopting a business strategy – for instance, selling feed or pesticides, running a slaughterhouse, or producing "value-added" products for sale. A minority went organic. These developments led to a growing social and economic divide

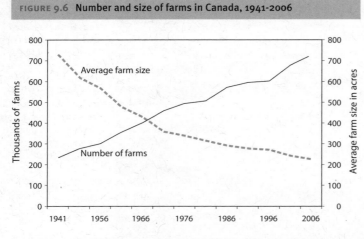

Source: Adapted from Agriculture and Agri-Food Canada, "Special Features: Census of Agriculture Summary," http://www4.agr.gc.ca/; Statistics Canada, Census of Agriculture, various years. Reproduced with the permission of the Minister of Public Works and Government Services Canada, 2012.

between small and large farms and conflicts over values within rural communities.

The Changing Nature of Food

As agriculture became more industrialized after the Second World War, food processing gradually moved from the farm to the factory. The first corporate food companies, such as General Foods, expanded in the 1920s, and food retailing expanded along with them. Large processors "created the first of many layers of middlemen between corporate growers and urban consumers" (Gabaccia 1998, 56). Large canning companies and meat packers either bought up farms or distributed contracts to farmers, who formalized their relations with corporate food processors to ensure access to the market. Over time, farmers had less and less control over contracts, partly because, as specialists, they formed

separate organizations that divided rather than united them and partly because of growing vertical integration – the process by which production and distribution come to be controlled by a single, more powerful company in an industry – among feed companies, contract producers, and marketing firms.

The growth of agribusiness and the integration of the wholesale, distribution, and retail sectors meant giant retail food chains, which advertised to influence consumer demand, also determined what farmers grew and what consumers ate. These chains developed huge supermarkets and were leaders in the modern food system. Spinoff industries such as institutional food companies that serviced large organizations (companies, governments, educational institutions, and even hospitals) developed close ties with increasingly diversified international food companies such as George Weston, Labatt Foods, Nestlé, and United Fruit. These companies, in turn, worked closely with service industries, such as companies that produced farm implements, seeds, animal feed, containers, or chemical food additives. This trend toward consolidation gave large corporate farms and food companies advantages over smaller farms and companies, and governments and marketing boards subsidized them in the interest of efficiency and modernization. By the early twenty-first century, five companies controlled 90 percent of the global grain supply, and three dominated the world tea market. Four large processing companies controlled 81 percent of American beef, and four multinationals (Proctor and Gamble, Kraft, Nestlé, and Sara Lee) controlled the world economy in coffee and kept prices low for poor producers and high for prosperous consumers.

The transformation of agriculture, food processing, and distribution systems decreased biodiversity and altered the nature of food by distributing more processed products in supermarkets and by supplying the expanding restaurant industry and fast food chains. Indeed, "the rise of consumer activity in the twentieth century ... essentially entailed the replacement of home-produced goods with industrially produced ones" (Varty 2009, 187). Despite the ever-growing range of goods on store shelves, North Americans became specialized eaters. Over a quarter of processed food in supermarkets had corn as its basis, and business consolidation meant 90 percent of milk in the United States came from a single breed of cow and eggs from a single breed of hen. The modern food production system was considered a marvel, but it was fundamentally unhealthy and ecologically unsound. Corporate concentration rendered the food chain permanently vulnerable to contamination, disease, and terrorism.

Modern food production has changed the composition, look, and taste of basic foods and created new ones. The fruits and vegetables developed by government-subsidized agricultural stations eased the picking process and transportation but had little flavour. Milk also underwent a similar transformation. In 1914, milk had to be pasteurized by law, an initiative that eliminated diseases such as tuberculosis, particularly among children. In later decades, however, other nutrients and additives were added so it would keep longer, look whiter, and travel well. Large companies distributed what was essentially a new product, with a new taste. In addition, farmers

WONDERBREAD

The history of Wonderbread, the first bread available ready-sliced as well as uniformly white and spongelike, parallels the history of corporate consolidation in the food industry. The bread was first produced in 1921 by Taggart Baking Company, an Indianapolis baking company that wrapped its bread in a package with colourful red, yellow, and blue balloons. When Continental Baking Company purchased Taggart in 1925, it became a national brand. The company began shipping the bread in sliced form in the 1930s and launched a marketing campaign to assure Americans that the bread would stay fresh. In the 1940s, Continental began to fortify its bread with vitamins and minerals and added nutritional information to its packaging. Wonderbread is now produced in Canada by Weston Bakeries, in the United States by Hostess, and in Mexico by Grupo Bimbo.

fed dairy cows steroids to produce more milk and antibiotics to prevent diseases. As the century came to a close, critics questioned the effect of these chemicals on the quality of milk and on consumers' health. It was only when consumers began to turn to organic milk produced by small farmers that natural milk products once again found a place on store shelves.

Industrial food processors also created food substitutes of partly or wholly reconstituted materials: "Milk and dairy-product substitutes, reconstituted from vegetable proteins, non-butter fats and other solids, are replacing liquid milk proteins in the markets for condensed and evaporated milk, cream powder, baby foods and desserts" (Goodman, Sorj, and Wilkinson 1987, 94). These new products – which include egg, cheese, meat, and fish substitutes – were processed to offend as few people as possible. As a result, they are bland. Refrigeration, quick-freezing techniques, and ever-larger grocery and big-box stores have only increased the range of processed foods available to consumers. In the 1950s, for instance, companies sold cake mixes and cereals to Canadians as new conveniences of the modern age. The TV dinner, invented by C.A. Swanson & Sons in 1953, was packaged to fit nicely on a TV tray. These frozen meals, along with other "instant" and canned foods, had a long shelf life but took up more space than fresh foods and meats in transportation vehicles and grocery store shelves. Frozen and convenience foods reflected advances in food technology and food science and the growing influence of "nutritionists." By using non-agricultural materials to create industrial substitutes for food, food companies reduced rural products to simple industrial inputs, which were easier to control, and opened the way to lessening or eliminating the rural production process.

Food companies laced processed foods with chemical additives to replace the nutrients lost during processing and transportation. Frozen peas were bright green, processed cheese was smooth, and even fresh foods such as oranges had colour added to their peels to make them more appealing to consumers. In the 1980s, a US study found that over 90 percent of households purchased manufactured or processed food items. Given that North Americans now consume food grown in artificially fertilized soil, sprayed with herbicides and pesticides, and "fortified" with chemicals and artificial ingredients, it is not surprising that they carry residues of numerous chemicals in their bodies.

Processed foods, the rise of the automobile, and the new consumer culture produced a food culture divorced from the land and the natural processes of gardening, livestock raising, and food preparation. Following the Second World War, people ate convenience foods quickly in kitchens with modern appliances. The microwave oven, invented by the US military during the war, entered homes in the 1960s, and companies introduced foods designed for it, such as vacuum-packed frozen meals and microwave popcorn. The fast food industry spread rapidly from the United States to Canada from the 1960s, appropriated certain immigrant food items such as pizza, and converted them into popular new food products. It enticed people to reduce their own food preparation and to eat out more; it broadened palates but lowered food quality. The number of meals consumed away from home also increased for social and cultural reasons. In the fast-paced modern era, families headed by two working parents or a single parent increased, and they patronized fast food establishments that offered inexpensive high-calorie foods such as pizza, burgers, and tacos. The food tasted good and could be consumed quickly as a snack in a car, but it had little nutritional value and was laden with sugar and fat.

In North America, globalization meant consumers could buy fresh foods and food products from around the world at low prices in all seasons. Canadians no longer had to eat seasonal foods or store root vegetables in cellars for consumption during the winter. Instead, for a cost, consumers could eat strawberries from California and asparagus from Mexico in December. The food served at Canadian tables increasingly travelled long distances at a high cost to the environment. Meanwhile, local growers struggled to find customers. Canada is

FAST FOOD NATIONS

Long associated with the automobile and sprawling suburbs, the fast food industry made it convenient for people to eat on the run, in their cars, and, frequently, alone. The resulting cultural changes were celebrated in films such as *American Graffiti* until Eric Schlosser published *Fast Food Nation* (2002) and Morgan Spurlock produced his documentary film *Super Size Me* (2004). Companies made huge profits by beaming ads at children, streamlining their production process and insisting on uniformity; focusing on quantity rather than quality; employing teenagers and seniors willing to accept part-time work, low wages, and no benefits; fighting any attempts at unionization; and maintaining a rapid turnover of employees.

The negative consequences of fast food provoked a re-evaluation of modern food culture. Obesity, even in small children, was a noticeable and growing problem among North Americans, who were also increasingly undernourished. According to health and nutritional experts, the "Western diet" has led to "Western diseases" such as heart disease and Type 2 diabetes, which are reaching epidemic proportions. Michael Pollan, author of books such as *In Defense of Food*, laments that North Americans have lost their ecological relationship to food. He advocates regaining it for health reasons and because food has historically been about "pleasure, about community, about family and spirituality, about our relationship to the natural world, and about expressing our identity" (Pollan 2008, 8). In other words, food is not only about culture but also about biology.

now part of a global system that feeds many people but has commodified food, limited biodiversity, and increasingly uses bioengineering. In poorer countries, agribusiness helped feed people but also created dependency, water contamination, soil erosion, and rural depopulation. In developed countries such as Canada, it changed the culture of food and deepened the gap between Canadians and their environment.

Bioengineered Food and Its Backlash

The mechanization of agriculture, development of hybrid plants, and use of chemicals to increase crop yields has liberated food production from its biological constraints, increased the capitalization of agriculture, and fuelled corporate concentration. Biotechnology represents another turning point in agriculture, one that fundamentally challenges its rural and biological basis. As large transnational corporations increasingly focus on biotechnology and genetic engineering, a future in which food is produced in factories out of nonfood and non-agricultural materials is becoming more feasible. These developments and their effects on food, farmers, and the environment are evident in the seed industry. Between 1984 and 1987, for instance, corporate leaders in the pesticides industry (Monsanto, Imperial Chemical Industries, and Dupont) bought up small seed companies. As these companies consolidated mail order seed companies, the number of nurseries decreased by a quarter in Canada and the United States, and the connection between biotechnology, agriculture, and food grew more intimate.

Corporations such as Monsanto had started to develop genetically engineered seeds in the 1970s. At the time, Monsanto was the agricultural subsidiary of Pharmacia, a large pharmaceutical company that had received approval to produce synthetic human insulin made from a genetically modified bacterium. With enormous confidence and a fair bit of idealism, if not apocalyptic fantasies, food engineers believed they had found the secret to defeating hunger. Scientists had been developing hybrids with particular marketable characteristics for years, but genetically modified organisms were something else – new organisms created by mingling the genes of species that would not combine or reproduce in nature.

In the 1980s, production companies argued that transgenic crops, crops that contain genetic material into which DNA from another organism has been artificially introduced, differed significantly from other plants, so much so that they could be patented. They sought patents to protect their intellectual property and investment in research and development. In the 1990s, when the registration of new agricultural products became lengthy and expensive, these same companies argued that their genetically modified plants did not differ significantly from those found in nature. Agriculture Canada and the US Department of Agriculture agreed with both arguments and issued patents on gene sequences but exempted them from the safety testing required for other new chemicals or food additives. In other words, the public potentially became the testing ground for genetically modified foods. Companies used technology to invent genetically modified seeds such as corn, canola, or soybeans that were resistant to certain pesticides and herbicides. Farmers, consequently, became dependent on companies such as Monsanto for both patented seeds *and* pesticides.

Although companies have focused on producing genetically modified soybeans and corn in the United States and canola in Canada, bioengineering is expanding to other plants and animals. Farmed salmon, for instance, have been genetically modified to make them more resistant to cold temperatures, and genetically modified organisms are used to produce numerous vitamins, flavourings, and additives. Fruits such as the Flavr Svr tomato, the first genetically modified food product approved by the American Food and Drug Administration (in 1994) for human consumption, ripen longer on the vine but remain firm, making shipping long distances possible. When the public rejected the tomato because of its flavour, Calgene, its producer, withdrew it from the market.

Although the industry promises to produce more varieties of genetically modified foods – such as melons with edible rinds, cheeses that mature in a week, and avocados with seeds in the skin rather than a pit – the effect of these organisms, on people and the environment, remains in question and the issue of food safety is a concern. When the Flavr Svr tomato was tested on rats, for instance, the rats developed stomach lesions. Calgene, however, distributed the product to the public. When Cornell University grew ten hectares of transgenic corn (intended for use in sweeteners for pop, glue for stamps, and texture for processed foods), it killed monarch butterflies. In the United States, the case of a woman who had a serious allergic reaction to genetically modified corn called Starlink came to the attention of the American government and the food industry. One study noted that "the knowledge base available for understanding transgenic organisms and their effects on health and on the environment is very limited" and that research was needed to understand food safety and environmental impacts. It also suggested that the use of genetically engineered (GE) plants to produce nonfoods such as vaccines or pharmaceuticals could affect all crops destined for human consumption: "It is reasonable to expect that such special GE products will inevitably enter the food chain." In light of this threat, many researchers are calling for studies on the possible environmental effects of genetically modified foods (McCalla et al. 2001, 1.2.1).

A SASKATCHEWAN FARMER TAKES ON MONSANTO

The growth of bioengineered crops raised political issues such as the viability of patents on plants, intellectual property rights, and the rights of small farmers in relation to large commercial companies. These issues were given a human face by Percy Schmeiser, a canola breeder and farmer from Bruno, Saskatchewan, who took on Monsanto when some of its genetically modified seeds blew into his fields in 1997 and contaminated his crops. In spring 1998, Monsanto accused Schmeiser of growing its patented Roundup Ready canola and sued him for patent infringement. Monsanto owns the rights to the DNA itself, and farmers who use the seed have to agree to buy new seed every year and pay a per-acre licensing fee. Schmeiser fought back, lost at the federal court level in 2001, and appealed the decision.

Schmeiser became an international symbol, known as the farmer who stood up to Monsanto and a spokesperson for the movement against the genetic engineering of food. In 2004, in the Supreme Court of Canada, his lawyer argued that "seeds and other life forms should remain within the realm of the commons," not subject to a corporate monopoly, and that "companies like Monsanto should be made liable for their pollution of the environment through genetic engineering, rather than the farmer being punished for having his land contaminated" (Adam 2004, 12). The Council of Can-

adians, the Sierra Club of Canada, and the National Farmers' Union served as intervenors because the case had vast implications. The Supreme Court's ruling in 2004 in favour of Monsanto was devastating. The court agreed that the plant is a higher life form that cannot be patented but argued that the patent does apply to the gene. The court found that Schmeiser had recognized Monsanto's seeds on his land and had not advised Monsanto to come and get them. Schmeiser paid no damages, which Monsanto demanded, because he had not acquired the seeds fraudulently or benefitted from them financially. His crop, however, was contaminated, and his lawyers advised him to destroy his own seeds.

Although Schmeiser lost, other cases will follow because traditional farming depends on farmers saving seeds produced on their own land for future crops. Terry Boehm of the National Farmers' Union stated, "This case was about preserving age-old agricultural practices such as seed saving and protecting farmers from being held responsible for the rampant contamination of our farm fields" (Canada Newswire 2004). The case also drew attention to the issue of biodiversity. At the time of the 2004 ruling, it was estimated that three hundred Canadian farmers were using Monsanto Roundup Ready canola. In 2005, genetically modified crops accounted for 95 percent of the canola grown in Canada.

FIGURE 9.7 Percy Schmeiser, 2009.
Courtesy John Schmeiser

Environmentalists have been outspoken critics of genetically modified crops, the aggressive legal actions of companies such as Monsanto against small farmers who resist their products, and corporate campaigns against labelling. They have criticized the Canadian and American governments for failing to provide the public with information about the new products and technologies, for their bias in favour of bioengineered food, for the absence of labels on processed foods listing genetically modified organisms, and for the lax testing of products before they enter the food chain. Nongovernmental organizations push for food labels so the public can choose whether to eat genetically modified organisms, but the companies that make the foods resist labelling. The issue is not only a matter of consumer choice but also one of intellectual property. Without labels, it is impossible to track genetically modified organisms; therefore, if a person becomes ill from a product, a company cannot legally be held accountable. North American governments resist labelling, despite overwhelming public support (95 percent in Canada). The European Union, by contrast, approved labelling as a precautionary principle and rejected imports without labels. In response, the United States threatened to sue the EU.

Scientists and environmentalists have also urged governments to test new products. In 1999, under the Food and Drugs Act, Health Canada approved forty-two genetically modified foods, and the federal government announced plans to create standards for the voluntary labelling of food. As Canadians demanded to know what they were eating, Greenpeace, the Council of Canadians, and the Sierra Club of Canada launched a campaign and asked Loblaws to remove genetically modified ingredients from its President's Choice and No Name brands. With some success, they urged international companies such as Kraft and Cadbury (now merged and part of the same company) to avoid the products, as there was no independent or verifiable long-term testing. In 2000, Ann Clark, a professor of plant agriculture at the University of Guelph, spoke out for Genetic Engineering Alert, a network of independent agricultural specialists not employed in the biotech industry. The group wanted to evaluate bioengineered products because it believed the Canadian government was doing an inadequate job. Clark pointed out that Canadians regularly ate the genetically modified organisms approved and listed on Health Canada's website, not because they approved of the foods but because they were not labelled. Seventy percent of these foods had not been tested for toxicity: the government had simply accepted the industries' assertions that they were safe. Only 30 percent had been tested for short-term health effects, and none had been tested as allergens or for their long-term effects. The government had assessed none of the foods independently in its own laboratories or through human or animal trials. Clark and her colleagues asked, who benefitted from inadequate testing? They advocated a regulatory framework to protect the public and allow for consumer choice.

In 2000, the federal government asked the Royal Society of Canada to convene an expert panel to advise it on developing a regulatory system for the use of biotechnology and bioengineered foods to ensure the safety

BIOTECHNOLOGY AND THE CANADIAN GOVERNMENT

In the late 1990s, the biotechnology industry launched a US ad campaign titled "Good Ideas Are Growing" to associate genetically modified foods in the public's mind with images of healthy crops, Third World prosperity, and corporate citizenship. Using public money, Canada launched a similar campaign. The Food Biotechnology Communications Network, based in Guelph, Ontario, produced a pamphlet titled "A Growing Appetite for Information" as an insert in *Canadian Living Magazine*. In 2001, the Canadian Food Inspection Agency, which is supposed to regulate the industry, likewise sent out a brochure, "Food Safety and You," in support of bioengineered food to every household. The *Canadian Living* insert promoted the sale of genetically engineered foods in Canada and abroad and quoted Canada's minister of agriculture and agri-food: "In Canada, we're taking a balanced approach to biotechnology. We're supporting the health, economic, and environmental benefits that we know will result from its use – particularly in medicine and food – while at the same time stringently regulating the approval of new products to mitigate the risks" (cited in Council for Biotechnology Information 2000, 12).

The Canadian Health Coalition accused the government of coordinating a multimillion-dollar public relations campaign to manufacture consent for bioengineering. The coalition's investigation, led by Bradford Duplisea, exposed the government's decade-long effort to turn Canada into a biotechnology powerhouse. In 1997, the government had even partnered with Monsanto to develop genetically engineered wheat, giving the company $500,000 and genetic material. The partnership ended in 2003 when the EU banned the importation of bioengineered food. To protect the public interest, the coalition advised that the promotion and regulation of biotechnology should be separated. The combination of promotional and regulatory activities within the department of Agriculture and Agri-Food Canada constitutes a conflict of interest that calls the department's credibility and independence as a regulator into question.

of new food products. The panel's report, which came out the following year, noted that the most significant potential risk of genetically modified organisms was their effect on gene flow in different sections of the environment (microorganisms, insects, and wild fish). Environmental assessments, therefore, had to be part of the Canadian regulatory process, and decisions on agricultural biotechnology had to be compatible with the Canadian Environmental Protection Act. The panel also addressed the conflict of interest among scientists, some of whom had an entrepreneurial interest in biotechnologies, and in regulatory agencies such as the Canadian Food Inspection Agency, which both promoted agricultural biotechnology and regulated it. It made a number of recommendations:

- rigorous testing of genetically engineered food and animal feed for both short- and long-term effects on human health
- an open, transparent regulatory process with independent scientific monitoring to ensure the promotion of independent research on potential health and environmental risks
- establishment of a Canadian Biotechnology Advisory Committee to review the domination of public research by private commercial interests
- application of a conservative "precautionary principle," whereby technologies would not be presumed safe
- the development of rigorous guidelines to protect food-producing animals from harm
- a system to track and register transgenic animals and separate those intended for pharmaceuticals from entering the food chain
- a moratorium on genetically engineered fish, with future production restricted to land-based facilities so as not to affect wild fish
- mandatory and voluntary labelling.

The Canadian government received the report and filed it away.

On agricultural and food issues, Canada consistently supported the United States – backed by Australia, Argentina, Chile, and Uruguay – in opposing strong regulations to protect the environment from the spread of genetically modified organisms. In 1999, more than 135 countries met in Colombia to negotiate a global treaty to govern their transfer, handling, and use. Canada and its allies insisted that regulations exclude all commodity crops, such as soya beans, corn, and canola, which accounted for over 90 percent of genetically modified organisms traded at that time. Several transnational companies that produced and marketed these products actively supported these countries. By 2005, Canada was one of the five top producers of biotech crops in the world, an industry worth an estimated US$44 billion (see Table 9.1).

Alternative Agriculture

The publication in 1962 of Rachel Carson's *Silent Spring*, a book about the overuse of pesticides, aroused public concern about pesticides and their potential adverse effects on food quality and public health. The book prompted the US and Canadian governments to ban the use of DDT and regulate the use of chemicals in crops and foods. It launched the modern environmental movement and its ongoing support for alternative agriculture.

Canadian Organic Growers was established in 1975 to help farmers grow whole foods locally without the use of chemicals. The organization offered organic growers and farmers, always a minority, information and advice. The organization's Reference Series included publications on subjects such as composting and the use of manure in organic agriculture; alternatives to medication for dairy cattle; and organic care of trees, shrubs, and roses. It began publishing *EcoFarm and Garden* in 1998, and it renamed the publication *Canadian Organic Grower Magazine* two years later. The organization filled a gap, for neither federal nor provincial departments of agriculture had advice, information, or trained personnel to assist organic growers. A pamphlet produced in 1990 informed readers that government bias against alternative farming systems meant "little or no financial assistance to see you through the lower-profit transition period," which would last at least three years (Canadian Organic Growers 2002). A new organic farmer, the organization cautioned, would have the support of neither the agriculture industry nor the international trade regime. Not even the University of Guelph's agricultural college offered courses on organic farming. After the organization spent more than two decades developing standards for organic farming and lobbying the government to oversee them, Canada enacted the Organic Products Regulations in 2009, which legally required

TABLE 9.1 Genetically modified food's share of crop plantings (as percent of total), 2005				
	Soybeans	Corn	Cotton	Canola
United States	93	52	79	82
Canada	60	65	–	95
Argentina	99	62	50	–
South Africa	65	27	95	–
Australia	–	–	90	–
China	–	–	65	–
Brazil	40	–	–	–
Uruguay	100	–	–	–

Source: Brookes and Barfoot (2006, 6).

all organic products to be certified according to Canadian Organic Standards.

Canadian Organic Growers made its philosophy clear in its publications. Its guide on making the transition to organic agriculture states, "To make the change from conventional to organic or ecological agriculture requires a fundamental change in the way of looking at your farming operation." It requires the "conviction that sustainability in agriculture is important" (Canadian Organic Growers 2002). According to the organization, organic agriculture supports biodiversity rather than monoculture and involves recycling wastes; creating fertile, productive soil by natural means; and operating without the use of synthetic pesticides or chemical fertilizers. Its 1999 "Position on Biotechnology" states, "In our view, genetic engineering (GE) runs contrary to the principles of caring for and protecting people and the ecosystems on which they depend. GE is a short-term, ill-conceived and oversimplified approach to agriculture; it does not respect natural systems."

Because of the persistent efforts of nutritionists and organizations such as Canadian Organic Growers and Greenpeace (which publicized that organic growers lacked government support whereas the Canadian government subsidized the biotechnology industry with about $400 million a year), organic farming became economically more viable (see Figure 9.8). By 1999, Canadian organic growers serviced a small but growing segment of consumers (about 1.5 percent). A more informed public increasingly understood the difference between industrial and organic agriculture. Small food outlets and farmers' markets supplied organic or wild

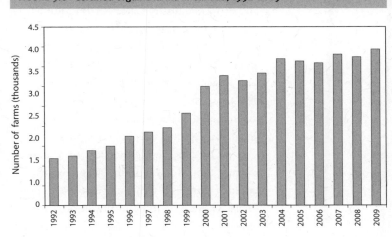

FIGURE 9.8   Certified organic farms in Canada, 1992-2009

Source: Agriculture and Agri-Food Canada, "Certified Organic Production Statistics for Canada, 2009," http://www4.agr.gc.ca/. Reproduced with the permission of the Minister of Public Works and Government Services Canada, 2012

products. As organic growers' share of the market increased, supermarkets set up sections for organic fruits and vegetables. The food, however, was often imported rather than local and produced by large-scale industrial organic farmers.

By the 1980s and 1990s, industrial agriculture was contested terrain and the focus of a number of grassroots movements. The community food-security movement emerged to help low-income people gain access to nutritional food from local organically produced sources. The movement supported alternative community-based food systems, which stand in contrast to the "dominant, long-distance, industrialized, highly concentrated, and globally reorganized system of food growing, processing, manufacturing, marketing and selling" (Gottlieb 1990, 184). To support the movement, organic community gardens in large city centres sometimes donated produce to food banks.

To counter the growth and predominance of fast food culture, Carlo Petrini founded the slow food movement in Italy in 1986. The movement began as a protest against the opening of a McDonald's restaurant in Rome and has since expanded to include over sixty-five thousand members in nearly fifty countries, including Canada. Members support local and regional cuisine, reject food homogeneity, and use gentle mockery to protest current food trends and insist on lengthy cooking times. They encourage people to purchase wholesome food locally and to eat it slowly in family or community groups. Slow Food Canada's mandate is captured in the slogan "Preserving Canadian Food Heritage."

Some Canadians have focused on maintaining biodiversity through the conservation of old plants and animal breeds. In 1975, for instance, a voluntary organization called the American Seed Savers Exchange formed to preserve and distribute heirloom seeds. By 2000, it had eight thousand members. In Canada, the Heritage Seed Program – now known as Seeds of Diversity Canada – was formed in 1984 at a Canadian Organic Growers conference by a network of organic farmers, gardeners, and consumers concerned about the loss of old plant varieties and their replacement with hybrids. The Heritage Seed Program expanded its activities in 1987, when Heather Apple launched a magazine and set up a living gene bank of endangered plants at her home in Uxbridge, Ontario. At the community level, the program sponsors Seedy Saturdays and develops preservation collections, such as a garlic collection based on Salt Spring Seeds and a preservation orchard on Salt Spring Island in British Columbia. Its apple varieties date back to the settlement era and include the Snow (Fameuse) apple, brought by French settlers to the area around Lake Champlain. The program has also agreed to grow out seeds from Agriculture Canada's Plant Gene Bank, established in 1970. In 2000, Seeds of Diversity Canada had 1,500 members and 1,580 varieties, half of which were not available commercially.

Members of seed exchange programs originally partnered with governments to protect Canada's biological heritage. They became politicized when multinational companies began to patent plants. Seeds of Diversity Canada is a strong opponent of genetically modified organisms, which it believes are potentially harmful to people and the environment. To combat monoculture and promote diversity, many gardeners stress the importance of growing indigenous plants, wildflowers, and grasses, and they work on roadside naturalization and beautification programs. They also educate the public about pesticide-free gardening, permaculture, and herbal remedies.

The urban garden movement, which began in Canada in the 1970s, has experimented

THE RETURN OF THE ZUCCA MELON

One of the most dramatic successes of the Seeds of Diversity Program has been finding and reviving the Zucca melon. Once grown as a commercial crop in British Columbia's southern Okanagan Valley and used to make candied peel between the 1930s and 1950s, the 60- to 120-pound melon disappeared when large seed companies stopped selling the variety in the 1970s. After a strenuous search, members of the Heritage Seed Program located a few in Sandwich, Illinois. The gourd was successfully grown out again in British Columbia, proving that "the grassroots grower can be a major player in the important task of preserving genetic diversity" (Rempal and Page 1992, 46). BC growers now meet annually and compete for the largest Zucca plant.

with rooftop gardens, and several Canadian communities, particularly in Montreal and Vancouver, have created organic gardens that not only "green" the city landscape but also feed people. They are reminiscent of early allotment gardens, which were set up in vacant urban areas to grow food for the poor or to provide growing space for people in apartments.

The environmental movement's scrutiny of food production began with questions about the use of herbicides and pesticides on crops, the treatment of farm animals, and the production methods of commercialized, intensive farming operations. More recently, its members have questioned the nature of animal feeds and opposed genetic engineering of food products. In the 1990s, activists began to criticize Health Canada and the Canadian Food Inspection Agency for having a close partnership with agribusiness. The federal government, they charged, had an out-of-date regulatory system, one that did not independently test and monitor new products to protect the health and safety of consumers and the environment.

FROM THE EARLY twentieth century, large corporations have created a new agricultural landscape characterized by functional uniform farms with fewer and fewer ties with the natural world. Biodiversity has been lost in the interest of mass producing cheap commodities using ever-evolving techniques, including cross breeding, herbicides and pesticides, consolidation, and biotechnology. Both governments and corporations trumpeted the latter as the beginning of a green revolution that would transform the way we feed the world. There are parallels between

the introduction of genetically modified organisms into modern ecosystems and the intermingling of organisms that accompanied the Columbian exchange, although in the latter case all the organisms were natural, not man-made. In both cases, new organisms entered new ecosystems with no knowledge of their effects.

Critics charge that government regulations favour large corporations and make it difficult for local or organic producers to grow and market their products. Consumers, they argue, have lost control of the food chain, and the result has been a food system that produces poor-quality food subject to periodic contamination. In the interest of better nutrition and food security, they encourage consumers to buy locally produced, nutritious, organic foods that are better for the environment and human health. The onus, they argue, should be placed on the producers of genetically modified foods to prove that their products are safe and healthful. In *Tough Choices: Living and Dying in the 21st Century,* Maureen McTeer argues that genetic engineering of the earth's plant, animal, and human organisms "reaches to the core of the natural order." In the current policy regime that favours corporations, the demand by environmentalists "for stringent legislated standards backed up with sanctions, as opposed to voluntary standards set by industry, is a real stumbling block in establishing an effective process for the regulation of genetically modified foods." Nevertheless, McTeer concludes that the rules governing genetically modified organisms need to include mechanisms to assess their impact on long-term health and pay compensation to persons harmed. These policy components "are part of the cost of doing business and the responsibility of companies using biotechnology." To achieve public protection she encourages the public to "fight to be included" because "decisions made now will determine who will have power and exercise control over the future" (McTeer 1999, 132).

Works Cited

Adam, Nadege. 2004. "Monsanto versus the People." *Canadian Perspectives,* Spring. http://www.canadians.org/.

Boyens, Ingeborg. 2003. "Dissecting Dinner: A Cook's Tour of What Goes in Our Mouths." *Literary Review of Canada* 11, 6: 8-9.

Brookes, Graham, and Peter Barfoot. 2006. "GM Crops: The First Ten Years Global – Socio-Economic and Environmental Impacts." ISAAA Brief No. 36. Ithaca, New York.

Canada Newswire. 2004. "Schmeiser Decision Causes Uproar around the World." 21 May. http://www.newswire.ca/en/index/.

Canadian Organic Growers. 1999. "COG's Position on Biotechnology." http://www/cog.ca/.

–. 2002. "From Conventional to Ecological Agriculture: A Guide to Crop Transition." Reference Series 6.

Council for Biotechnology Information. 2000. "Biotechnology: Good Ideas Are Growing." http://foodsafety.k-state.edu/articles/482/biotech_good_ideas.pdf.

Evans, Clifford. 2002. *The War on Weeds in the Prairie West: An Environmental History.* Calgary: University of Calgary Press.

Fleming, Donald. 1972. "Roots of the New Conservation Movement." *Perspectives in American History* 6: 7-91.

Gabaccia, Donna R. 1998. *We Are What We Eat: Ethnic Food and the Making of Americans.* Cambridge, MA: Harvard University Press.

Goodman, David, Bernardo Sorj, and John Wilkinson. 1987. *From Farming to Biotechnology: A Theory of Agro-Industrial Development.* Oxford: Basil Blackwell.

Gottlieb, Robert. 1990. *Environmentalism Unbound: Exploring New Pathways for Change.* Boston: MIT Press.

Leiss, William. 2004. "Two Stinking Cows: The Mismanagement of BSE Risk in North America." In *Mad Cows and Mother's Milk: The Perils of Poor Risk Communication,* edited by William Leiss and Douglas Powell, 229-61. Montreal and Kingston: McGill-Queen's University Press.

McCalla, Dennis R., Richard M. Beames, Hugh Lehman, and Bert R. Christie. 2001. "Regulation of Genetically Modified Food: A Submission to the Canadian Biotechnology Advisory Committee." 17 April. http://www.rsc.ca/.

McTeer, Maureen. 1999. *Tough Choices: Living and Dying in the 21st Century.* Toronto: Irwin Law.

Pollan, Michael. 2006. *The Omnivore's Dilemma: A Natural History of Four Meals.* New York: Penguin Books.

–. 2008. *In Defense of Food: An Eater's Manifesto.* New York: Penguin.

Rees, Ronald. 1988. *New and Naked Land: Making the Prairies Home.* Saskatoon: Western Producer Prairie Books.

Rempal, Sharon, and Cuyler Page. 1992. "Return of the Zucca Melon." *Heritage Seed Program,* December, 42-46.

Varty, John. 2009. "Trust in Bread and Bologna: Promoting Prairie Wheat in the Twentieth Century." In *Method and Meaning in Canadian Environmental History,* edited by Alan MacEachern and William J. Turkel, 182-95. Toronto: Nelson Education.

Wildfong, Bob. 2000. "The Chain of Seeds: Biodiversity and Agriculture," and "Appendix: Farm Animals – Diversity Is Declining (Jy Chiperzak)." In *Biodiversity in Canada: Ecology, Ideas, and Action,* edited by Stephen Bocking, 137-52. Peterborough: Broadview Press.

For Further Reading

Charles, Daniel. 2001. *Lords of the Harvest: Biotech, Big Money, and the Future of Food.* Cambridge, MA: Perseus Publishing.

Kimbrell, Andrew, ed. 2002. *Fatal Harvest Reader: The Tragedy of Industrial Agriculture.* Washington, DC: Island Press.

Kneen, Brewster. 1992. *The Rape of Canola.* Toronto: NC Press.

Laidlaw, Stuart. 2003. *Secret Ingredients: The Brave New World of Industrial Farming.* Toronto: McClelland and Stewart.

McIlwraith, Thomas F. 1997. *Looking for Old Ontario.* Toronto: University of Toronto Press.

Shiva, Vandana. 2000. *Stolen Harvest: The Hijacking of the Global Food Supply.* New York: South End Press.

The Revolution in Agriculture

Boyens, Ingeborg. 2003. "Dissecting Dinner: A Cook's Tour of What Goes in Our Mouths." *Literary Review of Canada* 11, 6: 8-9.

Evans, Clifford. 2002. *The War on Weeds in the Prairie West: An Environmental History.* Calgary: University of Calgary Press.

Fleming, Donald. 1972. "Roots of the New Conservation Movement." *Perspectives in American History* 6: 7-91.

Goodman, David, Bernardo Sorj, and John Wilkinson. 1987. *From Farming to Biotechnology: A Theory of Agro-Industrial Development.* Oxford: Basil Blackwell.

Gould, Annie. 1992. "The Horticultural Research Institute of Ontario." *Heritage Seed Program,* April, 24.

Kerr, Ernest A. 1994. "Vegetable Breeding at Stokes Seeds, Part IV: Sweet Corn." *Heritage Seed Program* 7, 2 (August): 20-22.

Leiss, William. 2004. "Two Stinking Cows: The Mismanagement of BSE Risk in North America." In *Mad Cows and Mother's Milk: The Perils of Poor Risk Communication,* edited by William Leiss and Douglas Powell, 229-61. Montreal and Kingston: McGill-Queen's University Press.

Merington, G., L. Winder, R. Parkinson, and M. Redman. 2002. *Agricultural Pollution: Environmental Problems and Practical Solutions.* London: Spron Press.

Wildfong, Bob. 2000. "The Chain of Seeds: Biodiversity and Agriculture," and "Appendix: Farm Animals – Diversity is Declining (Jy Chiperzak)." In *Biodiversity in Canada: Ecology, Ideas, and Action,* edited by Stephen Bocking, 137-52. Peterborough: Broadview Press.

The Altered Landscape of Farming

Canadian Organic Growers. 2002. "From Conventional to Ecological Agriculture: A Guide to Crop Transition." Reference Series 6.

Murphy, Tom. 1987. "Potato Capitalism: McCain and Industrial Farming in New Brunswick." In *People, Resources, and Power,* edited by Gary Burrill and I. McKay, 15-18. Fredericton: Acadiensis.

Potyondi, Barry. 1994. "Loss and Substitution: The Ecology of Production in South Western Saskatchewan, 1860-1930." *Journal of the Canadian Historical Association* 5: 213-35.

Statistics Canada. 2006a. Census of Agriculture, 2006.

–. 2006b. "The Financial Picture of Farms." http://www.statcan.gc.ca/.

Winson, Anthony. 1993. *The Intimate Commodity: Food and the Development of the Agro-Industrial Complex in Canada.* Toronto: Garamond Press.

The Changing Nature of Food

Boyens, Ingeborg. 2003. "Dissecting Dinner: A Cook's Tour of What Goes in Our Mouths." *Literary Review of Canada* 11, 6: 8-9.

Flannery, Tim. 2007. "We're Living on Corn." *New York Review of Books,* 28 June.

Gabaccia, Donna R. 1998. *We Are What We Eat: Ethnic Food and the Making of Americans.* Cambridge, MA: Harvard University Press.

Goodman, David, Bernardo Sorj, and John Wilkinson. 1987. *From Farming to Biotechnology: A Theory of Agro-Industrial Development.* Oxford: Basil Blackwell.

Hooker, Richard J. 1981. *Food and Drink in America: A History.* New York: Bobbs-Merrill.

Iacovetta, Franca, and Valerie Korinek. 2004. "Jell-O Salads, One-Stop Shopping, and Maria the Homemaker: The Gender Politics of Food." In *Sisters and Strangers: Immigrant, Ethnic, and Racialized Women in Canadian History,* edited by Marlene Epp, Franca Iacovetta, and Frances Swyripa, 190-230. Toronto: University of Toronto Press.

Mallet, Gina. 2004. *Last Chance to Eat: The Fate of the Taste in a Fast Food World.* Toronto: McClelland and Stewart.

McMullen, Ken. 2000. "The Truth about 'Frankenfood' Genetically Modified Organisms." *North Toronto Green Community Newsletter* 4 (Winter).

Mitchell, Don. 1975. *The Politics of Food.* Toronto: Lorimer.

Pim, Linda R. 1981. *The Invisible Additives: Environmental Contaminants in Our Food.* Toronto: Doubleday Canada.

Pollan, Michael. 2006. *The Omnivore's Dilemma: A Natural History of Four Meals.* New York: Penguin Books.

Reiter, Ester. 1996. *Making Fast Food.* Montreal and Kingston: McGill-Queen's University Press.

Schlosser, Eric. 2002. *Fast Food Nation: The Dark Side of the All-American Meal.* New York: Harper Perennial.

Steel, Carolyn. 2008. *Hungry City: How Food Shapes Our Lives.* London: Chatto and Windus.

Varty, John. 2009. "Trust in Bread and Bologna: Promoting Prairie Wheat in the Twentieth Century." In *Method and*

Meaning in Canadian Environmental History, edited by Alan MacEachern and William J. Turkel, 182-95. Toronto: Nelson Education.

Bioengineered Food and Its Backlash

Adam, Nadege. 2004. "Monsanto versus the People." *Canadian Perspectives,* Spring. http://www.canadians.org/.

Brookes, Graham, and Peter Barfoot. 2006. "GM Crops: The First Ten Years Global – Socio-Economic and Environmental Impacts." ISAAA Brief No. 36. Ithaca, New York.

Canada Newswire. 2004. "Schmeiser Decision Causes Uproar around the World." 21 May. http://www.newswire.ca/en/index/.

Council for Biotechnology Information. 2000. "Biotechnology: Good Ideas Are Growing." http://foodsafety.k-state.edu/articles/482/biotech_good_ideas.pdf.

Henig, Robin Marantz. 2001. *The Monk in the Garden: The Lost and Found Genius of Gregor Mendel, the Father of Genetics.* New York: A Mariner Book, Houghton Mifflin.

Kuyek, Devlin. 2007. *Good Crop/Bad Crop: Seed Politics and the Future of Food in Canada.* Toronto: Between the Lines.

Leiss, William, Douglas Powell, Angela Griffiths, and Katherine Barrett. 2004. "Gene Escape, or the Pall of Silence over Plant Biotechnology Risk." In *Mad Cows and Mother's Milk: The Perils of Poor Risk Communication,* edited by William Leiss and Douglas Powell, 153-81. Montreal and Kingston: McGill-Queen's University Press.

McCalla, Dennis R., Richard M. Beames, Hugh Lehman, and Bert R. Christie. 2001. "Regulation of Genetically Modified Food: A Submission to the Canadian Biotechnology Advisory Committee." 17 April. http://www.rsc.ca/.

McTeer, Maureen. 1999. *Tough Choices: Living and Dying in the 21st Century.* Toronto: Irwin Law.

Ridley, Matt. 2000. *Genome.* New York: Perennial.

Alternative Agriculture

Andrews, Geoff. 2008. *The Slow Food Story: Politics and Pleasure.* Montreal and Kingston: McGill-Queen's University Press.

Canadian Organic Growers. 2002. "From Conventional to Ecological Agriculture: A Guide to Crop Transition." Reference Series 6.

Garcia, Deborah Koons. 2004. *The Future of Food.* Mill Valley, CA: Lily Films.

Gottlieb, Robert. 1990. *Environmentalism Unbound: Exploring New Pathways for Change.* Boston: MIT Press.

Rempal, Sharon, and Cuyler Page. 1992. "Return of the Zucca Melon." *Heritage Seed Program,* December, 42-46.

PART 4

The Environmental Era

10

The Environmental Movement and Public Policy

The great arrogance of Western civilization in the industrial and postindustrial eras has been to imagine human beings existing somehow apart from the earth.

— WILLIAM CRONON, ENVIRONMENTAL HISTORIAN,
"INDIANS IN THE LAND," 1986

THE PUBLICATION OF Rachel Carson's *Silent Spring* in 1962 sparked the modern environmental movement in North America and drew attention to industrial agriculture's effect on food supplies and public health. Environmentalism drew on some of the ideas of early twentieth-century conservationists but had a broader reach and a larger conception of the interconnectedness of humans and nature in ecological systems and of environmental issues such as pollution from resources exploitation and industrial agriculture, acid rain and water conservation, and maintaining biodiversity. Environmentalists – unlike conservationists, who feared the future scarcity of resources – operated in a post-scarcity economy and questioned the effects of modernization and consumerism. Environmentalists not only fought to raise awareness about these issues, they also struggled to overcome the myth that constant economic growth, based on exploiting nature's storehouse, was good for business and the basis of prosperity.

Environmentalists faced opposition in the early decades of the movement, and governments responded slowly to their concerns. In the 1970s, environmentalism and high-profile environmental disasters influenced policy makers to lay out an environmental infrastructure to control the worst excesses of industry. Although the notion of sustainable development received statutory affirmation and institutional endorsements, its use as an enforceable legal standard was not implemented in the decades that followed, a time when multinational corporations exerted an ever-greater force on governments and when environmentalists were forced to go global to have their voices heard.

The New Environmentalism

Rachel Carson's book *Silent Spring* had a tremendous impact in North America, where it was welcomed by an audience "already anxious about the brave new world of chemicals and atomic energy" (Smith 2001, 733).

After serialization in *The New Yorker,* the book landed on the *New York Times*'s best-seller list, where it remained for thirty-one weeks. Thalidomide, a sedative drug used for morning sickness, had just been pulled from the market after it was found to be the cause of birth defects, and nuclear weapons testing, a constant feature of Cold War culture, had intensified fears about nuclear fallout. In *Silent Spring,* Carson, an American marine biologist, pointed out the dangers of the indiscriminate use of chemicals such as DDT and accused large agrochemical companies of poisoning the environment. Company spokespeople and many scientists condemned the book and its author, characterizing her as a hysterical spinster, a sentimentalist, and a faddist.

Unlike the conservationists who came before her, Carson used an ecological framework to describe changes in the environment. She used the analogy of a balance of nature to argue that air, soil, water, animals, and humans were interconnected and that damage to one would mean damage to all. *Silent Spring* sold well in Canada and drew attention to what Carson referred to as the "rivers of death" in New Brunswick's forested areas, places where aerial pesticide spray programs killed more fish than their target, the spruce budworm. Carson's groundbreaking book linked the issue of environmental pollution to public health and depicted the human species at a crossroads: "We stand now where two roads diverge ... The road we have long been traveling is deceptively easy, a smooth superhighway on which we progress with great speed, but at its end lies disaster. The other fork of the road – the one 'less traveled by' – offers our last, our only chance to reach a destination that assures the preservation of our earth" (Carson 1962, 244).

Carson's message sounded apocalyptic, but she backed up her research with detailed scientific evidence, particularly on the deleterious effects of DDT and other pesticides, which was listed in a bibliography meant to limit attacks. Her careful research – combined with her calm, deliberative manner on *CBS Reports* – was effective, not to mention remarkable for a person ill with cancer (she died in 1964 at the age of fifty-six). In the United States, President John F. Kennedy, in defiance of the wishes of the chemical industry and the Department of Agriculture, had the Science Advisory Committee investigate pesticide use. The committee vindicated Carson by concluding that "the accretion of residues in the environment can be controlled only by orderly reductions of persistent particles" (Lear 1997, 451). Pesticides were not eliminated, but their indiscriminate use was lessened. Canada banned DDT in 1969, and wildlife populations began to recover.

Unlike conservationists – who focused on first-generation environmental issues, including wildlife protection and the wise use of land and resources – members of the modern environmental movement such as Carson focused on the effects of human activity on the environment. They dealt with complex second-generation issues connected to postwar changes in the world of production, issues such as industrial air and water pollution, nuclear waste, carbon dioxide emissions, and the chemical content of processed foods. In the 1960s, individuals concerned about the long-term effects of environmental degradation and other aspects of so-called modernity adopted a new ethic based on an ecological approach to the environment. Ecology was holistic, concerned with the web of life, linked scientific disciplines, and valued nature. For both intellectual and emotional reasons, environmentalists worried about the exploitation of nature and opposed absolutist solutions to problems – for instance, developing an insecticide to wipe out a species, a drug to eradicate vectors of microbes, or an atom bomb to win the Cold War. These approaches, they argued, led to destruction and reflected intellectual arrogance and a will to master nature and control human destiny. This coarse ambition in the modern temperament had, they argued, fostered "immoderate and insatiable appetites and encouraged a hateful aggressiveness in all the relations of life" (Fleming 1972, 38). Human beings could develop new technologies to produce interesting, useful products and improve living standards, but they were less successful at moderating use or their own behaviour.

The idea that the environment required protection from humanity's hubris gained momentum within the 1960s counterculture, the cultural movement that overtook the Western world between 1956 and 1974 and was fuelled by the Vietnam War. The baby boom generation, which came of age during this period, found inspiration in the activism of individuals such as Carson and earlier naturalists' writings. They were also a generation that had no personal experience of war or depression and could afford to focus on quality-of-life issues. Environmentalism emerged simultaneously with the antiwar and anti-nuclear movements, the civil rights movement to desegregate the American South, and the free speech, feminist, and, later, gay liberation movements. In Canada,

the new spirit of tolerance ushered in after the moral shock of the Holocaust informed activism and led to human rights commissions, which promoted race, class, and gender equality in an increasingly multicultural society.

Whether they focused on pollution or preserving wildlife, environmentalists criticized the existing economic order. Hippies rejected the synthetic products and processed foods of the 1950s and sought alternatives such as organic foods, cosmetics not tested on animals, clothes made of natural fibres, and green sources of energy. They opposed a society based on unrestrained economic growth, profit, mass consumption, waste, and inequality and sought to integrate society and the environment in a new lifestyle based on a balance with nature. Some joined the back-to-the-land movement of organized organic farms and food co-ops; others became vegetarians, rode bicycles, and experimented with renewable energy. Counterculturalists avoided conflict, were self-reliant, set an example, and speculated about the possibility of developing a truly ecological society, one that was democratic rather than hierarchical and cooperative rather than competitive. Although utopian in certain respects and not lasting, the 1960s counterculture critiqued modern society's excesses and its potentially destructive effects and was compatible with environmentalism. Importantly, environmentalism evolved into a distinct movement by the end of the decade.

In the United States and Canada, over 20 million people gathered to mark the first Earth Day in 1970. In pressing for environmental protection, environmentalists motivated grassroots activist groups and sophisticated lobbyists. In 1972, the United Nations Conference on the Human Environment, which met in Stockholm, added a global dimension to the movement and has since been recognized as marking the beginning of modern political and public awareness of environmental problems. A Canadian businessman, Maurice Strong, chaired the meeting that drafted the conference's declaration; it established a program and administrative structure to coordinate international investigations into environmental problems.

Environmental Issues Defined

Environmental issues in Canada shifted over time from nuclear, water, and air pollution in the 1960s and 1970s to acid rain, the ozone layer, and forests and wildlife protection in the 1980s and 1990s. Thereafter, the focus moved to energy issues, biodiversity, and climate change. As soon as one environmental issue was partially resolved, such as the cleanup of phosphorus and algae in Lake Erie, new studies revealed further complications, including global implications. The more scientists learned, the more extensive environmental degradation they found. A number of high-profile events and publications fuelled environmentalism in Canada and around the world by drawing attention to emerging issues and problems. In 1963, for instance, under pressure from antiwar activists, nearly one hundred countries signed the first nuclear test ban treaty. The military's use of nuclear power linked the peace and environmental movements. Signatories agreed to test bombs underground but not in the atmosphere, the ocean, or in space. The opponents of nuclear bomb testing and power came from diverse backgrounds (see Figure 10.1). They ranged from the group of Quakers, ecologists, journalists, and hippies who founded Greenpeace in Vancouver in 1971 to the Mennonite and pacifist residents of Warman, Saskatchewan, who opposed the opening of a uranium refinery by Eldorado Mining and Refining.

In the mid- and late 1970s, the public in general began to question the nuclear industry's viability when unmarked radioactive nuclear dumps, unsafe uranium-mining practices, and unacknowledged radioactive spills came to light. Money wasted on three heavy-water plants in Cape Breton and the frequent malfunction of a reactor at Douglas Point also affected public opinion adversely, as did the meltdowns at Three Mile Island in 1979 and Chernobyl in 1986. In 1975, the Energy and Environment Committee of Montreal's Société pour vaincre la pollution published a booklet titled *Nuclear Power: Everything You Didn't Want to Know and Which They Wouldn't Tell You Anyway.* The organization raised awareness of problems in the nuclear industry and traced them to a secretive elite group of male scientists and bureaucrats. Unease about nuclear power was both reflected and enhanced by popular films such as *The China Syndrome* (1979) and *Silkwood* (1983).

The global dimension and interconnectedness of environmental issues were driven home further by a number of high-profile books. In 1972, the Club of Rome published *Limits to Growth,* a study paid for by the Volkswagen Foundation that reported the

FIGURE 10.1 Nuclear weapons policy became an issue after the bombing of Hiroshima in 1945 and extensive nuclear testing in the Pacific in the 1950s. Identified by their iconic "Ban the Bomb" symbol on buttons and signs, members of the movement held demonstrations such as this one on Parliament Hill to protest nuclear weapons testing.
Library and Archives Canada, e010836557

findings of MIT academics. Using computers, the group projected, accurately as it turns out, the environmental effects of exponential growth from industrialization, rapid population expansion, increased agricultural consumption, and the depletion of renewable resources. The study predicted rapid environmental deterioration and a catastrophic population-pollution-resources crisis that would threaten the future of civilization by 2050. To support life, it argued, the planet needed a "steady state of economic and ecological equilibrium" (Macdonald 1991, 102). By 1987, a solid definition of the modern concept of sustainability had been developed by the UN's Brundtland Commission: "Sustainable development is development that meets the needs of the present without compromising the ability of future generations to meet their own needs." The G7

JACK VALLENTYNE, ALIAS JOHNNY BIOSPHERE, ECO-WARRIOR

FIGURE 10.2 Jack Vallentyne, 1986
From the program of National Marine Educators' Association, Cleveland, OH, photographer unknown

Through books such as *The Algal Bowl* (1974) and presentations, scientist J.R. (Jack) Vallentyne contributed to the recovery of the Great Lakes in the 1970s and popularized the concept of banning phosphorus and chlorine-based chemicals to protect water sources and lakes. In 1978, at a presentation before the International Joint Commission in which he spoke in favour of an ecosystem approach, he argued that the Great Lakes could not adapt to the cumulative stresses of population growth, technology, and pollution: "Constant growth is an illusion. It's the myth of technological society. It's an illusion in the sense that nothing ever grows without limits, nothing ever grows constantly. It kills itself if it does" (Dempsey 2004, 192).

In the 1980s, Vallentyne took on the persona of Johnny Biosphere and began speaking to communities and students on the importance of protecting the biosphere and on "the danger humans posed to their own survival through unthinking devotion to growth" (Dempsey 2004, 191). He was the first Canadian to win the Rachel Carson Award from the Society of Environmental Toxicology and Chemistry.

endorsed this approach to environmental problems at its summit in Toronto the following year.

In 1973, E.F. Schumacher, a German economist, added the idea of smallness to modern environmentalism. His book, *Small Is Beautiful,* was a North American bestseller and touched a cord in the aftermath of the OPEC oil crisis. That same year, books such as Ellen Buchman Ewald's *Recipes for a Small Planet* and the *Canadian Whole Earth Catalogue* encouraged Canadians to live healthier, simpler lifestyles by eating locally and organically and by getting back to nature. Canada's own "eco-warrior," Jack Vallentyne, published *The Algal Bowl* the following year (see Figure 10.2). In it, he documented the issue of eutrophication in Lake Erie (see Chapter 8) for a lay audience. *Harrowsmith* magazine, which began publication in Camden East, Ontario, in 1976, was both a response and a spur to the back-to-the-land movement. Its approximately 100,000 subscribers devoured articles on vegetable gardening, alternative energy, and living ecologically. The magazine also published books about plants that could flourish in the Canadian environment. Canadian scientist David Suzuki (see Figure 10.3) added his voice to the environmental movement when he became the host of CBC's *The Nature of Things* in 1979.

New environmental issues in the 1980s and 1990s included the discovery of holes in the ozone layer, which exposed Earth to the

THE NATURE OF THINGS

In 2010, the Canadian Broadcasting Corporation celebrated fifty years of *The Nature of Things,* a program dedicated to documenting nature and the effects people have on it. When the show launched in 1960, it was a lone voice on environmental issues in Canada and helped frame debates and discussions for thousands of Canadians. The show was one of the first mainstream programs to present scientific evidence on a number of environmental issues, including nuclear power and genetic engineering.

sun's unfiltered ultraviolet rays. Scientists traced the damage to chlorofluorocarbons (CFCs), used in aerosol sprays, foam insulation, and electronic equipment cleaners. Consumers adapted by wearing hats, sunglasses, and protective UV sunblock and clothing, and the discovery led, in 1989, to the Montreal Protocol on Substances That Deplete the Ozone Layer, an international treaty designed to protect the ozone layer by abolishing the use of substances such as CFCs. Scientists also discovered that automobile emissions contributed to the greenhouse effect, the process by which the thermal radiation emitted by a planetary surface is absorbed by greenhouse gases in the atmosphere and radiated in all directions, including toward the planetary surface. The result is global warming.

The rapid destruction of the world's temperate rainforests and the loss of biodiversity that accompanied it also grabbed headlines and involved Canadian environmentalists abroad. These unique biospheres were important sources of new medicines and absorbed carbon dioxide in the atmosphere. Global rainforest destruction stemmed partly from the policies of the World Bank, which lent poor countries money, created debt, and then insisted on repayment with terms that caused the nations to destroy their resources to collect enough cash to pay the interest on the loans.

Canadian Environmentalism

The 1960s counterculture and the rise of environmentalism led to the creation of diverse reform groups across Canada. Environmental activists had limited resources, but

FIGURE 10.3 David Suzuki teaching a class at the University of British Columbia in 1971. Born in Vancouver in 1936, Suzuki is an award-winning scientist, environmentalist, and broadcaster who educates the public about the complexities of science and the interdependence of humans and the environment.
UBC Library Archives

they were savvy at gaining media attention. They favoured participatory politics and public consultation, a process articulated by student leaders in their campaign to democratize the governing structures of universities and supported, at least rhetorically, by politicians such as Pierre Trudeau, who became prime minister in 1968.

The green movement began in many countries simultaneously. In Canada, students and professors at the University of Toronto founded Pollution Probe in 1969 to try "to clean up the mess in which we now live and which threatens our survival" (Chant 1970, n.p.). Professor Donald Chant, an expert on natural alternatives to pesticides, led the group's successful fight to have DDT banned. The group also helped clean up Lake Erie

FIGURE 10.4 Early signs of environmental activism in Vancouver are evident in this 1969 billboard by Ben Metcalf, an activist, reporter, and founding member of Greenpeace.

Rex Weyler, photographer

and researched many pollution issues. Other organizations included A Society to Overcome Pollution (STOP) (1975, Montreal), the Canadian Coalition on Acid Rain (1981), and regional groups such as the Conservation Council of New Brunswick and the West Coast Environmental Law Association. Each group focused on particular issues, engaged citizens concerned about the environment, did public education work, and lobbied for policy and legislative change.

Canada's most famous environmental organization, Greenpeace, was formed in 1971 by Canadian and American activists in Vancouver (see Figure 10.4). It started with one leaking boat and a shoestring budget but quickly became a global nongovernmental organization. "Vancouver was the only place in the world where a political entity such as Greenpeace could have been born," wrote Robert Hunter, one of the founders (see Figure 10.5). "We had a critical mass of Americans who were really angry with their government. We had the right legal stuff, with sovereignty and anti-piracy rules on our side. We had the biggest concentration of tree-huggers, radicalized students, garbage-dump stoppers, shit-disturbing unionists, freeway fighters, pot smokers and growers, aging Trotskyites, condo killers, farmland savers, fish preservationists, animal rights activists, back-to-the-landers, vegetarians, nudists, Buddhists, and anti-spraying,

FIGURE 10.5 A meeting at the first Greenpeace public office in Vancouver, 1975. Around the table are Neil Hunter, Henry Payne, Leigh Wilkes, Rod Marining, Kurt Musgrove (hidden), and Bob Hunter. Standing by the door is Al Capp; leaning against the wall (right) is Bree Drummond

Rex Weyler, photographer

anti-pollution marchers and picketers in the country, per capita in the world" (Hunter 2004, 16). The organization came into being when members of its precursor, the Don't Make a Wave Committee, decided to sail an old fishing vessel, the *Phyllis Cormack,* into the US nuclear testing site at Amchitka, Alaska. Greenpeace was one of the first organizations to link the peace movement with budding environmental concerns through slogans such as "Ban the Bomb and Save the Redwoods! Nukes Harm Trees!"

The organization's focus on direct action and risky publicity stunts received worldwide attention, and it claimed success when the United States eventually abandoned testing in the Amchitka area. Its high-profile protests gained Greenpeace public support and led to the opening of more branches around the world. In 1979, Greenpeace's headquarters moved to Amsterdam, and in 1985 it reported that it had over 1 million members and had received donations of over $14 million annually. The small Canadian movement had evolved into an influential global organization led mostly by western Europeans and supported financially by donations.

Greenpeace sought to slow down and raise awareness about arms production by floating helium-filled balloons painted with the slogan "End the Arms Race" over the Soviet Union, during a time when Russians were insulated from world opinion. In 1985, when the organization launched a "peace flotilla" to protest French nuclear weapons testing in the South Pacific, photographer Fernando Pereira was killed by a bomb planted on the *Rainbow Warrior* by French agents. The incident led to the resignation of France's minister of defence, and Greenpeace gained

THE SEAL HUNT

Greenpeace won the undying hatred of some Newfoundlanders when it – along with the International Fund for Animal Welfare, the Fund for Animals, and the Sea Shepherd Conservation Society – focused on the seal hunt, which involved clubbing baby seals and overhunting them for their skins for fur coats. The seal hunt was part of Newfoundland's culture, a test of manhood for hunters whose bravery was celebrated as they went "to the ice" and worked in dangerous, treacherous waters. It created enormous wealth for a handful of merchants, but the absence of sustainable management policies led to depletion. In 1972, the number of Newfoundland–Gulf of St. Lawrence harp seals fell below 2 million. French actress Brigitte Bardot participated in Greenpeace's campaign, which began in 1976, when she flew to the North Atlantic in 1977 to draw attention to the seals' plight.

Following years of protest, the European Community, in 1982, banned the importation from Canada of white coat pelts and all harp seal products. The ban crippled the seal trade. In 1987, the Canadian government banned the commercial hunting of white coat pups but not molted pups (about thirty days old). The Department of Fisheries and Ocean's objective for harp seals was a long-term, sustainable harvest, but its record in managing fisheries was abysmal. It allowed a total allowable catch of 200,000 to 300,000 seals annually, even though it only had estimates of annual population levels. If the seal population dipped to 1.65 million, by its count, it would shut down the hunt. Environmentalists, however, argued that the government's quotas were too high. Even though the seal hunt continues, the Greenpeace campaign caused seal fur coats go out of fashion.

more members and adherents. Greenpeace also publicized and criticized the dumping of nuclear and other toxic wastes into lakes and oceans and the slaughter of whales and dolphins by commercial fishers. Its "Save the Whales" campaign won more Canadian supporters and led to the International Whaling Commission's adoption in 1982 of a global whaling moratorium and, in 1994, to the creation of the Antarctic Whale Sanctuary. Canada ended commercial whaling in 1971 and pulled out of the International Whaling Commission in 1982.

Whereas Greenpeace focused on international issues, other Canadian environmental groups had a local or regional focus and, from the 1970s, worked on many fronts and issues. In British Columbia, for instance, environmentalists sometimes allied with First Nations to combat the clear-cutting of forests, which threatened habitats with dangerous mudslides and soil erosion. Thousands of people worked in the province's sawmilling, logging, and pulp-and-paper industries, but environmentalists argued that the industry's unsustainable harvesting methods were ruining ecosystems. The forest industry, they revealed, was dominated by large multinational companies whose efficient technology had expanded and sped up production as the industry moved into new timber stands. Provincial royal commissions in 1943-45 and 1956 had created a forest management system that favoured giving large companies long-term leases, set annual government levels for timber cuts, and required companies to leave cut-over areas to nature or for reseeding or replanting. As corporate concentration increased, however, a sustained yield was not implemented, and reforestation was slow. The industry transformed the province's landscape as old-growth forests disappeared. Environmentalists fought to protect forests from clear-cutting, but collaboration between the lumber companies and the government facilitated the industry's expansion and informed policy decisions. Protests included confrontations in which protesters blocked timber roads, got arrested, lobbied governments, sought legal injunctions, and initiated legal cases. They sometimes also created conflicts between middle-class environmentalists and the unionized lumber workers over the issue of jobs.

Environmentalists convinced lumber companies and the BC government to protect some of the last remaining old-growth trees on Vancouver Island, at Cathedral Grove and in Pacific Rim National Park. In the 1990s, the province also doubled the amount of land protected in provincial parks, hired unemployed loggers to protect the forests, and supported more sustainable approaches to forestry. Yet it also allowed clear-cutting to continue. At the dawn of the twenty-first century, the United Nations declared Canada's forests essential to the health of the planet. Because they absorbed carbon dioxide through photosynthesis, any loss would contribute adversely to climate change.

Environmental Infrastructure and Inaction

A combination of environmentalism and high-profile environmental disasters influenced policy makers in North America to develop environmental infrastructure. In the United States, the Nixon (1969-74), Ford (1974-77), and Carter (1977-83) administrations passed landmark environmental legislation, including the National Environmental Policy Act (1970), to assess the ecological impact of large projects and to clean up chemical pollution from industries and municipalities. It set up the Environmental Protection Agency the following year, and more protective legislation followed, including the Clean Water Act (1972), the Endangered Species Act (1974), the Safe Drinking Water Act (1974), and amendments to the Clean Water Act (1977). After the Love Canal disaster (see Chapter 8), the US government created a superfund to clean up priority toxic sites and pay for citizens' relocation.

In Canada, where the power to pass laws relating to the environment is divided between the federal and provincial governments, Pierre Elliott Trudeau, prime minister from 1968 to 1979, established the Department of the Environment in 1971 to set environmental policy. The federal government enacted the Clean Air Act in 1971 and the Canada Water Act in 1972, and in 1972 both Canada and the United States signed the International Great Lakes Water Quality Agreement. Developing a coherent and comprehensive approach to the environment was complicated and limited, however, by the separation of powers. Fisheries and interprovincial trade and commerce fell under the purview of the federal government. The provinces had primary jurisdiction over natural resources, agriculture, forestry, mining, and hydroelectric development.

The vast infrastructure that emerged included federal and provincial environmental laws, regulations to administer pollution control policies, environmental departments and agencies, and environmental assessment procedures. The Department of the Environment, a complex regulatory body, had a mandate to protect the environment, but unlike the US Environmental Protection Agency, it also engaged in resource management. In its first four years, it developed *discretionary* assessment processes for large government and private projects, and it focused on air and water pollution, especially water quality and the use of phosphorus pollutants in the Great Lakes, projects that had some success (see Chapter 8).

The department's efforts to limit pollution elsewhere, however, were limited and reactive. From 1975 to 1986 – a decade defined by the energy crisis, high inflation, a recession, and pressure for restraint from businesses and the provinces – the department kept a low profile, lacked consistent leadership, faced institutional competition from other departments for financial resources, and encouraged the provinces to do frontline environmental regulation. The federal government passed the Environmental Contaminants Act in 1976 to control chemicals such as PCBs from entering the environment, but with limited resources and erratic research, implementation of the act and other policies was ineffective.

Defining and implementing a national environmental policy and infrastructure was complicated by the fact that the provinces and municipalities were also responsible for and passed legislation and regulations. When it came to water pollution, for instance, the Canada Water Act established the basic framework for federal-provincial cooperation on issues with water quality and policy, but there were overlaps and oversights that typified the governments' approach to all environmental issues. Unlike the United States, Canada had no national law or mandatory national standards to ensure safe drinking water, and the federal and provincial governments often had competing agendas or different interests. The federal Fisheries Act, for instance, prohibited the discharge of substances harmful to fish. In 1983, the federal government added steep penalties for firms that violated the act, which would be enforced by the Environmental Protection Service, a federal agency. The agency had the potential to get tough with polluters throughout Canada, but its focus was coastal, not inland, waters, and the provinces were opposed to the federal government taking measures against polluters in the pulp-and-paper industry. The provisions also contained a loophole by which companies could be exonerated if they could establish due diligence, that they had taken reasonable steps to avoid pollution. The Environmental Protection Service, although "new," also contained long-time personnel from the old regulatory brigade who reminded provincial officials in British Columbia and the Atlantic provinces of past jurisdictional conflicts pertaining to fisheries.

Developments at the provincial and municipal levels varied from province to city and from administration to administration, but provincial laws pertaining to inland lakes and rivers lacked a conservationist impulse. In 1970, for instance, Ontario premier John Robarts (1961-71) stated publicly that Canadians had a right to fresh air and clean water. Pollution, however, remained a low priority in his government: its budget for highway construction and repair that year was sixteen times larger than its budget for pollution control. The following year, however, the Ontario government did pass the Environmental Protection Act, supposedly to prevent the discharge of contaminants that impaired water quality, but companies such as Inco in Sudbury resisted. British Columbia, by contrast, took a licensing approach to local pollution control. The province established water quality standards and guidelines and issued permits that set outer limits on the amount of pollution a firm could discharge and defined the pollution-control equipment the company had to use. The firm was responsible for outlining its system of pollution control.

Informal cooperation among the federal and provincial governments worked better on larger crossborder areas than in local end-of-the-pipe pollution situations. Joint federal-provincial ecosystem programs – including the Great Lakes Initiative, St. Lawrence Vision 2000, the Fraser River Action Plan, the Atlantic Coastal Action Program, and Alberta's Northern Rivers Ecosystem Initiative – were set up to deal with serious water pollution, but neither level of government did much to put in place preventive ecological measures that would stop agricultural or urban runoff or airborne toxic chemicals

MUNICIPAL SEWAGE DUMPING

Municipal governments have implemented policies to improve sewage systems since the 1970s, yet success rates vary. The Sierra Legal Defence Fund, now Ecojustice, monitors water quality, and its National Sewage Report Card rates the discharges and treatment methods of twenty cities. Its reports have publicized the poor record of a number of cities and exposed their lack of compliance with regulations. In the 1990s, it publicized that Vancouver was simply dumping its sewage into the Fraser River and the ocean. In 1994, nearly half of Canadian municipalities had either failed to obtain or ignored provincial waste management permits. With pressure from the provincial and federal governments, some cities upgraded their treatment plants, but Halifax and Victoria continue to dump billions of litres of raw sewage into the ocean each year.

from entering the environment in the first place. The responsibility for instituting or improving sewage systems fell to municipal governments, not the provinces or Ottawa.

When it came to air pollution, the federal government developed standards and objectives, and these standards were incorporated into most provincial systems. Sections of the Clean Air Act set out the maximum allowable concentration of dangerous substances, including arsenic, mercury, and vinylchloride. In the late 1970s, the federal government banned the use of chlorofluorocarbons in aerosol cans, but it did little about industrial and municipal pollution, even though smog presented clear evidence that it was on the rise. The Environmental Contaminants Act designated substances likely to pose significant danger to the environment and authorized the government to ban them. Provincial air pollution measures focused on local actions. For instance, a company that planned to build a plant that would emit contaminants had to apply to the province for a building permit. Provincial standards and guidelines were based on federal objectives, and the provinces could issue control orders to protect the public from significant air pollution. Although both levels of government did little to limit car emissions, some provinces did institute inspections to get older vehicles off the road.

In the 1980s and 1990s, Brian Mulroney (prime minister 1984-93) was more interested in environmental issues than Jean Chrétien (prime minister 1993-2003), although Chrétien did commit Canada to the Kyoto Protocol (see Chapter 7). Both of their governments, however, concentrated on cost cutting, balancing budgets, creating jobs, and downsizing

government programs. Economic recovery took precedence over environmental protection. The Department of the Environment did, however, take a more activist position between 1986 and the early 1990s, when a series of disasters spurred it to action: the Bhopal gas leak in India in 1984, the Chernobyl nuclear meltdown in 1986, a PCB fire in Ville de Sainte-Basile-le-Grand in 1988, the *Exxon Valdez* oil spill in 1989, and the Hagarsville tire fire in 1990 (see Figure 10.6). In this context, in 1988, the department consolidated and updated Canada's environmental legislation in the Canadian Environmental Protection Act (CEPA), which sought to further regulate the entry of toxic chemicals into the environment, even though it excluded large groups of substances.

One issue that the federal government did address in the 1980s was the issue of acid rain and its effect on the Great Lakes, other water bodies, and terrestrial ecosystems. The Canadian Coalition on Acid Rain, which had 2 million members and the attention of the media, urged governments to act on both sides of the Canada-US border. In the United States, the Carter administration was unresponsive, and the Reagan administration argued that a "lack of scientific consensus" meant there could be no immediate action on controls. The government's claim flew in the face of a 1979 report that confirmed that Americans contributed five times more transboundary pollution than Canadians. Mulroney's election in 1984, particularly his good relations with President Reagan, however, put the issue on the US agenda. In 1985, Mulroney cleared roadblocks to an acid rain agreement with the United States with a

FIGURE 10.6 In February 1990, teenagers set a 7.3-hectare tire dump on fire in Hagarsvile, Ontario. The fire spewed toxic smoke for seventeen days, consumed 14 million scrap tires, took $13 million to put out, and forced four thousand people from their homes.
Boris Spremo, photographer, GetStock.com

commitment to reduce sulphur dioxide emissions and the entry of solid wastes, ozone-destroying CFCs, and pesticides into the environment. The Canadian government also agreed to bring its automobile and light truck emission standards up to those of the United States in 1987. It worked with the provinces to implement the regulations effectively, and it cooperated with other Western nations to reduce emissions. Following George Bush's election in 1988, Canada-US discussions culminated in amendments to the International Great Lakes Water Quality Agreement and to the Canada-United States Air Quality Agreement (1991). The two countries committed to reducing acid rain emissions by 50 percent (to 1980 levels) and to establishing a research and monitoring network.

On the international level, Canada briefly took a leadership role when it helped bring about the Montreal Protocol on ozone depletion, which countries around the world adopted and implemented. The following year, in 1988, when G7 leaders met in Toronto, Canada endorsed sustainable development in

principle, and the concept took centre stage in its Green Plan, which it announced in 1990. The government intended it as a five-year, $3 billion action plan to guide environmental policy and change the way the government dealt with environmental and sustainability issues. The plan had four chief goals: to regulate toxic substances, reduce waste by 50 percent by 2000, institute environmental assessments on all federal projects, and move toward sustainable development in the resource sector by 1995. Armed with its new plan, Canada played a leading role at the Rio Earth Summit, the United Nations Conference on Environment and Development, when it met in 1992 and endorsed sustainable development.

Five years later, however, the Green Plan had reached few of its goals. The plan had included no coercive instruments such as taxes and regulations to change behaviour or give Environment Canada a higher profile. When the government changed in 1993, the plan also lost the support of key players. Since then, successive reports by the Organisation for Economic Co-operation and Development (OECD) have declared Canada "an environmental straggler." Even though Canada signed the 1992 United Nations Conference on Environment and Development and the 2002 World Summit on Sustainable Development, it has maintained a poor environmental performance relative to other countries. A pioneer evaluation by David Boyd in 2001 found that the nation's record was among the worst (twenty-eighth out of twenty-nine countries). An evaluation completed by a team at Simon Fraser University for the David Suzuki Foundation in 2010 found that Canada ranked twenty-fourth out of twenty-five countries. It concluded that if Canada's environmental polices were comparable to those of the top three OECD countries, it would move from second-last to first place in the OECD. In other words, improvements are possible (see Table 10.1).

Canada's failure resulted from a combination of poor policy and lack of political will. The federal government passed legislation but failed to enforce it. Although Canadian citizens learned to recycle garbage as part of the successful blue-box program, and although some individuals made personal lifestyle changes to decrease their personal ecological footprint, governments favoured either business interests over the environment or a neoconservative agenda to balance budgets, cut down on public debt, and reduce their own regulatory and policy roles. The business lobby argued that environmental protection was too expensive and not compatible with a free market economy. Most companies failed to incorporate environmental sustainability into their business plans and continued to dump wastes and create pollution. Some

TABLE 10.1 Environmental performance rankings, developed countries			
Country	1992	2002	2010
Denmark	1	1	1
Sweden	2	5	2
Norway	3	7	3
Switzerland	6	3	4
Germany	18	4	5
Austria	9	2	6
Netherlands	20	6	7
Italy	12	9	8
United Kingdom	14	13	9
Finland	8	8	10
New Zealand	7	16	11
Korea	10	12	12
Spain	4	17	13
Japan	15	18	14
Greece	5	14	15
France	13	10	16
Ireland	16	19	17
Czech Republic	19	15	18
Portugal	11	11	19
Australia	17	23	20
Luxembourg	23	21	21
Iceland	21	20	22
Belgium	22	22	23
Canada	24	24	24
United States	25	25	25

Source: Gunton and Calbick (2010, 5).

companies, however, adhered to legal requirements because they understood the importance of maintaining a good public image and realized that environmental planning and programs could be cost-effective. Federal cutbacks, however, not only cut deeply into the research, monitoring, and enforcement budgets of environmental departments, they also shunted responsibility for the environment to the local level, where there were fewer resources to deal with issues.

PESTICIDE REGULATION SHIFTS TO THE CITIES

Following the Second World War, when Canadians moved to larger houses in the suburbs en masse, pesticide companies targeted homeowners as a new market. The Canadian Public Health Association warned that pesticides posed grave risks to human growth, reproduction, immunity, and neurological development, but its message was ignored for years. In 1991, the town of Hudson, Quebec, passed a bylaw banning the nonessential use of pesticides on public and private property. The law affected the lawn care industry, not farmers or foresters. In 1992, two companies, Spraytech and Chemlawn, were charged for violating the bylaw, and the case went to the Supreme Court. In 2001, the court upheld the municipality's right to pass such laws to protect public health. The decision increased the power of municipalities to regulate on environmental matters. Over the next five years, sixty-nine Canadian cities passed similar bylaws, and the case influenced developments in the United States.

In 2002, the federal government updated the Pest Control Products Act, but it did not eliminate pesticides for cosmetic use, even though the public supported fewer pesticides, standardized legislation for cosmetic pesticides use, and an alternative pesticide strategy. Many lawn care companies, however, began to adopt organic techniques and procedures.

Divisions in the Ranks and a New Global Outlook

The frustration that environmentalists and ordinary citizens felt as governments failed to take action on the environment led to fractures in the environmental movement, particularly in the United States, and the adoption of new strategies for change. South of the border, the environmental movement split between mainstream careerists, who left the movement to work for the state, and Earth First, an organization established in 1979 as a vehicle for direct action rather than traditional conservation. For instance, some activists engaged in a practice called monkey wrenching, in which they sabotaged logging efforts by spiking trees. Others engaged in acts of ecotage, such as destroying heavy machinery. This brief militant phase, however, led to internal divisions within Earth First when the majority declared its opposition to violence.

The environmental movement also became more complicated in the 1990s, when an American backlash against environmentalism gave birth to organizations such as the Yellow Ribbon Coalition, which favoured unfettered lumbering, mining in national parks, the abolition of the Endangered Species Act, and rolling back clean air, water quality, and pesticides legislation. Backed by the resource industries, but smaller than the Christian Right and the gun lobby, the coalition spoke out against all government regulation, particularly of private property. Its core activists were saboteurs who nearly killed a Greenpeace organizer when they placed a pipe bomb in her car. In the early twentieth-first century, a minority of Christian fundamentalists also condemned environmentalism as the new paganism.

These splits in the American environmental movement influenced some Canadian activists but did not lead to a profound fracture in the movement. A small minority briefly advocated violence. In 1982, for instance, a group called Direct Action blew up a hydro station on Vancouver Island, and the members of Greenpeace Canada split over the issue of the seal hunt. More commonly, environmentalists, frustrated by the failure of governments and agencies to implement existing policies, turned to legal action. The Sierra Legal Defence Fund (Ecojustice Canada, as of 2007), for instance, was established in 1990 to donate legal services to environmental organizations to litigate cases and establish precedents to reinforce existing legislation. Its members took inspiration from First Nations groups, which took governments to court in land claim lawsuits and to force the state to fulfill its treaty obligations.

The Sierra Legal Defence Fund's first case was against Fletcher Challenge, a multinational corporation from New Zealand, and MacMillan Bloedel, a Vancouver-based forestry company, which planned to log the Walbran Valley near Victoria, a nesting place of the marbled murrelet. The organization petitioned the federal government to do an environmental assessment to determine the effect of logging on the bird's habitat and to protect the bird under the Migratory Birds Convention Act, a tactic that had been used by environmentalists in the United States to save the California redwood.

Although litigation did not always succeed, cases launched by the Sierra Legal Defence Fund drew attention to issues and put pressure on governments. The group initiated cases against corporations for environmental violations and to protect endangered species, prevent water pollution, clean up toxic sites, and preserve wild lands. It sued governments to enforce their own laws. One case succeeded in stopping Vancouver from dumping raw sewage into Georgia Strait and Burrard Inlet. Other cases put pressure on governments to conduct environmental assessments. In a landmark decision in 1994, for instance, the Supreme Court of Canada ordered the federal government to do an environmental assessment of the James Bay Hydro Project. The Sierra Legal Defence Fund also defended citizen groups sued by large corporations in SLAPP (strategic law-suits against public participation) actions. These lawsuits were corporate attempts to bully citizens who opposed company actions. The Sierra Legal Defence Fund argued that these cases caused public attention to shift from the environmental issue at hand to the lawsuit.

The failure of governments to enforce or implement environmental assessment processes illustrated that, given a choice between creating jobs or protecting the environment, the economy won. In Quebec, for instance, in 1984, Noranda circumvented the provincial government's demand that it modernize its copper smelter in Rouyn by threatening to close down and fire 1,200 employees. In Ontario two years later, Kimberley-Clark threatened to close its plant in Terrace Bay if the government held it to its pollution-control deadline. The provincial government backed off. In Saskatchewan, the controversial Rafferty-Alameda Dam on the Souris River was subject only to voluntary federal government regulations until 1989, when the Canadian Wildlife Federation challenged the federal licence. The Federal Court decided the guidelines were legally enforceable, and in 1992 the Supreme Court of Canada decided such guidelines applied to provincial projects if they affected federal interests. This important decision implied that environmental assessments were necessary and should be taken seriously. In the early 1990s, however, Newfoundland approved the Hibernia offshore oil project without an intensive environmental impact study.

In the early 1990s, governments ignored environmental issues partly because of a recession and because poor management of public funds resulted in huge government deficits, but non-enforcement of environmental legislation was, to a certain degree, connected to globalization. Global corporations began to diverge in the 1980s from a postwar model in North America that had been shaped by Franklin Roosevelt's New Deal and the labour movement. The government guaranteed that companies would look after their employees' and communities' well-being through tax payments and negotiated collective agreements. Governments, in turn, would manage the social welfare state and regulate the private sector to uphold the public interest, which increasingly included the environment and public health. The 1980s, however, witnessed the rise of CEO capitalism. Corporations, which focused on creating short-term gains for shareholders (measured by market performance and dividends), reduced employees' wages, benefits, and pensions. Businesses lobbied successfully for reduced taxes and chipped away at the welfare state's social programs and government regulatory powers.

In the early 1990s, Canada's federal and provincial policy makers had to adjust to the new free trade regime negotiated under the Free Trade Agreement (1988), the North American Free Trade Agreement (1994), and the Free Trade Area of the Americas, which is still being negotiated. Canada was caught up in the wave of neoconservatism that swept developed countries, such as the United States and Britain. Its adherents supported small government, deregulation, union busting, lower taxes, balanced budgets, and reduced spending on social and environmental programs as panaceas to recession and unemployment. Government officials increas-

ingly embraced corporate concepts such as competitiveness, productivity, profitability, and attention to the bottom line. In Ontario, for instance, the Conservative Party, led by Mike Harris (premier from 1995 to 2002), cut social policies and spending on the environment without eliminating deficits. Following his government's defeat, urban infrastructure declined, and responsibility for tragedies such as the *E. coli* outbreak at Walkerton (see Chapter 8) could clearly be laid at the government's door. In Alberta, Ralph Klein's government (1992-2006) spent money on security against ecoterrorism rather than on protecting the environment. Although Klein promised a system of air pollution monitoring and a mechanism to resolve the dispute between ranchers and the oil and gas industry over gas flares (see Chapter 7), the contamination of ranchers' land continued.

In this context, environmental activists who campaigned to save old-growth forests or to prohibit genetically modified organisms from entering the food chain increasingly had to take on large multinational corporations "with budgets larger than most governments" (Pitelis and Sugden 2000, 72). The late twentieth century saw the rise of corporate mergers and the increased mobility of companies, leading to more control over producers and workers. Technological advances also led to further clear-cutting, overfishing, and new ways to manipulate plant and animal genes. This combination of technology and corporate consolidation to control the marketplace influenced global trade rules. Large companies also funded research, advertising, and conservative think-tanks to consolidate their power, maximize profits,

THE BATTLE OF SEATTLE AND FAIR TRADE

The Battle of Seattle, a 1999 protest against the World Trade Organization, brought together activists from diverse causes against the international trade regime. Friends of the Earth announced on its website that it was "working to prevent the WTO from overruling hard-won environmental laws." *The Nation* described the opposition to "the corporate-dominated trade regimen enforced by the WTO" as a red-green alliance of diverse protesters from many countries, a "phantasmagorical mix of tens of thousands of peaceful demon-strators – husky, red-jacketed steelworkers marching along-side costumed sea turtle im-personators, environmentalists with miners, human rights activists with small family farmers" (Cooper 1999, 1). Together, the teamsters and the turtles, the workers and the environmentalists managed to close down the WTO's opening sessions in Seattle and thrust the once-obscure issue of fair trade onto centre stage.

and increase executive bonuses. Faced with corporate lobbyists and companies that threatened to shut down rather than support social or environmental policies, many polit-icians supported corporate ideas about de-regulation, limited government intervention in the economy, and lax enforcement of occupational and environmental standards. As governments and corporations showed less interest in protecting the environment, environmentalists turned their attention to the lack of social and environmental policies in the new international free trade trade regime. Although environmentalists and members of the labour movement sometimes disagreed over the issue of jobs and were often divided culturally by class, they nevertheless joined with other activists – including Can-adian churches, the Council of Canadians, Aboriginal and women's groups, and many NGOs – to oppose the international trade regime's failure to include human rights, labour, and environmental standards in its trade rules.

In 1997, for instance, civil society groups challenged and temporarily halted the pro-posed Multilateral Agreement on Investment. This was a draft agreement among members of the Organisation for Economic Co-operation and Development that would give corporations precedence over elected govern-ments on issues that threatened their private investments. Opponents argued that the agreement would make it difficult for na-tional governments to regulate to protect the public interest. Maude Barlow and the Council of Canadians played a pivotal role in the campaign, using the Internet to mo-bilize people to pressure trade negotiators and governments. In response to the cam-paign, France announced in 1998 that it would not support the agreement. The cam-paign was the first successful example of use of the Internet to mobilize people to mass activism on a global scale.

In 1999, forty thousand activists, including Canadians, participated in the Battle of Seattle to protest the World Trade Organization

Conference of that year. The protesters argued that the organization was contributing to the widening gap between the rich and the poor. The protest "demonstrated the power of a convergence of class, environmental and other new social movement politics," including fair trade, an organized movement and market philosophy that seeks to help producers in developing countries by achieving higher prices for their goods and better, more sustainable environmental practices (Harter 2004, 83).

Limited Victories and New Strategies

Canadian environmentalists won limited victories but created a lasting movement. They educated the public about environmental protection, and the pressure they placed on governments resulted in environmental legislation and innovations such as the publication of air pollution indices after 1970. Their campaigns saved Lake Erie and led to more rigorous monitoring of the Great Lakes' water quality (see Chapter 8). Canadians eventually switched to unleaded gas, and in 1991 Canada and the United States agreed to monitor and reduce acid rain emissions (see Chapter 8). Canadian environmental law developed alongside the environmental movement, and its existence means there is "the potential ... for systematic preventive action" rather than ad hoc remedial initiatives (Benidickson 2002, 328): Liability can now be extended to institutions that ignore environmental standards, and the groundwork has been laid for expanding public participation in environmental decision making.

Armed with the goals of sustainability and biodiversity, some environmentalists in the 1990s experimented with new approaches. Realizing that solutions to environmental problems are unlikely unless corporate leaders come on board, they spoke of developing partnerships with business leaders, whom they referred to as stakeholders. On occasion, advisory committees representing diverse

ENVIRONMENTAL LAW

Law cases mounted by groups such as the Sierra Legal Defence Fund were only part of a larger web of interlocking treaties, conventions, legislation, regulations, and case law that forms the basis of environmental law. In the early 1970s, law schools in Canada began to offer environmental law courses, and the Canadian Environmental Law Association was founded to ensure that existing laws were being used to protect the environment. *Canadian Environmental Law News* began to report cases in 1972 and was followed by countless books and articles.

Environmental law encompasses different decision-making models, including administrative law, class action cases, and environmental assessment hearings. A traditional individual course of legal action involves the common law in trespass, negligence, and nuisance cases. In nuisance actions, the British case *Rylands v Fletcher* (1868) established the principle that persons who introduce dangerous substances onto their land and let them escape are liable for damages. The common law permits individuals to bring pollution problems to the courts. To sue, however, the claimant has to identify the injuries and prove who caused them. The claimant can sue only for the actual economic injury suffered, a severe restriction given that the costs of a lawsuit are so high. Early cases heard by the courts demonstrated that the common law was insufficient to solve modern environmental problems. This, in the 1970s, governments began to address this situation by passing legislation that is interpreted by environmental lawyers.

interests have reached agreements on pressing environmental problems. In 1994, for instance, environmentalists initiated a campaign to gain a moratorium on logging and grizzly bear hunting in British Columbia's Great Bear Rainforest, the largest expanse of coastal rainforest in the world. They enlisted German publishers, Home Depot, Ikea, and other companies in their efforts. These organizations and groups, in turn, put pressure on logging corporations by threatening to withdraw contracts. In 2005, four environmental groups, eight coastal First Nations, six international logging and pulp companies, and the BC government signed the Great Bear Rainforest Agreement, which laid out a long-term plan to maintain the ecosystem through sustainable logging practices and by providing alternative employment for loggers. This model of accommodating different, sometimes incompatible groups and bringing together people with diverse outlooks, backgrounds, experiences, identities, and training has since been applied to other issues such as parks.

Environmentalists also adopted the view in the 1980s and 1990s that governments should not simply react to crises – for instance, oil spills or public health tragedies – but should rather use environmental legislation to prevent disasters. In other words, they should institute measures that would force polluters rather than the public to pay for the consequences. Placing the onus for disasters on the instigators, they argued, would limit government expenditures, a position that is compatible with neoconservative policies that favour limited government and fiscal responsibility. This strategy was based on the realization that although such

TABLE 10.2 Federal election results for the Green Party, 1984-2011				
Election	Candidates nominated	Seats won	Total votes	% of popular vote
1984	60	0	26,921	0.21
1988	68	0	47,228	0.36
1993	79	0	32,979	0.24
1997	79	0	55,583	0.43
2000	111	0	104,402	0.81
2004	308	0	582,247	4.32
2006	308	0	665,940	4.48
2008	303	0	941,097	6.80
2011	304	1	576,221	3.91

Source: "History of Federal Elections since 1867," Parliament of Canada, http://www.parl.gc.ca/.

governments did not want to intervene to protect the environment, they also did not want to pay the price of environmental disasters.

Some environmentalists, such as Elizabeth May, argued that direct participation was the answer. Influenced by E.F. Schumacher's *Small Is Beautiful,* May, an author and activist, launched the Small Party in 1980 to raise awareness about the environment and the use of nuclear energy. Three years later, the Green Party of Canada was founded. May, the party's leader since 2006, became its first elected member of Parliament in 2011 (see Table 10.2). Party members believe in the election of green parties and have been influenced by such parties in the European Union, which gained influence by making environmentalism part of the political agenda. Despite its move toward freer trade, the EU retained certain social and environmental standards, implemented long-term energy policies, and supported Kyoto Protocol targets to reduce its carbon emissions. In Canada, the Green Party seeks to focus politics more on the environment and the need to take a path toward sustainability.

Environmentalists no longer view sustainability as an aspiration – they see it as a necessity in an age of climate change and relentless consumerism. Balancing the needs of the planet and public health with economic growth and private initiative is *the* issue of the twenty-first century. Global climate change has invaded the public consciousness through numerous vehicles, including media reports, books, and documentaries such as Al Gore's Academy-award-winning film *An Inconvenient Truth* (2006). American architect Paolo Soleri has commented, "Materialism is, by definition, the antithesis of green. We have this unstoppable, energetic, self-righteous drive that's innate in us, but which has been reoriented by limitless consumption. Per se, it doesn't have anything evil about it. It's a hindrance. But multiply that hindrance by millions, and you've got catastrophe" (Rose 2008, 27). The "environmental way of thinking" is often ignored by business and government leaders because it implies policies of restraint and conflicts with the status quo. Environmentalists therefore continue to espouse alternative values and lifestyles and embody cultural ideas inclusive of the natural world.

In 1972, when the Club of Rome published *Limits to Growth,* Jay W. Forrester, a scientist at the Sloan School of Management at MIT, was not optimistic about gaining acceptance for an equilibrium model because, he argued, "the growth instinct was enshrined in all contemporary institutions and many attitudes" (Fleming 1972, 73). But he recognized the need for profound changes and envisaged a more eclectic postcapitalistic world. "New

human purposes must be defined to replace the quest for economic advancement; the goals of nations and societies must be reformulated to become compatible with the philosophy of equilibrium" (Fleming 1972, 73). Since 2008, the world has experienced a global economic recession, the collapse and corruption of many financial institutions and corporations, and unprecedented environmental crises related to climate change, a crowded planet, and a degraded environment. New ways of living are needed if we are to repair the damage and renew human relations with the natural world.

SINCE THE 1970S, the environmental movement and nongovernmental organizations have demonstrated that they can be effective in the struggle to put in place laws and infrastructure to protect the environment. Indeed, such policy making got off to a heady start in Canada in the 1970s, when federal and provincial governments, inspired by developments in the United States, established new departments to focus on environmental issues as well as legislation to control pollution and the activities of corporations. In the 1980s and 1990s, however, the implementation of these policies was undermined by rising support for neoconservative values that favoured unregulated economic growth and consumerism. Politicians became less responsive to warnings from environmentalists and scientists about the degradation of the planet. They instead focused on deficit reduction and unemployment and viewed implementation of environmental policies as being in conflict with the core values of North American society – namely, continuous economic growth and consumerism. Many governments in Europe, by contrast, continued to advance environmental policies and took the lead on climate change initiatives, a strategy that reduced their nations' carbon levels and increased "green jobs" in new industries such as alternative energies. It remains to be seen if neglect of the environment in North America can continue. Fossil fuel resources, the predominant energy regime underpinning capitalism, will not last forever and produce too much carbon. The current global economy – based on a model of continuous economic growth, exploitation of resources, and a widening gap between rich and poor people and countries because of a shift in wealth since the 1980s – is not sustainable.

Works Cited

Benidickson, Jamie. 2002. *Essentials of Canadian Law: Environmental Law.* Toronto: Irwin Law.

Brundtland Commission. 1987. *Report of the World Commission on Environment and Development: Our Common Future.* Oxford: World Commission on Environment and Development.

Carson, Rachel. 1962. *Silent Spring.* New York: Crest Books.

Chant, Donald A., ed. 1970. *Pollution Probe.* Toronto: New Press.

Cooper, Marc. 1999. "Street Fight in Seattle." *The Nation,* 20 December, 1-2.

Cronon, William, in conversation with Richard White. 1986. "Indians in the Land." *American Heritage* 37 (August-September): 25.

Dempsey, Dave. 2004. *On the Brink: The Great Lakes in the 21st Century.* East Lansing: Michigan State University Press.

Fleming, Donald. 1972. "Roots of the New Conservation Movement." *Perspectives in American History* 6: 7-91.

Gunton, Thomas, and K.S. Calbick. 2010. *The Maple Leaf in the OECD: Canada's Environmental Performance* (Vancouver: David Suzuki Foundation).

Harter, John-Henry. 2004. "Environmental Justice for Whom? Class, New Social Movements, and the Environment: A Case Study of Greenpeace Canada, 1971-2000." *Labour/Le Travail* 54 (Fall): 83-119.

Hunter, Robert. 2004. *The Greenpeace to Amchitka: An Environmental Odyssey.* Vancouver: Arsenal Pulp Press.

Lear, Linda. 1997. *Rachel Carson: Witness for Nature.* New York: Henry Holt.

Macdonald, Doug. 1991. *The Politics of Pollution: Why Canadians Are Failing Their Environment.* Toronto: McClelland and Stewart.

Pitelis, Christos, and Roger Sugden. 2000. *The Nature of the Transnational Firm.* London: Routledge.

Rose, Steve. 2008. "This Is the Way We Should Live Now." *Guardian Weekly,* 12 September.

Smith, Michael B. 2001. "'Silence, Miss Carson!' Silence, Gender, and the Reception of *Silent Spring.*" *Feminist Studies* 27, 3: 733-52.

For Further Reading

Bateman, Robert. 2000. *Thinking Like a Mountain.* Toronto: Penguin Books.

Hays, Samuel P. 1987. *Beauty, Health and Permanence: Environmental Politics in the United States, 1955-1985.* Cambridge: Cambridge University Press.

Owram, Doug. 1996. *Born at the Right Time: A History of the Baby Boom Generation.* Toronto: University of Toronto Press.

Rome, Adam. 2003. "'Give Earth a Chance': The Environmental Movement and the Sixties." *Journal of American History* 90, 2: 525-54.

Solnit, David, Rebecca Solnit, and Anuradha Mittal. 2009. *The Story of the Battle of Seattle.* Oakland, CA: AK Press.

The New Environmentalism

Dempsey, Dave. 2004. *On the Brink: The Great Lakes in the 21st Century.* East Lansing: Michigan State University Press.

Fleming, Donald. 1972. "Roots of the New Conservation Movement." *Perspectives in American History* 6: 7-91.

Kirk, Andrew. 2002. "'Machines of Loving Grace:' Alternative Technology, Environment and Counter-Culture." In *Imagine Nation: The American Counterculture of the 1960s and '70s,* edited by Peter Braunstein and Michael William Doyle, 353-78. New York: Routledge.

Lear, Linda. 1997. *Rachel Carson: Witness for Nature.* New York: Henry Holt.

Macdonald, Doug. 1991. *The Politics of Pollution: Why Canadians Are Failing Their Environment.* Toronto: McClelland and Stewart.

Payne, Daniel. 1996. "The New Environmentalism and Rachel Carson's *Silent Spring.*" In *Voices in the Wilderness,* edited by Daniel Payne, 136-51. Lebanon, NH: University Press of New England.

Smith, Michael B. 2001. "'Silence, Miss Carson!' Silence, Gender, and the Reception of *Silent Spring.*" *Feminist Studies* 27, 3: 733-52.

Environmental Issues Defined

Boyle, Robert H., and R. Alexander Boyle. 1983. *Acid Rain.* New York: Nick Lyon Books.

Careless, Ric. 1997. *To Save the Wild Earth: Field Notes from the Environmental Frontline.* Vancouver: Raincoast Books.

MacIsaac, Ron, and Anne Champagne. 1994. *Clayoquot Mass Trials: Defending the Rainforest.* Gabriola Island: New Society Publishers.

Read, Jennifer. 1997. "'Let Us Heed the Voice of Youth': Laundry Detergents, Phosphates and the Emergence of the Environmental Movement in Ontario." *Journal of the Canadian Historical Association* 7: 131-49.

Warne, Kenneth. 2004. "Harp Seals: The Hunt for Balance." *National Geographic,* March, 50-67.

Canadian Environmentalism

Chant, Donald A., ed. 1970. *Pollution Probe.* Toronto: New Press.

Dale, Stephen. 1996. *McLuhan's Children: The Greenpeace Message and the Media.* Toronto: Between the Lines.

Hunter, Robert. 2004. *The Greenpeace to Amchitka: An Environmental Odyssey.* Vancouver: Arsenal Pulp Press.

Sunday Times Insight Team. 1986. *Rainbow Warrior: The French Attempt to Sink Greenpeace.* Toronto: Key Porter Books.

Weyler, Rex. 2004. *Greenpeace: How a Group of Ecologists, Journalists and Visionaries Changed the World.* Vancouver: Raincoast Books.

Environmental Infrastructure and Inaction

Boyd, David R. 2003. *Unnatural Law: Rethinking Canadian Environmental Law and Policy.* Vancouver: UBC Press.

David Suzuki Foundation. 2010. *The Maple Leaf in the OECD: Canada's Environmental Performance.* Vancouver: David Suzuki Foundation.

Doern, G. Bruce, and Thomas Conway. 1994. *The Greening of Canada: Federal Institutions and Decisions.* Toronto: University of Toronto Press.

Emond, D. Paul. 2008. "'Are We There Yet?' Reflections on the Success of the Environmental Law Movement in Ontario." *Osgoode Hall Law Journal* 46: 219-42.

Gale, Robert J.P. 1997. "Canada's Green Plan." In *Nationale Umweltpläne in ausgewählten Industrieländern* [National environmental plans of selected industrial countries], Submissions to the Enquete Commission "Protection of People and the Environment" for the Bundestag, 97-120. Berlin: Springer-Verlag.

MacQueen, Ken. 2005. "From Sea to Stinking Sea." *Maclean's,* 17 October, 21-26.

Pralle, Sarah. 2006. "'The Mouse That Roared': Agenda Setting in Canadian Pesticides Politics." *Policy Studies Journal* 34, 2: 171-94.

Sierra Legal Defence Fund Newsletter. 1995-97.

Valiante, Marcia. 2002. "Turf War: Municipal Powers, the Regulation of Pesticides and the Hudson Decision." *Journal of Environmental Law and Practice* 11: 327-58.

Winfield, Mark. 1994. "The Ultimate Horizontal Issue: The Environmental Policy Experiences of Alberta and Ontario, 1971-1993." *Canadian Journal of Political Science* 27, 1: 129-52.

Divisions in the Ranks and a New Global Outlook

Bronfenbrenner, Kate, and Tom Juravich. 1999. *Ravenswood: The Steelworkers' Victory and the Revival of American Labor.* Ithaca, NY: Cornell University Press/ILR Press.

Cooper, Marc. 1999. "Street Fight in Seattle." *The Nation,* 20 December, 1-2.

Council of Canadians. *Canadian Perspectives* (various issues).

Fraser Institute. 1993. *The NAFTA Network.* Bulletin, edited by John S.P. Robson.

Harter, John-Henry. 2004. "Environmental Justice for Whom? Class, New Social Movements, and the Environment: A Case Study of Greenpeace Canada, 1971-2000." *Labour/ Le Travail* 54 (Fall): 83-119.

Helvarg, David. 1994. *The War against the Greens.* San Francisco: Sierra Club.

Kazis, Richard, and Richard Crossman. 1982. *Fear at Work: Job Blackmail, Labor and the Environment.* New York: Pilgrim Press.

Manes, Christopher. 1990. *Green Rage: Radical Environmentalism and the Unmaking of Civilization.* New York: Little Brown.

Oreskes, Naomi, and Erik Conway. 2010. *Merchants of Doubt.* New York: Bloomsbury Press.

Pitelis, Christos, and Roger Sugden. 2000. *The Nature of the Transnational Firm.* London: Routledge.

Tollefson, Chris. 1994. "Strategic Lawsuits against Public Participation: Developing a Canadian Response." *Canadian Bar Review* 73, 2: 200-31.

Limited Victories and New Strategies

Homer-Dixon, Thomas. 2006. *The Upside of Down: Catastrophe, Creativity and the Renewal of Civilization.* Toronto: Knopf.

Rose, Steve. 2008. "This Is the Way We Should Live Now." *Guardian Weekly,* 12 September.

Sandberg, L. Anders, and Sverker Sorlin. 1998. *Sustainability: The Challenge – People, Power and the Environment.* Montreal: Black Rose Books.

11
Parks and Wildlife

National Parks are maintained for all the people – for the ill that they may be restored; for the well that they may be fortified and inspired by the sunshine, the fresh air, the beauty, and all the other healing, ennobling agencies of Nature. They exist in order that every citizen of Canada may satisfy his craving for Nature and Nature's Beauty; that he may absorb the poise and restfulness of the forests; that he may fill his soul with the brilliance of the wild flowers and the sublimity of the mountain peaks; that he may develop the buoyancy, the joy, and the activity that he sees in the wild animals; that he may stock his brain and mind with great thoughts, noble ideals; that he be made better, be healthier, and happier.

— JAMES HARKIN, COMMISSIONER OF NATIONAL PARKS, 1911-36, CITED BY BANFF-BOW VALLEY TASK FORCE

SINCE THEIR INCEPTION in the late nineteenth century, parks and wildlife preserves have taken on shifting meanings and have been manipulated to serve multiple purposes, whether it be resource development, public works projects, tourism and recreation, or fostering an aesthetic appreciation for nature among citizens. From the beginning, park administrators had diverse ideas about parks and had to contend with diverging expectations from politicians and the public about what a park should be. In Canada, the views of utilitarian conservationists held sway in parks and wildlife management. But in the 1960s, when public use and the number of parks expanded, scientific researchers, environmentalists, and animal-rights activists sparked action on Canadian parks by demanding a re-examination of parks policies and management and a role for the public in decision making. They also believed that parks should be a central component of policies to protect endangered species and ecosystems. Governments passed new parks policies, and parks officials met tourists' expectations with diverse recreational facilities and, occasionally, commercial concessions. But some park advocates came to see mass tourism as problematic for the natural environment and for wildlife within parks, particularly when tourists merely sought entertainment and treated the natural landscape as spectacle.

In the United States, environmentalists promoted the ideal of natural ecosystem management in parks and refuges. They directed managers to preserve all species and cease manipulating animal and plant life for special interest groups. In 1973, the US government passed the Endangered Species Act and funded preservation programs. That same year, Canada passed its Canada Wildlife Act. Six years later, it identified ecological integrity as a formal policy objective and embedded it fully into the amended National Parks Act (1988). Parks, however, continue to be not only places of complex, changing land-use policies and administrative practices but also places of shifting nature/culture relationships as citizens continue to project their varied hopes and dreams for Canada and its environment onto park landscapes.

Scientific Research and Evolving Attitudes toward Wildlife

Scientific research today plays an important role in the protection of wildlife. Attitudes toward research began to shift in the 1930s and 1940s as naturalists, park managers, and public servants alike acquired more scientific knowledge about animals. The federal government, for instance, held regular federal-provincial wildlife conferences and established the Canadian Wildlife Service in 1947 to initiate scientific research on certain species, implement existing federal legislation, work with parks to manage wildlife, and educate the public about wildlife conservation.

In the 1930s, the superintendent of Algonquin Provincial Park in Ontario, Frank MacDougall (1931-41), put wildlife management on a more scientific basis by initiating the first game surveys. Although he maintained a wolf extermination policy, he clamped down on poachers by using aircraft to survey the park. He also made fish management a priority. Research resulted in a ban on winter fishing as a conservation measure and a program to restock lakes. MacDougall worked with J.R. Dymond, a zoologist at the University of Toronto. Dymond's scientific research and ideas about ecology and preservation influenced the park's wildlife management policies and programs, which in 1934 grew to include a nature reserve or sanctuary. Over the next few decades, the park founded three of the earliest scientific facilities: the Harkness Lab of Fisheries Research (1936), the Wildlife Research Station (1938-39), and the Swan Lake Forest Research Station (1950).

The idea that humans should manipulate animals to meet their needs underpinned early wildlife management practices. With loss of habitat and decreasing species, however, game management began to change. As personnel at the Canadian Wildlife Service accumulated scientific information, completed animal surveys and reports, and studied protected species, they gradually developed less interventionist wildlife management plans informed by ecology. Like parks staff, they came to realize that predators such as coyotes and wolves were essential links in ecosystems. They noticed, for example, that when coyotes were destroyed on the Prairies, rabbits and gophers soon overpopulated the area. The Parks Branch began to use the language of animal ecology in the 1940s. It evaluated its predator policy in terms of population cycles, the balance of nature, and evidence of harm done. Park officials began

BISON RECOVERY IN CANADIAN PARKS

Canada's parks system played a crucial but complicated role in bison recovery. In Alberta, the provincial government established Wood Buffalo National Park in 1922 to protect wood bison (a darker, larger, northern subspecies of the North American buffalo), muskox, and caribou. Between 1924 and 1927, the government also devised a program to rehabilitate plains bison that involved shipping over six thousand from Buffalo Park in Wainwright, Alberta, to Wood Buffalo, where they interbred with wood bison. Historians Alexander Burnett and Tina Loo argue that this plan was a mistake because, by 1940, the "pure" wood bison genetic strain had almost disappeared. In addition, the Wainwright herd spread tuberculosis to the previously uninfected wood bison. The hybrid herd had to be culled, and the government eventually closed the park.

When a separate herd of pure wood bison was discovered in the 1960s, park managers worked to increase their numbers. They moved the herd to the isolated Mackenzie Bison Sanctuary, northwest of the Mackenzie River, and settled several other small herds of wood bison on sites in the Northwest. In 1987, the wood bison's status was downgraded from endangered to threatened, and the herds continue to reside in parks, conservation areas, and sanctuaries and zoos. The plains bison also remain threatened and are managed in several national parks, including Riding Mountain in Prince Albert, Grasslands in Saskatchewan, and Elk Island in Alberta. The bison live in wild (free range), semi-wild (fenced and managed but with relatively free movement), and captive (fenced in a small area) states. In 2003, the Nature Conservancy of Canada introduced fifty plains bison yearlings from Elk Island into a 13,000-acre (5,261 hectare) mixed-grass prairie preserve in Saskatchewan. It hoped to restore the ecological integrity of the ecosystem. This marked the first time plains bison had grazed on Canada's shortgrass

---

to hunt fewer animals, but in the 1950s, still influenced by livestock owners and hunting groups, they continued to eliminate bears and mountain lions, sometimes by poisoning them, and they nearly exterminated the wolf in parts of the country (see Figure 11.1). Their actions reflected the contradictory nature of wildlife management before the 1960s, a system in which certain animals were killed to protect others. When public attitudes changed, policy makers slowly implemented a new approach. Over time, some developed a more holistic view of the environment. They recognized that all species had value in ecosystems and that the protection of all wildlife was beneficial. This new approach was eventually incorporated into the Canada Wildlife Act of 1973.

Greater scientific knowledge about animal intelligence and behaviour changed the way people viewed animals. In the nineteenth century, most Canadians viewed wildlife either as food or as a source of recreation when it was hunted. Wildlife in national and provincial parks later became a tourist attraction. Early animal-rights activists such as Ernest Thompson Seton, an award-winning Canadian wildlife illustrator and naturalist,

FIGURE 11.1 Hunters posing with a wolf carcass in Algonquin Provincial Park, ca. 1940s. The first wolf bounty came into effect in Upper Canada in 1793, and Ontario did not end the bounty until 1972, by which time the wolf population had declined drastically. Eradication programs across Canada peaked in the 1950s and then eased as Canadians came to understand the importance of predators to ecosystems.
Archives of Ontario, 10011416

prairie since their near extinction. Commercial farms also began raising bison for their meat, which restaurants offered to customers with exotic tastes. Of the 230,000 bison in existence in Canada today, only about 1,000 are pure descendants of the original wild buffalo. The remainder contain some cattle DNA.

FIGURE 11.2 Buffalo in Wainwright National Park, Alberta, ca. 1909-14.
Glenbow Archives, NC-37-78

had attributed thought processes, emotions, and feelings to animals. Scientists, however, criticized his work as being anthropomorphic and sentimental. Attitudes changed in the 1970s with the emergence of both the environmental movement and the modern animal-rights movement. The public then started to perceive the increase in endangered or lost species as an environmental problem. Like activists in the nineteenth century, who founded humane societies for the protection of domestic and farm animals, animal-rights activists in the twentieth century struggled to change public opinion and were particularly critical of the inhumane use of animals in scientific research. Underlying their concern was the idea that although animals differed from human beings, they still had feelings, intelligence, and rights. The development of the science of animal welfare altered moral positions "by demonstrating the complexity and sophistication of animal behaviour and the capacity to suffer, which can go beyond merely experiencing pain" (Garner 2004, 5).

Animal-rights activists demanded change so animals could coexist with humans without being exploited by them. Although many scientists ridiculed such ideas, they gained traction, particularly among environmental-ists, who deplored the inhumane treatment of animals and the rapid loss of species. Some environmentalists supported vegetarianism, and all opposed the poor treatment of animals due to hunting.

PREDATORS IN LITERATURE, ART, AND FILM

Aldo Leopold, a prominent American wildlife manager, helped to change the way Americans and Canadians thought about predators and wildlife management. In 1933, his book *Game Management* presented the argument that animal populations should be manipulated and controlled to increase their numbers for sportsmen. Later, however, Leopold was influenced profoundly by ecology. In *A Sand County Almanac,* published in 1966, he wrote, "You cannot love game and hate predators," for "while a buck pulled down by wolves can be replaced in two or three years, a range pulled down by too many deer may fail of replacement in as many decades" (Leopold 1966, 132). The cowman who kills all the wolves, he argued, "is taking over the wolf's job of trimming the herd to fit the range." He concluded that such a cowman had "not learned to think like a mountain" or understand the web of life (Leopold 1966, 176).

In Canada, Farley Mowat published *Never Cry Wolf* to great acclaim in 1963, and the book was made into a film in 1983. Mowat, who had been hired in the late 1940s by the Canadian Wildlife Service to investigate the cause of declining caribou populations in the North, decried people's misunderstanding of the wolf and feared that wolfers and bounty hunters would destroy the entire Arctic wolf population. He is credited with transforming the public image of the wolf into a more positive one, a process that continued with films produced by Bill Mason for the National Film Board and by Robert Bateman's paintings and writing.

A National Wildlife Policy

Growing awareness of the depletion of wild-life species led to greater public support for wildlife protection. The modern environmental movement in the 1970s coincided with greater scientific knowledge about wildlife and more interest in ecology. Environmentalism (see Chapter 10) led to less hunting and angling by tourists and to the modern tourist industry's focus on ecotourism. In response to the environmental movement, first the United States and then Canada promoted an ecological approach to wildlife management in their parks and refuges, which involved recognizing the coexistence and interconnections among wildlife, humans, and nature. Armed with new scientific knowledge and new attitudes, parks administrators and the Wildlife Service developed policies to protect predators and paid closer attention to habitat programs. Although their approach became less interventionist, some micromanagement persisted well into the twentieth century. National parks, for example, donated wildlife species to organizations on request and received payment for their contributions. Park managers rationalized the policy on the grounds that they "knew how many of each animal population should be in each park, and therefore what numbers were 'surplus'" (MacEchern 2009, 206). In other words, they were not protecting wildlife, a part of their mandate, but continuing to use it as a commodity.

A more systematic approach to wildlife management took shape in the late 1960s and 1970s. David Munro, director of the Canadian Wildlife Service, was instrumental in synthesizing wildlife concerns and developing the National Wildlife Policy and Program. The policy included a variety of measures to manage wildlife, including more research, a habitat protection plan, the introduction of a game-bird hunting permit, and the Canadian Wildlife Act (1973). The goal of the legislation was to provoke concern for wildlife throughout the nation and within the provinces, which shared responsibility, and it set out a proactive role for the federal government. Canada signed the Convention on International Trade in Endangered Species of Wild Fauna and Flora (CITES) in 1975 and international agreements to protect polar bears in 1976.

In the early 1980s, the Canadian Wildlife Service developed successful recovery plans for the whooping crane and peregrine falcon. Under the North American Waterfowl Management Plan of 1986, it also worked to protect wetlands. Budget cuts, however, forced the agency to enter into partnerships with nongovernmental organizations such as the World Wildlife Fund to maintain programs. In the 1990s, animals were protected in an expanding array of wildlife areas, sanctuaries, and zoos, which had breeding programs for endangered species. When the federal government amended the Canadian Wildlife Act to include all plants and animals under the term *wildlife,* it openly recognized the importance of maintaining biodiversity and preserving ecosystems. The Canadian public, however, was often ahead of policy makers. Canadians, for instance, supported early initiatives to pass an Endangered Species Act, a movement that gained momentum in 1993, despite extensive government budget cutbacks. The first comprehensive endangered species bill was introduced in 1996, but it died on the order paper in 1997, when an election was called. The pattern was repeated in 2000 and 2001. The government tabled a revised Species at Risk bill in December 2001, and it passed the House of Commons on 11 June 2002.

Parks in the Age of Tourism and Conservation

Canada's wildlife policy reflected and evolved alongside parks policy. Since the 1930s, when Grey Owl drew national and international attention to Canada's parks, the focus has gradually shifted from utilitarian conservation to ecological preservation. This evolution was nowhere more apparent than in the 1930s at Algonquin Provincial Park under the administration of Frank MacDougall (see Figure 11.3), who later became the deputy minister of the Department of Lands and Forests. Before MacDougall's administration, park managers, influenced by the ideals of utilitarian conservation, viewed the park's abundant timber, wildlife, and fish as the basis for recreational activities and as revenue-producing assets. Without the benefit of research, their management led to overfishing, poaching, the extermination of predators, and a devastated landscape. The Gilmour Lumber Company, for instance, built a dam at the end of Tea Lake to raise the water level, and other companies built dams on park lakes for their spring log drives. The damage from floods and soil erosion was so extensive along shorelines that successive park superintendents complained. The

FIGURE 11.3 Frank MacDougall with his Beaver aircraft at Smoke Lake, 1950. Known as the "flying superintendent" of Algonquin Park, MacDougall was an important figure in the development of Ontario's park system and in the use of airplanes by the Department of Lands and Forests.

Courtesy Inna MacDougall

Provincial Parks Act of 1927 enforced logging bans on shorelines to protect watersheds, for park beautification, and to assist fire prevention. In 1929, cottagers on leased properties, which were later phased out, convinced the provincial government to create a shoreline timber reserve around Cache Lake to keep loggers at bay.

MacDougall imagined the park as a vast multiuser space, a place for resource exploitation, recreation, and most important, tourism. But he and his staff also believed in the benefits of scientific knowledge, experimented with new approaches to park management, and embraced early interpretive educational programs. In addition to launching initiatives in the field of wildlife preservation, MacDougall protected reserves of old-growth pine from loggers and established a wilderness area in

FIGURE 11.4 As the number of parks visitors increased, their food and garbage attracted wildlife, such as bears, which enthralled tourists but caused headaches for park administrators.

Glenbow Archives, Na-5611-81

1944 for silviculture research. To decrease potential conflicts between lumber interests and recreational users, he established forest reserves along canoe routes. The trees not only shaded the water and protected trout but also preserved the park's beauty. Mac-Dougall also expanded the park's programs for children in the 1930s and 1940s to include a naturalist program, special events, and publications about canoe routes, hiking trails, birds, and the park's history. MacDougall's work in the park reflected a growing concern with conservation and preservation.

Parks policy in the postwar period also reflected partisan politics, political infighting, and a desire to exploit the tourism side of parks to maximum effect. Fuelled by the postwar baby boom and car culture, the number of park users rose dramatically between 1940 and 1960, from 500,000 to 5.5 million (see Figure 11.4). This expansion was facilitated, in turn, by road building (inside and outside of parks) and regional development programs, particularly in Prince Edward Island and Newfoundland. At Jasper National Park and others, officials planned roads to highlight scenic views that would appeal to motoring tourists. In Ontario alone, the number of parks increased from 9 in 1954 to 261 in 1989. While public demand for more national and provincial parks increased, governments faced growing fiscal restraints, which caused them to lower operating budgets and increase user fees. In the 1960s, some parks began to phase out all or most resources exploitation and to expand tourism. At Algonquin Park, for instance, when resource extraction caused its wildlife protection programs to deteriorate, administrators stopped renewing leases for private or commercial purposes.

Population growth, urbanization, and automobiles not only fuelled tourism and the use of parks for recreational purposes, they also strengthened the preservationist ideal of wilderness protection. As policy makers and park administrators responded to competing pressures for more parks, more recreational facilities, and more wilderness conservation, parks policy and park landscapes entered an era of constant change. The United States led the way, initiating studies on different recreational models, all of which had complicated management plans. As the parks system expanded, the government implemented a zoning system to allocate parkland for different uses, depending on the kind and intensity of activity and the type of ecosystem. The government promoted more scientific research in parks and encouraged more coordination between national and state policy makers. The Wilderness Act (1964) enabled public land agencies to designate certain areas as wilderness or "landscape without roads" to satisfy the demands of backpackers, naturalists, and organizations such as the Sierra Club that supported the idea of wilderness protection. The wilderness parks made preservationists happy and were inexpensive to run in an era of budget cuts, but most people had no access to them.

The new approach to parks in the United States spread to Canada, but the Canadian approach was less proactive and more utilitarian, perhaps because citizens did not have a strong voice in policy making until the late 1960s. In addition, pro-development sentiments in Canada remained strong, as did the myth that Canada had unlimited wilderness. Park services grew in these decades to include campgrounds with water supply facilities, garbage disposal facilities, and greater police security. New service centres and winter programs also made the parks accessible on a year-round basis. In the West, concessionaires and snowplowing operators pressured for year-round recreation at Manning, Banff, and Jasper.

Recreational businesses – including campsites, trailer parks, and motels – in or near the parks mushroomed. These expanded services sometimes overwhelmed the parks' tourism services and destroyed the environment, particularly when careless visitors and resources workers littered and started fires that damaged trees and wildlife. The presence of more and more visitors complicated parks administration and increased conflicts among users, between parks officials and users, and between park administrators and their employees, who wanted better facilities and working conditions. One park superintendent at Jasper National Park warned that the park's existing operation status would not be able to meet the continued increase of tourists and their demands.

Throughout these decades, decision makers continued to reach arbitrary decisions about

DINOSAUR PROVINCIAL PARK

The expansion of parks and their different uses in the 1950s was reflected in the creation of Alberta's Steveville Provincial Park in 1959, renamed Dinosaur Provincial Park three years later. The park had a mandate to protect fossils and support scientific research in the province's badlands. The area had been of interest to scientists ever since Joseph B. Tyrrell, a geologist with the Geological Survey of Canada, explored the Red Deer River Valley in 1884 and discovered the fossilized remains of Albertosaurus, a distant cousin of Tyrannosaurus Rex. In 1916, Charles H. Sternberg excavated and shipped sixteen dinosaur skeletons to Ottawa. He then worked with the British Museum and collaborated with a Geological Survey of Canada topographer to map Steveville and the Deadlodge Canyon badlands.

Local people favoured the creation of a park because they wanted to protect the area's natural wonders, keep them in Alberta, and attract tourists. The park's first warden, Roy Fowler, an amateur fossil hunter since the 1920s, continued to collect specimens. In 1980, Dinosaur Provincial Park became the first site in Canada under provincial jurisdiction to be placed on UNESCO's World Heritage list.

the placement, purpose, and boundaries of parks. In the 1950s, for instance, the Parks Branch decided that Banff National Park should not expand spatially with urban sprawl; however, it planned for increased urban density to accommodate more tourists. In 1956, Cape Breton Highlands National Park lost a parcel of land to mining interests, and Fundy National Park had to give up land in 1958 for a hydro project. The project devastated the Chéticamp River in the 1970s. Provinces sometimes blocked the establishment of parks, excluded timber and mining lands, or placed parks in inappropriate areas. In the 1950s, for example, the Province of Ontario decided to create Inverhuron Provincial Park on Lake Huron as a recreational area for families in southwestern Ontario. It located the park, however, beside a federal-run experimental nuclear-generating station, Bruce Nuclear Power Development at Douglas Point. After years of gas releases from the nuclear complex, political prevarication, and a shroud of secrecy, the government transferred responsibility for the park in 1973 to Ontario Hydro "to comply with safety regulations imposed by the AECB (Atomic Energy Control Board)" (Parr 2006, 282). The decision was made in secret, and the energy utility subsequently closed the park to family camping, presumably because recreation and the generation of nuclear power could not coexist safely. Nuclear power took precedence over recreation. When park users protested, the government ignored their concerns. In the 1980s, the government of British Columbia actually developed a "park-in-waiting" policy that allowed natural resource companies to explore areas before they could be protected.

Preserving the Wilderness in Ontario

From the 1940s to the 1970s, Canadians claimed parks as their own – as an integral aspect of their natural identity – but they were deluded in their belief that Canadian parks were truly wild. The issue of wilderness parks and the creation of zones designated as "wilderness" in parks brought out conflicting and evolving ideas about nature. In 1931, the Federation of Ontario Naturalists, whose members viewed nature from an ecological perspective and had a preservationist outlook, lobbied the government to include wilderness areas, or nature reserves, in large parks such as Quetico Provincial Park and to protect park landscapes from businesses, tourists, and sportsmen. The federation opposed hunting and commercial activities within parks and sought nature reserves to protect wildlife. It also led the call for park zoning. In response to its campaigns, the provincial government passed the Wilderness Areas Act (1959), which employed the concept of sanctuary to preserve areas of natural or historical significance. Over the next three years, the provincial government established thirty-five wilderness areas. Forestry and mining interests within the Department of Lands and Forests, however, ensured that natural resources development would continue in wilderness areas larger than 259 hectares.

Calls for the protection and preservation of nature increased as the environmental movement's popular base expanded. The Federation of Ontario Naturalists in fact anticipated many of the ideas of modern environmentalists and, in 1963, founded the Nature Conservancy of Canada, a nonprofit organization with a mandate to protect "Canada's biodiversity through the purchase, donation, or placing of conservation easements on ecologically significant lands." The organization foreshadowed the work of the Algonquin Wildlands League, which became involved in tense standoffs with the government in the 1970s.

Organizations such as the Federation of Ontario Naturalists gained adherents as canoeists on holiday in the parks – under the impression that they were engaged in a rugged wilderness adventure – encountered loggers. These largely well-educated, middle-class, and influential urban men were outraged not only because the situation robbed them of their delusions but also because they believed the parks belonged to citizens, not resource companies. Support for wilderness parks came from urban elites who wanted to preserve a serene, rustic, contemplative environment for their fairly exclusive recreational activities. At the same time, pressure started to come from scientists and environmentalists who used the language of ecology to stress the importance of protecting nature, including wildlife habitats under stress.

Confrontations between wilderness preservationists and loggers in Algonquin, Quetico, Killarney, and Lake Superior Parks became heated in the late 1960s. Public pressure groups, such as the National and Provincial Parks Association of Canada and the Algonquin Wildlands League, aroused public support to protect parks from commercial interests and to include areas of protected wilderness. Between 1968 and 1974, this crusade to protect Ontario's wilderness, led by urbanites, stopped commercial logging in all provincial parks except Algonquin and

Lake Superior. The government also agreed to classify Quetico and Killarney as wilderness areas. In Algonquin Park, it preserved some wilderness in the interior, but tourism in the park expanded along Highway 60.

The struggle in Ontario inspired the Province of Alberta to pass the Wilderness Areas Act in 1971, which designated wilderness areas in provincial parks. British Columbia's first NDP government, elected in 1972, likewise responded to calls for new parks and conservation areas, a process that involved planning and zoning. The declared goal was environmental protection, but the government also hoped to divert attention away from the environmental damage associated with resource extraction and the lumber industry.

Finding a Balance

Preservationist views became more prominent and began to outweigh utilitarian conservation in the 1970s as Canadians visited national and provincial parks in ever-greater numbers, claimed the wilderness as their own, and learned about ecology and the importance of biodiversity. Federal and provincial policy makers found it easier to listen to and respond to public concerns about parks than other issues, such as resource development or climate change, because parks policy had fewer economic implications. The federal government established several large wilderness parks in the North, including Pukaswa (1978) in northern Ontario and Auyuittuq (1976) on Baffin Island (see Figure 11.5). Unlike more traditional national parks, these parks are fairly inaccessible and are visited only by a few people who want a true wilderness experience.

FIGURE 11.5 Named after an Inuktitut word meaning "land that never melts," Auyuittuq National Park is home to glaciers, the highest peaks in the Canadian Shield, marine shorelines along fiords, and Akshayuk Pass, a corridor used for travel by the Inuit for thousands of years. The park showcases the unique beauty and majesty of the Arctic.
Photograph by Ansgar Walk

Park officials, likewise influenced by the environmental movement, became strong advocates of wildlife and habitat protection, but they recognized that this goal was increasingly difficult as parks became more popular and as urban sprawl brought more people closer to designated areas. Policy makers and parks administrators responded to criticism by introducing public hearings and proposed plans. In 1967, in Ontario, for instance, the Parks Division developed a new policy framework to sort out confusion and conflicts in the province's parks. Its zoning system classified all parks and areas in each park as wilderness area, nature reserve, or waterway. It experienced difficulty implementing the plan, however, because northern resource industries opposed limitations on their activities. In 1978, the government produced two landmark documents, *Ontario Provincial Parks Policy* and *Ontario Provincial Parks Planning and Management Policies,* that provided a blueprint to administer land-use and parks policies. It implemented the plan in the 1980s with the designation of 6 wilderness and 3 historical parks, the creation of 155 parks for recreational purposes, and

the establishment of 74 nature reserves, which were open to "nonconforming" uses. Policy makers specified the purpose, goals, and objectives of parks for the first time: environmental protection, education, year-round tourism and recreation, and the preservation of heritage through the creation of "living museums." These goals reflected the ascendance of biology and ecology in parks policy. Zoning became a strategic parks management tool and a way of protecting green spaces.

Public pressure led governments at both the federal and provincial levels to phase out extractive industries such as lumbering and mining in most parks, although some commercial leases and freehold lands remained. Governments also continued to struggle to balance maintaining ecological integrity with recreational activities, but facilities continued to expand in the 1980s to accommodate rising numbers of visitors and automobile traffic. Encounters between tourists and wildlife in the parks became more common and made it more difficult to protect animals. At Banff, for example, grizzly bears started to change their behaviour as they fed on garbage and disrupted campsites. Park wardens were forced to remove animals from highly populated areas, and staff classified park space for different uses to avoid incompatible activities such as hiking and mountain biking or wilderness canoeing and fishing from a motorboat.

Problems associated with attempting to balance the maintenance of ecological integrity with tourism and recreation led to policy change at the federal level. In 1988, policy makers amended the National Parks Act, which had been passed in 1930 to clarify the role of the Parks Branch by giving it more authority to set aside and administer national historic sites as places for the people. The amendments made ecological integrity, or protecting intact ecosystems, a priority. In 1994, the federal government's policy statement likewise stressed the ecological role of national parks. The goal of policy was to ensure that natural ecological processes continued to function with minimal interference.

Armed with its new mandate, the federal government commissioned a study to investigate the environmental health of Banff National Park. The blistering report, released in 1996, disclosed that the park, which had received over 5 million visitors in 1995, was in crisis. The commission recommended managed use and reduced development; the demolition of some developed sites; the implementation of visitor quotas in wilderness areas; more wildlife overpasses on the Trans-Canada Highway, which runs through the park's sensitive montane area; restoration of aquatic diversity; and the cleanup of sewage in park waters. Although the government implemented some measures, unrestrained use of the park continued. The park suffered

from ad hoc decision making, the inconsistent application of the National Parks Act by Parks Canada, government cutbacks, and weak political will. By the end of the twentieth century, other parks in the national system had similar problems.

In 2000, Parliament amended the National Parks Act to make the restoration and maintenance of ecological integrity the *first* priority. It made Parks Canada more accountable for the health of the system and decided to review the *State of the Parks* reports every two years. Parks Canada developed a number of tools to enhance administrators' understanding of park resources, ecological processes, and the impact of human activities on the environment. These tools included a natural resources database that helped administrators monitor and manage ecosystems. It also adapted the zoning system to better balance preservation and use.

Park Politics

Maintaining a balance between preservation and use has faltered as parks policy has fallen victim to party politics. At the provincial level, provinces such as Ontario, British Columbia, and Newfoundland have experienced policy shifts with the election of successive administrations with different political outlooks. In Ontario, for example, conflicts in the Temagami region in the late 1980s over protecting old-growth forests, Aboriginal land claims, and land-use issues resulted in demonstrations by the Temagami Wilderness Association against clear-cutting. David Peterson's Liberal government (1985-90) upgraded preservation in wilderness and nature reserve parks and zones, but it permitted

PARK ZONING AND WILDERNESS AREA DECLARATION

Park zoning is a method for classifying the water and land in the park according to ecosystem and cultural resource protection requirements, and their capability and suitability for visitor experience opportunities.

Zoning provides direction for the activities of park managers and park visitors. The zones serve to guide visitors' perception of the park and where certain activities are appropriate.

Zoning System Summary

Zone	Purpose	Management
I Special preservation	Specific areas or features that deserve special preservation because they contain or support unique, threatened, or endangered natural or cultural features, or are among the best examples of the features that represent a natural region.	Preservation is the key consideration. Motorized access and circulation will not be permitted. Internal access is by non-motorized means.
II Wilderness	Extensive areas that are good representations of a natural region and that will be conserved in a wilderness state.	Outdoor recreation activities that are dependent upon and within the capacity of the park's ecosystems, and that equire few, if any, rudimentary services and facilities.
III Natural environment	Natural areas that can sustain low-density outdoor activities with a minimum of related facilities.	Outdoor recreation activities requiring minimal services and facilities of a rustic nature. Motorized access may be allowed, with public transit being preferred.
IV Outdoor recreation	Limited areas capable of accommodating a broad range of opportunities for understanding, appreciation, and enjoyment of the park's heritage values and related essential services and facilities.	Outdoor opportunities supported by facility development. The defining feature of this zone is direct access by motorized vehicles.
V Park services	Applied to communities in national parks that contain a concentration of visitor services and support facilities.	Not applicable to Bruce Peninsula National Park.

Source: Parks Canada.

sports fishing in sixty parks, Aboriginal hunting in certain areas, and logging in Algonquin and Lake Superior Provincial Parks. This policy, devised in 1988 to balance interests temporarily, left all parties disgruntled.

Bob Rae's NDP government (1990-95) focused on Aboriginal rights and introduced a new policy that permitted traditional hunting and fishing in Algonquin Park. The move shocked some environmentalists. The one-year agreement established hunting seasons and areas and set limits on the number of deer and moose hunted. It also restricted the use of motorized vehicles in these areas. Aboriginal claims on part of Quetico Provincial Park resulted in the interim use of three lakes for boat and canoe tours led by First Nations guides. The government recognized the need to harmonize Aboriginal rights and provincial parks policy by involving Aboriginal communities in the planning, management, and operation of some parks, particularly those in the North. Environmental groups, in turn, pushed for the protection of wildlife and old-growth forests in Temagami and the completion of the expanded parks system. Their efforts resulted in the creation of a sustainable forestry program, a wetlands policy, and an Environmental Bill of Rights (1994), which declared three founding principles: "(1) the people of Ontario recognize the inherent value of a natural environment, (2) the people of Ontario have a right to a healthful environment, and (3) the people of Ontario have as a common goal the protection, conservation, and restoration of the natural environment for the benefit of present and future generations."

When Mike Harris's Conservative government (1995-2002) took office in 1995, mineral exploration in the Temagami area resumed, the government sold some Crown lands, and it privatized the Elk Lake community forest. In 1999, the government's Living Legacy Land Use Strategy (Lands for Life) set a dangerous precedent. The strategy, which documents land-use policies for Crown lands in southern and mid-northern Ontario, had four objectives: to "(1) complete Ontario's system of parks and protected areas, (2) recognize land use needs for the resource-based tourism industry, (3) provide resource industries with greater land and resource certainty, and (4) enhance Ontario fishing, hunting, and other Crown land recreational activities." Although the plan expanded both the number of parks and hectares in the parks system, the underlying idea was that only land without economic value should be protected. If minerals were found on Crown land, they would be mined, and the mined-out area would then be returned to the parks system. Environmentalists rose in protest against the shift toward development on park land, and in 1999 the government, industry, and environmental groups signed the Ontario Forest Accord, in which each party pledged to seek a balance between land harvested or developed and land designated for protection.

In British Columbia, environmentalists battled to preserve parks from commercial exploitation and to save old-growth forests from decades of overcutting in the Walbran and Carmanah Valleys and at Clayoquot Sound (see Figure 11.6). Bill Bennett's Social Credit government (1975-86), however, resisted

FIRST NATIONS AND PARKS POLICY

In 1976, the federal government amended the National Parks Act to protect Aboriginal fishing and trapping rights. In places with an unresolved land claim, the legislation stated that no park could be established until the governments and First Nations reached a settlement. The amendment reversed nearly a century of driving Aboriginal peoples from their homes to make way for parks. Gradually, under political pressure, the British Columbia and federal governments involved Aboriginal communities in the creation of Gwaii Haanas National Park Reserve, established in 1988, and the Haida Heritage Site, established in 1992. The amendment also included them in a comprehensive land claims process, which determined the location, size, and Aboriginal hunting and fishing rights for new northern parks, such as Vuntut and Tuktut Nogait National Parks, both established in 1995.

pressure from environmentalists and supported large multinational companies intent on clear-cutting the forests. Bennett's government, and that of his successor, William Vander Zalm (1986-1991), ushered in a public and for-profit model for parks. With reduced budgets, BC Parks adopted market mechanisms such as outsourcing to private operators. By 1989, it had outsourced all operations and management of parks with motorized access to campsites, a highly developed infrastructure (including washrooms and visitor centres), and large numbers of visitors, particularly day visitors. BC Parks continued to set park fees but tried to keep them low. If there is a deficit, the department provides the private operators with additional funding. When there is a profit, the private operators retain it to a certain negotiated level. When Mike Harcourt's NDP government (1991-96) failed to end the clear-cutting of old-growth forests, environmentalists, through protest and negotiation,

FIGURE 11.6 Environmental groups have been fighting to protect the old-growth forests of Clayoquot Sound from logging since the 1980s. In the 1990s, citizens and activists blocked logging roads and chained themselves to log-removal equipment in some of the largest environmental protests ever seen in Canada.
Greenpeace Canada

convinced it to expand the parks system to protect some coastal old-growth stands and about 6 percent of productive forests. In 2011, BC Parks faced stiff opposition from the Wilderness Committee and the public, which stopped the development of 260 vacation homes next to the Juan de Fuca Trail in a park on the southwest coast of Vancouver Island.

In Newfoundland, party politics and the influence of neoliberal ideas in favour of reduced government spending and deregulation caused the province to dismantle its park system to reduce debt. Between 1995 and 1997, in a controversial move, the government offered forty-nine provincial parks to private interests to run, leaving only thirteen under its own control. By 2001, some of the privatized properties were no longer operating.

At the federal level, Stephen Harper's Conservative (2006-) government included parks in its plans to reduce the deficit. Parks Canada froze user fees at national parks and historic sites until 2013 for items ranging from entry and camping to the cost of fishing licences and the use of hot pools. The agency will try to find other ways to make money in the future as the cost of delivering services goes up.

IN A WORLD where humans put immense pressure on the environment, parks are a way to protect habitat and biodiversity. They also go a long way toward protecting the nation's natural heritage, if not the world's, for "Canada is the global steward of twenty percent of the planet's remaining wilderness" (McNamee 2003, 26). However, as historian James Murton points out, "Parks are inherently contradictory, places where nature is preserved from the very humanity that wants to visit and enjoy it" (Murton 2002-03, 111). Provincial and federal parks in Canada have been defined and shaped by an ongoing struggle to balance preservation with recreation and tourism. The future health of parks and Canadian wildlife depends on preserving that balance, but park administrators face many challenges, including vacillating public policy and the vagaries of party politics. Protecting parks against future environmental degradation will depend on a vigilant public to safeguard Canada's protected places.

Works Cited

Garner, Robert. 2004. *Animals, Politics and Morality.* Manchester: Manchester University Press.

Leopold, Aldo. 1966. *A Sand County Almanac.* New York: Oxford University Press.

MacEachern, Alan. 2009. "Lost in Shipping: Canadian National Parks and the International Donation of Wildlife." In *Method and Meaning in Canadian Environmental History,* edited by Alan MacEachern and William J. Turkel, 196-213. Toronto: Nelson Education.

McNamee, Kevin. 2003. "Preserving Canada's Wilderness Legacy: A Perspective on Protected Areas." In *Protected Places and the Regional Planning Imperative in North America,* edited by J.G. Nelson, J.C. Day, Lucy M. Sportza, James Louky, and Carlos Vasquez, 25-44. Calgary: University of Calgary Press.

Murton, James. 2002-03. "National Parks: What Are They Good For? A Review Essay." *BC Studies* 136 (Winter): 111-15.

Parr, Joy. 2006. "Smells Like? Sources of Uncertainty in the History of the Great Lakes Environment." *Environmental History* 11, 2: 269-99.

For Further Reading

Barringer, Mark Daniel. 2002. *Selling Yellowstone: Capitalism and the Construction of Nature.* Lawrence: University Press of Kansas.

Campbell, Claire. 2011. *A Century of Parks Canada, 1911-2011.* Calgary: University of Calgary Press.

Carr, Ethan. 1998. *Wilderness by Design: Landscape Architecture and the National Park Service.* Lincoln: University of Nebraska Press.

Cronon, William. 1995. "The Trouble with Wilderness." In *Uncommon Ground: Rethinking the Human Place in Nature,* 65-90. New York: W.W. Norton.

Dowie, Mark. 2009. *Conservation Refugees: The Hundred-Year Conflict between Global Conservation and Native Peoples.* Cambridge, MA: MIT Press.

MacEachern, Alan. 2001. *Natural Selections: National Parks in Atlantic Canada, 1935-1970.* Montreal and Kingston: McGill-Queen's University Press.

McNamee, Kevin. 2003. "Preserving Canada's Wilderness Legacy: A Perspective on Protected Areas." In *Protected Places and the Regional Planning Imperative in North America,* edited by J.G. Nelson, J.C. Day, Lucy M. Sportza, James Louky, and Carlos Vasquez, 25-44. Calgary: University of Calgary Press.

Stutchbury, Bridget. 2007. *Silence of the Songbirds: How We Are Losing the World's Songbirds and What We Can Do to Save Them.* Toronto: Harper Collins.

Sutter, Paul. 2004. *Driven Wild: How the Fight against Cars Launched the Modern Wilderness Movement.* Seattle: University of Washington Press.

Wishnant, Anne Mitchell. 2006. *Super-Scenic Motorway: A Blue Ridge Parkway History.* Chapel Hill: University of North Carolina Press.

Wright, H. Eleanor (Mooney). 2003. *Trailblazers of Algonquin Park.* Eganville: HEW Publishers.

Scientific Research and Evolving Attitudes toward Wildlife

Burnett, J. Alexander. 2003. *A Passion for Wildlife: The History of the Canadian Wildlife Service.* Vancouver: UBC Press.

Garner, Robert. 2004. *Animals, Politics and Morality.* Manchester: Manchester University Press.

Loo, Tina. 2006. *States of Nature: Conserving Canada's Wildlife in the Twentieth Century.* Vancouver: UBC Press.

MacDonald, Graham A. 1994. "Science and History at Elk Island National Park: Conservation and Its Contradictions." Paper presented at the annual meeting of the Canadian Historical Association, Calgary, March.

Mowat, Farley. 1963. *Never Cry Wolf.* Toronto: McClelland and Stewart.

Reid, Gordon. 1986. *Dinosaur Provincial Park.* Erin: Boston Mills Press.

Savage, Candace. 2005. "Back Home on the Range: Ranchers and Conservationists Join Forces to Return a Purebred Grass Guzzler to the Prairie." *Canadian Geographic,* January-February.

Seton, Ernest Thompson. 1977. *Wild Animals I Have Known.* Toronto: McClelland and Stewart.

Smith, Donald. 1990. *From the Land of Shadows: The Making of Grey Owl.* Saskatoon: Western Producer Books.

A National Wildlife Policy

Burnett, J. Alexander. 2003. *A Passion for Wildlife: The History of the Canadian Wildlife Service.* Vancouver: UBC Press.

MacEachern, Alan. 2009. "Lost in Shipping: Canadian National Parks and the International Donation of Wildlife." In *Method and Meaning in Canadian Environmental History,* edited by Alan MacEachern and William J. Turkel, 196-213. Toronto: Nelson Education.

Sandlos, John. 2008. *Hunters at the Margins: Native People and Wildlife Conservation in the Northwest Territories.* Vancouver: UBC Press.

Wilson, Jeremy. 1998. *Talk and Log: Wilderness Politics in British Columbia.* Vancouver: UBC Press.

Parks in the Age of Tourism and Conservation

Bella, Leslie. 1987. *Parks for Profit.* Montreal: Harvest House.

Buteau-Duitschaever, Windekind C., Bonnie McCutcheon, Paul F.J. Eagles, M.E. Havitz, and Troy D. Glover. 2010. "Park Visitors' Perceptions of Governance: A Comparison between Ontario and British Columbia Provincial Parks' Management Models." *Tourism Review* 65, 4: 31-50.

Killan, Gerald. 1993. *Protected Places: A History of Ontario's Provincial Parks System.* Toronto: Dundurn Press.

Nelson, J.G. 1973. "Canada's National Parks: Past, Present, Future." *Canadian Geographic Journal* 76, 3: 68-89.

Parr, Joy. 2006. "Smells Like? Sources of Uncertainty in the History of the Great Lakes Environment." *Environmental History* 11, 2: 269-99.

Searle, Rick. 2000. *Phantom Parks: The Struggle to Save Canada's National Parks.* Toronto: Key Porter Books.

Taylor, C.J. 2007. "The Changing Habitat of Jasper Tourism." In *Culturing Wilderness in Jasper National Park: Studies in Two Centuries of Human History in the Upper Athabasca River Watershed,* edited by Ian MacLaren, 199-232. Edmonton: University of Alberta Press.

—. 2010. *Jasper: A History of the Place and Its People.* Toronto: Fitzhenry and Whiteside.

Van Sickle, Kerry, and Paul F.J. Eagles. 1998. "Budgets, Pricing Policies and User Fees in Canadian Parks' Tourism." *Tourism Management* 19, 3: 225-35.

Wall, Sharon. 2009. *The Nurture of Nature: Childhood, Anti-modernism, and Ontario Summer Camps, 1920-55.* Vancouver: UBC Press.

Preserving the Wilderness in Ontario

Atkinson, Ken. 2003. "Wilderness and the Canadian Mind." *British Journal of Canadian Studies* 16, 2: 228-42.

Bray, Matt, and Ashley Thomson. 1990. *Temagami: A Debate on Wilderness.* Toronto: Dundurn Press.

Hodgins, Bruce W., and Jamie Benidickson. 1989. *The Temagami Experience: Recreation, Resources, and Aboriginal Rights in the Northern Ontario Wilderness.* Toronto: University of Toronto Press.

Killan, G., and G. Warecki. 1992. "Algonquin Wildlands League and the Emergence of Environmental Politics in Ontario, 1965-74." *Environmental History Review* 16, 4: 1-28.

Warecki, George. 2000. *Protecting Ontario's Wilderness: A History of Changing Ideas and Preservation Politics, 1927-1973.* New York: Peter Lang.

Finding a Balance

Allardyce, Gilbert. 1972. "The Vexed Question of Sawdust: River Pollution in Nineteenth-Century New Brunswick." *Dalhousie Review* 52, 2: 177-90.

Hodgins, Bruce W. 2006. "Aboriginal Peoples and Their Historic Right to Hunt: A Reasonable Symbiotic Relationship." In *The Culture of Hunting in Canada,* edited by Jean L. Manore and Dale G. Minor, 193-210. Vancouver: UBC Press.

McNamee, Kevin. 2003. "Preserving Canada's Wilderness Legacy: A Perspective on Protected Areas." In *Protected Places and the Regional Planning Imperative in North America,* edited by J.G. Nelson, J.C. Day, Lucy M. Sportza, James Louky, and Carlos Vasquez, 25-44. Calgary: University of Calgary Press.

Wilson, Roger. 1976. *The Land That Never Melts: Auyuittuq National Park.* Toronto: Peter Martin Associates/Indian and Northern Affairs/Pub. Centre, Supply and Services Canada.

Park Politics

Banff-Bow Valley Task Force. 1996. *Banff-Bow Valley: At the Crossroads.* Summary Report. Ottawa: Ministry of Supply and Services Canada.

Killan, Gerald. 1993. *Protected Places: A History of Ontario's Provincial Parks System.* Toronto: Dundurn Press.

Van Huizen, Philip. 2011. "'Panic Park': Environmental Protest and the Politics of Parks in British Columbia's Skagit Valley." *BC Studies* 170 (Summer): 67-92.

12
Coastal Fisheries

Unless the order of nature is overthrown, for centuries to come our fisheries will continue to be fertile.

— CANADIAN MINISTRY OF AGRICULTURE REPORT, 1885

The Fraser River's sockeye salmon are in trouble. And when the salmon are in trouble, we're all in trouble.

— DAVID SUZUKI AND FAISAL MOOLA, "UNCOVERING
THE MYSTERY OF BC'S DISAPPEARING SOCKEYE," 2009

BETWEEN 1992 AND 2009, two developments, on opposite sides of the country, shocked Canadians and the world and drew attention to the catastrophic effects of human activities on the environment. In 1992, the Canadian government announced a moratorium on the commercial fishing of northern cod, fished to near extinction off the coast of Newfoundland. In 2009, reports came out that the number of sockeye salmon returning to the Fraser River was one of the lowest in fifty years and that other salmon runs were endangered. These fisheries should have lasted forever, and throughout Canadian history most people assumed they would. Their loss not only threatened jobs and regional economies, the lifestyle of First Nations on the Pacific Coast, and a healthful food source, it also highlighted the interconnectedness of all things. Environmentalists asked, what chain of events would be set in motion if these

species were to disappear? What went wrong in the management of these two valuable resources? How can we rebuild what we have lost?

Early Warning Signs on the East Coast

Codfish were the key species in Newfoundland's seasonal commercial fishery, which expanded in the nineteenth century to dominate commerce in Newfoundland and New England. Nearly two hundred species of cod lived in the cold saltwater of the North Atlantic. Codfish were ideal for commercial fishing but did not interest sports fishers because they were bottom feeders and easy to catch. A migratory fish, cod swim long distances in large schools. In the late spring, they move into shallow waters along the shore in search of caplin, a small herring-like fish. In the nineteenth century, the cod

FIGURE 12.1 Codfish drying on flakes at Job Brothers and Company in St. John's, Newfoundland, 1906. Fish flakes, platforms for drying codfish, dotted the foreshores of fishing villages and small towns in rural Newfoundland.
Maritime History Archive, PF-315.361

fishery, the most productive in the world, appeared to be inexhaustible. It ranged from Greenland and Baffin Island in the north to the continental shelf of Labrador, Newfoundland, and the Gulf of St. Lawrence and down to the Grand Banks, situated off the coasts of Nova Scotia and Maine. The maintenance of fishing communities in Newfoundland and Labrador (see Figure 12.1) depended on the sustainability of the cod fishery, which continued to be abundant even as the fisheries expanded. But optimism, new fishing technologies, poor fisheries management, and the absence of conservation measures resulted in overfishing, not only of cod but of all species. "The history of the fishery for each species has been much the same, production remaining stable for a long time, then decreasing and becoming scarce after

a few years of extremely high catches" (Manchester 1970, 26).

Newfoundland's fishery fell under the management of the Department of Fisheries and Oceans in 1949, when Newfoundland joined Canada. Before its stewardship, cod catches had increased gradually as the number of permanent fishers in Newfoundland, who gained control of the inshore fishery in 1750, also increased. Prior to that year, annual cod catches were less than 100,000 tonnes. As cod exports increased, however, fishers began to express concern about catch failures, which plagued the inshore fishery in certain years between 1815 and 1840, in the 1860s, and in 1874. Concern about reduced inshore fishery catches led to an investigation by Henry Y. Hind, whose 1877 report resulted in the establishment of the Newfoundland

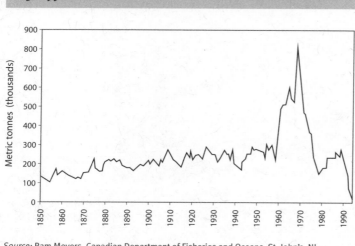

Source: Ram Meyers, Canadian Department of Fisheries and Oceans, St. John's, NL, http://www.fao.org/

to the banks, where they dropped off small dories with two-man crews who used hand-lines to catch the cod from the boat. Catches increased in size when offshore European fishers began to use long-lines, gill nets (large nets used to entangle fish), and steam-powered ships. To compete, Newfoundlanders adopted these more intensive methods to ensure continued access to merchant credit, which they needed to purchase necessities.

European fishers began to use trawlers, fishing vessels that catch fish in nets pulled behind them, after the First World War (see Figure 12.3). The first trawler, operated at Bath, Maine, in 1918, brought in a catch six times larger than the norm. The introduction of trawlers caused fish stocks to decline, first in the North Sea, then around Iceland, and finally, in the Grand Banks. In the absence of conservation practices, new technologies increased catches but depleted fish stocks in both the inshore and offshore fisheries and even in the waters of southeastern Labrador and the northeast coast of Newfoundland, places not fished regularly until the twentieth century. As catches increased, prices dropped. Fishers expressed concern about the future sustainability of the fishery, but the government failed to put conversation measures into place.

Technological developments led to the first diesel-powered trawlers in 1928, which coincided with the introduction of new products for consumers such as frozen fish fillets and fish sticks. During both world wars, when commercial fishing eased off, stocks improved. But the introduction of three innovations in the 1950s – huge factory trawlers, high-powered dragging nets, and fish freezers – ensured that stock depletion

Fisheries Commission in 1889 and the construction of a cod hatchery at Dildo, which produced eggs for release into Trinity Bay. In the twentieth century, overfishing led harvest rates to plummet as much as 40 to 50 percent. Catches increased from the 1880s to the 1910s to a peak of nearly 300,000 tonnes in 1910 but declined to around 150,000 tonnes in the 1940s (see Figure 12.2). In response, many fishers moved into the seal fishery or moved to a different fishing place. As a result, the spatial expansion of the shore, bank, and Labrador fisheries changed.

The expansion of the fishery before 1949 was fuelled not only by the growth of a local fishing population but also by technological breakthroughs and competition between local fishers in the inshore fishery and their European counterparts in the offshore fishery. Between the seventeenth century and the 1930s, local fishers typically travelled by large boats would continue. The new trawlers could process about six hundred tonnes of fish per day. Their enormous harvesting capacity meant cod catches got larger every year, even as the number of fishing nations in the off-shore fishery increased.

With larger ships, fishers focused on catching as many fish as possible. The industry became capital- rather than labour-intensive, but its participants still engaged in nineteenth-century thinking. Trawlers operated twenty-four hours a day, and fishers hauled their nets every four hours. The Spanish fleet out of Vigo practised pair fishing. Fishers hung a huge trawl between two ships. One crew operated the trawl while the other processed the fish. The two crews then switched roles

for the next haul. By this method, they ensured non-stop fishing. In the 1960s, fishers became even more efficient as they began to use radar and echo sounders to track schools of fish. In the 1980s, they added sonar or spotter aircraft to their arsenal. The environmental impact of trawlers extended beyond the size of the catches. Trawlers that dragged nets along the ocean floor created a desert. Marine biologists likened the process to clear-cutting the forest. The nets scooped up everything, including millions of fish that that were simply wasted if they had no commercial purpose.

As the number of trawlers in the offshore fisheries increased after the 1960s, inshore fishers complained to the government.

FIGURE 12.3 A trawler full of codfish off the Grand Banks, 1949. Trawlers enabled international fishing crews to bring in enormous catches. Newfoundland and Labrador's historic cod fisheries attracted local fishers and international fishing fleets with advanced technologies for almost five centuries before the Canadian government shut the industry down indefinitely in July 1992.

National Film Board of Canada, Library and Archives Canada, PA-110814

The government responded by redefining the offshore fishery several times and gradually extending its boundaries from 4.8 to 24.1 kilometres and finally, in 1976, to 322 kilometres offshore. The government took action to protect the inshore fishery, not as a conservationist measure. With the spatial limits of the inshore fishery expanded, the government allowed inshore fishers to use long-liners, large and powerful decked vessels. The long-liners replaced traditional open boats and had increasingly efficient gear: large gill nets, box-shaped cod traps, and long-lines (a single fishing line attached to hundreds of shorter baited lines). Some fishers used low-interest government loans to purchase the new vessels, a development that put pressure on those who maintained small boats. Meanwhile, technological innovations in the inshore fishery – such as mechanical tools to haul, bait, and set line trawls and to haul gill nets – increased the size of catches, as did new cod-trap designs. Competition for fish between inshore and offshore fishers also escalated along with disagreements with fishing nations such as Iceland and Britain.

Mismanaging the Cod Fishery

Managing fisheries is difficult. The International Commission for the Northwest Atlantic Fisheries began to explore the possibility of managing excesses in the Atlantic cod fishery in the 1950s. The commission came into being in 1950 when offshore-fishing nations began to entertain the possibility that the cod fishery could be depleted. The organization sought to protect and preserve fish resources on the basis of modern science. The establishment of the commission coincided with the Newfoundland fishery's falling under the purview of Fisheries and Oceans Canada. Before the mid-1960s, however, the fisheries remained quite open. There was no uniform licensing system, and there were few restrictions on catch levels or fishing capacity. Fisheries managers relied on various tools to control fishing: placing restrictions on the length of seasons, enforcing seasonal closures, setting minimum fish sizes, controlling the size of mesh in fish nets and other gear constraints, introducing special restricted gear areas, and setting maximum vessel sizes.

Fishing communities dependent on cod relied on Fisheries and Oceans to manage the fishery. Unfortunately, the department mismanaged the resource and allowed overfishing. Canada was not alone in this. No fish management regime in the world prevented exploitation: "As an open-access resource, fisheries were routinely overfished. Fishermen had no incentive to let fish remain in the sea where others might catch them. While all fishermen would be better off if they could refrain from catching young fish, which jeopardizes future fish stocks, any fisherman who did so lost fish to others who did not" (McNeill 2000, 237). The northern cod had no hope of recovering within this predatory fishing culture, and the department's and other organizations' efforts to establish harvesting regulations to conserve commercial fish species met with little success. In the 1950s, fishers began to demand stricter licensing to restrict the numbers of fishers and boats. The department extended limited-entry licensing to most major Atlantic fisheries under Canadian jurisdiction in 1973.

Within the system, the government fixed the number of allowable licences. Anyone who wanted to engage in commercial fishing had to buy an existing licence.

Between 1970 and 1974, the International Commission for the Northwest Atlantic Fisheries also introduced a total allowable catch limit and national quotas on cod for member nations to follow. The Canadian government, in 1976, followed suit with a new policy for commercial fisheries and developed the new policy framework to prepare for an expansion of its jurisdiction. It had declared the right to manage the fisheries in an exclusive economic zone that extended 340 kilometres (200 miles) offshore. The government wanted to reverse declining fish stocks by removing the presence of foreign fishing within the newly expanded inshore fishery and to achieve the "best use" of Canada's fish resources. However, the "absence of international fisheries regulations during peak offshore catches in the 1960s and early 1970s" and the failure of Canadian managers to control fish mortality in the 1980s so diminished the cod population that its recovery was almost impossible (Hutchings and Myers 1995, 75).

With only a limited knowledge of cod biology, scientists predicted the population would rebound from its low point in 1975. When Canada extended its fisheries jurisdiction in 1976, fish mortality decreased immediately because foreign trawler fleets could no longer fish the waters and because Canada did not as yet have trawlers. The fishery recovered temporarily and modestly between the late 1970s and 1985. But the quota system was based on faulty estimates and statistics. Fish are notoriously difficult to

COD ANNIHILATION IN HISTORICAL PERSPECTIVE

To gain a better perspective on the rapid decline of cod stocks in the twentieth century, consider this. It is estimated that fishers caught 8 million tonnes of northern cod between 1500 and 1750. Factory trawlers processed the same amount (probably a low estimate) in the brief fifteen-year period between 1960 and 1975. They reduced the number of cod available for harvesting by 82 percent, from an estimated 3,048,140 tonnes to 534,440 tonnes. The reproductive portion of the stock (codfish seven years and older) declined 94 percent, from about 1,625,675 tonnes to 94,492 tonnes, and the number of three-year-olds decreased from 1.016 billion to 69.09 million. The catch plummeted to 139,000 tons in 1978.

count, and the statistics gathered did not include illegal fishing (the so-called black catch) or discarded bycatches, which, by the 1990s, constituted one-third of recorded catches around the world. When it set quotas, Fisheries and Oceans overestimated the available stock, and it increased the total allowable catch even as scientists and inshore fishers warned of dangerously low stocks (see Figure 12.4). In 1992, John Crosbie, the minister of fisheries and oceans, set the quota at 187,969 tonnes, even though only 129,033 tonnes of fish had been caught the previous year. That same year, the government announced a moratorium on cod fishing and extended it the following year when the cod did not return in the spring. It then made the closure permanent.

The collapse of the Grand Banks cod fishery, which amounted to a 97 to 99 percent reduction in the species, has been described as "the worst fishery management failure in the world" (Boyd 2003, 198). The collapse had economic and ecological consequences, and the causes became clearer only after it had occurred. Over the next five years,

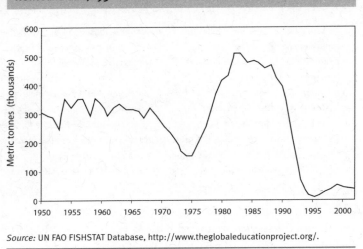

FIGURE 12.4 Collapse of Atlantic cod stocks off the coast of Newfoundland, 1950-2000

Source: UN FAO FISHSTAT Database, http://www.theglobaleducationproject.org/.

the moratorium resulted in the unemployment of forty thousand Maritimers and Quebecers. The federal government developed a five-year, nearly $2 million compensation program that paid fishery workers up to $382 a week during the moratorium, and it initiated plans, such as the Fisheries Alternatives Program, to create or maintain jobs and assist communities in diversifying, restructuring, and adjusting to the crisis. By 2003, federal aid amounted to $4 billion. Some fishers expressed disbelief that the cod were gone; others began fishing crab and lobster, which they also overfished.

One of the most devastating statistics released in 1992 was that the level of codfish spawning had been reduced to 1 percent of its historical maximum, "an ecological disaster of extraordinary magnitude" (Hutchings and Myers 1995, 82). The primary cause of the collapse was the failure to allow the stock to sustain itself. A maximum sustainable yield strategy would have allowed only 18 percent

of the estimated cod to be caught annually. But the government monitored the catch quota and harvesting ineffectively because it had developed a harmonious relationship with the offshore sector, which lobbied for higher quotas and cooperated with Fisheries and Oceans, and because its estimates did not take inshore fishing into consideration. Some of the data used by the department came from research vessels, but most of them came from the offshore-fishing vessels themselves. In 1986, the department had an observer on board most offshore vessels over a hundred feet long, but it ignored the inshore fishers, whom it found uncooperative and difficult to monitor because of the variety of vessels they used.

For the quota system to work, Fisheries and Oceans needed accurate statistics on catches. Its problems in data collection were exacerbated by its assumption that natural mortality in the fish would remain at a constant level, a wildly optimistic stance. Between 1978 and 1988, on the basis of catch rates and research surveys, government regulators assumed rising catch rates reflected an increase in the stock rather than an increase in fish harvesting. The commercial catch rate suggested that the stock had trebled, and their survey data indicated a 50-percent increase. The department therefore set a quota increase at the halfway point between the two results. Many inshore fishers recognized by the mid-1980s that the data were wrong, that they did not take into account underreporting, misreporting, and discarded catches. As a result of these miscalculations, by the early 1990s commercial fishers were removing from between 60 to 80 percent of the harvestable stock each year when 18 percent was the level for a sustainable management system. When two federal government reports in 1987 and 1990 confirmed that the department's estimates had gone awry, it lowered the total allowable catch. But it was too late.

The Collapse: A Postmortem

In explaining the 1992 collapse of the cod fishery, a former head of the Newfoundland Inshore Fishermen's Association concluded, "There's ... a historical problem here of not understanding the limits of nature, not understanding environmental risks" (Harris 1998, 150). At first, John Crosbie blamed oceanic conditions. The government then put forward several hypotheses that the data did not support. For instance, it suggested that increases to the natural mortality rate of cod had been caused not by stress or dramatic changes in the marine environment but rather by the mortality of the fish they fed on, such as plaice. The theory was rejected after cod were caught with full stomachs. It then suggested that cold water temperatures and changes in the ocean's salt levels had caused the cod to move south to warmer waters. The cod, however, had experienced similar conditions in the past and had not migrated. Others suggested that a confluence of factors – colder water temperatures, increased fish mortality from natural causes, fewer and weaker younger fish – played a role and conceded that the fishing rate had been high, but not high enough to bring about a total collapse. Environmentalists and some biologists greeted these excuses with skepticism.

One environmental factor was new. The high rate of cod eggs eaten by predators had been normal, but cod eggs had also died because of an increase in ultraviolet radiation caused by depletion of the ozone layer. The rate of natural population increase therefore declined. In other words, overfishing caused by a failure to adequately estimate stock levels was the primary cause of the collapse of the northern cod and other northwest Atlantic groundfish stocks. Although some observers suggested that the decline had been sudden, the indicators point to a gradual decline over many decades and more drastic decreases from the 1980s. Decreases in the inshore fishery after 1985 occurred as offshore fishing increased. Between 1986 and 1992, independent tagging studies demonstrated that the stock had declined seriously. Inshore fishers' "knowledge of the movement of fish" proved to be more accurate than the predictions of scientists, and most of the maritime community in Newfoundland criticized figures released by Oceans and Fisheries Canada (Matthews 1995, 93).

Before the collapse, scientists had little voice in the department's management decisions. Uncertain data, different opinions about fish stock health, and variations in environmental conditions were not discussed in the stock-assessment documents that management, in consultation with industry, used to make its decisions. After the collapse, scientists in Fisheries and Oceans Canada indicated that managers had converted their cautious scientific estimates into precise but inaccurate quotas of abundance for the sake of political expedience.

The federal government refused to restrict predatory technologies and the fleets' overcapacity and failed to develop an ecological approach to management, one that took into consideration marine biology and local knowledge. For instance, its limited-entry licensing system simply reduced the number of fishers, especially those who worked on a part-time or casual basis, rather than restricting the size of boats and methods of fishing. By arbitrarily introducing a new licensing system that divided fishers, the government created a more bureaucratic centralized policy, which excluded traditional local controls well known in Newfoundland communities and ignored local knowledge, which would prove to be more accurate than government fish data. The main focus of fisheries science at Fisheries and Oceans Canada shifted from marine biology to population dynamics and mathematics with complex models and data. Management reviewed and evaluated the status of the stock, one species at a time, and treated data on fishing, biology, and the environment separately. It made no attempt to evaluate the entire ecosystem or include behavioural ecology, population biology, or life history research in stock assessments of commercially harvested fish.

Since the collapse of the fishery, some researchers have advised managers to recognize the value of local ecological knowledge among fishers and local community stewardship, which they have not acted on. Others have advocated a neoliberal approach to privatize the fishery, which professional fishers would manage in a self-regulated free market. Both approaches see management as the solution, which Dean Bavington questions. To address the "unnatural history of managed annihilation in cod and other fisheries around the world," fishers and subsistence should take priority over industrial

fleets and commercial fisheries, and there should be a global ban on bottom trawling (Bavington 2010, 133).

After the cod fishery closed permanently in 1995, Brian Tobin, the minister of fisheries and oceans, criticized the Spanish for fishing endangered turbot stocks in international waters beyond the Canadian coastal limit and called for a sixty-day moratorium. The announcement was pure political grandstanding, since Canada itself did not have a sustainable fisheries policy. Instead of examining its policies, the Department of Fisheries and Oceans continued to license bottom draggers indiscriminately. In 2001, the Ecology Action Centre and Sierra Legal Defence Fund filed a lawsuit in Nova Scotia to try to force the department to exclude draggers from areas off the coast of southern Nova Scotia that had sensitive habitats. The government used legal technicalities to exclude expert witnesses. A journalist commented, "This hardly inspires confidence that Ottawa is truly interested in the sustainable use of Canada's fisheries" (Anderson 2003).

The Pacific Coast Fishery

Environmentalists, journalists, and the Canadian public linked the stunning collapse of the Atlantic cod fishery to the decline of wild salmon on the Pacific Coast, where salmon were and continue to be central to the culture and well-being of many First Nations. Pacific salmon live along the coast and are anadromous – that is, they are born in fresh water, migrate to the ocean, and return to their freshwater spawning grounds to reproduce. Tsimshian and Kwakwaka'wakw who lived

along the smaller rivers speared fish or
trapped them in weirs and offered prayers
and rituals so the salmon would return each
year. The Nisga'a worked the Nass River, and
the Gitksan fished on the Upper Skeena. The
Tsilhqot'in (Chilcotin) and Secwepemc
(Shuswap) farther south and the Haida on
Haida Gwaii enjoyed late summer runs of
salmon, and the Nuu-Chah-Nulth (Nootka)
fished from Vancouver Island. Coastal
peoples, using nets and harpoons, harvested
abundant catches that gave them the leisure
time to develop their distinctive art and
culture. They also traded salmon with peoples
along the Columbia River.

It is estimated that each family consumed
about one thousand salmon per year, or about
three-quarters of a million fish per year. However, they also harvested many more fish for
trade. Historians estimate that First Nations
traditionally caught as many fish as does the
commercial industry today, but their fishing
practices were sustainable (see Figure 12.5).
The salmon was a respected cultural icon,
and Aboriginal people's knowledge of its
habitat was extensive. First Nations had
dispersed fishing areas and engaged in practices that delayed fishing until after the fish
had spawned. Because First Nations had a
relatively small population and used basic
technology, salmon remained abundant.

After contact, Aboriginal people began to
fish more salmon to trade with Europeans,
and settlers increasingly captured a larger
share of the salmon fishery. The market for
salmon increased during the fur trade era.
In 1836, for instance, trading posts in New
Caledonia used about 67,500 salmon each
year. As the fur trade declined, the salmon

trade expanded. In 1864, William Hume
opened the first salmon cannery and produced
two thousand hand-hewn cans of salmon
each year. Alex Ewan of New Westminster
built the first salmon cannery on the Fraser
River six years later, and canneries quickly
spread up the coast and on Vancouver Island
despite unpredictable markets and prices (see
Figure 12.6). Business consolidation and
technological advances resulted in four

FIGURE 12.5 A fisherman
uses a dip net to catch
salmon. For generations,
First Nations used sus-
tainable methods to
harvest salmon for food
and trade each year.
BC Archives, D-06014

companies operating ninety-four canneries in 1917. Faster transportation and improved canning techniques put pressure on the larger salmon runs.

In the nineteenth century, the salmon runs occurred in three areas: the Fraser River in the south, the Nass and Skeena Rivers in the north, and the Rivers and Smith Inlets in between. It is estimated that between 120 and 160 million salmon returned each year to spawn in the Fraser River. The Skeena, the second largest area of salmon production after the Fraser, provided 20 percent of the total catch, and the northern waters, taken together, produced more than the Fraser. In the early twentieth century, between 1.5 and 3.0 million sockeye salmon returned annually to Rivers Inlet, and a large run occurred about every four years. From Alaska to Washington State, routes were filled "with

the merciless sifting of the seine nets or the strangling web of gillnets" (McKervill 1967, 99). In the short season, during the main run of salmon in July, fishers and canners rushed to catch as many fish and make as much money as possible.

The management of salmon fisheries in British Columbia, both tidal and freshwater, fell to Fisheries and Oceans Canada. Early inspectors reported that salmon were being overfished, and commissions in 1887, 1892, and 1897 reported that fishers were wasting salmon and flouting rules. By then, the heyday of the salmon-canning industry had ended. Only forty-two canneries remained in 1942. Capital investment, however, increased in the commercial industry, even as the number of fish declined. In 1960, over four hundred seiners, fishers who employ large nets that hang vertically from floaters

FIGURE 12.6 Salmon fishers waiting to unload at a BC cannery.
BC Archives, D-04026

SOCIAL INEQUALITIES IN THE CANNERIES

The expansion of the salmon fishery changed the character of life on the coast. It introduced "clanking cans, tumbling presses, steam," and the stench of fish and offal-polluted water (McKervill 1967, 53). The canneries employed Aboriginal, Chinese, and Japanese workers, who lived in rows of unsanitary shacks nearby. When the canners formed an association to protect their interests in 1893, workers organized the Fishermen's Protective and Benevolent Association, but its first strike failed because there was a lack of unity among Asian, Aboriginal, and white workers. Although it began as an inclusive organization, the association gradually came to represent only non-Aboriginal workers.

FIGURE 12.7 Shacks housed Aboriginal workers behind the cannery at Friendly Cove in Nootka Sound, 1930s.
BC Archives, A-08869

to capture fish, worked the coast, and the gill-net fleet consisted of over 4,500 fishing boats and 3,000 trawlers.

Declining Salmon Populations

It is estimated that salmon populations – captured by commercial, Aboriginal, and recreational fishers – declined by 80 to 90 percent in the twentieth century. Overfishing and competition among fishers in the commercial salmon fishery contributed to declining salmon runs. Yukon and British Columbia had lost at least 142 salmon runs by 1990, and hundreds more approached near collapse. The region's commercial catch of Pacific salmon fell 75 percent, from 40 million to 10 million, and salmon populations disappeared from 40 percent of the rivers where they once spawned. The capture of Canadian-bound salmon by American fishers at Puget Sound also contributed to reduced runs, as did railway construction and landslides, both natural and man-made, which disrupted salmon migrations. For instance, a landslide in 1913 at Hell's Gate on the Fraser River blocked the salmon's migration route, and millions died without spawning. Inexplicably, the problem was not fixed until the 1940s. Hydro dams built for irrigation and power generation likewise prevented salmon from reaching the upper sections of large rivers

The commercial fishery encroached on Aboriginal people, whose ancestral right to fish for food was restricted by law. The government required Aboriginal fishers to obtain permission and permits from local fishery officers, and it limited their fishing to times and places that did not compete with commercial interests. In this restrictive environment, the number of Aboriginal fishers declined from 3,084 in 1883 to 2,300 in 1962, about 14 percent of the total number of fishers. After the Supreme Court ruled in *Calder* (1973) that First Nations in British Columbia had unextinguished Aboriginal rights, the federal government began to negotiate comprehensive claims agreements. Fishing rights formed part of the claims, and Aboriginal groups reasserted their position in the salmon industry. The *Derrickson* case (1976) recognized Aboriginal peoples' right to fish under Fisheries Act regulations, and the *Sparrow* (1990) decision affirmed that the Constitution protected rights in existence in 1982, including fishing rights. In the interest of conservation, the Supreme Court stated that the priority for Aboriginal fishers should be food.

and streams. Fishways were eventually built on dams to assist salmon around barriers, but they were not always successful. When lumber company dams were demolished in the 1950s, the catch increased significantly.

In general, however, fish populations continued to decrease, even as Fisheries and Oceans passed regulations to control the size of net mesh and limit fishing seasons and areas. In 1964, the government established a 4.8-kilometre territorial limit off the coast, which it extended to 19.3 kilometres in 1970 to define a larger Canadian territory. Between 1980 and 1984, it closed Rivers Inlet, but the measure had little effect. More than 3 million sockeye travelled to the area to spawn in the 1970s. In 1999, fewer than 3,600 sockeye did so. The collapse of the central coast sockeye run, the third largest in the province, amounted to the collapse of an entire ecosystem. Not only were fishers, canners, and sports fishers deprived of fish, local animals such as birds and grizzly bears that depended on the river for nourishment starved. Some of the bears that entered the town of Oweekeno in search of food were shot.

Mismanagement in the Salmon Fishery

As was the case in the Atlantic cod fishery, the salmon fishery had been subject to mismanagement from the earliest years of the commercial fishery. As wild stocks declined, policy makers and fishery managers in the 1970s increasingly focused on aquaculture, the cultivation of aquatic plants or animals for food, as a solution to declining salmon runs. They were influenced by developments in the United States, where policy makers refused to regulate salmon fishing on the Columbia River and instead advocated using scientific techniques to "make more salmon." Fish culturalists hoped to simplify and manipulate nature to produce fish in a more efficient, convenient, and profitable way. A Canadian, Samuel Wilmot, had built the first salmon hatchery, located near Lake Ontario, in 1867, and an American, Livingston Stone, successfully transplanted salmon eggs from New Brunswick to New England the following year. American policy makers moved quickly to establish hatcheries, even though they had a relatively low success rate in producing fish that survived release into the wild. They deflected criticism by blaming the failure on nature or predation by seals, sea lions, cormorants, and even songbirds. Hatcheries, regardless of whether they were successful, enabled policy makers to claim they were taking action even as they ignored conservation and other serious environmental issues.

Canadian policy makers were slower to embrace the concept of aquaculture and engaged in more rigorous research, but they eventually came to see it as the solution to declining salmon runs. John Babcock, a Californian who served as the BC fisheries commissioner in 1901-05 and deputy commissioner in 1907-10, opposed pond raising and favoured hatchery practices that followed "as closely as possible the footsteps of nature" (Taylor 1999, 210). He opposed fingerling (young salmon) programs that relied on unnatural foods that led to gastric parasites and caused the salmon fry to miss the spring floods that carried them to sea. A sockeye salmon hatchery was set up at Cultus Lake, but in 1934, following a number of scientific reports that cast doubt on the effectiveness of hatchery programs, the Biological Board of Canada recommended terminating Canada's hatchery program. The federal government shut down all of its hatcheries in 1937, not because the hatcheries disrupted and reshaped stream ecology, but because the board favoured finding new stocks and developing better fishing tools and methods to better exploit existing stocks.

When salmon stocks began to decline noticeably in the 1970s, the fish culture industry emerged as an adjunct to the commercial fishery. Policy makers supported the establishment of fish hatcheries and farms – raising fish in tanks and enclosures for commercial gain – because they sent a message that the government was addressing the problem, and the Department of Oceans and Fisheries applauded the trend because it provided employment in coastal communities. The science of raising farmed salmon was perfected in Norway in the 1970s to take

pressure off declining wild salmon stocks. Scotland and Ireland entered the business in the 1980s, and Canadians soon began farming Atlantic salmon on the Pacific Coast. Established in 1979, the Canadian Salmon Enhancement Program also employed many strategies to increase the freshwater survival of coho, chinook, and chum salmon in British Columbia. This work included the establishment of eighteen fish hatcheries on many major rivers, along with the development of fishways and spawning channels. Fish farming likewise became a huge business – the total output in Canada grew from $7 million to over $259 million between 1984 and 1999, when the value of the cultivated harvest exceeded by eleven times that of the wild Pacific salmon catch (see Figures 12.8 and 12.9). By 2005, BC's salmon-farming industry was

FIGURE 12.8 **Aquaculture production in Canada by tonnage and value, 1990-2009**

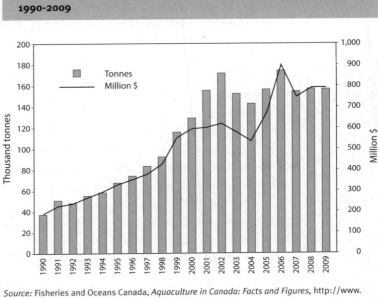

Source: Fisheries and Oceans Canada, *Aquaculture in Canada: Facts and Figures,* http://www.dfo-mpo.gc.ca/; Statistics Canada (2009)

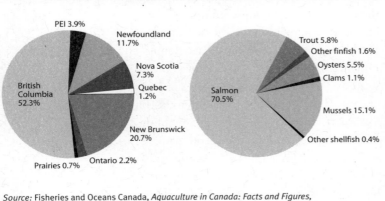

FIGURE 12.9   Aquaculture output by province and species, 2009

Source: Fisheries and Oceans Canada, *Aquaculture in Canada: Facts and Figures*, http://www.dfo-mpo.gc.ca/; Statistics Canada (2009)

the fourth largest in the world. Eighty-five farms were valued at $400 million and provided approximately four thousand people with jobs.

Aquaculture never took an ecological approach, and despite protests from environmentalists, aquaculture scientists blithely introduced Atlantic salmon to the West Coast and Pacific salmon to the East Coast, even though the fish were different species. These practices harmed both farmed fish and wild salmon. Fisheries and Oceans claimed that Atlantic salmon could not survive in the wild on the West Coast, yet they were increasingly discovered in BC's streams and in rivers as far north as the Bering Sea, where they compete for food and space with wild Pacific salmon. Within fish farms, scientists bred salmon to meet standards for industrial salmon, and they fed penned fish antibiotics to ward off diseases. Because the flesh of the final product was tasteless and grey, it had to be dyed red to look like wild salmon. When the medicated feed entered the larger aquatic

environment, it had an adverse effect on other sea life. Likewise, when large amounts of fish excrement, high in nitrogen, entered the sea, it created dead zones below the farms. In 2004, *Science* magazine also reported that farmed salmon contained higher levels of toxins than wild salmon. Scientists speculated that the high levels of fish oil fed to farmed salmon to increase their levels of Omega-3 fatty acids made them susceptible to chemical residues. Salmon farms, which were stocked year-round with hundreds of thousands of fish in net-cages, also developed diseases that spread to wild salmon. In 2005, a report by the Royal Society of Britain linked higher levels of sea lice among wild salmon to salmon farms. The lice attach themselves to young salmon as they make their way out to sea, causing many to die because their immature bodies cannot withstand the attack.

The Department of Fisheries and Oceans, which is responsible for protecting salmon and their habitats, took no action on fish farms and monitored them inadequately. It repeated the same management patterns that led to disaster in the East Coast cod fishery, and, like its American counterpart who managed the commercial fishery on the Columbia River, it used fish culture as a quick fix to sustain catches in the commercial and sports fisheries and for the food industry. The department consistently gave priority to economic development rather than creating a regulated, sustainable West Coast fishery. Following the example of Newfoundland's cod fishery, as the number of Pacific salmon declined, the management system became more complicated and time consuming without becoming more effective. Political conflicts between levels of government, between

Canadians and Americans, and among fishers who resisted regulations such as permits and set fishing seasons made coming to an agreement on developing a sustainable fishery difficult.

The Department of Oceans and Fisheries was quick to protest that it needed more research to take action, yet it ignored scientists' warnings about declining wild salmon, and it produced little research to fulfill its mandate to protect fish. In 1995, for instance, biologist Carl Walters, in a report on the salmon fishery for the David Suzuki Foundation, recommended reducing fishing fleets by 50 percent and making commercial fishers help pay for intensive conservation measures. A few months later, a critical report by John Fraser, a former fisheries minister, charged the Department of Fisheries and Oceans with "glaring organizational flaws and bureaucratic ineptitude" (Howard 1995). Fraser stated that the department had failed to enforce fishing regulations and had ignored its constitutional responsibility and its first priority, to be the guardian of the salmon fishery. He recommended that the department find methods to estimate fish numbers more accurately and become conservative in determining its quotas. He commented, "The public is not interested in different stakeholders blaming each other. The public knows that we have lost the Atlantic cod, at least for many, many years, and most of the public believes that is a national Canadian scandal. Most of the public here wonder if we are on the verge of doing the same with the salmon" (Cernetig 1995).

Although the federal government announced it would rebuild wild salmon stock by protecting habitats and removing migratory barriers, and although it ordered reduced catches of declining species such as sockeye salmon in 2000, scientists at Simon Fraser University's Institute of Fisheries Analysis argued that its wild salmon policy did not "firmly and explicitly commit Fisheries and Oceans to the protection of wild salmon" (Institute of Fisheries Analysis 2000, 1). The institute advocated using salmon-cultivation techniques *only* as a last resort to preserve at-risk populations. After more consultation, Fisheries and Oceans produced "A Policy Framework for Conservation of Wild Pacific Salmon: Wild Salmon Policy" in 2005. Its stated goal was to "restore and maintain healthy, diverse salmon populations and habitats of five species of Pacific Salmon" through sustainable resource management. The Canadian Wildlife Federation criticized the policy because it refused to recognize salmon aquaculture as a significant source of stress on wild salmon and because the department monitored environmental problems in fish farms ineffectively and implemented its regulations in an unsustainable way. Frustrated environmentalists argued that the government's policies of both promoting and regulating the aquaculture industry were incompatible.

When the Fraser River salmon failed to return to British Columbia in 2009, the government established the Cohen Commission to investigate their mysterious disappearance. When millions of sockeye unexpectedly returned the following year, Fisheries and Oceans immediately increased the total allowable catch without understanding why numbers were up. Salmon behaviour in recent years is a complex mystery. Yet, even though we do not know the exact cause of every salmon population decline, scientists do understand the major threats. The government should take precautionary actions to curtail activities that we know harm salmon even as it researches abrupt population declines. Canada's Wild Salmon Policy provides the tools to do this, but the government has been slow to fund and implement it and has ignored the negative impact of commercial aquaculture.

THE CONFLUENCE OF variables that contributed to the disappearance of fish on both the East and West Coasts supports the need for more holistic, ecosystem-based approaches to fisheries management. The Department of Fisheries and Oceans focused consistently on short-term economic growth, on the demands of large commercial fishers rather than the needs of local communities and the health of ecosystems. On both coasts, despite its mandate to protect the fisheries, it did not adopt sustainable policies. It favoured quota limitation and fleet reduction in the 1990s by cutting out smaller fishers and giving precedence to industrial fleets. It consistently passed inadequate, poorly monitored policies that paid little attention to scientists or the public interest. Today, fishers and First Nations in British Columbia are working together to develop more sustainable harvesting techniques, and scientists are experimenting with closed-containment salmon farms. These new approaches take local ecological knowledge into consideration and the future of local communities seriously. The poor management of Canada's fisheries resulted in a 90-percent reduction of fish stocks and mass unemployment because the long-term sustainability of fish resources and communities was never a priority. A more sustainable fisheries policy would include anti-pollution measures to improve fish habitats, downsizing and regulating the fishing industry to allow fish to reproduce, and strict regulation of aquaculture.

Works Cited

Anderson, Mitchell. 2003. "The Cod's Gone, Yet the Deadly Draggers Remain." *Globe and Mail,* 30 April.

Bavington, Dean. 2010. *Managed Annihilation: An Unnatural History of the Newfoundland Cod Collapse.* Vancouver: UBC Press.

Boyd, David R. 2003. *Unnatural Law: Rethinking Canadian Environmental Law and Policy.* Vancouver: UBC Press.

Cernetig, Miro. 1995. "Tobin Vows to Overhaul BC Fishery." *Globe and Mail,* 8 March.

Harris, Michael. 1998. *Lament for an Ocean: The Collapse of the Atlantic Cod Fishery, a True Crime Story.* Toronto: McClelland and Stewart.

Howard, Ross. 1995. "Pacific Fishery Facing Collapse, Report Warns." *Globe and Mail,* 1 February.

Hutchings, Jeffery A., and Ransom A. Myers. 1995. "The Biological Collapse of Atlantic Cod Off Newfoundland and Labrador: An Exploration of Historical Changes in Exploitation, Harvesting, Technology, and Management." In *The North Atlantic Fisheries: Successes, Failures, and Challenges,* edited by Ragnar Arnason and Lawrence Felt, 37-93. Charlottetown: Institute of Island Studies.

Institute of Fisheries Analysis. 2000. "Fisheries and Oceans' 'Wild Salmon Policy': A View from the Perspective of Science." Simon Fraser University, Burnaby.

Manchester, Lorne. 1970. *Canada's Fisheries.* Toronto: McGraw-Hill.

Matthews, David Ralph. 1995. "Commons versus Open Access: The Collapse of Canada's East Coast Fishery." *The Ecologist* 25, 2-3: 86-92.

McKervill, Hugh W. 1967. *The Salmon People: The Story of Canada's West Coast Fishing Industry.* Sidney, BC: Gray's Publishing.

McNeill, John R. 2000. *Something New under the Sun: An Environmental History of the Twentieth-Century World.* New York: W.W. Norton.

Suzuki, David, and Faisal Moola. 2009. "Uncovering the Mystery of BC's Disappearing Sockeye." Straight.com, 25 August.

Taylor, James E., III. 1999. *Making Salmon: An Environmental History of the Northwest Fisheries Crisis.* Seattle: University of Washington Press.

For Further Reading

Alexander, David. 1990. "Newfoundland's Traditional Economy and Development to 1934." In *Acadiensis Reader,* 2nd ed., edited by P.A. Buckner and David Frank, 1-33. Fredericton: Acadiensis Press.

Ellis, Richard. 2003. *The Empty Ocean: Plundering the World's Marine Life.* Washington, DC: Island Press/Shearwater Books.

Evenden, Matthew D. 2004. *Fish versus Power: An Environmental History of the Fraser River.* New York: Cambridge University Press.

Rogers, Raymond A. 1995. *The Oceans Are Emptying: Fish Wars and Sustainability.* Montreal: Black Rose Books.

Ryan, Shannon. 1985. "Fishery to Colony: A Newfoundland Watershed, 1793-1815." In *Acadiensis Reader,* 1st ed., edited by P.A. Buckner and David Frank, 138-56. Fredericton: Acadiensis Press.

Young, Nathan, and Ralph Matthews. 2010. *The Aquaculture Controversy in Canada: Activism, Policy, and Contested Science.* Vancouver: UBC Press.

Early Warning Signs on the East Coast

Cadigan, Sean T. 1999. "Failed Proposals for Fisheries Management and Conservation in Newfoundland, 1855-1880." In *Fishing Places and Fishing People: Traditions and Issues in Canadian Small-Scale Fisheries,* edited by Dianne Newell and Rosemary E. Ommer, 147-69. Toronto: University of Toronto Press.

Ommer, Rosemary. 1994. "One Hundred Years of Fishery Crises in Newfoundland." *Acadiensis* 23 (Summer) : 5-20.

Mismanaging the Cod Fishery

Bavington, Dean. 2010. *Managed Annihilation: An Unnatural History of the Newfoundland Cod Collapse.* Vancouver: UBC Press.

Hutchings, Jeffery A., and Ransom A. Myers. 1995. "The Biological Collapse of Atlantic Cod Off Newfoundland and Labrador: An Exploration of Historical Changes in Exploitation, Harvesting, Technology, and Management." In *The North Atlantic Fisheries: Successes, Failures, and Challenges,* edited by Ragnar Arnason and Lawrence Felt, 37-93. Charlottetown: Institute of Island Studies.

Manchester, Lorne. 1970. *Canada's Fisheries.* Toronto: McGraw-Hill.

The Collapse: A Postmortem

Anderson, Mitchell. 2003. "The Cod's Gone, Yet the Deadly Draggers Remain." *Globe and Mail,* 30 April.

Bavington, Dean. 2010. *Managed Annihilation: An Unnatural History of the Newfoundland Cod Collapse.* Vancouver: UBC Press.

Chantraine, P. 1993. *The Last Cod Fish: Life and Death of the Newfoundland Way of Life.* St. John's: Jesperson.

Harris, Michael. 1998. *Lament for an Ocean: The Collapse of the Atlantic Cod Fishery, a True Crime Story.* Toronto: McClelland and Stewart.

Hutchings, Jeffrey A. 1999. "The Biological Collapse of Newfoundland's Northern Cod." In *Fishing Places and Fishing People: Traditions and Issues in Canadian Small-Scale Fisheries,* edited by Dianne Newell and Rosemary E. Ommer, 39-93. Toronto: University of Toronto Press.

Kennedy, John. 1997. "At the Crossroads: Newfoundland and Labrador Communities in a Changing International Context." *Canadian Review of Sociology and Anthropology* 34, 3: 297-318.

Matthews, David Ralph. 1995. "Commons versus Open Access: The Collapse of Canada's East Coast Fishery." *The Ecologist* 25, 2-3: 86-92.

The Pacific Coast Fishery

McKervill, Hugh W. 1967. *The Salmon People: The Story of Canada's West Coast Fishing Industry.* Sidney, BC: Gray's Publishing.

Millerd, F.W. 1988. "Windjammers to Eighteen Wheelers: The Impact of Transportation Technology on the Development of British Columbia's Fishing Industry." *BC Studies* 78: 28-52.

Newell, Dianne. 1989. *The Development of the Pacific Salmon-Canning Industry: A Grown Man's Game.* Montreal and Kingston: McGill-Queen's University Press.

–. 1993. *Tangled Webs of History: Indians and the Law in Canada's Pacific Coast Fisheries*. Toronto: University of Toronto Press.

Declining Salmon Populations
Brown, Dennis. 2005. *Salmon Wars: The Battle for the West Coast Salmon Fishery*. Madeira Park, BC: Harbour Publishing.
Cone, J. 1995. *A Common Fate: Endangered Salmon and the People of the Pacific Northwest*. New York: Henry Holt.

Mismanagement in the Salmon Fishery
Canadian Wildlife Federation. 2005. "Brief on the Wild Salmon Policy." 18 February.
Cernetig, Miro. 1995. "Tobin Vows to Overhaul BC Fishery." *Globe and Mail,* 8 March.

Howard, Ross. 1995. "Pacific Fishery Facing Collapse, Report Warns." *Globe and Mail,* 1 February.
Institute of Fisheries Analysis. 2000. "Fisheries and Oceans' 'Wild Salmon Policy': A View from the Perspective of Science." Simon Fraser University, Burnaby.
Knudsen, E. Eric, Donald McDonald, Dudley W. Reiser, Cleveland R. Steward, and Jack E. Williams. 1999. *Sustainable Fisheries Management: Pacific Salmon*. Boca Raton, FL: CRC Press.
Taylor, James E., III. 1999. *Making Salmon: An Environmental History of the Northwest Fisheries Crisis*. Seattle: University of Washington Press.

13

The North and Climate Change

*We must on this, our last frontier proceed only with the most complete
knowledge of and concern for flora and fauna of the North, for the biomass
of the forest and the tundra.*

— THOMAS BERGER, CANADIAN LAWYER AND JURIST,
MACKENZIE VALLEY PIPELINE INQUIRY, 1977

CANADA'S NORTH – ITS Arctic and Subarctic regions – is in transition. It is not only Canada's last resources development frontier but also the country's (and the world's) barometer to measure the pace and effects of climate change. Until the twentieth century, the people of the North – Inuit, Dene, and Metis – and their environment were largely insulated from the vast changes that accompanied European settlement. Over the last hundred years, however, incursions into the North by hunters, governments, and resource companies have changed the relationship between people and their environment and drawn attention to the region's fragility. The Mackenzie Valley Pipeline Inquiry in the 1970s brought these issues to light, and its report reflected not only growing environmental awareness but also the importance of integrating local ecological knowledge into environmental assessments of future development plans. Today, the effects of climate change in the North are occurring at a rate twice that experienced by the rest of the

world. As the region's ice recedes, new resources are being exposed, intensifying both exploration and competing sovereignty claims among northern nations. Canada's minimal climate change policy, which is guided by the incompatible goals of protecting the North and exploiting its resources, has proved inadequate in dealing with this unfolding situation.

Canadian Sovereignty in the North

Canada's Arctic and Subarctic lands, those inland and coastal areas north of the treeline, comprise nearly 40 percent of the country's landmass. The landscape is unique. Above the treeline lies the taiga, a partially forested area that separates the treeless tundra to the north from boreal forest to the south. The treeline runs east on a diagonal from the Beaufort Sea in the northwest to northern Hudson Bay and through the Ungava Peninsula in Quebec and Labrador. Until recently, the region was occupied almost exclusively by Inuit and Dene people, who over centuries learned to adapt to the harsh climate and environment and build economies and cultures centred on the region's abundant flora and fauna, particularly seal, whale, caribou, and waterfowl.

The Inuit had only limited contact with Europeans for two hundred years after the Hudson's Bay Company first arrived in the North in 1670. In the late nineteenth century, the company had 250 posts and stores in the North, but the fur trade adapted its operations to the Inuit and Dene's seasonal rhythms. Christian churches had likewise established outposts in the North, from which missionaries tried to acculturate Aboriginal people. These outposts also provided early education, health, and welfare services sustained by government grants. Following the creation and entry of Northwest Territories and Yukon into Confederation – in 1870 and 1898, respectively – federal police established a few posts, patrolled the region, and dealt with emergencies. The Indian Affairs Department negotiated Treaty 8 (a comprehensive treaty that covers northern Saskatchewan, Alberta, and British Columbia and the southern portions of Northwest Territories) in 1899 and Treaty 11 (negotiated with the Dene in Northwest Territories following the discovery of oil in the Mackenzie Valley) in 1921. Unlike in the south, however, the treaties were not followed by an influx of white settlers. Inuit and Dene continued to rely on wildlife for subsistence, and their culture, well-being, identity, and art continued to centre on their traditional lifestyle. Nevertheless, increased trade introduced local people to Western diseases such as typhoid, tuberculosis, and influenza, which were passed up the corridors

of disease transmission, first by fur traders and whalers and then by southerners who came to build transportation, communications, and resources infrastructure.

Governmental institutions in the Arctic were limited until its oil was discovered and other nations began to pose a threat to Canadian sovereignty. The Council of the North-West Territories, created in 1870, met infrequently. In 1905, a commissioner who represented the minister of the interior had an appointed four-person council. The council had no indigenous members and was moribund until 1921. With the discovery of gold in the North and the resulting influx of population, in 1898 Ottawa passed the Yukon Territory Act to constitute Yukon as separate and distinct from the North-West Territories. As in the NWT, the council, however, made few decisions because Ottawa set policy for the North.

Between 1913 and 1918, in response to competing claims from other nations, the federal government launched the Canadian Arctic Expedition to explore, gather information, and assert Canadian sovereignty in the North (see Figure 13.1). The expedition, which found two new islands, was led by explorer Vilhjalmur Stefansson and included specialists in anthropology, biology, and earth sciences. It had three mandates: to explore and map the western Arctic coast and islands, to survey local peoples, and to document the region's resources.

Infrastructure and Resource Development

The new knowledge gathered by the Canadian Arctic Expedition made southern legislators enthusiastic about opening the

FIGURE 13.1 John Cox, a scientist with the Canadian Arctic Expedition, takes latitude measurements at Cape Barrow, Northwest Territories (now Nunavut). In addition to asserting sovereignty, the expedition provided Canada with more knowledge of its northern landscape, peoples, and wildlife.
Canadian Museum of Civilization, 43279

THE CANADIAN ARCTIC EXPEDITION

Using depth soundings through ice, the Canadian Arctic Expedition mapped the edge of the continental shelf, including the western Arctic coast and islands. Members of the expedition gathered information from meteorological, magnetic, and marine biological investigations and documented the geography, geology, resources, wildlife, and people of the Mackenzie River Delta and other areas. They paid particular attention to promising trade routes and copper deposits. The expedition had a considerable impact on the Inuit and Inuvialuit, to whom new tools, guns, and utensils were introduced. Members also drew local people into the fox trade, an industry that led to increased use of Banks Island by the Inuvialuit. The expedition collected thousands of specimens of animals, plants, fossils, rocks, and artifacts and produced fourteen volumes of research, countless photos, and film footage.

North to development and also attracted the attention of resource companies. Between the 1920s and 1960s, mining and fishing companies transformed the Canadian Subarctic, particularly around its large lakes – Lake Athabasca, Great Slave Lake, and Great Bear Lake. The Canadian state, including politicians, administrators, and scientists, facilitated their efforts. The government received royalties in return for providing companies with access to northern resources. It also gave companies tax breaks and government-backed securities to underwrite the costs of exploration and development. This collaborative process between government and business led to the creation of industrial infrastructure – roads, communications networks, and airports – and to the growth of towns.

As these companies moved into the North, they had to adapt exploration and mining technologies to local conditions, including ice, muskeg, and sudden seasonal changes. They sometimes relied on local knowledge, for example, hiring indigenous guides and boat pilots, but they typically viewed the region (in a pattern familiar from the colonial period) as a no man's land that was theirs to use as they liked, often disdaining local people's customs, observations, and understanding of the Arctic environment. After the Canadian Geological Survey mapped the region's minerals in 1916-17 as part of the larger Arctic Expedition, entrepreneurs began exploring for gold, silver, uranium, nickel, and radium near Great Slave Lake, Lake Athabasca, and Great Bear Lake. The Port Radium mine opened near

FIGURE 13.2 The first oil well in Norman Wells, Northwest Territories, 1925. The well initially produced small amounts of oil but over time experienced booms and busts that shaped the local community. Norman Wells today is a small town with links to both Yellowknife and Inuvik, but it may expand in the future along with greater oil production in the Arctic.
NWT Archives, Canada, Department of the Interior fonds, G-1979-001: 0232

the latter in 1933, signalling "the arrival of international capital interested in the application of industrial fuels and technologies to Subarctic resource exploitation ... and thus ... the twentieth-century industrial transformation of the Northwest" (Piper 2009, 39). The twentieth-century industrial model led companies to exploit certain resources and remove them on barges, roads, or in airplanes to markets. In the Great Slave Lake area, as elsewhere, the creation of mines stimulated the growth of urban communities such as Yellowknife, where bush pilots and mechanics built makeshift hangars, small-business owners opened log cabin warehouses, and workers slept in tents. A portable sawmill was barged across the lake to cut lumber for hotels, restaurants, and permanent warehouses, a process repeated in other northern mining towns.

Oil and gas exploration and development began in earnest in the 1920s. In 1911, fur trader J.K. Cornwall had reported oil seepages at Fort Norman. Three years later, P.O. Bosworth staked three oil leases on the northeastern bank of the Mackenzie River, an area where only a few thousand Dene, some fur traders, and missionaries lived. Imperial Oil, through its subsidiary the Northwest Company, bought Bosworth's leases and in 1919 sent a crew into the blackfly-infested muskeg to drill its first well. The company struck oil in 1920 north of Fort Norman and built a small steam-powered gasoline and diesel oil refinery (see Figure 13.2). It chartered two single-engine German Junkers aircraft with floats or skis to land on water or snow to transport men and equipment from Edmonton. This was the first regular industrial air service in Canada. The isolated Norman Wells field

was a small producer that supplied fuel locally to riverboats and floatplanes. It closed
temporarily in 1925 because there was little
local demand for oil. In the 1930s, however,
a market for Norman Wells crude opened up
at the Port Radium mines and at the Con
and Negus mines at Yellowknife. In 1944, the
Norman Wells field was linked to Whitehorse.
The field therefore became part of the US
CANOL pipeline project, which in turn
supplied both the Alaska Highway project
(completed by the US army during the war)
and the North West Staging Route (an air
route from Edmonton to Fairbanks, Alaska,
with airports built during the war).

Geological surveys, military operations,
resource exploration and development, and
patrols depended on a vast infrastructure of
airlines, roads, highways, and pipelines. The
Canadian Air Board began to develop an
Arctic industry in 1919, building airports for
bush pilots and early commercial pilots and
upgrading the stations for weather reporting.
In the 1930s, it installed radio beacons along
the main flight routes, which expanded during the Second World War. Highways and
communications networks grew during the
Cold War to include continental defence
infrastructure such as Distant Early Warning
(DEW) monitoring stations, and the United
States improved, straightened, and upgraded
nearly 1,560 kilometres of the original Alaska
Highway and built 725 kilometres of new
road. The Canadian government likewise
built the Mackenzie and Cassiar Highways
and improved the NorthWest Staging Route
and phone lines to upgrade communication
networks in the North. In the 1950s, it also
increased its involvement in the Arctic,

spurred by Prime Minister Diefenbaker's
"northern vision" of national development.
This expanding infrastructure gradually ended the region's isolation and facilitated the
influx of goods and people. These changes
encouraged Aboriginal people to take up
wage employment and become involved in
a money-based economy. They also created
pollution, altered landscapes, and led to
government programs that pressured
Aboriginal people to adapt to a less mobile
existence.

The Environmental Consequences of Development

The development of the North had an immediate adverse effect on people, wildlife,
and the land. As in the rest of Canada, resource development had a detrimental impact on the environment, precipitating air,
soil, and water pollution that disrupted the
region's fragile ecosystems and, in turn, contributed to climate change (see Figure 13.3).
For example, although Eldorado Mines
efficiently recycled and reused water and
wastes, it still did much damage to the environment starting in the 1930s, when it
dumped uranium-silver mine tailings into
Great Bear Lake and several other lakes that
were converted into tailing containment
ponds (see Chapter 7). Canada promoted
and supported northern development through
grants and tax concessions to resource companies, but it often ignored their exploitive
treatment of the environment and the waste
they left behind when they moved on to
new, more economically viable areas or when
they declared bankruptcy to avoid cleanup

FIGURE 13.3 The Pine Point Mine, an open pit lead and zinc mine south of Great Slave Lake, was a joint venture between the Canadian government and Cominco that was developed in the 1950s. A modern town appeared beside the mine in the 1960s, but Cominco closed the mine in 1988. The town shut down, and all the buildings were either removed or demolished.
NWT Archives, Canada, Department of the Interior fonds, N-1987-021: 0056

responsibilities. When the wartime CANOL pipeline project ended in 1945, for example, crews deserted their camp across the river from Norman Wells. It rotted and rusted until 1977, when the Canadian government recognized the wreckage as a hazard and razed it.

Development projects brought in people, food, and fossil fuels but also contributed to cultural dislocation. In the postwar period, about twenty new towns appeared as part of the development process, and as they began to dot the landscape, local people moved to them for part of the year to take up jobs as wage earners. By the 1970s, most Inuit lived in rows of prefabricated buildings, which included basic amenities, schools, and nursing

stations. The men travelled to camps to hunt but left their families behind. As Inuit and Dene became more reliant on wages, without secure employment, unemployment increased. Life in town also meant eating more nontraditional foods and a more sedentary lifestyle, both of which had health implications. The problems associated with this trend were compounded by the effects of contagious diseases, the depletion of local wildlife, and the government's failure to take local knowledge into consideration in its minimal attempts to deal with environmental degradation.

Diseases, first introduced by whalers, fur traders, and missionaries, continued to ravage Inuit and Dene communities as labourers moved north to work in the resources sector or to service infrastructure. In 1942, for instance, measles spread from Alaska Highway crews to local populations. The following year, indigenous people suffered dysentery, jaundice, German measles, and meningococcic meningitis. In the 1950s, personnel at an air base in Labrador spread measles that devastated Inuit along Ungava Bay in northern Quebec. The North's small, dispersed, and isolated populations helped contain epidemics, but the climate and malnutrition enhanced the effects of disease, despite government efforts to provide medical care.

The arrival of non-Aboriginal people likewise put pressure on the region's wildlife. For instance, when American explorer Robert Peary decided to "live off the country" on Ellesmere Island during his excursions to the North Pole, he hired northern Greenlanders to hunt for his crew. They overhunted the muskox population, and its precipitous decline influenced early conservation efforts,

including a 1917 hunting ban. Both muskox and caribou populations also began to decline when Inuit, Dene, and Metis switched from spears and bows and arrows to rifles. The Mackenzie Delta caribou nearly disappeared because of overhunting by local people and by American whaling crews. When conservation officers performed aerial surveys of barren ground caribou following the Second World War, they discovered that a species that had once existed in the millions had been reduced to thousands.

Although declines in species populations had multiple causes – including local and commercial hunting, industrial projects, and climate change – scientists employed by the federal government blamed Inuit and Dene hunting practices and their reliance on Arctic animals for clothing and food. In essence, policy makers and wildlife managers problematized Aboriginal hunting and culture. By the early twentieth century, hunting in Western culture had become the preserve

BUILDING THE ALASKA HIGHWAY

The Alaska Highway was built during the Second World War to connect Alaska to military bases in the southern states. The highway cut through Canada, and its construction not only involved the importation of large American work crews – forty-six thousand soldiers and civilian contractors – into the Arctic, it also stimulated other construction projects, including telephone, telegraph, and radio communications networks.

Using bulldozers, sometimes five in a row, the crews blasted through forests and cleared peat moss covering permafrost. When the unprotected permafrost began to melt, vehicles got trapped in the muskeg. To correct the problem, the crews built corduroy or log roads across the taiga, upon which they then built the highway. Crews were told they were "conquering the wilderness to help defeat an evil enemy," the Japanese (Twichell

1992, 170). To build the base at Hay River, the crews blasted out rapids, blew up cliffs, and built over portages. The soldiers' cigarette butts caused extensive fires that destroyed thousands of hectares of forests, and leaks from pipelines threatened drinking water. Local people were dismayed by the waste and destruction. Crews left behind supplies, including huge uneaten caches of meat, they abandoned equipment to rust, and they

threw out bedding supplies rather than distributing them to the community. Alcohol also became a problem because, even though it was illegal to sell it to Aboriginal people, some of the soldiers traded alcohol for food or sex.

REINDEER FARMING: A FAILED EXPERIMENT

The Canadian government participated in a number of unsuccessful experiments in game ranching and wildlife conservation in the North, the most famous example being the importation of reindeer.

Vilhjalmur Stefansson, for instance, convinced both the government and private interests to introduce the reindeer to Canada to supplement indigenous people's diets as caribou populations declined. In 1932,

the government established Reindeer Station in the Mackenzie Valley as the headquarters of its project to introduce reindeer farming to the North. It arranged for 3,442 reindeer to be herded from

Alaska. Intended to transform nomadic Inuit into herders, the project was unsuccessful. The herds were sold back to the government in 1956, and the station was abandoned in 1969.

FIGURE 13.4 Reindeer Station on the Mackenzie River Delta, ca. 1936. Established by the Canadian government in the 1930s, the station was used to manage reindeer who had survived a five-year trek from Alaska to the Mackenzie River Delta. The reindeer grazed on a huge reserve east of the delta, on the former site of a Hudson's Bay Company trading post.
NWT Archives, Canada, Department of the Interior fonds, N-1979-050: 0313

of the rich, and transportation infrastructure opened Yukon to commercial and big game hunting. The arrival of non-Aboriginal hunters in turn led to game laws, trapline registration, and a new view of wildlife as an export commodity rather than a staple. The conservation ethos, such as it was, prevented local control or use of protected wildlife. Aboriginal peoples' traditions of self-government remained strong, however, and they resisted outside ideas about wildlife.

Following the Second World War, the government tried to protect wildlife and fisheries from overharvesting, but its efforts proved to be both inadequate and insensitive to the needs and traditions of indigenous hunters. For instance, wildlife managers interpreted local practices such as mass caribou killings at river crossings as "wanton

slaughter." In reality, Aboriginal hunters left the carcasses to freeze or ferment for later use. When wildlife managers conducted research and created sanctuaries and parks to protect caribou, they often disrupted Aboriginal hunting practices and, in extreme cases, forced communities to relocate. Indigenous people and the government tried to manage hunting through a system of quotas that would allow for subsistence hunting and, if numbers were high enough, a commercial hunt. Inuit argued, however, that the research methods employed by wildlife biologists were flawed and biased since they did not take local knowledge about animal behaviour and movements into consideration in their population surveys.

The same criticisms held true for the government's fisheries regulations. Fishing in local lakes and rivers was sustainable when conducted by local populations and sports fishers, but the commercial fishery, which focused on Arctic char and whitefish, was not. Administrators favoured scientific models and commercial fishing companies over Aboriginal people's local knowledge and warnings about overfishing. The result was environmental pollution as companies dumped fish waste in the North's vast but ecologically fragile lakes. Indigenous peoples' persistent adherence to their own fishing and hunting methods, despite pressures from resources companies, and their knowledge of wildlife not only informed their astute criticisms of the commercial Arctic fisheries and quota policies for hunters, it also led them to communicate their wishes and needs concerning the proposed Mackenzie Valley Pipeline.

The Mackenzie Valley (Berger) Pipeline Inquiry

The Mackenzie Valley Pipeline Inquiry was a turning point in northern resources development. Commissioned by the federal government in 1974 to investigate the social, environmental, and economic impact of a proposed pipeline through Yukon and the Mackenzie River Valley to Alberta, the inquiry was the government's first serious attempt to examine the impact of development on local people and the northern environment.

International oil companies had discovered billions of cubic metres of oil and gas in Alaska's Prudhoe Bay and in Canada's Mackenzie Delta in 1968. The discovery came at a time when environmentalists were raising awareness about the damage caused

THE THELON WILDLIFE SANCTUARY AND FIRST NATIONS

In the early twentieth century, the federal government, responding to demands from conservationists, established wildlife sanctuaries (see Chapter 4). The sanctuaries helped spread the idea of wildlife preservation throughout the country, but their establishment also interfered with Aboriginal hunting rights in certain areas. In 1927, for example, the government created the Thelon Wildlife Sanctuary, the largest and most remote wildlife refuge in North America. Located near Great Slave Lake, in "one of the last great, unaltered ecosystems" in the world, the refuge had a mandate to protect large northern mammals such as migratory caribou and muskox, whose numbers were declining partly from habitat loss but also from overhunting ("The Thelon Wildlife Sanctuary" n.d.). The sanctuary's remoteness, however, left it without a true wildlife management policy by either level of government. It was closed to development and protected from hunters, including Aboriginal people.

In the 1970s, the sanctuary came under pressure from First Nations and from large transnational mining companies that wanted to develop the area. Today, hunters work with officials to administer northern parks' wildlife policy and the sanctuary. The Nunavut Land Claims Agreement of 1992 led to a management plan to give indigenous hunters access to the sanctuary. The plan's advisory committee was composed of representatives from both government and local communities, and the plan was subject to the federal government's Species at Risk Act (2003) and the Nunavut Wildlife Act (2003). The Wildlife Act specifies that local hunter and trapper organizations are to manage and regulate the harvesting of wildlife. Co-management requires that environmentalists respect local knowledge and that Aboriginal people augment their expertise with knowledge of modern ecology. Environmentalists and Aboriginal groups sometimes disagree about wildlife management issues because they have different priorities. Aboriginal people want to maintain their hunting culture, whereas environmentalists want to protect and preserve wildlife species.

by oil and gas exploration and development and by pipeline projects. The 1973 OPEC oil embargo, which caused a sharp rise in oil prices, however, spread concern about oil supply and stimulated pipeline development plants. The proposed pipeline would solve logistical problems with shipping, facilitate on-site oil and gas refining, and spur further explorations for offshore oil. In 1973, following much debate, the Nixon administration in the United States authorized construction of the Trans-Alaska Pipeline from Alaska's North Slope to the Port of Valdez in southern Alaska. Tankers would then ship the oil to the southern states. Meanwhile, in Canada, the federal government introduced guidelines for Arctic pipelines in 1970 and broadened them in 1972. Companies such as Dome and an international consortium called Arctic Gas, both subsidized by the government, explored the idea of a pipeline corridor from the North. Two consortiums, Canadian Arctic Gas Pipeline and Foothills Pipe Lines, eventually put forward detailed proposals. The first consortium proposed two pipelines: one from Prudhoe Bay, Alaska, through

northern Yukon to the Mackenzie River Delta in Northwest Territories, and another through the Mackenzie Valley to Alberta. The second consortium proposed a single pipeline through the Mackenzie Valley.

Although the federal government favoured the construction of a pipeline, it appointed Justice Thomas Berger as commissioner to head the Mackenzie Valley Pipeline Inquiry in response to pressure from the environmental movement, Aboriginal groups, and the NDP, which held the balance of power in the House of Commons between 1972 and 1974. It remains unclear why Prime Minister Trudeau appointed Berger, a former leader of the NDP in British Columbia and a champion of Aboriginal rights, to head the commission to evaluate the pipeline proposals (see Figure 13.5). Berger's "Magic Circus," as contemporary pundits named his public commission meetings in the Arctic, departed from past approaches. The inquiry examined the engineering science of northern pipelines; the geology, geography, and ecology of the Mackenzie Valley; environmental protection issues; and the future of indigenous peoples. In an innovative process, it heard three hundred experts in Yellowknife, visited thirty-five communities, received one thousand submissions, and listened to seventeen hundred witnesses in seven languages at informal well-publicized hearings. The inquiry increased Canadians' awareness of the North and stimulated local peoples' self-awareness, which influenced future northern development. This approach brought Aboriginal people and public interest groups into the decision-making process, and subsidies helped them to make their presentations effective. During the hearings, pipeline supporters

FIGURE 13.5 Chief Justice Berger of the Supreme Court of British Columbia strikes a pensive pose as he listens to testimony on 6 March 1974 during the Mackenzie Valley Pipeline Inquiry in Yellowknife.
Canadian Press, staff reporter

characterized these groups as radical, but their appearance at the hearings was very professional.

Berger, an effective communicator, learned that the North was a region of conflicting goals and aspirations. Aboriginal groups would oppose the pipeline until their land claims were settled. Canadian Arctic Gas Pipeline wanted Aboriginal claims excluded from the inquiry, however. The territorial council supported the pipeline, but Wally Frith, a Metis from Fort McPherson and the first Aboriginal member of Parliament for Northwest Territories, opposed it. The local business community, largely non-Aboriginal, supported the proposed pipeline because its members believed it would advance industry. Berger assumed that gas and oil in the western Arctic could be transported through the Mackenzie Valley, but he sought the best way to protect the environment and Aboriginal peoples' interests. In consultation with Inuit and Dene, the commission learned that policy makers, companies, and government officials often ignored Aboriginal institutions and languages, values, and customs to focus on short-term gains for non-Aboriginal people.

The pipeline would require a huge infrastructure of wharves, warehouses, storage sites, airstrips, roads, and boats. Building it would require 130 gravel operations, 6,000 pipeline workers, and 1,200 workers to build gas plants and gathering systems. Building the pipeline's estimated six hundred river and stream crossings would depend on the importation of countless aircraft, tractors, earthmovers, trucks, and trailers. The proposed project posed major engineering challenges, but the construction plans were uncertain

because the pipeline would carry frozen gas underground. Berger discussed the possibility of frost heave and damaged piping when frozen gas hit an unfrozen section. Pipeline construction was scheduled for winter, but delays or cost overruns could cause work to stretch into the summer, when the environmental impact would, potentially, be greater.

The inquiry also investigated the pipeline's effect on wildlife and habitats. It learned that the proposed pipeline from Prudhoe Bay, Alaska, would cross flats and adversely affect the routes and livelihoods of migratory birds such as ducks, geese, and loons and of raptors, including peregrine falcons and golden eagles. These species used the coastal plains in Yukon and Alaska as a staging area for their long southern migrations in the fall. The pipeline's coastal route would also run through the Porcupine caribou's calving range, the last remaining in the world. The interior route would pass through the caribou herd's winter range, likewise reducing its numbers and undermining the Old Crow people's economy. The delta region, where fish, birds, and mammals fed and reproduced was also a calving area for white whales in the summer.

The owners of small businesses argued that the pipeline would create growth and jobs for Aboriginal people. Yet Aboriginal people pointed out that sustenance and income from hunting, fishing, and trapping remained important in the North, whereas large-scale projects to tap nonrenewable resources rarely provided permanent employment for many. The commission learned that once the pipeline was completed, only 250 people would be required to operate it, and that the jobs would be of a technical nature and probably filled by qualified personnel from the south. Aboriginal groups understood the pipeline would provide only short-term employment and advised the commission that strengthening their more reliable traditional economy was more important. They also testified that they feared the influx of workers required by the project would increase social problems, damage the land, and harm their identities. Berger concluded that their fears were well founded because increased alcoholism, crime, violence, and welfare dependency often accompanied the rapid expansion of the wage system. Inuit and Dene presentations reflected a new energy and sense of leadership. Besides addressing land claims and land-use issues, presenters discussed renewable and nonrenewable resources, schools, health and social services, and the future restructuring of political institutions in the North.

After the hearings, Berger wrote his report quickly because he wanted to influence the National Energy Board before it released its report. The first volume went to Minister Warren Allmand in April 1977, and the second was released in November. *Northern Frontier, Northern Homeland* was a landmark report. The commission concluded that the proposed route across northern Yukon would affect the environment to such an extent that the government should not approve it. The pipeline would destroy land vital to the survival of large numbers of mammals, birds, and fish, and this land would need to be protected from use to preserve habitats, species, and local economies. It concluded that the route proposed by the second consortium would not threaten wildlife populations as much but would require more assessments of Aboriginal peoples' social and economic needs. The government, it advised, should not give the proposal its unqualified support or financial guarantees until these environmental concerns were addressed. Berger recommended designating Yukon territory north of the Porcupine River as a national wilderness park. The government established Ivvavik National Park in 1984 and Vuntut National Park in 1995 with constitutional guarantees.

After rejecting the idea of building an oil and gas corridor across the delta, the commission instead recommended creating a bird sanctuary in the outer delta and a whale sanctuary in the West Mackenzie Bay for calving. Protecting the area would depend on controlling the timing and extent of Dome Petroleum's exploratory drilling in the Beaufort Sea because the proliferation of wells increased the risk of oil spills that could devastate the delta habitat and its wildlife. Berger's report recommended strict limits on oil and gas facilities and that the government independently assess the feasibility, desirability, and impact of a series of proposals for northern oil and gas exploration and development. To do so, the government would need an ongoing comprehensive program of northern science and research.

Berger decided the pipeline should not precede the settlement of Aboriginal claims. Aboriginal people needed time to organize a new partnership of interests to achieve their goals and to develop their institutions to deal with the social consequences of a pipeline. The pipeline's immediate construction, he argued, would set back the Inuvik and other delta communities. Although orderly exploratory drilling in the delta and the Beaufort Sea could continue, Berger did

FIGURE 13.6 The confluence of the Smoky and Peace Rivers, part of the Mackenzie River system in Alberta. Like other regions in the river system, this area, now a provincial park, is the home of many types of birds and contains important wildlife corridors for large animals.
Mhalifu

not believe the exploitation of nonrenewable resources by large companies with technology would be the basis of the North's future economy. Rather, a renewable resource economy would strengthen Aboriginal peoples' traditional economy, enabling them to participate in the industrial system without becoming completely dependent on it. In Berger's view, a "rational program of northern development" based on northern peoples' ideals and aspirations would result in a diversified economy. Nevertheless, in 1983, Norman Wells expanded operations when Exxon's engineers built six artificial islands in the middle of the Mackenzie River to tap into the oil under the river and constructed a twelve-inch pipeline to carry the crude to

transfer terminals in western Alberta. The company's islands, buildings, and drilling derricks made huge incursions in the environment.

THE COMMITTEE FOR THE ORIGINAL PEOPLES' ENTITLEMENT

The Mackenzie Valley Pipeline Inquiry focused the nation's attention on Aboriginal issues in the North and the region's fragile environment. In 1970, the Committee for the Original Peoples' Entitlement was established to protect traditional lands and ways of life from mineral and petroleum exploration. The committee participated actively in the inquiry and negotiated the first land claim, in 1984, for the Inuvialuit. It also safeguarded the interests of Inuvialuit through organizations such as the Inuvialuit Games Council and the Inuvialuit Development Corporation. In the 1980s, it pressed for self-government, which resulted in the founding of Nunavut in 1999. From 1994, Aboriginal peoples and the government negotiated and settled other Arctic land claims.

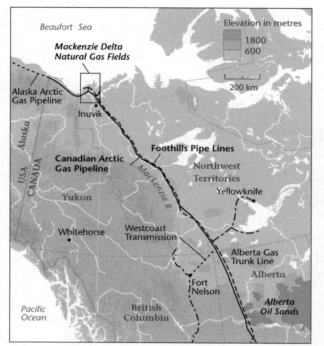

FIGURE 13.7 This map shows the routes of the proposed Mackenzie Valley Pipeline, and the one route Justice Berger accepted but whose development he recommended be postponed

The commission's report postponed pipeline construction in the Mackenzie Valley for ten years until Aboriginal claims were settled (see Figure 13.7). The inquiry was "a unique and valuable experiment in participatory – or advocatory – democracy" (Peacock 1977, 182). The report's impact was profound in that for the first time a large development project was postponed by the federal government. In response to the report, the National Energy Board accepted the second consortium's proposal. By the time it made its decision, however, rising oil and gas prices and inflation had caused the project to be abandoned, and a new proposal was not agreed upon for thirty years.

Companies began to seriously consider a pipeline again in the 1990s. The Mackenzie Natural Gas Pipeline Project Group, which comprised a number of exploration and development companies, proposed a pipeline along the Mackenzie Valley to link gas-producing wells to an existing pipeline in northwestern Alberta. Its backers discovered three natural gas fields in the Mackenzie Delta but recognized that development needed the cooperation of companies, Aboriginal communities, regulatory agencies, and governments. In 1998, the Mackenzie Valley Resource Management Act established the Mackenzie Valley Environmental Impact Review Board to assess proposals. Oil and gas groups opened negotiations with the Aboriginal Pipeline Group, which represented the Inuvialuit, Sahtu, and Gwich'in, and they signed an agreement in 2003 that gave Aboriginal people one-third ownership of the project. In 2011, Cabinet approved the pipeline, and the National Energy Board granted final approval, which concluded the regulatory process. The pipeline's future, however, remains uncertain. Although the companies signed agreements with the three First Nations in the Aboriginal Pipeline Group, they did not sign an agreement with the Dehcho, who hold land along the pipeline route. The Dehcho had not reached a land claims agreement with the federal government and expressed dismay when the government, in 2010, unilaterally terminated the ecological protection of Edéhzhíe (Horn Plateau) on their land in Northwest Territories, an action that made minerals beneath the surface available for prospecting and mining. The Dehcho interpreted this action as a betrayal of trust.

Global Warming

Although the Mackenzie Valley Pipeline Inquiry opened the way for a more inclusive approach to environmental issues in the North, global warming since the 1970s has proven to be a nearly insurmountable problem, one that challenges even Aboriginal peoples' knowledge and adaptive strategies. Images of huge glaciers breaking and melting in the ocean, of polar bears stranded on tiny ice floes, or of seals huddling on shore as islands of ice melt now symbolize for many the dramatic effects of a global trend. With melting occurring more quickly than scientists expected, the urgency for action on climate change is apparent.

The link between developments in the North and climate change caught the attention of Canadians when the Intergovernmental Panel on Climate Change noted in its 2007 report that "warming of the climate system is unequivocal" and is largely the result of human activity. Although climate change is a global phenomenon, the panel concluded that its effects are greater at higher northern latitudes, where "average Arctic temperatures have increased at almost twice the global average rate in the past 100 years" (IPCC 2007, 30). As glaciers, ice caps, and polar sheets melt, the sea level rises. Since 1978, annual average Arctic sea ice has receded by 2.7 percent per decade. In 2004, a scientific report presented to the Arctic Council predicted that global warming would profoundly change the North's climate, wildlife, and people. If too much permafrost melts, it will expose deeply buried ice that isolates an estimated 400 billion tonnes of frozen methane deposits. If these deposits release into the atmosphere, they would, in turn, contribute to global warming.

Melting sea ice and global warming have already had an effect on the North's wildlife and, by extension, the Aboriginal communities who depend upon it. Polar bears, for example, depend on floes, sheets of floating ice, to hunt seals. As the sea ice melts, they are forced ashore, where they spend the summer fasting because they do not know how to forage for food on land. If the ice caps continue to melt sooner and form later, polar bears will become too thin to reproduce. Warmer temperatures have also caused the treeline to move north, drawing new species such as beavers and brown bears from the south. Their arrival is changing the species composition of the North's ecosystems and, in combination with melting sea ice, the rhythms of the hunt. The Intergovernmental Panel on Climate Change predicts this trend will probably have a detrimental effect on the North as "barriers to species invasions are lowered" (IPCC 2007, 52). In the long-term, climate change will also have a detrimental impact on Aboriginal communities.

A growing awareness of the effects of climate change on the North has inspired

CARIBOU: AN EARLY WARNING SIGN OF GLOBAL WARMING

Caribou, once a mainstay of Inuit and Dene peoples in the Arctic, are being killed off by global warming. Although regional fluctuations in caribou populations are normal, half of the global caribou population has disappeared in the past fifty years. Canada is home to half of the current total population. In 2009, a study revealed that twenty-nine of the country's existing fifty-seven herds were not self-sustaining. Their disappearance will be devastating for northern people who continue to rely on them for food and clothing. Scientists speculate that, in addition to the damaging effects of hunting and industrial development on the caribou's habitat, global warming has caused snow to fall as freezing rain and form ice that covers the caribou's main food, lichen. Warmer temperatures also bring more mosquitoes and flies, which pester caribou while they forage, causing them to lose weight so they have trouble reproducing and caring for calves.

environmental historians to focus more attention on the North and to expand their research to include the modern period. Stephen Bocking, who has studied the role of scientists in the Arctic from the 1940s to the 1970s, suggests that understanding the work of scientists, particularly those working out in the landscape, will not only make for better analyses of both historical and contemporary changes overtaking the North, it will also increase attention to the issue of climate change as an environmental and public policy issue.

Climate Change and Public Policy

Global warming in the North is a harbinger of things to come, a wake-up call to national governments to work together to ensure the future of humanity and the planet's survival. In 1988, Canada hosted an international science conference at Montreal titled "The Changing Atmosphere: Implications for Global Security" that led to the Montreal Protocol (see Chapter 10), an admission that climate change was a problem and that a target should be set for carbon emission reductions. The Rio Conference, held in 1992, reaffirmed this need and, through the United Nations Framework Convention on Climate Change, set a target for a 20-percent reduction in emissions by 2005. The treaty set no mandatory limits on greenhouse gas emissions but instead provided for updates, or protocols, that would set mandatory emission limits.

Immediate political action on the issue was delayed, however, as governments continued to spend millions on subsidies for the fossil fuels industry. Interest groups such as Exxon Mobil also financially supported and encouraged climate change deniers, and the media persisted in reporting "both sides" of the issue even though overwhelming evidence revealed that climate change was already well under way. President George W. Bush's administration supported the efforts of climate deniers as the Pentagon toyed with the idea of trying to manipulate the climate by funding geoengineering as a quick fix to prevent global warming without changing the current economy or consumer culture. Examples included such solar radiation management techniques as stratospheric sulfur aerosols, space mirrors, and cloud reflectivity enhancement. Environmentalists, by contrast, focused on conservation and reducing greenhouse gas emissions, and Al Gore stressed the urgency for action on climate change. As governments missed the target set at the Rio Conference, the Intergovernmental Panel on Climate Change concluded in 2007 that "a wide variety of national policies and instruments are available to governments to create the incentives for mitigation action" (IPCC 2007, 73). These policies and instruments include global cooperation, regulations and targets on emission levels, carbon taxes, tradable emission permits, financial incentives such as subsidies and tax credits, voluntary agreements, educational awareness campaigns, and research and development of new technologies.

In 2002, the Canadian government under Jean Chrétien had agreed to ratify the Kyoto Protocol to achieve "stabilization of greenhouse gas concentrations in the atmosphere at a level that would prevent dangerous anthropogenic interference with the climate system." The protocol had been adopted in December 1997, and it went into force in February 2005. The United States did not ratify the protocol. Upon ratification, Canada agreed to reduce emissions by 6 percent below 1990 levels by the end of the five-year commitment period of 2008-12. Because Canadian emissions rose 15 percent between 1990 and 1999, however, this amounted to a 30-percent reduction. The government planned to meet the target through a combination of incentives, regulations, and tax measures.

Canada's role in climate change negotiations has not been exemplary. In the introduction to the Canadian edition of his book *Heat: How to Stop the Planet from Burning,* George Monbiot accused Stephen Harper's Conservative government of political cowardice for not trying to meet its Kyoto targets, and he blamed Rona Ambrose, minister of the environment and daughter of an oil executive, of filibustering the entire Kyoto Protocol. In March 2006, Ambrose noted that Canada's greenhouse gas emissions were up by 24 percent since ratifying Kyoto. The Harper government at first pledged to develop a made-in-Canada climate change program. It then insisted it would act in accordance with US policy and later threatened to withdraw Canada from the Kyoto Protocol, which his majority government did in 2011. In October 2006, the Harper government introduced the Clean Air Act, which promised to cut greenhouse gas emissions in half by 2050. A year earlier, in July 2005, the government had endorsed the Asia-Pacific Partnership on Clean Development and Climate, an alternative to Kyoto supported by Australia, the United States, Japan, China, India, and South

Korea. The partnership encouraged private-public partnerships in any initiatives to deal with climate change. Harper insisted that China and India, both large polluters who had not signed the Kyoto Protocol, must sign either the protocol or its successor and argued that developing nations must contribute to carbon reduction as much as developed nations, whose economies were responsible for the bulk of carbon emissions.

Canada's policy on climate change has been slow, inadequate, focused on voluntarism, and since the election of the Conservative government, virtually nonexistent. The federal government gave millions of dollars in tax breaks annually to the oil and gas industry – the source of the majority of carbon emissions – but it spent little on alternative energy sources. The federal government released *Climate Change Plan for Canada* in 2002, but its policies have not prevented emissions from rising rapidly since the 1990s, largely because of the Alberta tar sands, which it actively supports and does not regulate. To support the coal and oil and gas industries, it tried to get an agreement to allow Canada a 25-percent increase in emissions at home. The plan failed but demonstrated the government's priorities. Canadian programs contained no financial penalties for greenhouse gas producers and no regulated limit on industrial emissions.

Canada's minimal policy on climate change has emphasized information programs – energy-efficiency labels, advertising, building audits – and subsidies such as efficiency grants to homeowners to voluntarily reduce greenhouse gas emissions. Such programs may change the behaviour of a few but are ineffective in shifting the economy away

CARBON TRADING

Under the Kyoto Protocol, countries can use a trading system to help meet the accord's goal of reducing the world's greenhouse gas emissions. Countries can buy credits, the right to emit a certain amount of carbon dioxide, from countries that exceed their reduction targets. Countries that cut their emissions get credits: one credit for each tonne of reduced emissions. Critics argue that countries should not be allowed to earn credits for anything but real energy reduc-tions – in other words, buying a forest should not count. The carbon-trading system, they argue, is also limited because some of the world's biggest polluters – the United States, China, and India – have either failed to ratify the accord or are not included because they are considered developing countries. As the weaknesses of this approach became more apparent, support for carbon trading to reduce emissions will continue to decline.

from its dependence on fossil fuels. The federal government also cut some programs. In 2009, a report from England disclosed that out of twelve comparable nations, Canada ranked the lowest in policy development and implementation of action to mitigate climate change. Ironically, although the United States has not signed the Kyoto Protocol, its emissions record is better than Canada's. It has spent money on emissions reduction strategies and alternative energy businesses, and local governments and states have initiated their own more aggressive programs. Between 1995 and 2003, the United States reduced air pollution emissions by 45.0 percent, whereas Canada's reduction was only 1.8 percent. If US industry continues to be pressured by government-sponsored research-funding agencies to become more energy-efficient, "Canadian industries will indeed become uncompetitive with the US" (Sallot 2005, A7). President Barack Obama has linked energy efficiency to economic recovery measures, but action has been slow.

Canada has not followed a similar approach and is unlikely to do so.

The Canadian government's policy on climate change continues an age-old pattern: "Successive federal governments ... have engaged in a depressing mixture of bold international commitments and targets and a complete absence of any serious steps aimed at ensuring that emissions would decline" (Robinson 2007, 14). Emissions increased as Harper backed away from Kyoto, supported voluntarism, and delayed action until the Obama administration's position on climate change was clear. In 2009, Canada and the United States agreed to open a dialogue on developing a North American approach to reducing greenhouse gases and exploring cleaner energy technologies, but no action resulted. In the meantime, the Canadian government refused to tackle the oil and gas industry – particularly Alberta's oil sands, which President Obama called "dirty oil" – or encourage alternative energy technologies or sustainable energy policies. Public frustration led one environmental group to take the federal government to court for missing its Kyoto targets.

In 2011, Canada invoked its legal right to withdraw and pulled out of the Kyoto Protocol on climate change. The federal government hoped to avoid $14 billion in penalties for not achieving its Kyoto targets. Meanwhile, the Durban Platform – a deal struck at the United Nations Climate Change Conference held in Durban, South Africa, in 2011, which includes the United States and China – set the stage for a new binding agreement that would require both developed and developing countries to cut their carbon emissions. The terms need to be agreed upon by 2015 and will come into effect in 2020. Canada, however, will not commit to the extension of the Kyoto Protocol included in the new plan.

The unwillingness and apparent inability of governments in Canada to act effectively on climate change reflects disagreements over what must be done and the strength of the ongoing business-government relationship. Government promotes and protects older industries such as automobiles and oil that remain central to the current politico-economic regime. These groups are in no hurry to change the status quo from which they derive wealth, and many politicians share their interests. It took the global financial crisis of 2008 to convince policy makers that structural changes in the automotive industry were necessary. The meltdown resulted in more active regulation of the economy and some limited support for alternative energy companies. Climate change makes new approaches and new technologies essential but still difficult to achieve. Nonetheless, advanced global capitalism is not sustainable in its current form.

IN CANADA, THE Arctic's melting ice caps have stimulated policy makers' concerns about sovereignty in the North and the future of the Northwest Passage, which is likely to become a busy shipping channel as the ice recedes. They have shown less concern about what the melting ice means and even less interest in committing to action on climate change. But action is necessary to protect the public and to give people time to adapt. We do not want to hit a point of no return. As James Hansen of NASA commented in the *New York Times* in 2005, "The Earth's climate is nearing, but has not passed, a tipping point beyond which it will be impossible to avoid climate change with far-ranging undesirable consequences. These include not only the loss of the Arctic as we know it, with all that implies for wildlife and indigenous peoples, but losses on a much vaster scale due to rising seas ... This grim scenario can be halted if the growth of greenhouse gas emissions is slowed in the first quarter of this century."

Works Cited
Hansen, James. 2005. "It's Not Too Late." *New York Times,* 13 December.
IPCC (Intergovernmental Panel on Climate Change). 2007. *Climate Change 2007: Synthesis Report.* http://www.ipcc.ch/.
Peacock, Donald. 1977. *People, Peregrines, and Arctic Pipelines: The Critical Battle to Build Canada's Northern Gas Pipelines.* Vancouver: J.J. Douglas.
Piper, Liza. 2009. *The Industrial Transformation of Subarctic Canada.* Vancouver: UBC Press.
Robinson, John. 2007. "Clearing the Air on Climate Change." *Literary Review of Canada,* 14 October.

Sallot, Jeff. 2005. "Canada Lags on Air-Pollution Cleanup Compared with US, Coalition Finds." *Globe and Mail,* 13 October.
"The Thelon Wildlife Sanctuary: Northwest Territories and Nunavut, Canada." N.d. http://www.thelon.com/sanctuary.htm.
Twichell, Heath. 1992. *Northwest Epic: The Building of the Alaska Highway.* New York: St. Martin's Press.

For Further Reading
Brody, Hugh. 2000. *The Other Side of Eden: Hunters, Farmers, and the Shaping of the World.* Vancouver: Douglas and McIntyre.

Dick, Lyle. 2001. *Muskox Land: Ellesmere Island in the Age of Contact.* Calgary: University of Calgary Press.

Flannery, Tim. 2006. *The Weather Makers: How We Are Changing the Climate and What It Means for Life on Earth.* Toronto: Harper Collins.

Sandlos, John. 2008. *Hunters at the Margins: Native People and Wildlife Conservation in the Northwest Territories.* Vancouver: UBC Press.

Zellen, Barry Scott. 2009. *Arctic Doom, Arctic Boom: The Geopolitics of Climate Change in the Arctic.* Santa Barbara: ABC-Clio.

Canadian Sovereignty in the North

Coates, Kenneth S., P. Whitney Lackenbauer, William R. Morrison, and Greg Poelzer. 2008. "The New North in Canadian History and Historiography." *History Compass* 6, 2: 639-58.

Diubaldo, Richard J. 1998. *Stefansson and the Canadian Arctic.* Montreal and Kingston: McGill-Queen's University Press.

Evenden, Matthew. 2009. "Mapping Cold War Canada: George Kimble's *Canadian Military Geography,* 1949." In *Method and Meaning in Canadian Environmental History,* edited by Alan MacEachern and William J. Turkel, 254-70. Toronto: Nelson Education.

Grant, Shelagh D. 2010. *Polar Imperative: A History of Arctic Sovereignty in North America.* Vancouver: Douglas and McIntyre.

Page, Robert. 1986. *Northern Development: The Canadian Dilemma.* Toronto: McClelland and Stewart.

Piper, Liza. 2009. *The Industrial Transformation of Subarctic Canada.* Vancouver: UBC Press.

Piper, Liza, and John Sandlos. 2007. "A Broken Frontier: Ecological Imperialism in the Canadian North." *Environmental History* 12, 4: 759-95.

Zaslow, Morris. 1971. *The Opening of the Canadian North, 1870-1914.* Toronto: University of Toronto Press.

–. 1988. *The Northward Expansion of Canada, 1914-1967.* Toronto: McClelland and Stewart.

Infrastructure and Resource Development

Dick, Lyle. 2009. "People and Animals in the Arctic: Mediating between Indigenous and Western Knowledge." In *Method and Meaning in Canadian Environmental History,* edited by Alan MacEachern and William J. Turkel, 76-101. Toronto: Nelson Education.

Hamilton, John David. 1994. *Arctic Revolution: Social Change in the North-West Territories, 1935-1994.* Toronto: Dundurn Press.

Kerr, D., and D.W. Holdsworth. 1987. *Historical Atlas of Canada.* Vol. 3, *Addressing the Twentieth Century.* Toronto: University of Toronto Press.

McCandless, Robert G. 1985. *Yukon Wildlife: A Social History.* Edmonton: University of Alberta Press.

Twichell, Heath. 1992. *Northwest Epic: The Building of the Alaska Highway.* New York: St. Martin's Press.

The Environmental Consequences of Development

Indian Country Today Media Network. 2011. "Caribou Is the Canary in the Coal Mine." Indian Country Today Media Network.com, 11 February. http://indiancountrytoday medianetwork.com/.

Mackenzie Valley Environmental Impact Review Board. *Annual Report, 1999-2000.* http://www.reviewboard.ca/.

Pilgrim, Sarah, and Jules N. Pretty. 2010. *Nature and Culture: Rebuilding Lost Connections.* London: Earthscan Canada.

Twichell, Heath. 1992. *Northwest Epic: The Building of the Alaska Highway.* New York: St. Martin's Press.

The Mackenzie Valley (Berger) Pipeline Inquiry

Berger, Thomas R. 2002. *One Man's Justice: A Life in the Law.* Vancouver: Douglas and McIntyre.

Berger, Thomas R., and Mackenzie Valley Pipeline Inquiry. 1977. *Northern Frontier, Northern Homeland: The Report of the Mackenzie Valley Pipeline Inquiry.* 2 vols. Ottawa: Printing and Publishing Supply and Services Canada.

Peacock, Donald. 1977. *People, Peregrines, and Arctic Pipelines: The Critical Battle to Build Canada's Northern Gas Pipelines.* Vancouver: J.J. Douglas.

Watkins, Mel. 1977. *Dene Nation: The Colony Within.* Toronto: University of Toronto Press.

Global Warming

Adam, David, and Leo Hickman. 2009. "Scientists: Act Now or Face Climate Catastrophe." *Guardian Weekly,* 20-26 March.

Bocking, Stephen. 2007. "Science and Spaces in the Northern Environment." *Environmental* History 12, 4: 867-94.

Dunaway, Finis. 2009. "Seeing Global Warming: Contemporary Art and the Fate of the Planet." *Environmental History* 14, 1: 9-31.

Fagan, Brian. 2000. *The Little Ice Age: How Climate Made History, 1300-1850.* New York: Basic Books.

–. 2008. *The Great Warming: Climate Change and the Rise and Fall of Civilizations.* New York: Bloomsbury Press.

Fleming, James Rodger. 1998. *Historical Perspectives on Climate Change.* New York: Oxford University Press.

Fleming, James Rodger, Vladimir Jankovic, and Deborah R. Coen. 2006. *Intimate Universality: Local and Global Themes in the History of Weather and Climate.* Sagamore Beach: Science History Publications.

Gore, Al. 2006. *An Inconvenient Truth: The Planetary Emergency of Global Warming and What We Can Do about It.* Emmaus, PA: Rodale.

Indian Country Today Media Network. 2011. "Caribou Is the Canary in the Coal Mine." Indian Country Today Media Network.com, 11 February. http://indiancountrytoday medianetwork.com/.

Climate Change and Public Policy

Bowen, Mark. 2008. *Censoring Science: Inside the Political Attack on Dr. James Hansen and the Truth about Global Warming.* New York: Dutton.

Gore, Al. 2006. *An Inconvenient Truth: The Planetary Emergency of Global Warming and What We Can Do about It.* Emmaus, PA: Rodale.

Hill, Stephen, and William Leiss. 2004. "A Night at the Climate Casino: Canada and the Kyoto Quagmire." In *Mad Cows and Mothers Milk: The Perils of Poor Risk Communication,* edited by William Leiss and Stephen Hill, 262-95. Montreal and Kingston: McGill-Queen's University Press

Hoggan, James. 2009. *Climate Cover-Up: The Crusade to Deny Global Warming.* Vancouver: Greystone Books.

IPCC (Intergovernmental Panel on Climate Change). 2007. *Climate Change 2007: Synthesis Report.* http://www.ipcc.ch/.

Jaccard, Marc. 2005. *Sustainable Fossil Fuels: The Unusual Suspect in the Quest for Clean and Enduring Energy.* New York: Cambridge University Press.

Monbiot, George. 2006. *Heat: How to Stop the Planet from Burning.* Toronto: Doubleday Canada.

Oreskes, Naomi, and Erik M. Conway. 2010. *Merchants of Doubt: How a Handful of Scientists Obscured the Truth on Issues from Tobacco Smoke to Global Warming.* New York: Bloomsbury Press.

Robinson, John. 2007. "Clearing the Air on Climate Change." *Literary Review of Canada,* October.

Sallot, Jeff. 2005. "Canada Lags on Air-Pollution Cleanup Compared with U.S., Coalition Finds." *Globe and Mail,* 13 October, A7.

Simpson, Jeffrey, Marc Jaccard, and Nic Rivers. 2007. *Hot Air: Meeting Canada's Climate Change Challenge.* Toronto: McClelland and Stewart.

Weart, Spencer R. 2008. *The Discovery of Global Warming.* Cambridge, MA: Harvard University Press.

Webster, Paul. 2006. "Canada's Dirty Little Kyoto Strategy." *Globe and Mail,* 3 June.

Conclusion

Our responsibility for the spaceship earth is increasing with the growth in our ability to modify natural systems.

— BOYCE RICHARDSON, WRITER, *JAMES BAY: THE PLOT TO DROWN THE NORTH WOODS*, 1972

NATURE IS A dynamic, constantly changing phenomenon. Sixty-five million years ago, northern North America was a completely different world than it is today, inhabited by enormous animals, unusual plants, and no people. A meteor brought the dinosaur age to an end, but the natural world recovered over millions of years. After the Ice Age, the first people to arrive in the region encountered a landscape that had evolved beyond recognition. When Christopher Columbus landed in the "New World," sparking an age of European imperialism and exploitation, he also precipitated the Columbian exchange, which stimulated profound changes in North American ecosystems as peoples, plants, animals, and bacteria from separate continents intermingled with dramatic results.

We have come full circle. Today, global warming, a human-made rather than a cosmic event, is precipitating a profound transformation on Earth. Although the effects of climate change are most apparent in the Arctic, global warming has already disrupted weather patterns around the world. If greenhouse gas emissions are not reduced, the extinction of more species will result. In this sixth era of extinction, the present extinction rate is "likely more than 50 times and less than 500 times the prehuman baseline" (Wilson 2006, 79). A reading of environmental history suggests that what is likely, but not inevitable, is that the planet will survive, but many species will disappear, and humans will not necessarily be exempt.

Throughout Canadian history, human beings in northern North America have exploited the environment on two levels: the collective-economic and the individual-cultural. They developed the area's natural resources largely without a concern for conservation, and decision makers rarely showed a concern for the environment. The establishment of close ties between businesses and governments fuelled empire- and nation-building efforts in a new country, and for years politicians viewed the public interest as synonymous with corporate interests. But today these ties are outmoded. With the emergence of the conservation and environmental movements in the twentieth century, politicians took some responsibility for protecting the environment by passing environmental legislation. Yet large corporations continued to overexploit the environment without being held accountable to society as a whole. Beaver and large game populations were hunted to near extinction, and the salmon and cod fisheries collapsed. The development of the agricultural, lumber, mining, manufacturing, and energy sectors precipitated habitat destruction and excessive, largely unregulated pollution. Yet successive governments in Canada were reluctant to enforce existing environmental legislation and environmental standards.

Vast economic and cultural changes in Canada, particularly since the end of the Second World War, were grounded in earlier practices and attitudes toward nature. Canadians now live in a modern, advanced global economy dependent on fossil fuels, automobiles, and consumer culture. This way of life is not sustainable, and despite our improved understanding of environmental issues, the limits to growth continue to be ignored. Corporate leaders, politicians, consumers, and the mainstream media have either forgotten or chosen to ignore the fact that nature underpins our society. Our advanced technology and consumer culture may implode, as some scholars and prominent Canadians such as David Suzuki and Margaret Atwood have mused.

Climate change is a threat that has forced us to realize that the planet, though resilient, is fragile. In the twenty-first century, new ideas, new technologies, and different policy approaches and goals will perhaps facilitate the creation of a more sustainable society to combat climate change. The nature and structure of a sustainable society are unclear, but developing them is necessary and requires the application of environmental values; more eclectic, inclusive decision-making structures; and alternative economic and energy regimes. Business plans will probably need to incorporate assessments of environmental costs and strategies to deal with waste responsibly. Tax policies or fines may move businesses and society in a new direction, but only if there is political will.

Although inertia, tradition, and entrenched interests have prevented Canada from developing effective environmental protection measures at the policy level, culture has also contributed to inaction at the individual level. Notions of superiority and entitlement accompanied European colonizers to the New World, and they have persisted among political and economic elites from the early settlement period into the contemporary era. Such values underpinned the exploitation of Aboriginal people, labourers, women, and immigrants that accompanied these developments, and they carried over to the environment. The centrality of consumerism in modern Canadian society has led to spending habits and lifestyle choices – for example, opting for cars over public transportation and large houses over smaller ones – that are impeding our ability to create a healthy environment for future generations.

Although people in high-income brackets enjoy a high standard of living, the corporatization, commodification, quantification, and standardization of goods and services have actually led to a decline in living standards in terms of diversity, variety, and the quality of goods. We are reluctant to give up products that are harmful to the environment and our health because we associate them with status or because they make our lives easier. Cars are an obvious example. Only a minority of consumers have adopted alternative or "green" approaches to transportation, food and energy consumption, and other facets of everyday life. In a society premised on economic growth, one that views consumption as the main driver of the economy, governments do not have a stake in encouraging consumers to seek sustainable alternatives. Yet some individuals are choosing to walk more, ride bicycles, give up plastic bags, and participate in local food movements. They are ahead of politicians in their awareness of environmental issues, their desire for environmentally friendly policies, and their willingness to question their consumer habits and rethink their relationship to the natural world.

Throughout Canadian history, alternative ideas have frequently come from the margins. Conservationists and environmentalists were minorities. They included activists who defended old-growth forests against clearcutting, farmers who responded to agribusiness by producing organic food, First Nations who questioned the government's management of fisheries and wildlife, and peaceniks who hoped to protect the planet from nuclear testing. Their ideas eventually entered the mainstream, but their struggles revealed that changing the way people think often requires education – whether through the formal education system, courts of law, books, films, or documentaries – and the enactment and enforcement of public policies that regulate producers and encourage sustainable living. Information is power, and individuals educated about the state of the planet will have the tools necessary to examine their own lifestyles and live as stewards of the land. Individuals can make a difference and contribute to the well-being of future generations. As consumers, we can apply enormous pressure on companies, advertisers, and media to produce products and project lifestyles that are not harmful to the environment. As citizens in a democracy with a high literacy rate, Canadians still have the right to speak up, communicate with one another in their communities, and present positive alternatives. Support for meaningful environmental legislation is a positive process.

The history of the relationship among human beings, nature, and other species is cause for pessimism. As a group, environmental historians tend to be negative about modernity and the current state of the world. It is the historian's job to study the past and, if possible, find patterns that illuminate the present. In Canadian history, human ideas about economics, politics, religion, and human-nature relationships were often about control of nature and of people. The current climate change crisis may stimulate innovation and free policy makers and consumers from this mindset. Environmentalists challenge the status quo and recognize the need to adapt our modern lifestyles to take a gentler approach toward the planet. As biologist E.O. Wilson wrote recently, "Life on this planet can stand no more plundering" (Wilson 2006, 99). Creating a truly sustainable society will require a new set of values because, as David Suzuki (2003, ix) concludes, "The overarching crisis resides in the modern, urban human mind, in the values and beliefs that are driving much of our destructiveness."

WHILE WRITING THIS book, I also strove to create environmentally healthy places – one wood lot, meadow, and garden at a time. Each individual, with effort, can live harmoniously with the environment and with wildlife. My own journey has been a satisfying experience, and I encourage others to take it up. In 1992, Helen Caldicott, an Australian physican, author, and anti-nuclear activist, stated, "Hope for the earth lies not with leaders but in your own heart and soul ... if you love this planet" (Caldicott 1992, 203). We can all learn from environmentalism, which seeks in nature the values of equilibrium, moderation, and renewal so that we can reduce the destructive effects of aggressive capitalism and excessive consumption. Canadian society requires new, creative, eclectic, and inclusive ideas, and decision-making approaches that lead to more sustainable ways for people to live and work in the twenty-first century.

Works Cited

Caldicott, Helen. 1992. *If You Love This Planet: A Plan To Heal the Earth*. New York: W.W. Norton.

Richardson, Boyce. 1972. *James Bay: The Plot to Drown the North Woods*. San Francisco/ Toronto: Sierra Club/ Clarke Irwin.

Suzuki, David. 2003. *The David Suzuki Reader*. Vancouver: Greystone Books.

Wilson, E.O. 2006. *The Creation: An Appeal to Save Life on Earth*. New York: W.W. Norton.

Index

A

abundance/superabundance, 23, 24, 32, 53, 64, 65, 96, 97, 101, 106, 109, 110

acid rain, 147, 149, 197, 212, 243, 246, 255, 256, 262

activism
1960s, 245, 261, 328
animal rights, 268, 270, 271
Ban the Bomb movement, 247, 251
Council of Canadians, 261

adaptation, 15, 19, 20

agriculture. *See* farming

air quality/smog, 120, 129, 132, 133, 144, 147, 148, 149, 150, 182

Alpine Club of Canada, 108

alternative ideas, 328

Arctic/Subarctic North, 18, 120, 121, 134, 305, 326
Baffin Island, 134
Canadian Arctic Expedition, 306, 307
climate change, 305, 323
community, 315
development, 307, 317
diseases, 306, 310, 311
drilling, Beaufort Sea, 316
environmental adaptation, 307, 311, 315, 319
environmental hazards, 310, 311
fisheries, 312, 313
incursions, 305
indigenous people, 305, 306, 307, 308, 309, 312, 313, 315, 316, 318, 319, 323
culture, 310, 311
hunting, 311
Innu, 208
Inuit, 178, 278, 306

land claims, 316, 318
Committee for the Original Peoples' Entitlement, 317
Thule, 18, 19
infrastructure, 306, 307, 309
air industry, 309
Alaska Highway, 309, 311
communications, 309, 311
landscape, 305
missionaries, 306
policy, 307, 309, 311, 312
pollution, 309, 312
protection, 305
renewable resources, 317
resources development, 305, 307
CANOL project, 309, 310
mines, 309
oil and gas, 308, 314, 317
sovereignty, 305, 323
technology, 308
towns, 310
wage economy, 309, 310
waste, 309, 311
wildlife, 306, 310, 311, 312, 319, 323
managers, 312
Yellowknife, 132, 308, 309, 314
Yukon, 312

asteroid, 11,

atomic energy boards, 176, 177, 178, 179, 180, 181, 182

Atwood, Margaret, 327

automobile/car, 107, 109, 140, 153, 163, 224, 228, 229, 327, 328
accidents, 146, 147, 148
advertising, 144, 146, 147, 148
branch plants, 143

car types
early, 141, 142
electric, 142, 149, 150, 183
hybrid, 149, 150, 157
hydrogen, 183
Model T, 142
Russell, 143
SUV, 148, 150, 173
companies, 141, 143, 147, 149, 150
culture, 144, 146, 156, 274
dependency, 140, 146, 156, 327
design, 144
driving, 146
emissions, 147, 148, 149, 185, 197, 249, 255
environmental effects, 146, 147, 148
gas stations, 144, 150, 151
health, 141
lead, 148, 149, 262
mass production, 141, 142, 144
mobility, 140, 150
ownership numbers, 143, 144
parking, 146, 151, 156
parts, 144
regulations, 146, 147, 148, 150, 256
traffic, 144, 145, 147, 156

B

Beothuk, 18-21, 23

Beringia, 13, 14
Bering land bridge, 14

biodiversity, 12, 96, 152, 199, 215, 218, 219, 221, 224, 226, 229, 231, 235, 236, 237, 243, 246, 249, 262, 272, 277, 282

biology, 215

Bluefish Caves, 14

business-government relationship, 116, 120, 129, 130, 133, 137, 145, 148, 169, 175, 176, 195, 197, 198, 207, 212, 222, 232, 233, 237, 252, 257, 261, 264, 292, 307, 309, 310, 323, 326

C

Caldicott, Helen, 329
Calgary, 78
Canada, 35, 40
Canadian Shield, 4, 42, 120, 121, 130, 132, 181, 278
carbon capture, 165, 184
carbon emissions, 12, 147, 165
cars. *See* automobile/car
Carson, Rachel, 5, 234, 244, 245
    award, 248
    Silent Spring, 5, 234, 244
cities/municipalities, 4, 75, 76, 96, 105, 168, 172, 191, 255
    animals in, 83, 84
    beautification/town planning, 92, 93, 190, 192
    cultural influences, 76-77
    design, 150
    filth, 82, 86, 93, 191
    garbage, 82, 86, 88
    hinterlands, 76, 80
    housing/slums, 82, 151, 174
    infrastructure, 81, 82, 89, 167, 193, 194
    markets, 79
    reform/public health, 76, 86, 87, 90, 93
    sanitation, 79, 86, 87, 88
    sewers/waterworks, 88-90, 93, 106, 152, 191, 193, 194
    urban development, 79, 87, 93, 188
    urban growth, 76, 79, 80
    urban sprawl, 151, 278
    walking, 76
    waste disposal, 84, 86, 87, 88, 89, 191, 192, 193
climate, 121, 215
climate change, 5, 11, 12, 14, 18, 33, 96, 140, 145, 148, 149, 150, 156, 157, 165, 175, 176, 182, 185, 246, 252, 264, 265, 277, 305, 309, 326, 327, 328

adaptation to, 323
Arctic temperatures, 319
Canada's role, 321-23
carbon emissions, 321
carbon trading, 322
climate deniers, 320
effect on wildlife, 319
global warming, 12, 13, 14, 20, 189, 249, 318, 319, 326
IPCC report 2007, 319
melting glaciers, 319
oil and gas industry subsidies, 321
policy, 320, 321, 322
politics, 320, 322
public security, 323
tipping point, 323
US approach, 322
climate zones, 54
Clovis people, 14
Columbian exchange, 2, 28, 35, 237, 326
comet, 14
Commission of Conservation, 92, 104-6, 108, 113, 115, 164, 166
communities, 16, 28, 46, 52, 65, 79, 140, 150, 179, 190, 202, 206, 207, 302, 303
    commercial, 76, 81
    community groups/NGOs, 212
conflict, 19, 20, 21, 23, 31, 193, 207, 210, 224, 245, 252, 275, 277, 278
conservation, 33, 67, 103, 104, 115, 116, 168, 182, 190, 199, 236, 243, 328
    American movement, 96, 98-99,
    Canadian movement, 93, 103, 109, 111, 116, 327
    forest, 97, 103
    plants/animal breeds, 236
    preservation, 93, 99, 111, 272, 275, 276, 277
    reform/regulation, 100, 101, 191
    utilitarian, 99, 116, 268, 273, 275, 277
    wise use, 244
consumer, 35, 150, 155, 156, 173, 219, 221, 226, 228, 232, 235, 237, 288, 328
commodities, 24, 32, 61, 63, 167, 168, 169, 222, 229, 237, 272
consumption, 142, 144, 148, 150, 152, 183, 218, 243, 245, 247, 264, 327, 329

culture, 140, 147, 152, 327
    society, 140, 170
consumerism. *See* consumer
contact, 2, 25, 27, 28, 32, 35, 41, 42
continental drift, 12
Cootes Paradise Project, 200
cottage, 109, 140, 273
counterculture, 156, 245, 249, 264
    back-to-the-land movement, 248
crops, 40, 51, 52, 54, 115, 184, 215, 216, 218, 219, 220, 224, 230, 237
    canola, 230, 231
    damage, 149
    grains, 219
    Marquis, 58
    pest control, 218, 220
    Red Fife, 58
    spraying, 218
    transgenic, 229, 234
    wheat, 51, 52, 216, 225
Crown land, 4, 63, 64, 103, 281
culture, 16, 19, 26, 128, 207, 208, 327
    art, 16, 18
    ceremonies, 16, 19
    consumer. *See* consumer
    hunting, 33
    medicine wheels, 16
    notions of superiority, 327
    pottery, 32
    religion, 16, 19, 27
    shock, 42

D

dams, 34, 65, 66, 99, 105, 128, 163, 164, 165, 166, 169, 188, 189, 204, 207, 273, 297
    artificial lakes, 204, 206, 211
    projects, hydroelectricity, 169, 200, 204, 208, 212
        Churchill Falls, 204
        Columbia River Project, 204, 205, 207
        environmental impact of, 203, 204, 206, 208, 209, 210, 211
        James Bay Hydroelectricity Project, 169, 208, 209, 259
        James Bay and Northern Quebec Agreement (JBNQA), 210, 211

Peace River Project, 206
relocation/disruption of people, 202, 204, 205, 207, 208, 209
St. Lawrence Seaway, 201, 202, 203, 205, 207, 212
workers, 210
DDT, 5, 219, 234, 244, 249
disease, 21, 28, 29, 32, 33, 35, 42, 83, 86, 89, 90, 93, 105, 128, 227, 300
environmental, 149, 177, 209
mercury, 209
occupational, 124, 133, 136, 177
Dominion Lands Act, 102
Ducks Unlimited, 199, 200

E

early peoples, 14
Earth Day, 5, 245
ecology, 3, 28, 29, 33, 40, 46, 97, 115, 209, 219, 224, 227, 243, 244, 245, 250, 269, 272, 277, 278, 294, 300
animal ecology, 269
ecological society, 245
economic alternatives, 327
economic growth, 5, 96, 116, 153, 175, 183, 184, 185, 207, 243, 245, 247, 248, 264, 265, 302, 328
ecosystem programs, 254, 302
ecosystems, 14, 34, 35, 43, 59, 96, 125, 128, 169, 174, 178, 188, 192, 196, 197, 198, 199, 200, 201, 203, 204, 205, 211, 219, 235, 237, 248, 252, 268, 272, 294, 298, 309, 326
ecotourism, 115, 272
Edmonton, 78, 89
energy, 76, 79, 147, 185, 202, 246, 327
biofuels, 183
coal, 122, 125, 163, 164
conservation, 182
consumption, 154, 164, 182, 183, 185
efficiency, 183, 184
electricity, 81, 105, 115, 122, 125, 136, 141, 142, 163, 164, 165, 166, 176, 183, 184, 201, 204, 205, 206, 208, 209, 210
blackouts, 182

fossil fuels, 140, 145, 156, 163, 164, 170, 182, 184, 185, 197, 265, 313, 327
gas, 81, 140, 141, 142, 148, 163, 164, 171, 172, 183
gas flares, 171
hydrogen, 183
kerosene, 170
nuclear, 168, 175, 176, 180, 181, 182, 243, 246, 276
CANDU reactor, 176, 180
Chernobyl, 246
moratorium, 181
power reactors, 180, 205
waste, 180, 181, 182
oil, 142, 148, 173, 174, 175, 184, 308
Imperial Oil, 170, 175
peak, 175
oilfields and wells, 170
Athabasca, 173
Hibernia, 172
Leduc Oil Well, 170, 171
Norman Wells, 308, 317
Pembina, 172
Redwater, 172
surveyors, 172
Turner Valley, 170
renewable/alternative, 168, 182, 183, 184, 205, 245, 248, 265, 327
solar, 184,
steam, 81, 141, 163
whale oil, 170
wind, 184
windmills, 163, 184
wood, 163
environmental
awareness, 305
degradation, 152, 155, 156, 165, 173, 174, 178, 181, 183, 185, 192, 196, 197, 201, 207, 210, 212, 244, 283, 309
disruption, 188, 206, 253, 255
exploitation, 326
infrastructure, 243, 252, 253, 264
health, 129, 133, 134, 180, 181, 195, 196, 197, 198, 212, 237
partnerships, 262
Great Bear Rainforest Agreement, 263

performance, 257
protection, 116, 148, 245
standards, 261, 327
environmental assessments, 233, 259, 305
environmental costs, 327
environmental history, 75, 326, 328
definition, 1
development, 3
historiography, 1-2, 75, 100
history of the North, 320
environmental justice, 2
environmental law, 262
environmental legislation, 233, 243, 250, 252, 253, 255, 263, 280, 327, 328
jurisdiction, 253, 254
litigation, 259
provincial laws, 254, 255, 280
environmental movement (modern), 96, 100, 109, 137, 194, 207, 234, 237, 243, 262, 272, 276, 278, 327
fractures, 258
global, 246,
environmental organizations, 250, 251, 252
environmental policy, 253, 327
environmentalism, 2, 116, 156, 243, 245, 248, 249, 258, 264, 272, 327, 328, 329
environmentalists, 130, 168, 182, 188, 193, 198, 203, 208, 210, 212, 223, 224, 232, 237, 243, 245, 252, 258, 262, 264, 268, 271, 277, 280, 281, 286, 293, 300, 301, 320, 328
media savvy, 249, 251
opposition to, 243
equilibrium, 264
extinction, 11, 14,

F

farmers (habitants), 43-49, 51, 58, 67, 110, 113, 116, 129, 144, 179, 215, 216, 219, 224, 225, 231, 270
gentlemen, 60
immigrants, 217
markets, 52, 59, 235
organic, 234, 328
Schmeiser, Percy, 231

farming (agriculture), 15, 17, 28, 40, 41, 43, 47, 49, 58, 60, 96, 97, 115, 125, 188, 193, 199, 215, 216, 327
agribusiness, 215, 218, 222, 224, 226
alternative, 234
animal breeding, 221
animal gestation, 215
barns, 222
breeding, 216, 217
commercial/industrial, 52, 59, 60, 216, 217, 218, 219, 221, 224, 226, 237, 243
dairy production, 51, 60
extensive, 50, 53
farms, 47, 48, 59, 64, 199, 206
    corporate/factory, 53, 219, 221
    experimental, 58, 216, 217, 218, 227
        Ontario Agricultural College, 216, 218
    family, 225
    mixed-farming, 68
    organic, 235, 245
    size of, 52, 58, 59, 225, 226
fertilizers, 215, 219, 235
green revolution, 218, 219, 237
growing season, 215
hybrids, 58, 215, 217, 218, 219, 220, 224, 229, 237
    genetics, 216
    Mendel, George, 216
    Preston, Isabella, 218
legislation, 216, 218, 222, 234
livestock, 28, 40, 50-52, 54, 112, 179, 199, 215, 221, 222, 227, 228
mad cow disease, 223
mechanization, 52, 58, 59, 215, 218, 219, 220, 224, 229
methods, 49, 50, 54, 207, 216, 219, 237
monoculture, 58, 59, 68, 215, 218, 220, 224, 235, 236
orchards, 60, 236
organic, 215, 225
patents, 220, 224, 230, 231, 236
pesticides/herbicides, 219, 220, 229, 230, 234, 235, 237
regulation, 105, 216, 218, 222, 234
research/science, 216, 218, 219, 220, 221

seeds, 219, 220, 229, 230, 231, 236
    Monsanto, 229, 231, 232, 233
    Seeds of Diversity Canada, 224
standards, 217, 218, 234
state of, 51
subsistence, 43, 50, 51, 54, 60
wine, 217
Federation of Ontario Naturalists (FON), 276, 277
Fernow, Bernhard, 99
fibres, natural, 245
fire, 2, 19, 23, 26, 47, 48, 53, 55, 59, 80, 88, 124, 195, 212, 275, 311
    prevention of, 98, 100, 102, 103, 104, 108, 115, 273
fish, 4, 16, 22, 23, 24, 40, 65, 66, 67, 115, 128, 189, 195, 199, 202, 206, 209, 244, 281, 296
    cod, 22, 23, 286, 287, 290
    decline, 297, 299, 301
    First Nations, 295,
    Hell's Gate, 297
    runs, 296, 298
    salmon, 15, 16, 111, 113, 125, 126, 128, 191, 203, 206, 207, 230, 286, 294, 299, 300, 301
fisheries, 16, 22, 23, 40, 41, 207, 286, 307
    aquaculture, 298, 299, 300, 301, 302, 303
    blame/politics, 293, 294, 300
    canneries, 295, 296, 297
    catches, 287, 288, 289, 290, 291, 292, 293
    cod moratorium, 286, 291, 292
    collapse, 291, 292, 298, 301, 327
        economic effects, 292, 303
    commercial/companies, 191, 288, 291, 292, 295, 296, 299, 300, 302
    dragging nets, 289
    farms, 299, 300, 302
    Grand Banks, 288
    habitat, 295, 300, 301, 303
    hatcheries, 113, 288, 298, 299
    industry, 96, 211
    inshore/offshore, 287, 288, 290, 291, 293
    investigation, 288, 290
    licenses, 290, 291, 294,
    local knowledge, 294

management, 113, 269, 286, 287, 288, 290, 292, 293, 294, 296, 298, 300, 303, 328
neoliberal privatization, 294
overfishing, 188, 189, 191, 206, 273, 286, 287, 288, 289, 290, 292, 293, 296, 297
protection, 190, 290, 301, 302
quotas, 291, 292, 302
radar, 289
regulation/policy, 190, 290, 291, 298, 300, 301, 302, 303
scientists, 293, 294, 300, 301, 302, 303
seal, 288
spatial expansion, 288, 290, 291, 298
sustainability, 287, 288, 292, 293, 294, 295, 302
technology, 288, 290, 293, 295, 295, 296
trawlers, 288, 289, 291, 294
waste, 289
fishers, 15, 23, 30, 41, 53, 102, 191, 208, 210, 286, 288, 291, 294, 295, 296, 298, 303
floods/flood control, 153, 189, 199, 201, 202, 205, 206, 207, 208, 209, 210, 211, 273
food, 16, 20, 33, 83, 110, 112, 113, 126, 128, 134, 146, 156, 190, 215, 220, 243, 274, 286, 300
additives, 222, 227, 228
alternative, 215, 235, 328
biotechnology, 215, 221, 224, 229, 232, 233, 237, 238
    DNA, 221
    Genetic Engineering Alert, 232
    genetic manipulation, 221, 231, 237
chain, 219, 221, 227, 232, 237
corporate consolidation, 226, 227, 229, 237
corporate organization, 215, 222, 226, 227, 228, 229, 237
costs, 215
culture, 228, 229
diets, 219
fast food, 146, 221, 227, 228, 229, 235
    Frankenfoods, 223
    microwave, 228
    obesity, 229
    TV dinner, 228
    Wonderbread, 227

genetically modified, 230, 232, 233, 234, 235, 237
  effects, 230, 237
heritage, 236
intellectual property, 220, 230, 231, 232
international market, 215, 218, 222, 224, 228
labels, 222, 232
local, 215, 235, 236, 237
organic, 237, 245
  Canadian Organic Growers (COG), 234, 235, 236
potato, 50, 51
preparation, 228
processed, 215, 218, 220, 221, 226, 227, 228, 232, 244, 245
  chemicals, 219, 227, 228, 234, 243, 244
production, 215, 218, 237
products, 218, 221, 222, 224, 227, 235
quality, 227, 228, 234, 237
regulation, 219, 222, 233, 237
research/science, 216
retailers/supermarkets, 226, 227, 228, 235
security, 215, 223, 232, 235, 237
slow food movement, 235
standards, 216, 218, 222, 224
substitutes, 227
unsustainable, 215
forest, 4, 23, 25, 34, 40, 43, 48, 65, 67, 121, 152, 174
  boreal, 14, 23, 46, 62, 189
  clearcutting, 252, 281
  clearing, 43, 46, 47, 64, 65, 97
  deforestation, 46, 61, 64, 67, 97, 98, 105, 209
  industry, 96, 97, 199
  limits, 97, 101
  management, 67, 97, 98, 115, 116
  old-growth, 46, 60, 63, 64, 97, 100, 273, 279, 281, 282, 328
  privatize, 281
  protection of, 100, 101, 108, 111, 116, 246
  rainforest destruction, 249
  rangers/foresters, 101, 108
  reforestation, 101
  regulations, 98, 252

renewable, 101
reserves, 44, 98, 101-4, 108, 111, 113, 273, 274
secondary growth, 63, 100
silviculture, 115
spraying, 244
trees, 16, 23, 25, 28, 46, 57, 58, 60, 61, 64, 67, 92, 97, 102, 103, 115, 128, 149, 190, 208, 274, 275
Fort McMurray, 173, 174
free trade, 167, 168, 260
  deregulation, 167
  Free Trade Agreement (FTA), 168
  North American Free Trade Agreements (NAFTA), 173
  privatization, 167, 168
fur trade, 22, 23, 29-33, 35, 40, 49, 56, 96, 126, 170, 295
  Metis, 35, 54, 56
  swan trade, 34

G

gardens, 17, 28, 49, 51-53, 58, 60, 82, 93, 228, 236, 248
  allotment, 237
  organic, 237
  rooftop, 237
Geological Survey of Canada, 120, 121, 216, 307
  mapping, 121
  reports, 121
globalization, 260, 327
  capitalism, 329
  CEO capitalism, 260
grants, land, 43, 44, 45
grasslands, 16, 20, 30, 32, 40, 55, 57, 58
Great Bear Lake, 128, 178, 307, 309
Great Lakes, 17, 30, 80, 177, 188, 189, 190, 191, 192, 193, 194, 195, 198, 203, 204, 212, 253
  acid rain, 197, 255
  alien species, 192, 200, 202, 203
    alewives, 203
    lamprey, 202
    zebra mussels, 203
  anglers, 192, 280, 298

boundary, 189
  companies, 197, 198
  fish, 189, 191, 192, 193, 194, 196, 200, 203
  fisheries, 190, 191, 192, 193
  hatcheries, 192
  Lake Erie, 192, 198, 246, 250, 262
    algae, 193
    eutrophication, 193
    detergents, 193, 194
    phosphorus, 193, 194, 198, 248
  management, 192, 197
  manipulation, 192, 204
  pollution, 192, 193, 194, 197, 198, 200
  recovery, 248
  regulation, 262
  transportation, 189
  waste, 191, 193
    toxic, 194, 195, 196
  water, 193
Great Slave Lake, 120, 128, 132, 307, 308, 310
green industry, jobs, 176, 182, 265, 328
greenhouse gases, 12, 149, 165, 171, 174, 211, 249, 320, 326
Green Party of Canada, 263
Greenland, 12, 21, 287
Greenpeace, 5, 232, 235, 246, 250, 258
  anti-nuclear campaigns, 251, 328
  Rainbow Warrior, 251
  seal hunt, 251
  whales, 251
Grey Owl, 109, 273
Group of Seven, 109

H

Hagarsville tire fire, 255, 256
Halifax, 43, 90, 254
Hamilton, 86, 88, 90, 190, 191, 192, 200
Head-Smashed-In-Buffalo-Jump, 16
Hind, Henry Youle, 54, 111
Hippies, 245
historians
  Berger, Carl, 3
  Cook, Ramsay, 2
  Cronon, William, 2, 28, 243
  Crosby, Alfred, 2, 29
  Grove, Richard, 1

McNeill, John, 1
Melosi, Martin, 2
Worster, Donald, 1
historical geography, 3
Homo sapiens, 14
horse, 17, 34, 52, 84, 140, 146
households, 153
houses, 16, 48-49, 58
Hudson Bay, 30, 31, 120, 126
Hudson's Bay Company (HBC), 30, 33, 34, 35, 53-56, 64, 124, 126, 170, 306, 312
hunter-gatherers, 15, 17, 41, 43
hunters, 5, 14, 16, 17, 30, 32, 35, 53, 102, 110, 208, 210, 270, 271, 272, 280
   conservation, 111
   hunting ethic, 111
   regulation of, 96, 110, 111, 112, 114
   sportsmen, 110, 111, 112, 113, 114, 116, 271
   tourism, 111, 281

I

Ice Age, 4, 12, 35, 326
ice sheets, 13, 14
imperialism, 21, 24, 26, 29, 30, 32, 40, 326
indigenous (Aboriginal) people, 2, 11, 15, 16, 17, 18, 20, 26-35, 40, 42, 47, 48, 53, 57, 60, 67, 76, 106, 112, 113, 114, 121, 122, 126, 128, 129, 132, 134, 137, 163, 169, 174, 177, 178, 188, 189, 195, 199, 202, 206, 208, 209, 210, 211, 252, 259, 279, 280, 286, 294, 298, 303, 327, 328
   Huron, 17
   Serpent River First Nation, 177, 178
industrialism, 67, 75, 79, 80, 84, 91, 93, 96, 106, 111, 121, 128, 129, 140, 155, 163, 167, 169, 183, 185, 188, 190, 192, 197, 199, 201, 243, 247, 308
   accidents, 86
   hazardous waste, 155, 191, 192
   factories, 75, 79, 190, 192
   industrial time, 85
   Taylorism, 85
inequality, 245, 265
irrigation, 201, 204, 205

J

jobs versus environment, 259
Joly, Henri-Gustave, 97

K

Kane, Paul, 54
Keeling Curve, 12
Kingston, 88
Kyoto Protocol, 5, 150, 175, 182, 255, 263, 320, 321, 322
   Durban Platform, 322

L

land title, 42
   land grants, 77
   squatters, 43
Laurentian theory, 3
Limits to Growth, 246, 264
limits to growth, 327
Little Ice Age, 21, 23, 54
lobbyists, 246
loggers, 61-63, 65, 252, 277
logging companies/lumber industry, 61-64, 252, 273, 327
   environmental destruction, 64-66, 104, 189
   log drives, 62, 65
   markets, 61, 64
   regulation, 102, 252
   sawdust, 65-67
   sawmills, 61, 63, 64, 66, 189
   waste, 101, 115
London, Ontario, 89, 93
lumber, 115
   cuts, 98, 102
   leases, 98, 102, 105, 108
   products, 61, 63, 64, 67

M

Mackenzie River, 31
Mackenzie River Valley, 14
Mackenzie Valley Pipeline Inquiry, 305, 313
   Berger, Tom, 314
   companies, 314
   development, impact of, 313, 314
   effect on people, 313, 314, 315, 318

environmental impact, 316
   protection, 314
infrastructure, 315
land claims, 316
report 316, 318
revival of pipelines, 318
routes of pipelines, 318
wildlife, 316
Macoun, John, 3
mammals, 14
mammoth, 13, 14
manufacturing, 122, 123, 140, 144, 149, 153, 164, 183, 195, 327
Mesozoic era, 11
metropolitanism, 3, 76
Miner, Jack, 113, 114
minerals, 25, 104, 121
miners, 124, 126, 128, 130, 133, 136, 137, 178
   occupational health, 120, 133, 134, 136, 137, 177, 178
mining, 104, 120, 121, 307, 327
   abandoned sites, 130, 135
   asbestos, 121, 131, 132, 133
   coal, 122-25, 128
   copper, 130
   culture, 135
   deposits, 121, 122, 124
   environmental damage, 122, 124, 125, 126, 128, 129, 130, 131, 132, 134, 136, 177
   gold, 126, 127, 128, 132
      gold rush, 55, 59, 64, 128
   hazardous waste, 120, 123, 124, 125, 130, 131, 134, 136, 137, 177, 178, 179
   infrastructure, 122
   nickel, 130
   ore, 124, 128, 178
   practices, 246
   prospectors, 120, 121, 135
   reclamation, 125, 130, 131, 137
   regulation of, 105, 124, 129, 136, 179
   silver, 131
   smelter/refinery, 128, 129; 179
   sulphur, 123, 125
   tailings, 124, 130, 131, 137, 177, 178
   towns, 120, 124, 126, 129, 131, 134, 177, 178

types and processes, 122, 124, 126, 127, 128, 130, 131, 137, 177
uranium, 134, 136, 175, 182, 246
  radiation, 177, 178, 181
  yellowcake, 177
Mining Watch Canada, 137
modernity, 211, 224, 243, 244, 328
Montreal, 30, 42, 76, 77, 82, 87, 90, 91, 92, 151, 201, 203
Montreal Protocol, 249, 256
Muir, John, 99, 100
multinational corporations, 243, 252, 260, 281, 327
  corporate consolidation, 260

N

National Energy Board (NEB), 169
  National Energy Program (NEP), 173
National Museum of Canada (later Canadian Museum of Civilization), 122
National Parks Association, 108
naturalists, 98, 100, 106, 109, 111
nature, 2, 91, 92, 96, 100, 106, 215, 219, 222, 229, 243, 245, 268, 276, 282, 293, 326, 327
Nature Conservancy of Canada, 276
Nature of Things, 248
navigation/shipping, 201, 202, 205
  canals, 188, 190, 200, 201, 202
neoconservatism, 257, 260, 264
  neoliberal ideas, 282
Norse, 20
  trade, 20, 21
north, 4, 305
North West Company (NWC), 30, 31, 54, 170
Northwest Passage, 24, 25, 30
nuclear tests, 5, 244, 246
  treaty, 246

O

Ontario Water Resources Commission, 177, 193, 194, 195
Ottawa, 93
ozone layer, 246, 249, 293

P

packaging, 155
Palliser, John, 54
  expedition, 55
  Palliser's Triangle, 55
parks, 4, 91
  Algonquin Provincial Park, 102, 112, 269, 273, 274, 277, 280
  Auyuittuq National Park, 278
  Banff, 106, 107, 115, 276, 278, 279
  beautification, 273, 274
  boundaries/placement, 276, 281
  camps, 109
  cemeteries, 92
  city, 90-93
  commercial concessions, 268, 275, 278, 281
  Dinosaur provincial park, 275
  doctrine of usefulness, 106, 268
  education/heritage programs, 273, 274, 278
  facilities/services, 108, 274, 275, 281
  Gwaii Haanas National Park Reserve, 281
  legislation, 269, 275, 278, 279, 280
  MacDougall, Frank, 273
  multiuser, 273
  national, 96, 99, 102, 105, 106, 108, 109, 113, 116, 140, 252, 268, 272, 278, 279, 281, 316
  Olmstead, Frederick Law, 92
  Parks Branch, 108, 113, 114, 269
  Point Pelee, 113
  policy/management, 268, 272, 273, 274, 277, 278, 279, 280, 281
    ecological integrity, 269, 278, 279
    First Nations, 281
    natural ecosystem, 269, 279
    privatization, 282
    user fees, 282
    zones, 274, 276, 278, 279, 280
  politics, 108, 274, 279, 281, 282, 283
  protection of, 277, 279, 282, 283
    Algonquin Wildlands League, 277
  public's role, 268, 275, 278, 283
  purposes, 268
  Quetico, 102, 276, 280

regulation of, 106,
revenue, 273, 274
scientific research, 269, 273, 275
tourism/recreation, 106, 107, 108, 115, 150, 268, 273, 274, 275, 278, 279, 281, 282
wardens, 108, 112, 113, 114, 279
wilderness, 273, 274, 276, 277, 278, 279, 279, 280, 316
Yosemite, 100,
pesticides, 153, 244, 258
Phyllis Cormack, 5, 251
Pinchot, Gifford, 98, 99, 103
pipelines, 134, 148, 172, 173, 313, 314
Pleistocene era, 13
political will, 257, 279
pollution, 66, 67, 76, 80, 84, 85, 87, 90, 93, 101, 104, 120, 121, 124, 129, 130, 134, 137, 140, 145, 146, 148, 149, 152, 155, 156, 174, 177, 185, 188, 189, 190, 191, 193, 194, 195, 196, 197, 198, 200, 202, 219, 231, 244, 245, 246, 248, 253, 254, 302, 327
  air standards, 255
  radioactive spills, 246
Pollution Probe, 149, 194, 249
population, 17, 20, 26, 28, 29, 40, 41, 79, 80, 83, 126, 128, 151, 153, 190, 191, 193, 247, 248
  baby boom, 140, 144, 153, 245, 274
  immigration, 153
products, 153, 155
  oil-based, 170
  plastics, 170
professions, new, 99, 116
public policy, 56, 58, 61, 63, 64, 66, 67, 79, 96, 101, 102, 103, 106, 112, 113, 115, 116, 125, 129, 145, 148, 156, 157, 166, 167, 169, 172, 179, 181, 188, 196, 197, 198, 208, 212, 219, 233, 234, 237, 243, 250, 253, 256, 257, 283, 327, 328

Q

quality of life, 245

R

racism, 60, 128

regions, 14, 15, 17, 18, 42, 185, 286
  Alberta, 164, 170, 172, 173, 175, 185, 275
  British Columbia, 59, 102, 124, 126, 127,
      128, 135, 145, 150, 167, 168, 204, 207,
      254, 263, 275, 286, 295-6,
    development, 274
    ecological, 42, 53
  Manitoba, 166, 167
  New Brunswick, 244
  Newfoundland and Labrador, 18, 20, 21,
      23, 40, 251, 274, 282, 286, 287, 289
  Nova Scotia, 122, 123, 164, 287
  Ontario, 102, 130, 134, 167, 170, 175, 176,
      179, 201, 207, 210, 217, 254, 278, 280
  Ottawa Valley, 61, 66
  Prairies, 53, 54, 57, 78, 89, 102, 115, 121,
      124, 170, 224, 225, 231, 269
  Prince Edward Island (PEI), 274
  Quebec, 130, 131, 166, 167, 169, 201,
      208-11, 258
  Yukon, 13, 14, 128, 131, 145
reserves, Native, 43, 57, 67, 208
resources, 33, 104, 120, 166, 188, 212, 277,
      326
  conservation of, 98, 100, 105
  depletion, 96, 185, 247, 277
  exploitation, 22, 46, 76, 96, 98, 243, 265,
      281
  management, 29, 96, 210,
  waste, 47, 53, 64, 66, 67, 97, 98, 101, 169
rivers, 15, 30, 31, 43, 54, 55, 61, 126, 129, 169,
      171, 174, 201, 202, 204, 207, 208, 209,
      210, 211, 296, 317
Roosevelt, Teddy (Theodore), 98, 99, 100,
      104
Royal Society of Canada, 232, 233

S
seeds, 28, 49, 51, 54
  Seeds of Diversity Canada (Heritage Seed
      Program), 236
settlement, 25, 40, 41, 49, 54-56, 58, 67, 126,
      188, 190
settlements, 41, 49, 53, 61, 63, 64, 76, 98,
      121, 207, 224
  Acadia, 41

New France, 41, 42, 47-49
Plaisance, 41
Red River, 54, 77
  Resistance 1869-70, 56
St. John's, 41
Thirteen Colonies, 41
Upper Canada/Canada West, 47, 50, 51
West (Prairies), 53, 56, 57, 78, 79
  Northwest Rebellion, 1885
settlers, 2, 29, 40, 42, 46, 57, 60, 61, 65, 76,
      113, 163, 189, 295
  immigrants, 45, 57, 60, 80, 93
  Loyalists, 42, 44, 50, 51, 77, 202
  rural workers, 80
Sierra Club, 100, 110, 148,
Sierra Club of Canada, 123, 150, 232, 275
Sierra Legal Defence Fund (Ecojustice),
      198, 210, 254, 258, 259, 262, 294
Sifton, Clifford, 103, 104, 105, 106, 164, 166
soil, 42, 51, 53, 57, 59, 60, 65, 66, 115, 116,
      120, 121, 125, 199, 219, 235 ·
  erosion, 58, 59, 66, 115, 125, 153, 189, 229,
      252, 273
species extinction, 326
standard of living, 153, 164, 167, 245, 327,
      328
Stefansson, Vilhjalmur, 25, 306, 312
stewardship, 5
Stewart, Elihu, 102, 103
suburbs, 80-82, 140, 149, 150, 151, 153, 156,
      207, 229
  Don Mills, 152
  environmental impact, 152
  housing, 152, 153
  services, 152
  shopping malls, 151, 155, 156
Sudbury, 130
surveys, 40, 43, 44, 45, 55, 56, 67
sustainability, 156, 183, 235, 251, 257, 262,
      264, 328, 329
  sustainable development, 4, 182, 243, 247,
      256
  sustainable society, 5, 96, 140, 157, 182,
      185, 247, 327, 328
  unsustainable, 175, 182, 252, 265, 323, 327
Suzuki, David, 248, 249, 327

T
tar ponds, Sydney, 123, 124, 125
  Athabasca, 174
technology, 5, 15, 20, 21, 23, 27, 46, 52, 58,
      62, 120, 123, 132, 134, 135, 150, 153,
      155, 165, 167, 173, 175, 176, 185, 191,
      201, 203, 204, 207, 211, 215, 219, 245,
      248, 252, 260, 287, 327
Thalidomide, 244
Three Mile Island, 246
timber leases, 64
  licences, 61, 64
tobacco, 17
Toronto, 43, 80, 81, 84, 90, 92, 93, 151,
      152
  Toronto Carrying-Place Trail, 76, 77
  York, 77
toxic waste, 195, 196
  chemicals, 255
  Love Canal, 195
  Mercury, 195
  PCBs, 195
trade, 15, 23, 25, 31, 35, 41, 42, 46, 202
Traill, Catharine Parr, 52, 65, 199
transportation, 4, 31, 40, 51, 55, 64, 76, 78,
      79, 141, 157, 163, 215, 227
  airlines, 120, 121, 132, 145, 209, 289, 309
  bicycle, 140, 141, 142, 245, 328
    cycling, 141, 157
  canoe, 17, 18, 28, 277, 280
  mass transit, 146, 157
  railways, 40, 55, 57, 79, 80, 81, 85-86, 120,
      122, 128, 130, 131, 137, 140, 145, 147,
      190, 202
  roads, 31, 40, 126, 128, 140, 141, 142, 144,
      145, 146, 147, 149, 156, 190, 199, 202,
      209, 224, 274, 279, 309
    Trans-Canada Highway, 145, 146
  street railways, 81, 151
treaties, 35, 42, 45, 57, 306

U
unions, 130, 133, 134, 136, 137, 168

V
Vallentyne, Jack (Johnny Biosphere), 248

Vancouver, 78, 82, 89, 90, 92, 93, 128, 156, 183, 250, 254, 259
Vancouver Island, 59, 60, 124, 252, 258, 282
ventilation, 79
Victoria, 78, 128, 254

W

waste, 245
  nuclear, 244
  recycling, 235
water, 4, 23, 40, 57, 86, 87, 115, 120, 121, 125, 140, 166, 174, 181, 188, 198, 210, 212, 243
  contamination, 178, 179, 229
  control, 204
  diversion, 189, 204, 206, 209, 211
  irrigation, 115
  legislation, 194, 195, 196, 197, 199, 205, 206, 211, 212
  manipulation, 188, 200, 204, 206, 212
  quality, 194, 198, 212, 253, 254
  regulations, 203
  temperature, 211
  Walkerton, 198, 199, 260
  waste recipient, 188, 212
watersheds, 5, 104, 177, 273
waterways, 65, 67, 78, 79, 126, 128, 164, 167, 188, 198, 199, 200, 206, 208, 212, 279
  Niagara Falls, 164, 165, 167, 201, 204
weather, 25
weeds, 28, 51, 58, 59, 219, 220

wetlands, 66, 80, 153, 188, 189, 190, 199, 200, 272
whales, 22, 23
wilderness, 24, 44-47, 54, 58, 60, 67, 91, 100, 106, 112, 275, 276, 277, 282
  preservation, 99, 101, 276, 277, 279
  Temagami, 279, 281
  Wilderness Committee, 282
wildlife, 24, 30, 32, 33, 34, 46, 53, 59, 65, 67, 96, 108, 121, 125, 128, 192, 193, 194, 199, 210, 278, 279
  bear, 274, 298, 319
  beaver, 30, 31, 33, 34, 65, 109, 110, 189, 199, 319, 327
  birds, 24, 59, 99, 111, 112, 113, 114, 174, 189, 199, 259, 272, 274, 298
  bison, buffalo, 16, 30, 32, 34, 55, 109, 114, 271
    hunt, 34, 35, 56, 110
    robes, 34, 35
  bounties, 110
  breeding programs, 272
  Canadian Wildlife Service, 269, 272
  caribou, 128, 311, 319
  commodity, 272
  depletion/extinction of, 110, 112, 128, 153, 174, 177, 189, 206, 207, 209, 269, 271, 275, 326, 327
  endangered species, 268, 269, 271, 272
  game, 327

  habitat, 110, 152, 174, 207, 252, 269, 272, 278
  legislation, 269, 270, 272, 273, 276
  Leopold, Aldo, 271
  management of, 96, 108, 112, 113, 114, 269, 270, 272, 313, 328
  Mowat, Farley, 271
  muskox, 311
  poaching, 102, 112, 269, 273
  predators, 110, 111, 114, 115, 269, 270, 272, 273
  preserves/sanctuaries, 104, 111, 112, 114, 268, 272, 276, 316
    Thelon, 313
  protection of, 96, 101, 102, 104, 105, 106, 109, 111, 112, 113, 114, 115, 116, 199, 245, 246, 270, 272, 273, 278
  recovery, 244, 272
  reindeer, 312
  scientific research, 269, 272
  seals, 18, 22, 41, 251
  tourist attraction, 270
  wolf extermination policy, 269, 270
    bounty, 270, 271
    wolf, 110, 112, 269, 270, 271
Winnipeg, 78
Wisconsin Glacial Episode, 13
World Bank, 249
World Trade Organization (WTO), 133
  Battle of Seattle, 261-62

Printed and bound in Canada by Friesens

Set in Garamond and Meta by Artegraphica Design Co. Ltd.

Text design: Irma Rodriguez

Copy editor: Lesley Erickson

Proofreader: Deborah Kerr

Cartographer: Eric Leinberger